DEVASTATION AND LAUGHTER

Satire, Power, and Culture in the Early Soviet State, 1920s–1930s

In *Devastation and Laughter*, Annie Gérin explores the use of satire in the visual arts, theatre, cinema, and the circus under Lenin and Stalin. Gérin traces the rise and decline of the genre and argues that the use of satire in official Soviet art and propaganda was neither marginal nor untheorized. The author sheds light on the texts written in the 1920s and 1930s by Anatoly Lunacharsky, the Soviet Commissar of Enlightenment, and the impact his writings had on satirists. While the Avant-Garde and Socialist Realism were necessarily forward-looking and utopian, satire afforded artists the means to examine critically past and present subjects, themes, and practice. *Devastation and Laughter* is the first work to bring Soviet theoretical writings on the use of satire to the attention of scholars outside of Russia. By introducing important bodies of work that have largely been overlooked in the fields of art history and film and theatre history, Annie Gérin provides a nuanced and alternative reading of early Soviet art.

ANNIE GÉRIN is the Dean of Fine Arts at Concordia University.

Devastation and Laughter

Satire, Power, and Culture in the Early Soviet State, 1920s–1930s

ANNIE GÉRIN

UNIVERSITY OF TORONTO PRESS
Toronto Buffalo London

Reprinted in paperback 2021

ISBN 978-1-4875-0243-0 (cloth)
ISBN 978-1-4875-2654-2 (paper)

Library and Archives Canada Cataloguing in Publication

Title: Devastation and laughter : satire, power, and culture in the early Soviet state, 1920s–1930s / Annie Gérin.

Names: Gérin, Annie, 1969– author.

Description: Paperback reprint. Originally published 2018. | Includes bibliographical references and index.

Identifiers: Canadiana 20200397168 | ISBN 9781487526542 (softcover)

Subjects: LCSH: Satire, Soviet. | LCSH: Arts, Soviet. | LCSH: Soviet Union – Intellectual life – 1917–1970. | LCSH: Laughter – Soviet Union. | LCSH: Art and state – Soviet Union. | LCSH: Satire in art.

Classification: LCC NX556.A1 G47 2021 | DDC 700.947–dc23

This book has been published with the help of a grant from the Federation for the Humanities and Social Sciences, through the Awards to Scholarly Publications Program, using funds provided by the Social Sciences and Humanities Research Council of Canada.

University of Toronto Press acknowledges the financial assistance to its publishing program of the Canada Council for the Arts and the Ontario Arts Council, an agency of the Government of Ontario.

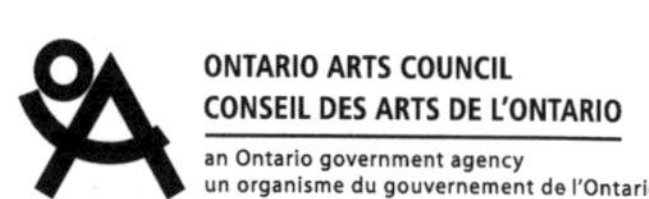

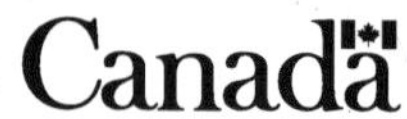

For Peter and Maya, both excellent laughers.

In memory of David King (1943–2016), without whom this book would have never happened.

Invocation by Laughter

O, burst out laughing, laughers!
O, laugh out loud, laughers!
You who laugh with laughs and you who laugh it up laughishly,
O, laugh out loud, laugheringly!
O, belaughable laughingstocks – the laughter of laughering laughers!
O, unlaugh it enlaughingly, the laughter of onlaughing laughermen!
Laughterling, laughterling,
Uplaugh, downlaugh, laughlings, laughlings,
Laughsies, laughsies.
O, burst out laughing, laughers!
O, laugh out loud, laughers!

Velimir Khlebnikov, 1908–1909

First published in N.I. Kulbin (ed.), *Studiya impressionistov,* vol. 1 (Saint Petersburg: Izdatelstvo N.I. Butkovskoi, 1910), 47.

Table of Contents

Illustrations

Colour Plates

Colour plates follow page 190

Note on Transliteration, Translation, and Dates

Whenever possible, the transliteration of Russian names and titles complies with the British Standard System, modified to omit hard and soft signs. The only exceptions to that rule pertain to familiar names that have acquired a recognized English spelling, and to material quoted from sources using other transliteration systems. Unless specified, translations are by the author.

In February 1918, Russia shifted from the Julian to the Gregorian calendar. Unless specified, all dates before February 1918 refer to the Julian calendar, while those after February 1918 refer to the Gregorian calendar.

Acknowledgments

A chance encounter can change the course of a research career. In my case, it was meeting David King (1943–2016) at the *Dom knigi* bookstore in Moscow in 1998. We became fast friends, and David opened his collection to me. Through him I discovered and gained access to lesser-known examples of visual culture that were to become central to my research. I am grateful for his friendship, his astute eye and mind, and for providing the majority of the images printed in this book.

I am truly obliged to my students and research assistants, who participated in various stages of the project: Analays Alvarez Hernandez, Marie-France Bisson, Maria Bondarenko, Erika Couto, Karen Harutyunyan, Renée-Claude Landry, Géraldine Lavoie-Dugré, Maude Nadeau, Sergei Smoliakov, Julie Richard, Maria Silina, Melina Waters, and Sasha Zaitseva. I am grateful to Richard Ratzlaff and Stephen Shapiro, my editors, to Terry Teskey who did a brilliant job of smoothing out rough corners at the copyediting stage, and to the entire University of Toronto Press team. I also want to thank the anonymous readers who provided insight and constructive comments on the manuscript, Valerie Wade in London, Clive Coward and Chris Sutherns at the Tate for helping with images, and the employees of the Russian State Library, the Russian State Archive of Literature and Art (RGALI) and the Russian State Archive of Socio-political History (RGASPI), as well as the Centre interuniversitaire d'études sur les lettres, les arts et les traditions (CÉLAT), the Federation for the Humanities and Social Sciences, and the Social Sciences and Humanities Research Council of Canada (SSHRC) for their generous support.

Finally, I must express my very profound gratitude to my family and friends, in particular my mother, Raymonde, who read the manuscript from cover to cover, and my partner Peter who now knows more than he ever wanted about Anatoly Lunacharsky and the Soviet satirical scene. Your unfailing support and continuous encouragement throughout the years have made this book possible.

DEVASTATION AND LAUGHTER

Satire, Power, and Culture in the Early Soviet State,
1920s–1930s

Introduction: Devastation and Laughter

Laughter has always been an important element in social processes. The role of laughter is as important as ever in our struggle, the last struggle for the emancipation of human beings.

A.V. Lunacharsky[1]

"We don't have laughter for laughter's sake, simple belly-laughs that bare all teeth, just like we don't have art for art's sake. Here, art and laughter are implements of battle."[2] These words were written in 1938 by graphic satirist Dmitrii Orlov, better known by his pen name Dmitrii Moor. Since the days of the October Revolution, Moor had been prosperously employed as an artist-satirist, producing posters for the state and contributing images to several Soviet satirical journals (Plate 1). For him the harnessing of graphic satire to state propaganda – the belligerent laughter he spoke of – could be nothing but positive. Not only did it allow him to feed and clothe his family (no small feat in a period marked by civil war, famine and dearth), it afforded satire – and therefore satirists – an important social status.

During the same years, Nadezhda Mandelstam occupied a very different position on the Soviet social map. She had joined in deportation her husband, the poet Osip Mandelstam, arrested for the first time in 1934 for composing an epigram that bluntly poked fun at Stalin and then again in 1938, accused this time of counter-revolutionary activities.[3] In her memoirs of a life half spent in internal exile, forced out of Moscow by the Stalinist regime, she recalled bitterly the prevalence of state-sponsored satire, which she felt had

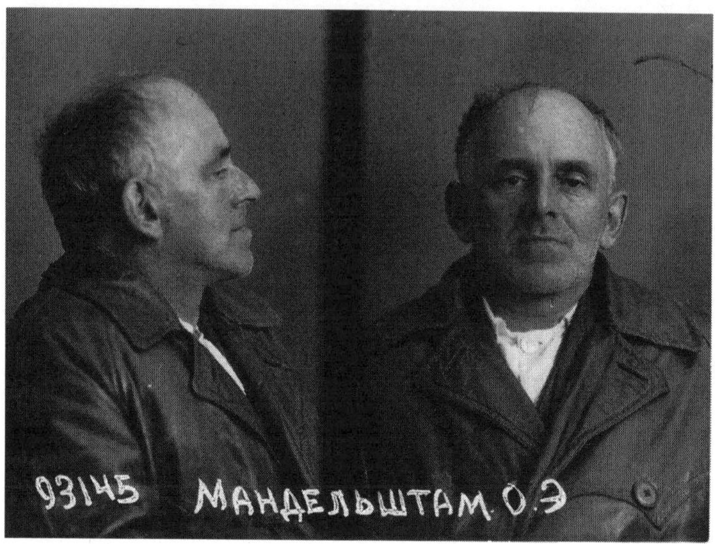

0.1 Police photograph of the poet Osip Mandelstam taken on his arrest
in 1938. Part of the David King Collection. Presented to Tate Archive
by David King 2016.

become an official sort of laughter at the expense of poetic wit. "In
the twenties," she wrote, "humour disappeared altogether, except
insofar as it was made to serve, during the next fifty years, as a well-
paid propaganda technique."[4]

But laughter, whether it be satirical, humorous, absurd, or otherwise, never disappeared in the Soviet Union. In 1920, in the midst
of the Civil War, Anatoly Lunacharsky, then People's Commissar of
Enlightenment, marvelled at the resilience of his people and their capacity to find mirth in the everyday: "We live in a hungry and cold
country that was recently torn to shreds. Yet, I often hear laughter,
I often see laughing faces on the streets."[5] Among its innumerable
forms, there were harmless humorous ditties, kitschy calendars, and
"politically correct" plays and animation films. There were also political jokes, oppositional to the regime, whispered behind closed
doors. In the 1930s, at the height of the Stalinist purges, these were
taken very seriously; they could send their utterer to the forced labour
camps of Kolyma. And there was official, state-sponsored satire, put
to the service of propaganda.

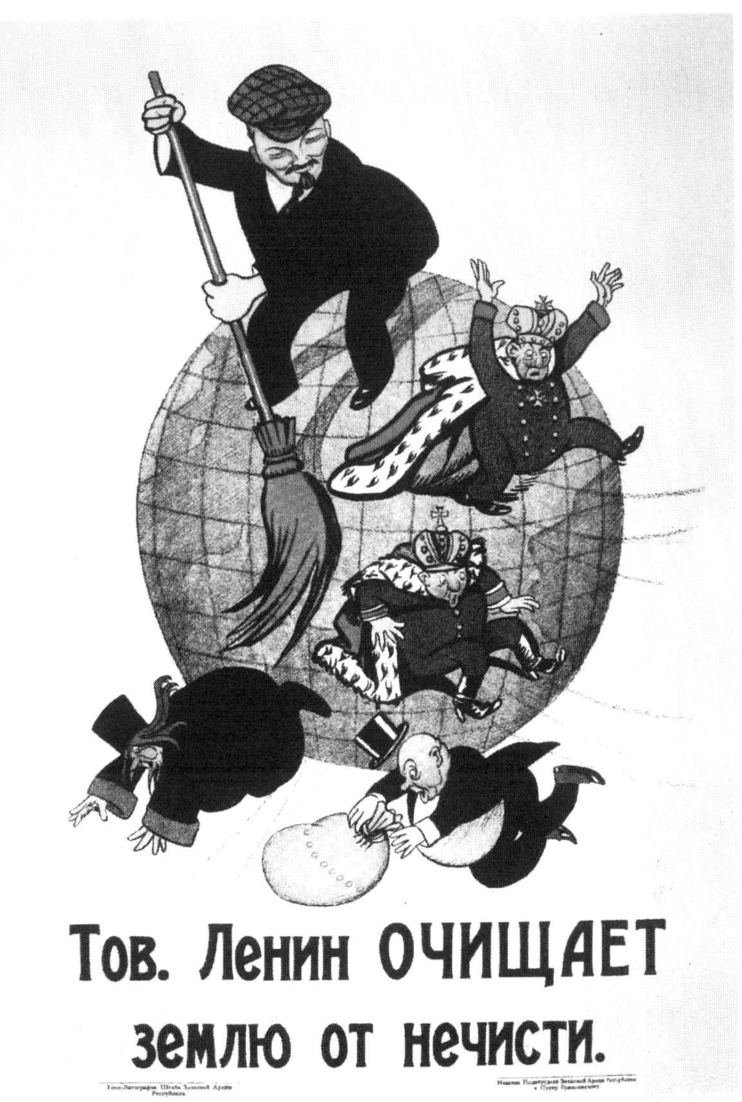

0.2 "Comrade Lenin Is Sweeping the Scum off the Earth," poster by Viktor Deni, 1920. Part of the David King Collection. Presented to Tate Archive by David King 2016.

The Soviet system produced, in its early years, tremendous amounts of hope, energy, and joy. But it also engendered suffering, repression, and fear. It is against this complex backdrop of devastation and laughter that the subject of this book takes shape.

This study is about Soviet state-sponsored satire in the visual arts, cinema, theatre, and the circus in the 1920s and 1930s. It focuses on visual manifestations of laughter, rather than on the satirical literature of Ilf and Petrov, Mikhail Zoshchenko, Mikhail Bulgakov, or Daniil Kharms, which has garnered some degree of interest from scholars over the past decades.

I started to think about visual uses of satire several years ago when I encountered for the first time the satirical antireligious journal *Bezbozhnik u stanka* (*Godless at the Workbench*, 1923–31). The aforementioned Dmitrii Moor was this richly illustrated publication's artistic director. Regular contributors included prominent artists, such as Aleksandr Deineka, Mikhail Cheremnykh, and Aleksandr Radakov, who had experimented with abstraction in the 1910s or were to later join the ranks of socialist realism. They frequently maintained parallel "serious" and "unserious" practices. Yet their satirical production is – to this day – conspicuously absent from the glossy-paged monographs dedicated to their work. After this initial contact, Soviet satirical images started to appear with greater frequency in my field of vision. In fact, I realized they were everywhere: in journals, posters, films, collages, and even (although less frequently) in paintings and photographs.

The two main motivations for writing this book are to address the scarcity of Soviet visual satire in art historical research and to question certain assumptions about Soviet culture, largely disseminated in scholarship and in mass media. I am a child of the Cold War. Like many of my generation, I have had bleak and drab images of Soviet Russia imprinted onto my retinae from the earliest age. As a teenager, I regularly saw on television people in ratty beige overcoats queuing for bread against grey winter skies. I saw broken-down Ladas on unkempt roads and oversized glasses sitting on the noses of bored bureaucrats. I saw worried faces, gigantic ballistic missiles parading across Red Square, and the rushed evacuation of Chernobyl. Laughter never made the news and Russia did not seem like a fun place at all. As an art historian, I studied the Russian avant-garde – rayonism, suprematism, constructivism – and then socialist realism. For all its utopian impulses and earnestness, Soviet art never seemed much fun either. But as I found out traipsing around Russia for the past few decades, the reality is much more complex than it appears from the other side of the globe. I also realized, when I started to think critically about laughter, that it can play various and sometimes apparently incompatible roles.

Theories of Laughter

There are two main difficulties associated with the study of laughter. The first is rooted in language. Scholars often make no distinction between the humorous, the absurd, the witty, the satirical, the farcical, and the jocular. These are all understood as variants of humour linked by a common purpose, the production of laughter or amusement. As we will see throughout this book, the particular brand of laughter matters greatly. It provides more than a tone or intensity – it is a rhetorical mode, made to produce specific affects and effects. In my general analysis, I have used the word "laughter" as an umbrella term; *smekh* was in fact the word used most widely in Soviet theoretical and critical writings in the 1920s and 1930s. This preference for "laughter" over "humour" or any other term was no doubt borrowed directly from the title of Henri Bergson's *Laughter*, first published in French in 1899 as a series of three articles in *La revue de Paris*, and translated into Russian the following year. Satire, humour, irony, parody, and other key terms will be defined as we go.

The second difficulty is interpretive. Laughter is the fiefdom of deeply cultural and contextual forms and it draws on topical themes, vocabularies, and images. Therefore, early-twentieth-century wit might seem unfunny to our twenty-first-century eyes and intellects. We may not recognize the sources of parodies or know their targets. We may not fully understand the general context or the importance of norms being transgressed in a satirical work. Umberto Eco once remarked, with regard to the telling of jokes, that "what remains compulsory, in order to produce a comic effect, is the prohibition of spelling out the norm. It must be presupposed both by the utterer and by the audience. If the speaker spells it out, he is a fool or a jerk; if the audience does not know it, there is no comic effect."[6] Obviously, this judicious remark on the art of jokesmanship does not apply to the interpretation of laughter in the context of scholarly research. In fact, the opposite is true.

To unlock the potential richness of laughter in visual works and link them to broader visual, cultural, political, and intellectual frameworks,

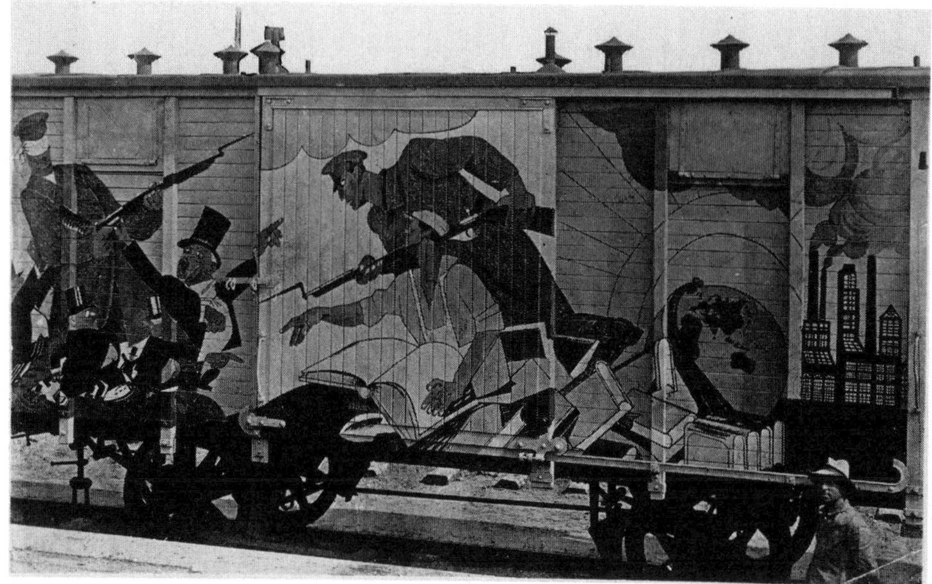

0.3 Agitational train decorated with satirical propaganda played an important role in the acculturation process in the 1920s. Part of the David King Collection. Presented to Tate Archive by David King 2016.

we will need to establish contexts and conduct meticulous descriptions, iconographical analyses and investigations of norms and traditions, as well as examine the formal mechanisms that produce laughter outcomes in a given work. This restitution will always be imperfect, however. It is impossible to recreate for the contemporary viewer the initial affective response that captured those who first saw a given work in full colour, at proper scale, and displayed in its original setting.

Bearing all this in mind, we can gain valuable insight into society from the study of laughter, since it targets everyday practices and values by playing with expectations. It puts the finger on nodes of tension to poke fun at norms and rules, rebel against them, exacerbate potential dissensus, or endorse escapism. It also sheds light on hopes and aspirations, as well as on the dark corners of the human soul, where shame and hatred are relegated. In other words, it amuses, distracts, celebrates, informs, attacks, and chastises; it partakes in complex processes of acculturation.

Contemporary scholarship on laughter divides theoretical approaches in three main streams: superiority theory, relief theory, and incongruity theory.[7] Superiority theory goes back to Plato, Aristotle, and Quintilian, who believed humans take pleasure in laughing at deformed, ugly, or morally inferior individuals or at the misfortunes of others.[8] For Thomas Hobbes, who built on the Aristotelian tradition, "The passion of Laughter is nothing else but a suddaine Glory arising from suddaine Conception of some Eminency in our selves by Comparison with the Infirmityes of others, or with our owne formerly."[9] At the turn of the twentieth century, Henri Bergson emphasized the aggressive feelings that also fuel this condescending laughter. "In this sense, laughter cannot be absolutely just. Nor should it be kind-hearted either. Its function is to intimidate by humiliating. Now, it would not succeed in doing this, had not nature implanted for that very purpose, even in the best of men, a spark of spitefulness or, at all events, of mischief."[10]

Relief theory appeared in the nineteenth century in the work of Herbert Spencer. Spencer approached laughter from the angle of psychophysiology. He understood it as "the discharge of arrested feelings into the muscular system" that happens when a concentrated subject is suddenly distracted or liberated from stress. "Laughter naturally results only when consciousness is, unawares, transferred from great things to small."[11] Sigmund Freud's work in *Jokes and Their Relation to the Unconscious* (1905) shifted relief theory towards the unconscious.[12] Freud argued that laughter occurs as the symptom of an economy of psychic energy that is achieved when forbidden thoughts or feelings (that would usually need to be repressed in deference to society) are expressed as a joke.

Finally, the incongruity theory can be traced to Aristotle's *Rhetoric*, but it was rediscovered and expanded upon periodically over the centuries by Francis Hutcheson, Immanuel Kant, Arthur Schopenhauer, Søren Kierkegaard, Arthur Koestler, and others.[13] While the previous theories can be considered affective, incongruity theory can be understood as cognitive or structural. It proposes that laughter arises from the failure of perceptions to match expectations. Schopenhauer emphasized the element of surprise caused by the mismatch: "The greater and more unexpected this incongruity in the apprehension of the person laughing, the more violent will be this laughter."[14] In the context of visual satire, incongruities leading to bursts of laughter will be found in the subject matter of a given work (either intrinsically in relation to its context or other representations), but they will also arise from its formal components: composition, style, colour, scale, and liberties taken with conventions of representation.

These three main approaches are by no means exhaustive. Other theories have been developed to address, for example, a presumed evolutionary advantage of people graced with a good sense of humour,[15] the benevolence of laughers in certain situations (what Michael Billig calls "the nice guy theory"),[16] or the morphological aspects of laughter, as in Vladimir Propp's formalist method.[17] Furthermore, superiority, relief, and incongruity theories are not impervious to one another. Freud speaks of the cruelty and tendentiousness of laughter, and the feeling of self-importance it may provide; Spencer mentions how incongruity may be the source of emotional demobilization, and Hobbes comments on the potential relief caused by the expression of disdain over others. The Russian understanding of laughter that emerged and evolved in the early part of the twentieth century, the backbone of this book, borrows from all three theories.

Weapons and Tools

If, as Moor observed, Soviet laughter is an implement of battle, it then needs to be considered in terms of its rhetorical potential, as intentional and conscious communication holding certain impelling qualities. In his book *Institutio Oratoria*, Quintilian adopted this point of view. He argued orators should seek the production of laughter in their speeches for its effectiveness as a means of persuasion: "I now turn to a very different talent, namely that which dispels the graver emotions of the judge by exciting his laughter, frequently diverts his attention from the facts of the case, and sometimes even refreshes him and revives him when he has begun to be bored or wearied by the case."[18] Three crucial points about the use of laughter as a rhetorical device are brought to the fore in Quintilian's account. First, skilled orators can use laughter to alleviate tension; it may also ease the discussion of emotional or rebarbative topics. Second, used judiciously, laughter can be effective at creating diversions, or shifting the audience's attention away from facts that may hinder the speaker's objectives. Third, if the audience lose interest, laughter holds the potential to draw their attention back to the topic at hand.

But there is more. Under the guises of laughter certain things can be expressed that would otherwise be silenced altogether. Furthermore, particular cognitive or signifying relationships can be created within a "community of laughers." For example, irony allows the audience to engage actively in the (re)construction of meaning, as they figure out that the orator is saying the opposite of what she actually means. This waggish investment in signification processes creates a bond between the speaker and her public, who need to be "in the know" to a certain degree to understand the ironic twist. Parody functions differently: it mimics a form while displacing its intent. It allows the audience to playfully rework conceptions about people, ideas, and things they might have previously taken for granted. As the parodic configuration circulates, it then contaminates the source from which it draws. For those exposed to the parody, the signifying integrity of the original is therefore compromised. Satire functions as a broader category that can integrate either irony and parody or both (or none). It has very specific goals: to destroy, punish, or correct. By ridiculing its subject, it aims to discredit it, to reveal inconsistencies, vices, and ineptitudes. The desired effect is either the eventual rejection by the audience of the target of satire or the reformation of the shamed victim.

Rhetoric appeals to reason – and to passion. Therefore, for laughter to be effective in a propaganda context, ideology needs to combine with affect: fear, anger, contempt, distress, disgust, interest, shame, surprise, but also joy or amusement. Affects are adaptive responses to external stimuli. While they can – and do – draw on the cognitive and other information-processing systems in the brain, they have a much more immediate function, which has lead scholars to describe them as extra-textual and extra-iconographic: "as such, affects are not to do with knowledge or meaning; indeed, they occur on a different *asignifying* register."[19] Without subscribing to this mind/body split that would enable us to understand affects as autonomous, let's just say that as opposed to fully articulated interpretations, affects can take place at the threshold of awareness.[20] In other words, affective responses – rooted in instinct as well as in experience of fear or pleasure – occur as reflex and are later modulated by more complex thought processes. They contribute a significant psychophysiological dimension to the layered character of interpretation. While the turn to affect is relatively recent in humanities scholarship, it is Bergson – along with Baruch Spinoza, William James, and Freud – who stands as a philosophical precursor of affect theory. His writings were readily available in Russia during the first decades of the twentieth century; and they were greatly influential on early Soviet artistic and intellectual production, including the theorizations of laughter.[21]

Affective responses are precisely what differentiate the workings of artistic and satirical works of propaganda from straightforward, earnest ones. In the 1920s, for example, the satirical antireligious journal *Bezbozhnik u stanka* coexisted with several "serious" antireligious and atheist publications, including *Bezbozhnik* (*Godless*, 1923–41) and *Ateist*

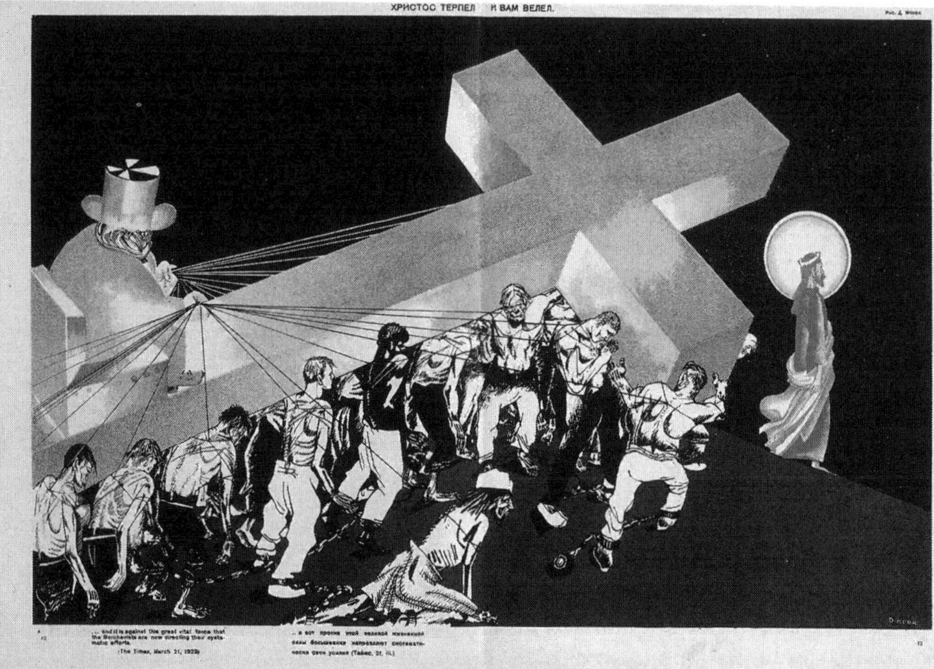

0.4 "Christ suffered for you and showed you the way," centrefold by Dmitrii Moor for the journal *Bezbozhnik u stanka*, Nos. 9–10, 1923. Part of the David King Collection. Presented to Tate Archive by David King 2016.

(*The Atheist*, 1922–30). The latter two provided their readers with rigorous argumentation denouncing all religions as historical constructions, miracles as fallacies, and religious institutions as exploitative. These journals were meant to add water to the atheist mill and supply antireligious activists with arguments they could then serve to their audiences. But what *Bezbozhnik u stanka* could do that these other journals could not was to drive its viewers into a circuit of deep feeling and response. *Bezbozhnik u stanka* stirred up affect: indignation, hatred, or shame at having been duped in the past. It propelled the viewer into a situation, a state of being, intensity, passion, or empathy. It shifted the critique from the intellect to the experienced, the felt, the lived, and this is precisely why it became so successful as an "implement of battle." And indeed, for Gilles Deleuze and Félix Guattari, "Affect is the active discharge of emotion, the counterattack … Weapons are affect and affects weapons."[22]

During the years that followed the 1917 October Revolution, remarkable social changes occurred as Russia shifted from a tsarist, theocratic, and capitalist country to a Bolshevik, atheist, and socialist one. This profound transformation entailed more than the nationalization of banks, industry, and private property. It required the shredding of the established social order and the creation of a new, socialist master narrative, a process that spilled onto every plane of public and private life. Under the guidance of the state and its People's Commissariat of Enlightenment, Soviet citizens were called upon to rework their relation to history, the collective, and the everyday. No ideological rock was left unturned with regard to consumption, work, spirituality, knowledge, and the body. In the course of this acculturation process that characterizes early Soviet Russia, sharpened weapons and tools became indispensable. These took the shape of words, images, symbols, rituals, and representations of all kinds. They were used by politicians, theoreticians, and artists to destroy the old, making way for the foundation of new Socialist Russia. Among these, visual satire played a prominent role.

In *A Thousand Plateaus*, Gilles Deleuze and Félix Guattari pointed out that "a distinction can always be made between weapons and tools on the basis of their usage (destroying people or producing goods). But although this extrinsic distinction explains certain secondary adaptations of a technological object, it does not preclude a general convertibility between the two groups, to the extent that it seems very difficult to propose an intrinsic difference between weapon and tool."[23] In the Russian language, the corresponding words are *oruzhie* (weapon) and *orudie* (tool). While they originated from different etymological roots, the shifting character highlighted by Deleuze and Guattari is nevertheless reflected in their current usage. *Oruzhie* came from the verb *rugat* (Slavic root *rog*), which means to scold, insult, mock. *Orudie* originally meant "work," "instrument," "equipment," and derives from the Slavic root *"red."* However, their phonetic proximity was the cause of semantic contamination during the eighteenth century. *Oruzhie* then developed a new signification, as a hostile means to proceed, or a tool for destruction.[24] Furthermore, as we will see in the first chapter of this book, in early Soviet writings on laughter, the two words are used almost interchangeably. Satire, in particular, is understood as holding the potential to destroy petit bourgeois attitudes, wipe out superstitions, and punish opportunism, while simultaneously structuring appropriate responses to internal and external threats and contributing to the overall socialist construction of the new. All this is achieved through the rhetorics of laughter.

Overview of the Book

In 1930, Anatoly Lunacharsky, People's Commissar of Enlightenment from 1917 to 1929, set up a government commission to study satirical genres in literature, visual arts, music, theatre, and film. He was himself working on a book manuscript provisionally titled "Laughter as a Weapon in Class Struggle," which he never completed. Because of his administrative appointment, Lunacharsky was the principal patron of the arts in the early Soviet period and the main middleman between political leaders such as Vladimir Lenin, Leon Trotsky, and Joseph Stalin on the one hand, and artists such as Vladimir Mayakovsky, Kazimir Malevich, Marc Chagall, Aleksandr Rodchenko, Vassilii Kandinsky, Sergei Eisenstein, and Vsevolod Meyerhold on the other. Throughout his career as commissar, Lunacharsky was instrumental in the production of much satirical work through the allocation of government contracts and commissions to artists. He also wrote art criticism and theoretical texts that encouraged the use of satire and humour by Soviet artists, as weapons against enemies of the regime and as tools for acculturation and social change in the context of the emerging Soviet Union. This work, inspired by prevalent theories of laughter (mainly those of Freud, Bergson, Spencer, Sully, and Lipps), revisits them through the lens of Marxism and translates them into a very specific Soviet language and worldview. Although these texts were originally published in Soviet journals and later reprinted in Soviet anthologies of Lunacharsky's writings, they remain virtually unknown. Chapter 1, "Anatoly Lunacharsky and the Power of Laughter," offers a historical and critical study of Lunacharsky's theoretical work on laughter.

Early Soviet interest in a political culture of satire influenced popular art forms and media, from literature to painting and music, from theatre to cinema and the circus. But its most pervasive visual expression was without a doubt print culture, as satire became ubiquitous in broadsheets, posters, periodicals, and books that disseminated mass propaganda in the early years of the regime. Print culture had been harnessed to mould public opinion and collective self-image for centuries in Russia as elsewhere. In Soviet Russia, the mass reproduction of images and text was understood as a tool that could play a considerable role in popular mobilization and acculturation. Chapter 2, "Soviet Satirical Print Culture: A Serious Affair," highlights the crucial importance of print culture as a support for visual propaganda. It does so by tracing a history of Soviet illustrated satirical journals and Civil War–time posters.

Chapters 3 and 4 build on the preceding one, but reflect on the specificity of the circus, theatre, and cinema, about which Lunacharsky wrote a great deal, and which the Soviet government also considered important means for propaganda and acculturation. There is, however, one important difference between these forms and the ones discussed in chapter 2. Most circus acts and theatre plays shown in Russia in the 1920s had been written and choreographed before the Revolution. Similarly, during the period, most cinemas were privately owned and showed imported films (Charlie Chaplin and Mary Pickford comedies being particularly appreciated). This caused Lunacharsky, in a text dealing specifically with humour and satire in cinema, to nuance his enthusiasm for the use of laughter, and distinguish between socialist and bourgeois (and potentially dangerous) satire. These two chapters also examine the gradual constitution of a Soviet "satirical scene," the decline of satire in the late 1920s, and the efflorescence of optimistic comedies produced in the early 1930s for the stage and the silver screen, in particular films by Grigory Aleksandrov and Ivan Pyryev.

While theatre and cinema can be considered literary forms from the point of view of play/screen writing, the emphasis here will be on scenography and how the visual can be exploited for satirical purposes in these mediums. And indeed, as Richard Taylor astutely pointed out with regard to films, during the 1920s "cinema *was*, of course, still silent. It was therefore a purely *visual* medium of communication and of necessity combining simplicity with directness in its appeal to mass audiences."[25]

The fifth chapter, "The Strategies and Targets of Satire," can be considered a methodological one. Here, I identify various strategies developed and adopted by Soviet satirists in the visual arts – including the visual aspects of circus, theatre, and cinema. These strategies can be grouped into four broad categories: caricature, collage, parody, and irony. After defining these terms and determining how each functions pragmatically in relation to the vaster genre of satire, the chapter moves on to three case studies that highlight the scapegoats and types of subject matter most fertile for Soviet satirical practices, and the broader goals artists aimed at through their sardonic treatment of a given theme. These are the so-called Campaign against the Everyday, the antireligious crusade, and the drive against Trotsky and Trotskyism.

Several artists worked simultaneously in satirical and earnest genres, depending on the objectives that shaped the artworks they were producing. The final chapter of this book, "The Rhetorics of Satire and

Socialist Realism," examines early Soviet debates around satire and the notion of realism in order to propose that the use of humour and satire offered artists alternative and complementary rhetorical modes in the context of propaganda art. While the avant-garde and socialist realism were necessarily forward looking and utopian in their goals and strategies, satire and humour afforded artists the means to critically examine past and present subjects, themes, and practices.

The book concludes with a translation of one of Lunacharsky's key texts, "On Laughter" (1931), a speech given on 30 January 1931 during the inaugural meeting of the Commission for the Study of Satirical Genres at the Academy of Sciences of the USSR. It offers a summary of the theorization of laughter Lunacharsky developed over roughly two decades, and that underpinned public debates about Soviet satire in the 1920s and early 1930s.

Anatoly Lunacharsky and the Soviet Satirical Scene

An important figure crosses the pages of this book and guides the reader through different aspects of Soviet state-funded laughter. It is that of Anatoly Vassilievich Lunacharsky.

Born in 1875, Lunacharsky became a Marxist at the age of fifteen. Interested in philosophy, he pursued his studies in Switzerland, France, and Italy, reading Marxist theory, French materialism and phenomenology, as well as German nineteenth-century idealist philosophy. He was particularly drawn to the teachings of critical positivists Richard Avenarius and Ernst Mach, and to Henri Bergson's metaphysics of experience. While in Europe, he met prominent socialists including Rosa Luxemburg, Leo Jogiches, Georgii Plekahnov, Alexandr Bogdanov, Leon Trotsky, and Vladimir Lenin, and joined the Russian Social Democratic Labour Party. In 1903 the party split into Bolsheviks, led by Vladimir Lenin, and Mensheviks, who followed Julius Martov. Lunacharsky sided with the Bolsheviks. When the Bolsheviks, in 1908, divided into Lenin's followers and those who supported Bogdanov, Lunacharsky joined the second group. With Bogdanov and Maxim Gorky, Lunacharsky then contributed to the elaboration of the "God-building" theory (*bogostroitelstvo*), which was immediately denounced by Lenin in his book *Materialism and Empiriocriticism* (1909).

Like many exiled Russian Marxists, Lunacharsky returned to Russia in February 1917. The day following the October Revolution, he was appointed People's Commissar of Enlightenment and remained in that

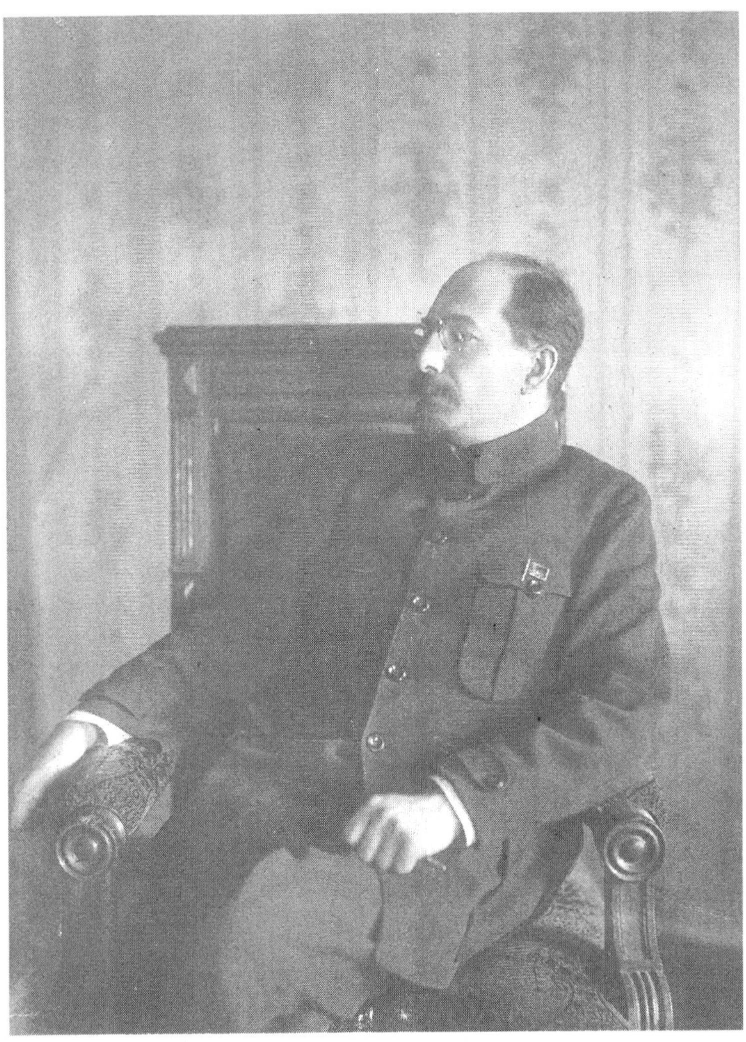

0.5 Portrait of Anatoly Lunacharsky, 1920s. Lunacharsky was People's Commissar of Enlightenment from 1917 to 1929. Part of the David King Collection. Presented to Tate Archive by David King 2016.

position until 1929. This function entrusted him with oversight of Soviet propaganda, education, and the arts. Known to be an art connoisseur and a shrewd critic, he was clearly the right man for the job. But his liberal ways and his broad interests in psychology, affect, phenomenology, and idealism often sparked misgivings in more orthodox Bolsheviks; they also periodically put him at odds with Lenin.

So why did Lenin appoint Lunacharsky to the key position of People's Commissar and keep him on, despite all their differences? Lunacharsky was smart, sensitive, a brilliant orator, and a passionate defender of the new. Lenin trusted and esteemed him. As he put it to the Soviet writer Viktor Shulgin in 1920: "I advise you also to respect him. He is drawn towards the future with his whole being. That is why there is such joy and laughter in him. And he is ready to share that joy and laughter with everyone."[26]

With his appointment as commissar, Lunacharsky found himself in the position of needing to pull together a bureaucratic team from scratch. The call was immediately sent out to all educators and artists. Those who had been close to the pre-revolutionary cultural institutions remained cautious. They essentially refused to cooperate. The artists who chose to join the People's Commissariat of Enlightenment all had certain things in common. They were young, they were forward thinking, they felt sympathy for the regime, they nurtured ambitions for the social role of art – and most already knew each other, for having frequented Saint Petersburg's and Moscow's avant-garde circles and their futurist cabarets.

Many of these also became the protagonists of a Soviet satirical scene during the 1920s – and now of this book. They include, among others, dynamic personalities such as poet Vladimir Mayakovsky, film-maker Sergei Eisenstein, and theatre director Vsevolod Meyerhold. Their friendships and collaborations influenced their creative work – across the mediums – as they shared satirical themes, iconography, and strategies for inducing laughter.

This book is about the deliberate use of laughter for purposes of acculturation in Soviet Russia in the 1920s and 1930s. It was designed to showcase primary sources: decrees, statements, and debates, as well as artworks in a variety of mediums. Indeed, the main arguments that structure this book are made by the protagonists of the story told here: Anatoly Lunacharsky, Vladimir Mayakovsky, Mikhail Koltsov, and many others.

Chapter One

Anatoly Lunacharsky and the Power of Laughter

Throughout history laughter resounds. It may be a roaring cannonade or an original music, accompanied by the clanking of little bells.

A.V. Lunacharsky[1]

In the spring of 1930, three years before his untimely death, Anatoly Lunacharsky, People's Commissar of Enlightenment from 1917 to 1929,[2] created a governmental commission for the study of satirical genres in literature and art, under the auspices of the Social Sciences Division of the Soviet Academy of Sciences. Lunacharsky had recently been nominated academician. He had also been appointed to a committee charged with the restructuring of the Academy, with the purpose of updating its work in relation to contemporary social and scientific imperatives.[3]

A preliminary document describing the goals and objectives of the "Commission for the Study of Satirical Genres in Western Europe" was drafted on 22 May 1930 by Lunacharsky with the help of Aleksandr Morozov, a young historian of literature who was to become the commission's secretary and its only permanent employee.[4] In the months that followed, the organ was renamed "Commission for the Study of Satirical Genres" to better reflect an extended mandate; its geographical and historical focus was expanded to encompass Latin America,

---

An earlier version of this chapter was published in French as "On rit au Narkompros: Anatoli Lounatcharski et la théorie du rire soviétique," *RACAR: Revue d'art canadienne/ Canadian Art Review* 37, no. 1 (2012): 41–52. This version has been substantially revised and augmented.

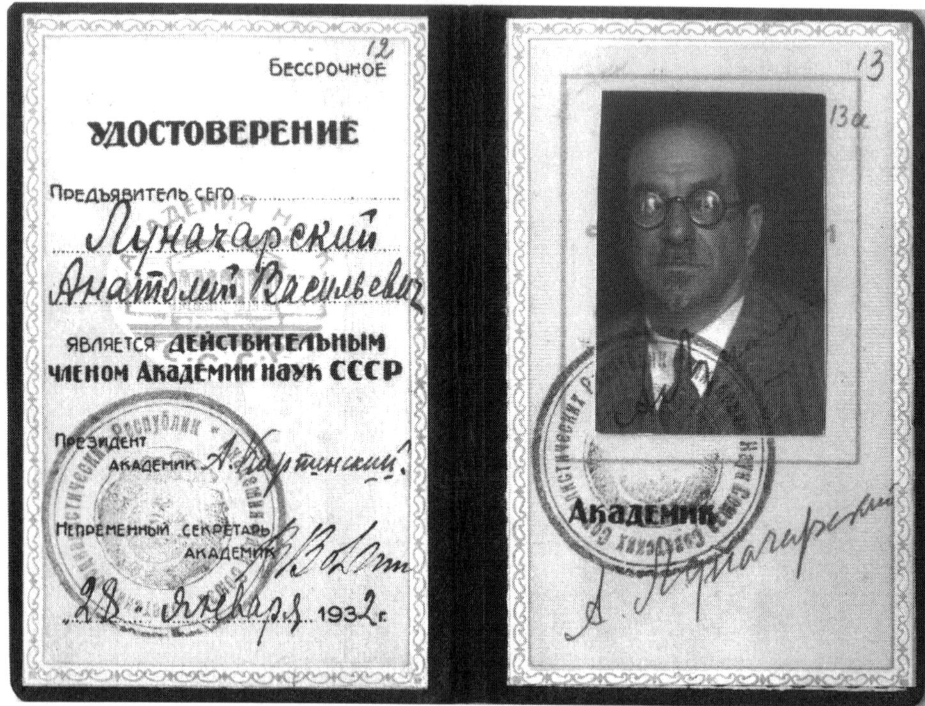

1.1 Anatoly Lunacharsky's Academy of Science identification document
for the year 1932. Russian State Archive of Literature and Art.

historical Russia, and the Soviet Union, and its scholarly objectives
developed from connoisseurship and the Marxist analysis of satire to
embrace epistemological, rhetorical, and other theoretical concerns. Em-
ploying intermittently established scholars and graduate students, its
main tasks were to study the reciprocal action established, in a variety
of historical contexts, between the development of satire and broader
social processes, and to build a reference library. The library – or Satire
Cabinet, as it was referred to – was to collect and preserve textual and
visual documents testifying to historical practices of satire, theoretical
works in a variety of languages, and examples of international satirical journals, manuscripts, artworks, photographs, and the like. The re-
defined objectives were presented by Lunacharsky on 30 January 1931
at the first working session of the commission, in a speech titled "On
Laughter" ("*O smekhe*"), which is reproduced in its entirety at the end
of this book.

Five weeks later, the creation of the commission was announced to the greater public; a letter signed by Lunacharsky was published in the 6 March 1931 issue of the Soviet Union's leading literary journal *Literaturnaya gazeta*.[5] As well as inviting readers to contribute to the Satire Cabinet by donating theoretical works and issues of foreign satirical journals such as *Punch* (1841–1992), *Simplissimus* (1896–1967), *Le Charivari* (1832–1937), *L'Assiette au beurre* (1901–12), *Kladderadatsch* (1848–1944), and *L'Asino* (1892–1925), the letter put an end to a two-year debate that had taken place in the journal about whether or not satire was still relevant or necessary in Soviet arts and literature.[6]

Lunacharsky's decision to channel scarce state resources into the study of satire seems incongruous from today's post-Soviet vantage point. Moreover, the very idea of distinguished members of the Academy of Sciences reflecting on a rhetorical mode most often associated with dissent, opposition, and rogue waggery seems absurd. But satirical genres may not have been considered so trivial in the emerging Soviet Union. Satire may in fact have been deemed a crucial weapon or tool in the struggle for acculturation that mobilized countless artists, theoreticians, and state workers. This first chapter outlines how satire was understood in the Soviet Russia of the 1920s and 1930s, and how it came to be viewed as an important political instrument. It does so by focusing on Anatoly Lunacharsky's theoretical writings and involvement in the literary and artistic scene of his day. It also builds on a history that demonstrates that satire had held a privileged position in Russian public discourse and practice since the eighteenth century.

Laughter and Satire in Tsarist Russia

Throughout its history, Russia has been the theatre of many and varied public manifestation of a comic nature. The best know is the enduring medieval carnival *Maslenitsa*. Celebrated for several weeks during the pre-Lent period, it is no doubt what inspired Mikhail Bakhtin in his writings on the carnivalesque. For Bakhtin, while carnivalesque laughter "remained outside all official spheres and outside all official strict forms of social relation"[7] – be they religious cult, state ceremonies, or etiquette – it nevertheless played an essential role in medieval culture. It served as a safety valve in an otherwise repressive and austere culture. It also held apotropaic virtues, warding off harmful and malevolent influences, while affording temporary victory over terror of God, fear of nature, and cultural taboo. Medieval laughter – parodies of Christian ritual, mocking of church and political hierarchy, comic processions, burlesque spectacles, irreverent ditties, grotesque pantomimes, festive madness, *diableries* and public obscenities – was most often coupled with feast. "It coincided with the permission for meat, fat, and sexual intercourse. The festive liberation of laughter and body was in sharp contrast with the stringencies of Lent."[8] As Dianne Ecklund Farrell remarks, "Within the festive life, popular humor constituted an alternative view and way of life. The festive life was everything that ordinary life was not – hence the popular saying 'that's not life, that's *Maslenitsa*.'"[9]

In Russia, this carnivalesque form exceeded the realm of the popular. In the second half of the seventeenth century it migrated to the court of Peter the Great, where it was made to contribute to the strengthening of tsarist rule. The "Transfigured Kingdom" consisted of a parodic theatralization of ecclesiastic ritual and court culture. During the feast, the tsar and his entourage would ordain false patriarchs and priests. They would engage in mock ritual, subverting ceremonies, ridiculing and renouncing God. While many contemporaries denounced the indecencies of the young tsar, select members of the nobility partook in the unholy bacchanalia, while "the properly ordained ecclesiastical officials not only would do nothing to forbid the tsar and his retinue from carrying on in this way but would even 'drink and act merry with them.'"[10] Ernest Zitser argues this carnivalesque celebration played an important role in the consolidation of Peter the Great's power. "By implicating courtiers in taboo-breaking bacchanalian mysteries," he writes, "the tsar and his advisers also attempted to induct select members of the muscovite elite into a new order of distinction between nobility and baseness, sacrality and profanity, tradition and modernity, thereby challenging them to confront, internalize and implement Peter's charismatic scenario of power."[11]

Other deep-rooted manifestations of laughter included *chastushki*, two- or four-line rhymed humorous poems, often set to music. During the Soviet period, the state appropriated this vernacular practice, publishing booklets of "ideologically appropriate" *chastushki*. The *lubok* also proved to be enduring. A popular visual art form that developed in the second half of the seventeenth century, it is characterized by simple and often amusing graphics and narratives derived from folktales, religious stories, and occasionally current events. Portraying the comic, the absurd, and carnivalesque reversals (such as domesticated animals overpowering humans), early *lubki* prints (whether woodcuts, engravings, or etchings) were used mainly for entertainment and decoration.

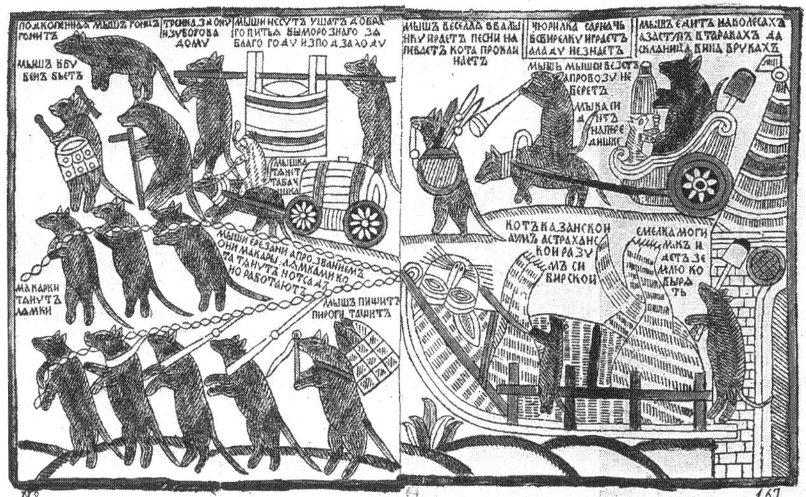

1.2 *Mice Burying the Cat*, anonymous *lubok*, circa 1725. Public domain; source, Wikimedia.

Medieval laughter tended to be farcical, irreverent, and inclusive. It turned the world upside down, subverting all hierarchies, dogmas, and moral norms, directed at all and implicating everyone; no one could extract themselves from the wholeness of the carnivalesque world. Most importantly, as Mikhail Bakhtin points out, it was ambivalent. It was gay, triumphant, and at the same time mocking. It all at once degraded, denied, sanctioned, and revived.[12]

In the eighteenth century, however, public laughter underwent crucial changes.[13] Ushered in by the didactic impulse of the Enlightenment, satire made its debut as medieval humour increasingly gave way to biting and divisive forms of laughter, usually charged with some social or political object lesson. Satire was used to mock and ridicule in order to denounce, exclude, expose, or chastise vice or excesses. As Michael Gardiner explains, referring to Bakhtin, this modern type of laughter reduced "genuine carnival laughter to 'cold' irony and sarcasm, whereupon it loses its vital power, its status as a positive, regenerating force."[14] Just like carnival, *chastushki* and *lubki* were also contaminated by the satirical spirit; they progressively became didactic instruments and political tools. *Mice Burying the Cat*, for example, is considered to be one of Russia's first works of printed satire. As Matthew Cullerne Bown argues, the cat in this image refers to Peter the Great, who passed away in 1725. He is rendered identifiable by his whiskers, "a reference to Peter's [controversial] adoption of the European fashion of a moustache rather than the traditional Russian Beard."[15]

The period of Catherine the Great's rule (1762–96) is often considered the Golden Age of the Russian Empire. A notable example of enlightened despot, she cultivated correspondences with Voltaire, Diderot, and d'Alembert, the French encyclopaedists who later cemented her reputation in their writings. Catherine also had standing as a patron of the arts and advocate for education. She founded a number of educational institutions, including the Smolny Institute, Russia's first academic establishment for women; and the Hermitage Museum, Russia's most important art gallery, began as the tsarina's personal collection.

Catherine the Great also penned comedies, essays, and memoirs. She celebrated the didactic and moral virtues of satire, and collected examples of European graphic and literary wit, such as the works of Rabelais, Molière, Jonathan Swift, Geoffrey Chaucer, and William Hogarth. In the first years of her reign, she founded and directed one of Russia's first satirical journals, *Vsyakaya vsyachina* (*All Sorts and Sundries*, 1769–70), in which she penned articles anonymously.[16] She also encouraged the publication of a dozen satirical periodical publications by freeing editors from preliminary censorship.[17] Satirical journals rapidly became immensely popular with the educated public, allowing for the mass circulation of critical ideas and the assessment of dissent.

Vsyakaya vsyachina ridiculed what it perceived as the outmoded morals and manners of the Russian gentry. It engaged in intellectual debates about education and serfdom, and served its readers a moralizing satire about good citizenry. It also came out against divergent social positions, primarily by attacking progressive satiric journals, in particular *Adskaya pochta* (*Mail from Hell*, 1769), *Truten* (*The Drone*, 1769–70), and *I to i syo* (*This and That*, 1769). Not only did all these publications participate in current debates, they also shaped and cultivated satirical practices as a means of promoting discussion in the developing public sphere. Only a few topics were off-limits: the tsarina, her government and public officials, and the bureaucracy.[18]

In the nineteenth century, satire – and the more general preoccupation with the social role of laughter that accompanied it – developed into a key topic of erudite deliberation for the emergent intelligentsia, most particularly in socialist circles. In fact, a critical, satirical spirit came to be understood as the touchstone of Russian intellectual culture. Dating the emergence of Russian literature to the middle of the eighteenth century, Vissarion Belinsky wrote in 1845 that "the satirical tradition was never interrupted in Russian literature."[19] "It has always constituted the most vigorous, or rather the only vigorous trend in our literature," added Nikolai Chernyshevsky in 1855.[20] In 1859, Nikolai Dobrolyubov summed it up by simply stating that "our literature started out satirical, continued to be satirical, and stands today on satire."[21] The crucial social role and significance of satire also became a topic for reflection, inasmuch as it was understood as having the capacity to participate in historical processes. In this vein, Aleksandr Herzen succinctly explained in1858 that "laughter is one of the most powerful tools against all that is outdated and hangs on to God knows what, the great ruins that frighten the weak and hinder the development of a new life."[22]

The chime of satire resounded constantly throughout the nineteenth century, responding to popular taste as well as political events. It manifested itself in the literature of Mikhail Saltykov-Shchedrin, Aleksandr Pushkin, Nikolai Gogol, and even Anton Chekhov. It also found its way into visual arts practices, in particular in the works of critical realist artists such as Ilya Repin, Vasily Surikov, Pavel Fedotov, Vasily Perov, and Vasily Pukirev, some of whom would join the *Peredvizhniki*[23] movement in 1863 and establish the stylistic basis of what would become Soviet socialist realism in the 1930s. They sought to portray Russian social life through a realist lens, often critical of inequities and injustices, often with sardonic undertones. *The Unequal Marriage* (1862) is typical of this satirical impulse (Plate 2). The genre painting depicts the wedding ceremony of a young, visibly unhappy girl to an elderly, high-ranking official. The work clearly denounces the subaltern position women occupied in mid-nineteenth-century Russian culture and ridicules in one fell swoop patriarchy, bureaucratic complacency, and corruption of the clergy. Vasily Perov's *A Religious Procession at Easter* (1861) was removed from an 1862 exhibition held in Moscow "because it portrayed the clergy rolling drunk,"[24] and with an unambiguously mocking intent.

The satirical trend in literature and the visual arts that was widespread in the second half of the nineteenth century, influenced by the critical writings of Belinsky, Chernyshevsky, Dobrolyubov, and Herzen, was intended to arouse dormant social consciousness and revolutionize society. These ideas infiltrated popular culture, as stand-up comedy involving social commentary became increasingly popular towards the turn of the century. Influenced by the circus as well as satirical journals,

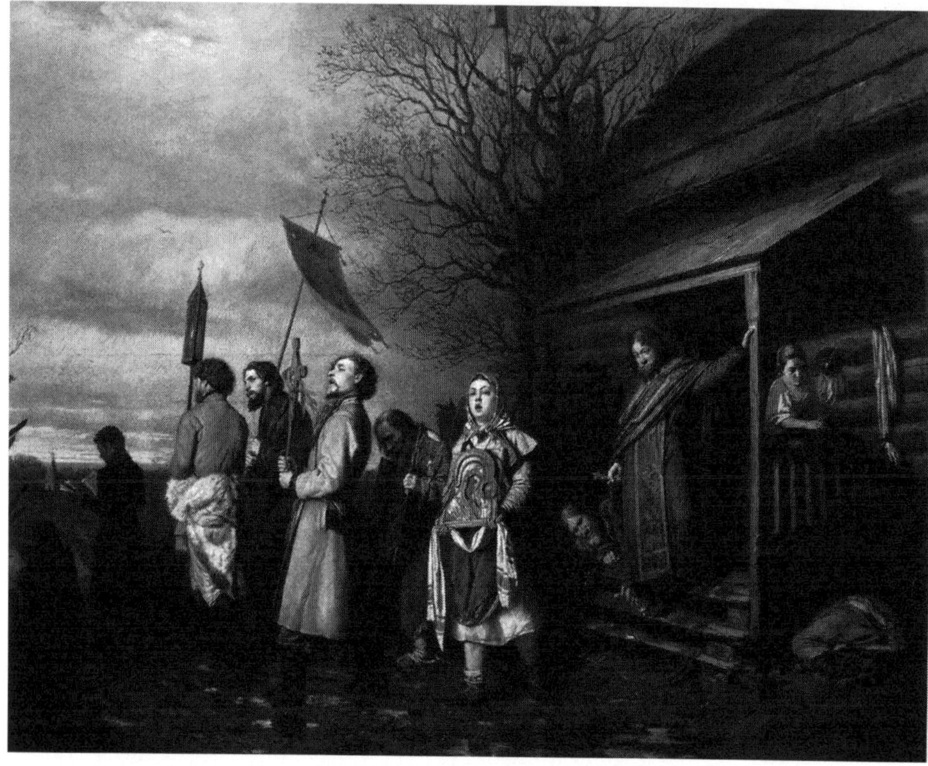

1.3 Vasily Perov, *A Religious Procession at Easter*, 1861. The State
Tretyakov Gallery.

stand-up often became topical, reacting to current events. As a Russian
critic once pointed out, "a joke for a nightclub routine must originate in
the morning newspaper."[25]

Enter Lunacharsky

As a young Marxist intellectual, Anatoly Lunacharsky bathed in this
critical tradition; he nurtured from the onset a keen interest in satirical and comic genres. From 1912 to 1914, while in exile in France, he
published his first series of articles dedicated to the cultural specificity of laughter, comparing comedy in the national theatre traditions of
France, Ireland, and England.[26] He also penned art criticism, review-
ing recent exhibitions of French graphic satire.[27] In these early days

Lunacharsky's understanding of laughter was limited to a strict sociological grid, much indebted to the writings of Belinsky, Chernyshevsky, Dobrolyubov, and Herzen. But following his intellectual incursions into the varied fields of art, philosophy, and psychology, his gaze and his analysis both sharpened.

During the 1920s and early 1930s, Lunacharsky, who in 1917 had become Soviet Russia's first People's Commissar of Enlightenment, wrote a series of theoretical texts testifying to his sustained interest in the fields of satire, humour, and laughter in general, as well as his theoretical grasp of the subject. These texts were strongly influenced by the principal theories of laughter then circulating in the European intellectual circles around which he gravitated. Lunacharsky read in the original the recent works of authors as diverse as the French philosopher Henri Bergson, the English philosopher, biologist, and sociologist Herbert Spencer, the Austrian neurologist Sigmund Freud, the English psychologist James Sully, and the German philosopher Theodor Lipps.[28] Leon Trotsky, in a commemorative text about Lunacharsky published in January 1934, just a few days after his death, remarked on the commissar's insatiable appetite for fashionable ideas and theories: "His glance wandered right and left. Lunacharsky was too receptive to each and every philosophical and political novelty to fail to be attracted by it and to play with it."[29] Lunacharsky's intellectual curiosity was also observed by François Champarnaud in his study of the Soviet Cultural Revolution. Casting a critical gaze on the commissar's intellectual production, he noted disapprovingly that "there is indeed a kind of dilettantism in Lunacharsky, as well as permeability. As a result, in his analyses, he often disappears behind the author he examines."[30]

If this unflattering comment allows us now to notice certain affectations that pepper Lunacharsky's writings, it is, however, important to underline that his evolving conception of laughter draws its originality from a very personal adaptation of European and Russian conceptions and theories, and their operationalization in the emerging Soviet context. It is also crucial to note that Lunacharsky's understanding of laughter is meticulously articulated within the Marxist conception of art that the commissar was developing during the same period.

Lunacharsky on Art

For Lunacharsky, art was first and foremost a social fact. It developed in close, dialectical relation with economic, political, and cultural processes. "First, according to Marxism as a social theory, art is a defined superstructure, emerging from a distinct framework of social relations of production, which are determined by the predominant forms of labour of a given historical period."[31] As a superstructure, art was therefore considered to be constituent of the world of ideologies, just like political thought, philosophy, and religion. And "among all these ideologies, art plays an eminent role. It is an organisation of social thought."[32] Furthermore, anchoring his thought in a Tolstoyan perspective, which defined art as communication or the social distribution of emotion,[33] Lunacharsky afforded it an affective and performative role. Art therefore acquired the potential to act as a catalyst by triggering emotions via viewers' senses as well as their intellect:

> *Aesthetic power* means, first and foremost, the organisation of expressive resources in such a way that they act directly upon the feelings of men, and change those feelings. And art is the highest expression of this kind of agitational work, this way of affecting emotionally those around you. That is why art is of such immense importance – it summons up, fosters and organises the sympathies of the individual for what is around him; it makes us understand, love, hate, feel a lively reaction to the existence of other people, of animals, of things, to the past and to the future; and if we can make use of the old art for this purpose, taking from it those elements which are appropriate to our purpose, how much more ought we to want to develop our own art, which will express *our* ideas, *our* principles, *our* views, and which will be of gigantic significance educationally.[34]

It is not surprising that, in the passage above, Lunacharsky avoided describing or qualifying in any concrete way emerging Soviet art practices. Indeed, in the thirteen years during which he occupied the duties of People's Commissar of Enlightenment, he worked with artists of all tendencies, refusing to openly favour one artistic movement over another or to impose a restrictive directive line with regard to either form or content. Furthermore, on multiple occasions he insisted on the essential neutrality of the People's Commissariat of Enlightenment (Narkompros) in relation to aesthetic matters, an attitude to which can be attributed the phenomenal artistic development and the diversity of practices that characterizes the first decade of the post-revolutionary Russian art world.

> Dozens of times have I said and repeated that the People's Commissariat of Enlightenment must demonstrate impartiality in relation to the different

tendencies that populate the art world. As for questions of form, the taste and preferences of the People's Commissar and other government officials should never be part of the equation. Let all artists and artistic groups evolve freely! Never let a single tendency push another aside, boasting titles of glory gained by tradition or by contemporary, fashionable success![35]

Finally, if for Lunacharsky art could serve as a vessel for education and propaganda, he was convinced that, for a work of art to deliver an affective as well as an intellectual impact, it had to be of great artistic quality. Indeed, in several of his texts, the commissar explicitly rejected propaganda that was banal, overly didactic or of inferior artistic quality. He often insisted on the fact that "it would be very imprudent to hang paper flowers to the bare branches of an early spring. To protect with blind obstinacy pseudo-artistic revolutionary [artworks] would result in such a policy."[36]

Lunacharsky on Laughter

In this context, Lunacharsky's writings shed a favourable light on certain literary and artistic practices that fall under the general heading of "laughter,"[37] whether they be historical or contemporary, local or foreign. He became acutely interested in the works of Jonathan Swift, Nikolai Gogol, Anatole France, Ilf and Petrov, Mikhail Saltykov-Shchedrin, George Grosz, Vsevolod Meyerhold, and Vladimir Mayakovsky, to name but a few. In the specific works he chose to examine, he particularly appreciated the deployment of satirical strategies, the effect of which he described in his expressive and often convoluted prose as "an aggressive laughter that hits the target,"[38] laughter that "kills with the venom of its poisoned arrows,"[39] through which the "screeching of chastisement becomes audible,"[40] and that announces "the thunder of an upcoming battle."[41] In order to impart even more sharpness to his descriptions of satire, Lunacharsky clearly distinguished this incisive and quarrelsome form of laughter from humour, which he described, following Sigmund Freud and James Sully, as the more generous laughter of those who "fully understand the burden of existence, and seek to afford themselves and others a short respite."[42]

In addition to introducing the most recent theories of laughter to the Soviet readership, he also penned a number of texts that encouraged artists of all tendencies to integrate satirical strategies into their artistic practice. He did so because, following Belinsky, Chernyshevsky,

Dobrolyubov, and Herzen, he considered that certain forms of laughter, and chiefly satire, were particularly well-suited instruments for the critical analysis of social processes in revolutionary times, and could therefore be harnessed for the purposes of propaganda art. As he underscored in his above-mentioned speech at the first meeting of the Commission for the Study of Satirical Genres: "Laughter is a tool, I would even dare to say a critical tool, which can either serve the objectives of auto-discipline for a social class; or alternatively, that can allow this class to exert pressure on other classes."[43]

Two main axes of theoretical reflection structure Lunacharsky's intellectual work on laughter: the psychophysiology of laughter and the social role of satire. These conceptions evolved gradually over a period of twenty years, combining a theoretical reflection with a more practical engagement that involved his practice as an art critic, a literary critic, a playwright, and, of course, People's Commissar of Enlightenment. Furthermore, as Aymeric Monville astutely remarks, one should never forget that Lunacharsky's theoretical writings emerged in a very particular historical moment, framed by specific political, social, and cultural conditions. "Let's imagine ourselves in this context of urgency. Let's understand that these are the tasks of a minister of culture, working in the service of a country barely coming out of feudalism, in which more than fifty percent of the inhabitants are illiterate. His mandate is to wage battle on two fronts: a democratic struggle for literacy throughout the country, and the passage from a reactionary culture to a revolutionary one."[44]

Lunacharsky broached for the first time in formal terms the psychophysiology of laughter in a text introducing the Irish satirical writer Jonathan Swift to the Soviet readership.[45] Here, references to the work of English philosopher, biologist, and sociologist Herbert Spencer are explicit, in particular to his 1863 essay "The Physiology of Laughter." For Spencer, laughter is a reflex, a physiological reaction caused by nervous and muscular excitation. And this involuntary response is the product of very particular circumstances. Laughter occurs when a subject, strongly absorbed by a thought, a feeling, or an emotion, is unexpectedly disturbed. The nervous flux caused by the emotive engagement, following appropriate physiological channels, is then also abruptly interrupted. If the subject's concentration is immediately redirected towards an equally captivating sentiment, then the nervous energy will follow other, more appropriate channels. However, if there is no alternative release route, then the subject's nervous energy is boisterously discharged in the form of a laughter reflex. As Herbert Spencer explains: "The discharge of arrested feelings into the muscular system, takes place only in the absence of other adequate channels – [it] does not take place if there arise other feelings equal in amount to those arrested … Laughter naturally results only when consciousness is, unawares, transferred from great things to small."[46] But if Spencer does not ascribe to laughter any particular emotional or moral value, other than the sudden relaxation of an absorbed mind and body, for the Marxist thinker there needs to be more: "Even the most rigorous psychophysiological analysis, establishing under what circumstances laughter occurs and what it means in biological terms, cannot resolve the problem of the social and historical character of laughter (even if psychobiological analysis can shed light on this problem)."[47]

In order to gauge the cultural and political character and value of laughter as a social phenomenon, Lunacharsky then turns to the work of the English psychologist James Sully, from which he draws psychological motivations that transform laughter into expressions of nervousness or fear.[48] He also integrates Sigmund Freud's discussion of the tendentious or aggressive potential of laughter,[49] as well as the understanding developed by German philosopher Theodor Lipps of laughter as a creative feat that serves the main purpose of establishing the superiority of the one who laughs over the object of his ridicule.[50] Finally, borrowing from Freud's principles of psychic expenditure and economy, described first in *The Joke and Its Relation to the Unconscious* and some twenty years later in *Humour*,[51] Lunacharsky portrays a subject suddenly liberated from stress by tendentious laughter. The subject, recognizing in the satirical work the evocation of an enemy, is immediately mobilized by fear and hatred. But certain traits, certain features of the characterization render the threat ridiculous. The mismatch between the initial reaction and the realization of its inanity causes swift demobilization and hence laughter. The expenditure of feeling that is economized turns into pleasure for the subject, who can also vicariously express emotions via the satirical work, with minimal affective outlay: "We now understand why laughter is such a merry and pleasant experience. You were armed to face stress or a threat; and were abruptly demobilized. You then quickly returned to a state of equilibrium. A good strong laugh that shakes your belly is the proof that, at the moment, you have no serious enemies."[52]

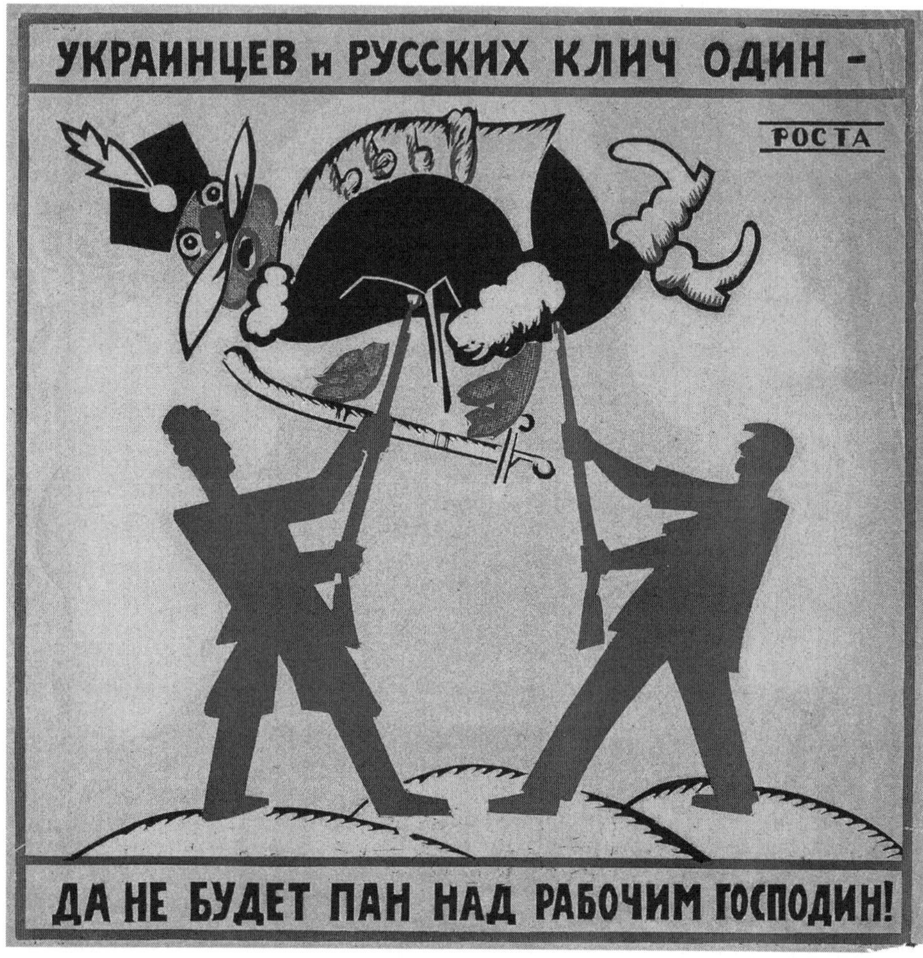

1.4 "Ukrainians and Russians have a common war cry – Pan will not be the master of the worker!" ROSTA window by Vladimir Mayakovsky, 1920. The poster satirizes the landowners of Poland (referred to by the term *pan*), Soviet Russia's enemies in the context of the Russo-Polish War. Part of the David King Collection. Presented to Tate Archive by David King 2016.

Beyond psychophysiology, Lunacharsky seeks, as any good Marxist intellectual would, to understand laughter in its social dimension. This aspect of his work borrows heavily from that of Henri Bergson, who explains in the very first pages of his seminal book *Laughter: An Essay on the Meaning of the Comic* that "to understand laughter, we must put it back into its natural environment, which is society, and above all we must determine the utility of its function, which is a social one. Such, let us say at once, will be the leading idea of all our investigations. Laughter must answer to certain requirements of life in common. It must have a *social* signification."[53]

In the particular context of the Soviet Union of the 1920s, the role of the satirist is therefore to guide the Soviet public towards preoccupations that are political or economic in nature, or linked to the practice of everyday life in an emerging Soviet state. Building on the psychophysiology of laughter as a corner stone, the satirist must first mobilize the attention of his public by portraying a subject that is at once contemporary, captivating, and menacing. In other words, he must produce affect. But he must also weave into the structure or form of the satirical composition he creates elements of ridicule, comic, caricature, or grotesque, which will unexpectedly trigger amusement and the sudden relaxation of the mind and body, therefore sparking laughter. It is this successful demobilization that, for Lunacharsky, allows the satirist to foreshadow the victory of the laugher over his enemy.

So then, what is a satirist? First and foremost, he is a very keen observer. He has noticed several revolting features about society that oppress you. You, his readers, his public, do not yet see these revolting features or are not paying sufficient attention to them. The publicist, in writing in a serious vein and drawing your attention to this evil, views it as an important and serious obstacle to the normal course of affairs. In a way, he attempts to frighten you. A satirist differs from the "serious" publicist in that he wants you to laugh at once at this evil, thereby giving you to understand that you are the victor, that this evil is miserable, weak, and does not merit serious attention, that it is far beneath you, that you can just laugh it off, that you are morally superior to this evil. Thus, the satirist's method is to launch an attack against an enemy, while simultaneously declaring him already vanquished and making a laughingstock of him.[54]

In Lunacharsky's work, laughter is thus much more than the mere result of enjoyment, tomfoolery, or entertainment. It is a weapon and a tool; it destroys the outmoded, the residual, and the deviant and contributes to building the new. By its belligerent attitude, laughter can also aim at garnering social gains. Indeed, "He who laughs established his superiority in relation to those he subjects to mockery; he attempts to reveal his opponent's weaker traits, and to reveal weakness can be an important manoeuver in social interactions."[55] Furthermore, laughter holds the potential of being an agent of social regulation, and consequently serves the goal of auto-discipline within a group. As Bergson explains, laughter casts the spotlight on "an individual or collective imperfection which calls for an immediate corrective. This corrective is laughter, a social gesture that singles out and represses a special kind of absentmindedness in men and in events."[56] In other words, laughter can contribute to social order, by establishing or consolidating norms. It does so by calling upon public opinion (a powerful tool in class struggle), which ridicules or punishes lapses, mistakes, and infractions: "For laughter to be effective, the laugher himself must first and foremost be convinced of the insignificance of his enemy. Secondly, laughter should attack the self-esteem of its target. Thirdly, in the eyes of its witnesses, mockery should be convincing; it should attract sympathy for the satirist's attempt to break his enemy."[57]

For Lunacharsky, satirical laughter is never kind. A powerful weapon in revolutionary times, it exposes, disarms, humiliates, defeats, and conquers. It must often be cruel. "To say that 'we're just having a laugh' is misleading," he writes. "To say that you are laughable actually means that I see you as degraded, it means I won't even honour you with serious criticism."[58] But, as Bergson explains, this cruelty strikes a chord in human beings. "In this sense, laughter cannot be absolutely just. Nor should it be kind-hearted either. Its function is to intimidate by humiliating. Now, it would not succeed in doing this, had not nature implanted for that very purpose, even in the best of men, a spark of spitefulness or, at all events, of mischief." [59]

Lunacharsky's 1931 speech at the Commission for the Study of Satirical Genres explicitly addresses this potential of laughter to strengthen social tendencies and correct ideological deviation, particularly in a revolutionary context:

Laughter has always been an important element in social processes. The role of laughter is as important as ever in our struggle, the last struggle for the emancipation of human beings.

We will therefore be happy and proud if we succeed in defining and analysing the historical development of laughter through concrete examples, and thereby fashion sharp tools for our humorists and our satirists.[60]

Shaping and Nurturing Soviet Laughter

Throughout his career as commissar, Lunacharsky was involved, whether from close or afar, in the production of satirical artworks. As a playwright he wrote a number of satirical pieces; as a historian and critic he commented on the most prominent satirists, of past epochs and of his day; as a popular theoretician he educated producers of satire and publics, and encouraged them to push their own critical understanding further. But perhaps most importantly, Lunacharsky was the man at the head of the People's Commissariat of Enlightenment, through which seasoned and emerging satirists received governmental commissions to produce their works. Let's not forget that after the October Revolution the private art market, still in its infancy at the beginning of the twentieth century, was suffocated by nationalization policies and the effects of the Civil War. In this context, the Narkompros became, for all intents and purposes, the main employer for Soviet artists, and the most important patron of artworks and works of propaganda.

Several artworks facilitated by Lunacharsky will be examined in the following chapters. The strategies developed by artists and the subjects that satirical forms privileged will also warrant discussion. But before we conclude this chapter, a few remarks remain to be made about Lunacharsky and his involvement in shaping and nurturing a Soviet culture of laughter and satire.

First and foremost, Lunacharsky appreciated and valued laughter. Several acquaintances and friends recall, in their various memoirs and tributes to the commissar, how he enjoyed reading humorous and satirical literature, how he truly loved to hear and tell jokes. During the event commemorating the thirtieth anniversary of Lunacharsky's death, in 1963, Soviet author Lev Nikulin recounted how Lunacharsky always accepted with good grace being the target of a witty anecdote.[61] In his account, Vladimir Mayakovsky, employed at the Narkompros during the 1920s, seems to have been the constant perpetrator of "friendly jests" directed against the commissar. The number of caricatures published in the journals *Krokodil, Prozhektor,* and *Begemot,* which make light of Lunacharsky's graphomania, idealism, and excessive enthusiasm, also testify to the commissar's openness in matters of laughter. Poking fun at a high-ranking official might have been perilous from the mid-1930s until Stalin's death, as Osip Mandelstam's experience sadly demonstrates. But the situation was different in the 1920s. As Nikulin explained, "These were days when people who understood and loved Soviet power could make jokes, and no one would be offended by them."[62]

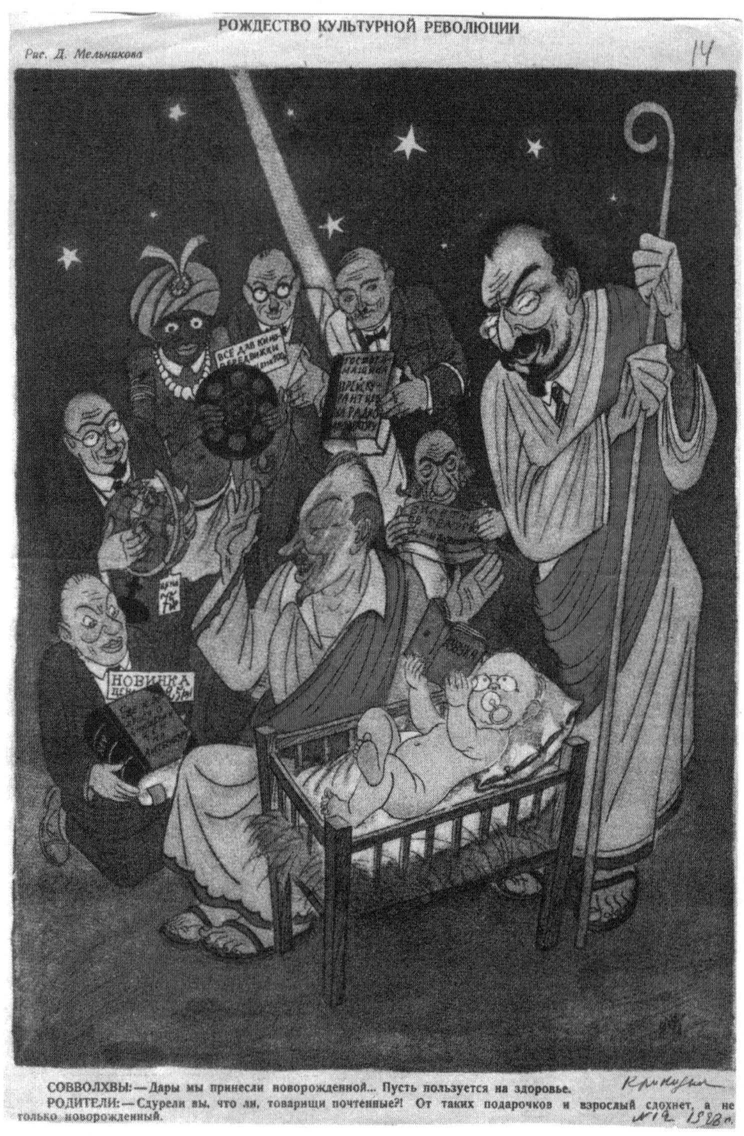

1.5 "The Birth of the Cultural Revolution" by D. Melnikov, *Krokodil* 12 (1928), p. 7. Bureaucrats resembling the Magi bring the child literature, cinema, theatre tickets, and other symbols of Soviet culture, as Anatoly Lunacharsky, to the right, watches over him. Part of the David King Collection. Presented to Tate Archive by David King 2016.

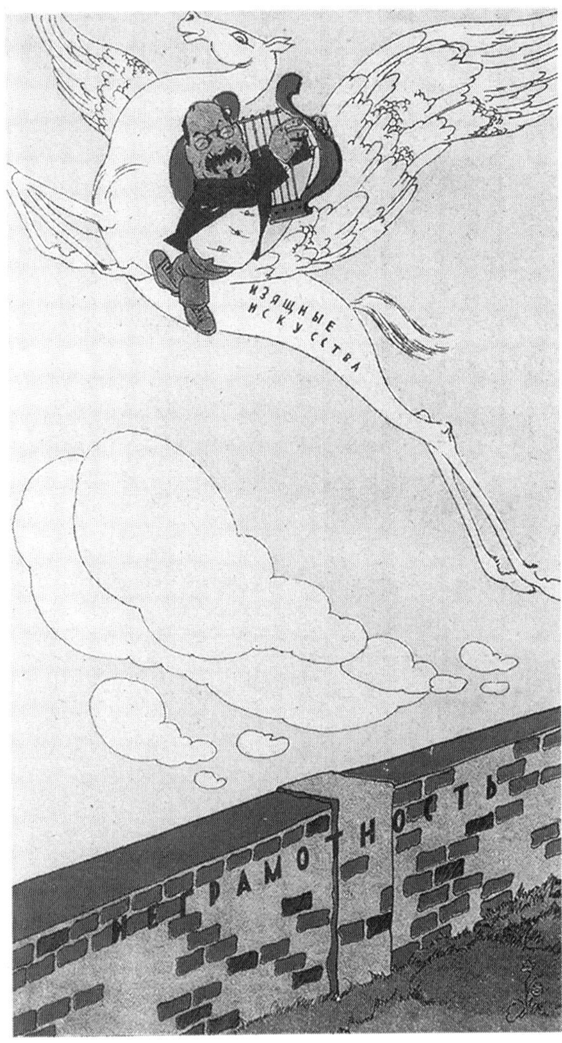

1.6 Anatoly Lunacharsky sitting on Pegasus, the horse of the ancient Greek muses, playing the harp. They leap over the barrier of illiteracy. *Krokodil* 13 (1929), p. 7, by M. Khrapkovsky. Part of the David King Collection. Presented to Tate Archive by David King 2016.

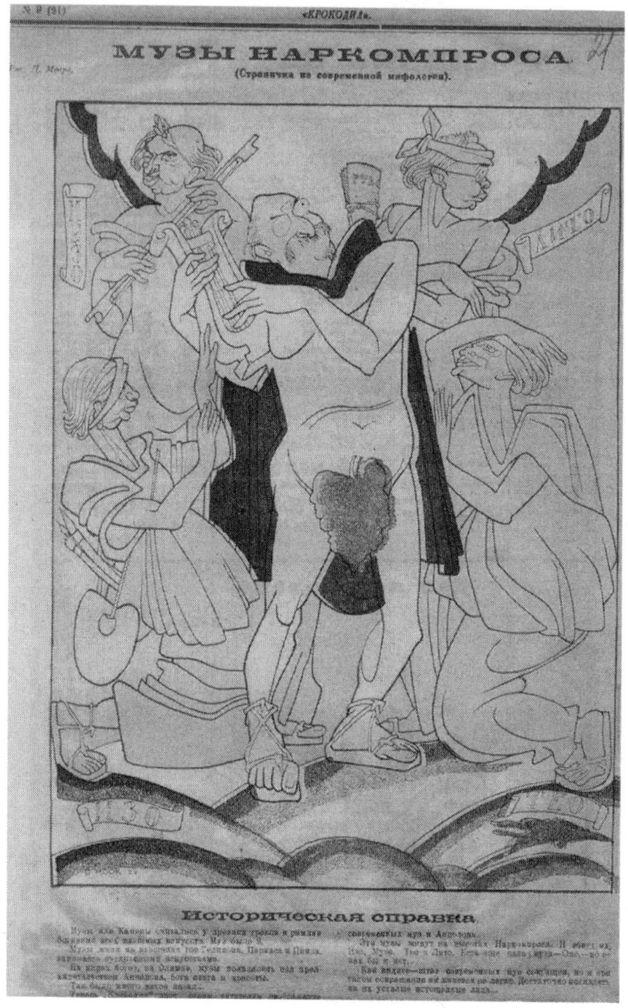

1.7 "The Muses of the Narkompros." The muses represent music, literature, theatre, and the visual arts. *Krokodil* 9 (1922), p. 18, by Dmitrii Moor. Part of the David King Collection. Presented to Tate Archive by David King 2016.

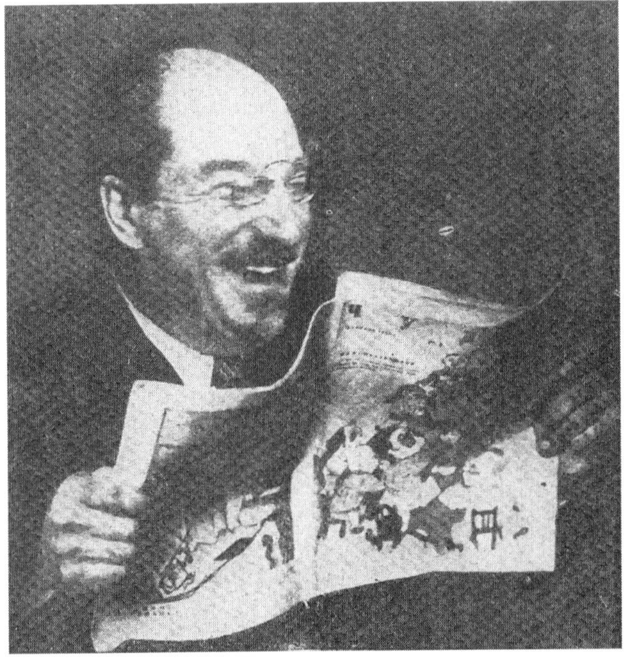

1.8 Anatoly Lunacharsky reading the satirical journal *Chudak* (*The Oddball*), *Chudak* 11 (1929), p. 15. Part of the David King Collection. Presented to Tate Archive by David King 2016.

The keen interest in laughter Anatoly Lunacharsky developed in his youth accompanied him throughout his life. After he resigned from his post as commissar, this interest grew even stronger. A few months after the creation of the Commission for Study of Satirical Genres, Lunacharsky travelled to Germany. On 26 September 1930 he wrote his wife, the actress Natalya Rozenel, about how he imagined the following years of his life:

If fate continues to lead me down the same paths, which I happily travelled in the past, then all is clear. It is clear that I need to detach myself, physically and mentally, from my former "duties" and "administration," and from intense political activity (although, in this respect, the last 13 years [at the Narkompros] have been tremendously beneficial). It is also clear that my new circumstances will guide me towards Europe ... I was asked to write a book about Lenin, which will focus on contemporary wisdom. Aside from this, I want to write "Laughter as a Weapon in Class Struggle," in which I'll be able to outline my conception of aesthetics. If I have enough strength, I will then turn my attention to a third book, which I haven't titled yet. This one will be a history and theory of wisdom.[63]

Lunacharsky passed away in December 1933 in Menton, France, on his way to take up the post of Soviet ambassador to Spain. His remains were returned to Moscow where his urn was buried in the Kremlin Wall Necropolis, alongside Bolshevik revolutionaries. The Commission for the Study of Satirical Genres, which owed its very existence to the enthusiasm of the former commissar, was dissolved. His book on laughter was never finished. His preparatory notes are preserved in the State Archives of Art and Literature in Moscow.[64]

Chapter Two

Soviet Satirical Print Culture: A Serious Affair

Satire can be taken to extremely high degrees of malevolence, which makes laughter poisonous, biting ... your laughter also proves that you consider the evil that you mock so deep and harmful that you cannot hide your irritation and animosity.

A.V. Lunacharsky[1]

An interest in a political culture of satire manifested itself in Soviet Russia from the onset. It was soon to encompass artistic production in a variety of art forms and media, from literature to painting and music, from theatre to cinema and circus. Its most notable expression, however, was surely print culture: broadsheets, posters, periodicals, and books. These served as a privileged means for the dissemination of mass propaganda in the early years of the regime.

But this use of the print medium was not at all new. In Russia as elsewhere, print culture had served to mould public opinion and collective self-image for centuries. What is particular to the Soviet context is that the government viewed the mass reproduction of images, text, and rhetoric as a tool that could play a considerable role in popular mobilization and acculturation. This chapter highlights the crucial importance of print culture as a support for visual propaganda, in particular in the first decades that followed the October Revolution, by tracing

---

An earlier version of this chapter was published in French as "Rire rouge: La presse satirique en Russie soviétique," *Ridiculosa* (special issue, 2013): 56–93. This version has been substantially revised and augmented.

a history of Russian and Soviet illustrated satirical journals and Civil War–time posters.

The Decree on the Freedom of the Press: October 1917

On 27 October 1917, the Council of People's Commissars released a decree restricting freedom of the press. The council had that day met for the first time, and the Revolution was two days old. The celerity with which measures were taken to control the publishing industry is a clear indicator of the importance print culture held in the eyes of the Bolsheviks. The "Decree on the Freedom of the Press" was immediately followed by the confiscation and nationalization of paper and ink supplies, specialized machinery and print shops.

It is important to note from the outset that liberty of the press had always been a relative concept in Russia, in particular since the instauration of the first censorship law in 1804 by Alexander I. This censorship rule was maintained with an iron hand, except in short periods of political instability when unbridled print culture flourished, in particular between November 1905 and March 1906 and for a few months in 1917, between the abdication of the tsar and the October Revolution.[2]

The October 1917 decree constituted an urgent measure, targeting specifically counter-revolutionary presses of all stripes, "those inciting to open resistance or disobedience towards the Workers' and Peasants' Government; those sowing confusion by means of calumny and perversion of facts; those inciting to criminal actions punishable by penal laws."[3] The decree also drew the public's attention to the fact that, at that time, the great majority of the Russian media were controlled by bourgeois interests. In revolutionary times, freedom of the press would hence be tantamount to the encouragement of counter-revolutionary propaganda. On this aspect, the decree is clear:

> Everyone knows that the bourgeois press is one of the most powerful weapons of the bourgeoisie. It was impossible to leave this weapon in the hands of the enemy at a time when the press is no less dangerous than bombs and machine guns, in this critical moment when the new order, that of the workers and peasants, is in process of consolidation. This is why temporary and extraordinary measures have been adopted for the purpose of cutting off the stream of rubbish and calumny in which the yellow and green press would like to drown the recent victory of the people.[4]

Even if, in fact, freedom of the press was never re-established in the Soviet Union, the document was nevertheless explicit about the topical and provisional nature of the restrictions: "The present decree is temporary and will be revoked by special *order* when normal conditions of social life return."[5]

The diktat, which produced a de facto state monopoly in the field of publishing, immediately fell under attack from all sides, even from within the Council of People's Commissars.[6] The Bolshevik government had in the past positioned itself in favour of freedom of expression and freedom of the press.[7] It was now accused of negating the most fundamental principles of its own political program. Lenin's government was therefore made to explain itself on a number of occasions, in particular during the period of the Civil War (1917–23), when its authority was particularly fragile. It did so mainly through the pen of Anatoly Lunacharsky, the People's Commissar of Enlightenment, the official in charge of education, arts, and propaganda.

In a text published in 1921, the commissar took stock of the current debate on the freedom of the press. "People are telling unbelievable stories," he wrote. "They say that the revolutionaries, having fought for the freedom of expression refused to them under the old regime, are in turn denying it to others – this is absolute philistinism."[8] For Lunacharsky, the regulation of the print industry in the period that followed the Revolution was of crucial importance. At a time when radio had not yet become a major means for mass communication, periodical publications were the single most efficient medium the state could harness to communicate with the population. This remained true despite the difficulties caused by the necessary reorganization of the printing industry after the Revolution and during the Civil War. Furthermore, since the party considered words and images as crucial tools and weapons in the context of mass propaganda, the control of print material also became an essential means of maintaining relative social peace. For Lunacharsky, "Words are weapons. Just as the revolutionary government cannot tolerate everybody running around with handguns and machine guns because some could in fact be menacing enemies, the state cannot tolerate freedom of printed propaganda."[9] In fact, the commissar even considered censorship of certain literary and artistic publications as the necessary flip side of an efficient Bolshevik propaganda machine: "If the government strives to establish and encourage various forms of artistic propaganda, then it is obligated to strike down artistic counter-propaganda."[10] In any case, he concluded, freedom of the press in bourgeois society is pure illusion. Writers have always depended on those who finance their work – the nationalization of the publishing industry marks no exception.

The Bolshevik satirical illustrated press was born in this context of censorship. Inspired by the tradition inaugurated in Russia in the eighteenth century during the reign of Catherine the Great, it modelled itself on the satirical periodicals that appeared in large numbers during the events of 1905.

Antecedents of the Soviet Satirical Press: Bloody Sunday 1905

A torrent of anti-tsarist satirical periodicals appeared in the fall of 1905, in the wake of Bloody Sunday (5 January 1905), a peaceful demonstration in which over 30,000 citizens participated. The demonstrators called for the liberation of all imprisoned revolutionaries, better labour conditions, the concession of land to peasants, and the suppression of censorship. The imperial guards opened fire on the protesters, an act of excessive violence that caused thousands to be wounded and killed. This murderous gunning down sent a clear signal to the workers of Saint Petersburg about the lack of cooperation they could expect from their government. In turn, they called a strike, which rapidly reached its apogee with 150,000 strikers. From then on, a series of industrial actions, affecting the majority of industries, sparked across Russia. Strikes became increasingly radical until the ratification of the October 1905 Manifesto on the Improvement of the State Order, as it was officially known, which pledged to constitute a parliament and to grant certain civic liberties to the people, including freedom of religion, speech, and assembly. In reality, the manifesto did not significantly increase these liberties; the tsar continued to exercise the power of veto on the government and dissolved it several times.

In the publishing industry, the youthful and politically united printers' guild established itself at the forefront of the struggle. Starting in January 1905, typesetters had illegally been producing subversive books and periodicals. Then, during a meeting held in October, journalists and typesetters jointly decided that they would no longer voluntarily submit themselves to preliminary censorship. In an even bolder resolution, they moved to no longer "address any claims for freedom to the government, but to institute such freedoms ourselves, without permission."[11]

If the October Manifesto, signed by Tsar Nicholas II on 17 October 1905, supposedly granted freedom of expression, in reality censorship on print matter remained effective. While most industries resumed operations, the strike in the print industry continued. Tensions escalated when, on 19 October, the Saint Petersburg Soviet declared that only publications refusing to surrender themselves to censorship would be published. On 30 October, a new decree issued by the government finally explicitly recognized freedom of the press. That freedom nevertheless remained only partial: ministers and other officials could be named and openly criticized, but the tsar could never be mentioned without the authorization of censors, and his positions could never be debated or opposed. The weakened censorship apparatus allowed all kinds of materials and contents to seep through its loosened fingers. Censored publications were even sold on the streets of Saint Petersburg, without reprisal. Because of their more ambiguous nature, images in particular managed to escape repressive measures, providing a topical supplement to the more or less veiled meaning of unsympathetic texts. At this time, illustrated periodicals seized their role as a privileged site for critique, debate, and opposition.

During the very days that followed the October 30 decree, hundreds of writers and artists placed themselves under the banners of a variety of satirical illustrated journals, such as *Pulemet* (*The Machine Gun*, 1905–06), *Zhupel* (*The Bogeyman*, 1905–06), *Gudok* (*The Whistle*, 1906–07), *Skorpion* (*Scorpion*, 1906), *Knut* (*The Knout*, 1906–07), *Buksir* (*The Tugboat*, 1907), *Signaly* (*Signals*, 1906), and *Strely* (*Arrows*, 1906). Between 1905 and 1908, over four hundred satirical journals were created, serving as barometer of public opinion. But they were all short lived, disappearing abruptly under the hammer of censorship, re-established in full force and effect in 1906.[12]

Of all the periodicals to emerge in the first decade of the twentieth century, one illustrated satirical journal stands apart, first because of its ten-year lifespan – remarkable for that period – and second because it survived the October 1917 Revolution and, for close to a year, Soviet censorship. This journal is the weekly *Satirikon* (*The Satyricon*, 1908–14), which morphed into *Novyi satirikon* (*The New Satyricon*, 1914–18) following a rebellion of its main contributors in 1914.[13] During the First World War, the journal became the voice of the liberal intelligentsia and a forum for Russia's patriotic voices. Then, at the beginning of 1917, *Novyi satirikon* adopted an aggressively anti-Bolshevik stance, which consolidated and became more militant with the Bolsheviks' seizure of

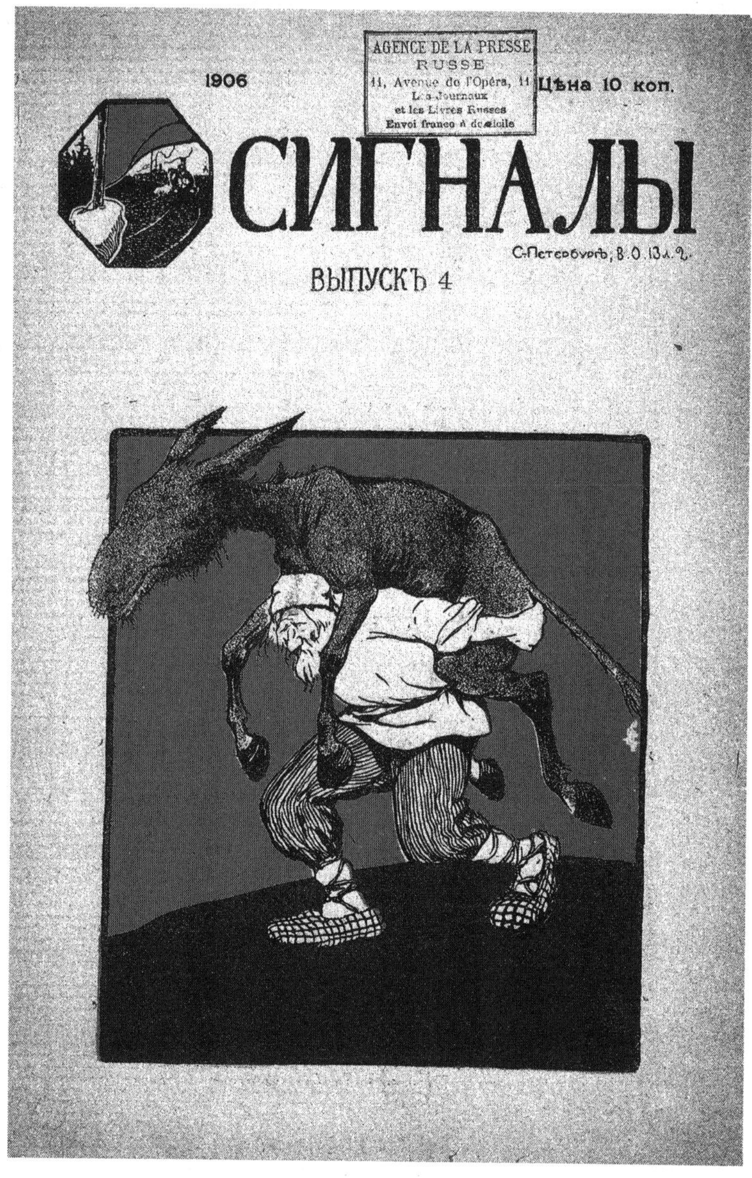

2.1 *Signaly* (*Signals*), no. 4 (1906), cover. Part of the David King Collection. Presented to Tate Archive by David King 2016.

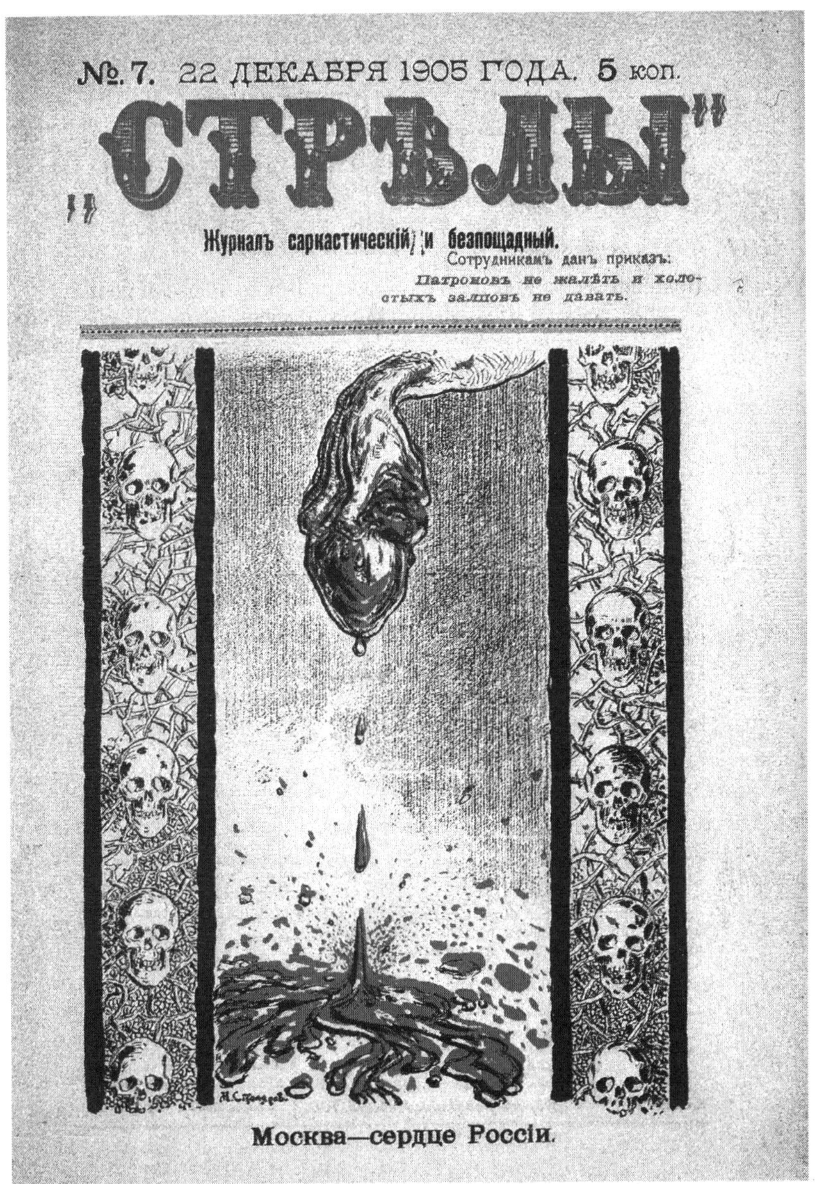

2.2 *Strely* (*Arrows*), no. 7 (1906), cover. "Moscow – The heart of Russia." Part of the David King Collection. Presented to Tate Archive by David King 2016.

power in October. The tone of *Novyi satirikon*'s particular brand of satire was most often ironic and sarcastic. The December 1917 issue, titled "N. Satirikon Thanks the Bolsheviks for ...," exemplifies this strategy that uses crude overstatements to imply the exact opposite of what it explicitly states. On the journal's cover, a Bolshevik is represented as an enormous, brutish man slouching on a gigantic chair, ostentatiously placed on a monumental pedestal. This image eerily prefigures the throne room scene orchestrated ten years later by film-maker Sergei Eisenstein for his historical dramatization *October* (1928). At the bottom-right corner, a satyr proclaims: "*Novyi satirikon* thanks the Bolsheviks for ... see page 2." Pages 2 to 9 provide striking and fully ironic visual examples of what the new government should be thanked for: liberating Russia from foreign capital; isolating it on European soil; freeing the state apparatus from unnecessary – as well as necessary – bureaucracy; sending the Russian population roaming on a long and uncertain path; and the like. The journal survived until August 1918, when it was prohibited by the Revolutionary Tribunal of the Press,[14] and hence deprived of paper and ink.

With the liquidation of *Novyi satirikon*, Russian satirical press became almost non-existent. There were a few attempts to create journals espousing Bolshevik ideological positions: *Balalaika* (*The Balalaika*, 1918), *Bich* (*The Whip*, 1916–18), *Gilotina* (*The Guillotine*, 1918–19), and *Krasnyi dyavol* (*The Red Devil*, 1918–19), to name a few. A small number of short-lived publications distributed exclusively to Red Army soldiers at the front also surfaced, such as *Krasnyi shmel* (*The Red Bumblebee*, 1920) and *Krasnaya zvezda* (*The Red Star*, 1921–22). But, as Sergei Stykalin explains, during the period of the Civil War that followed the Revolution, material conditions were extraordinarily unfavourable to this type of venture, and no journal managed to publish with regularity.[15] Everything was lacking: paper, ink, and lead type as well as trained personnel. It is only with the end of the Civil War that new satirical publications appeared and managed to publish issues in a more or less regular rhythm, finally allowing for the constitution of a necessary solid readership base.

Civil War-Time Satirical Posters

Since satirical journals lacked the means to rapidly and effectively communicate political and social events during the Civil War, they were replaced with large-scale satirical posters, which provided quick and

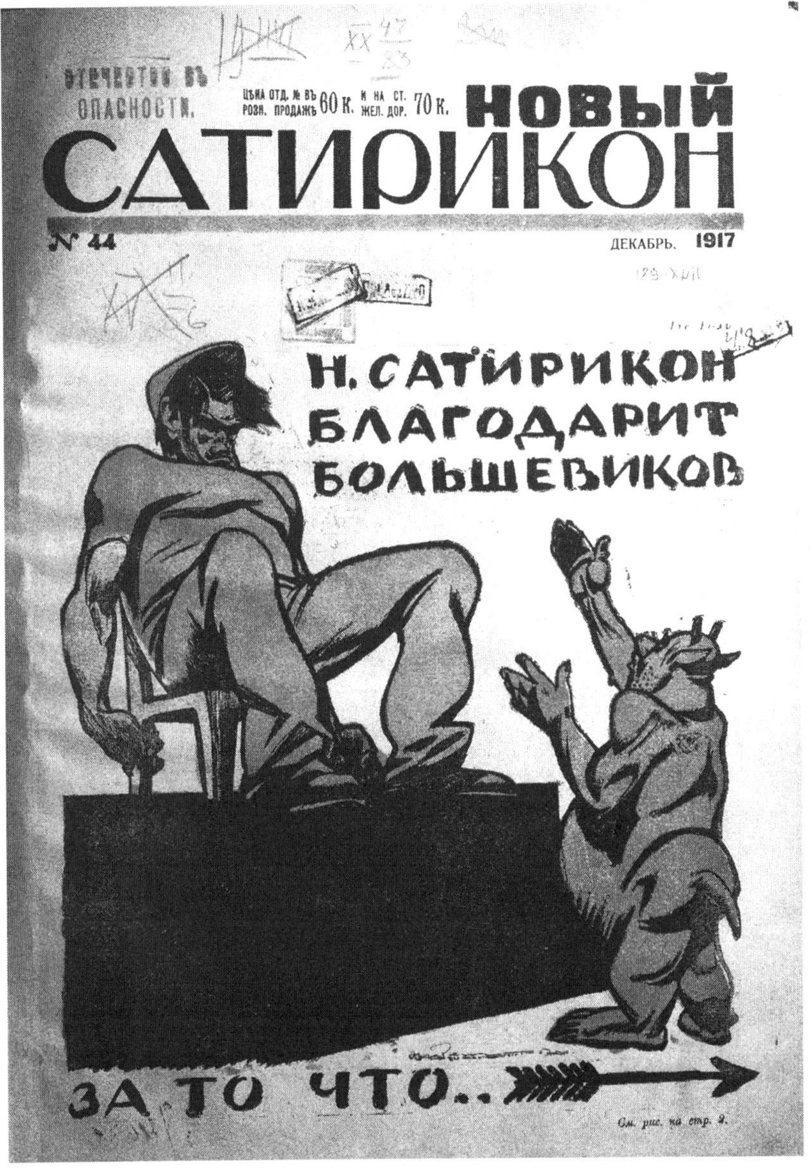

2.3 "N. Satirikon Thanks the Bolsheviks for …" *Novyi satirikon* 44 (1917), cover. Russian State Library.

inexpensive dissemination of information. These were produced by a variety of presses working under Soviet jurisdiction. According to Stephen White, between 1918 and 1921 well over thirty-six hundred posters were produced on a variety of themes. Of these, the majority were printed (57.5 per cent) and the remainder hand crafted.[16]

Visual satirists Viktor Deni and Dmitrii Moor contributed hundreds of posters, often with print runs that reached one hundred thousand copies. "The League of Nations," for example, is a satirical poster designed by Viktor Deni. It was produced in Moscow by the publishing organ of the Revolutionary Military Council, the supreme military authority of Soviet Russia, chaired by Leon Trotsky. This particular image denounces and mocks the newly formed League of Nations. It portrays France, the United States, and Great Britain as jowly, portly capitalists, their bellies resembling money bags; they sit on gilded thrones atop a heap of distorted bodies wearing measly rags. In the background, gallows project their dark silhouette against a blood red sky. Such posters were meant to concentrate into one caricatural image large amounts of information. This one identified the League's protagonists, clearly marked their ideological/economic allegiances, exposed the colonial roots of their prosperity, and denounced the hypocrisy of their peaceful mission. In other words, it discredited the League through laughter. The seriousness of this wartime satire is underscored by a warning printed at the bottom-right edge of the frame: "Anyone who tears down this poster or covers it up is performing a counter-revolutionary action."

A Dmitrii Moor poster from the same period shows a mighty trio formed of a soldier, an industrial worker, and a peasant sweeping away cowering enemies of the regime into a comical procession. "The People's Court" (1919, also published under the auspices of the Revolutionary Military Council), parodies the boustrophedonic structure used in Russia throughout the tsarist period to depict royal, religious, or military processions in their entirety (Plate 3). Following the trajectory shaped like an elongated and reversed S, the viewer can appreciate the panoply of parading wrongdoers the young regime had to contend with: top-hat-wearing capitalists, kulaks, antagonist military officials, representatives of several religions, and figures emblematic of corruption, such as Grigori Rasputin, the self-proclaimed holy man assassinated in 1916, dragging behind him naked women clutching at his feet.

Not all posters produced during the Civil War period were satirical, obviously. Many drew on allegory and myth to produce symbols of struggle and victory. Some were meant to elicit tears by showing the misery of

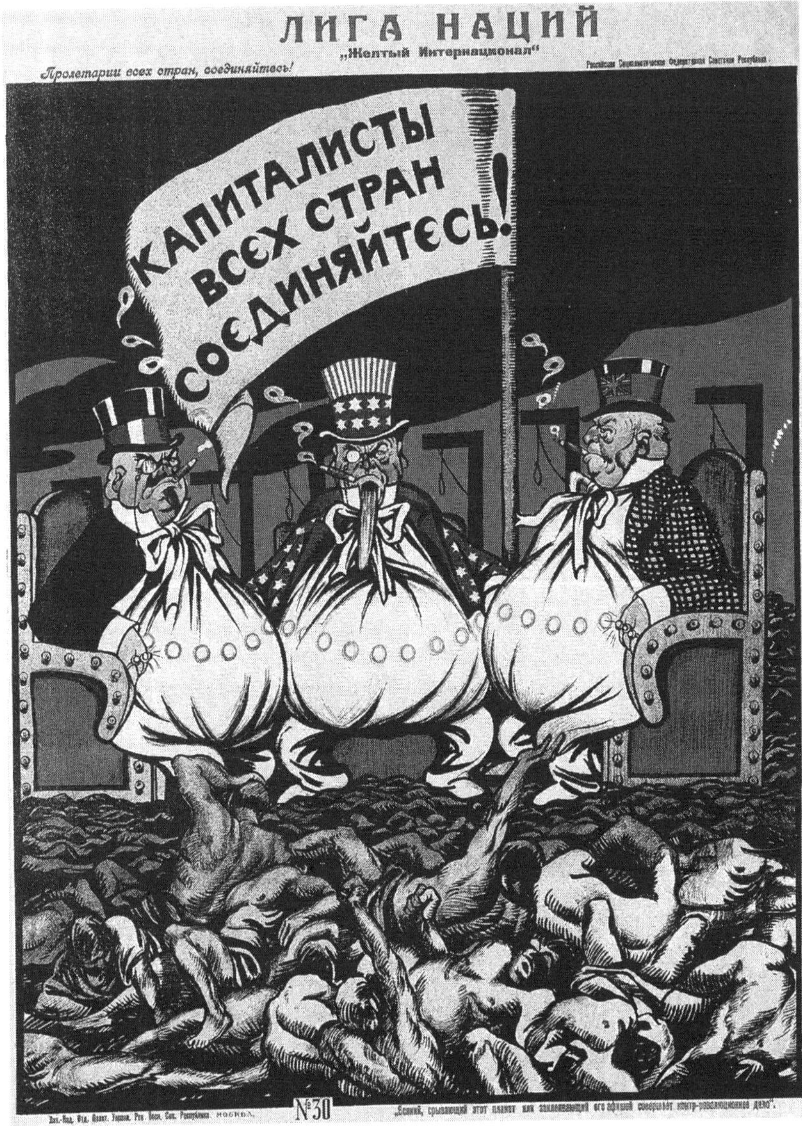

2.4 "The League of Nations,"1920, poster by Viktor Deni. Corpulent figures representing France, the United States, and England sit on a pile of emaciated corpses. On the flag, the slogan reads: "Capitalists of the World Unite." Part of the David King Collection. Presented to Tate Archive by David King 2016.

the oppressed. Others were designed to inspire, featuring heroic youthful male and female workers earnestly looking to the future. But as one rapidly notices when looking at a variety of Civil War–time posters, satire played a very specific role in the propaganda arsenal: it became a specialized tool used to discredit or shame enemies of the regime through ridicule.

The most important publisher of satirical posters during the Civil War period was, without a doubt, the newly constituted Russian Telegraph Agency (ROSTA),[17] an organ working under the auspices of the Narkompros. It produced "ROSTA windows" between September 1919 and January 1922.[18] These were propaganda posters or groups of posters, usually displayed in the morning in the windows (hence their name) of the Telegraphic Agency, train stations, kiosks, and empty storefronts across the country. Several windows were produced each day. In particular circumstances, they could react immediately to urgent news received from the front and be posted within the hour. In order to accelerate the production process (and because of material shortages), the posters were made by hand. At first they were copied with carbon paper. They were later painted with cut-out stencils made from cardboard and occasionally put through a printing press. This allowed for rapid duplication, with circulation reaching 150 to 300 copies.[19] The development of stencils also made it possible for artists to share templates or repurpose successful imagery for use in other windows. Artists adapted to their needs time-honoured visual strategies borrowed from 1905 political journals and from popular arts, in particular *lubki*. In ROSTA windows, visual satire was always accompanied by slogans, often taking the form of rhymes, puns, and *chastushki*, which could be set to music and repurposed as ditties.

Several well-known artists contributed to the production of the windows, working in Moscow or in the regional offices of the Telegraphic Agency: satirists Mikhail Cheremnykh, Ivan Maliutin, and Dmitrii Moor; avant-garde artists Kazimir Malevich, El Lissitzky, Marc Chagall, and Vladimir Lebedev; and artists who would later be associated with socialist realism, but who cut their teeth on ROSTA windows. Painter Aleksandr Deineka, best known for the monumental mosaics he produced in the 1930s for the Moscow Metro, started out at the Kursk regional ROSTA office. The futurist poet Vladimir Mayakovsky also contributed numerous images (for more than four hundred posters) and signed the texts of nearly 90 per cent of the estimated sixteen hundred different windows produced over three years. His experience working at ROSTA is described in a book published posthumously in 1932 under the title *Groznyi smekh* (*Menacing Laughter*).[20]

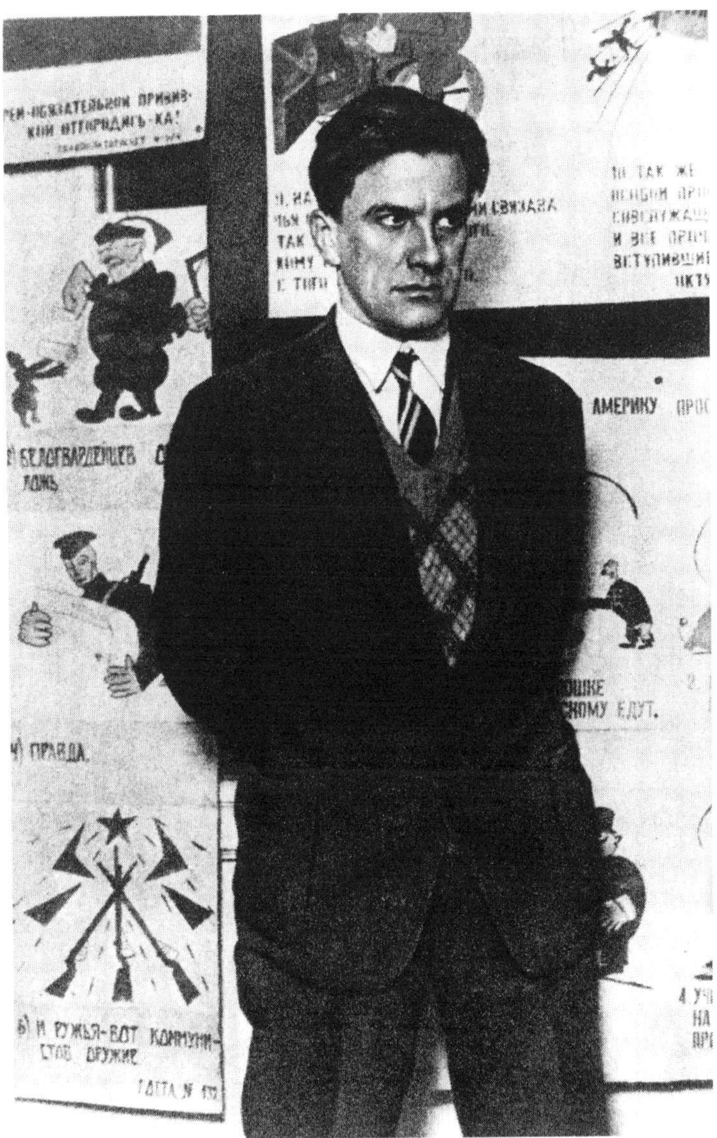

2.5 Vladimir Mayakovsky standing in front of ROSTA windows at the
Russian Telegraph Agency, circa 1920. Part of the David King Collection.
Presented to Tate Archive by David King 2016.

In ROSTA windows, a range of caricatural figures, whose exaggerated features made them easy to interpret by the largely illiterate masses, circulated freely. They portray enemies of the regime as hateful, stupid, and ridiculous. The most prominent satirical character is the foreign general covered in absurd medals and gold trimming, hands dripping with blood. He keeps company with the pot-bellied capitalist in his black dinner jacket and top hat, dragging along an enormous money sack, and the priest, his nose red and bulbous from alcohol abuse, stealing from peasants their meagre crops. There are also positive, yet equally inflated, characters. The most recurrent by far are the Bolshevik worker and the Red Army soldier, both tall, strong, heroic, generous, valuing learning, and determined to partake in the construction of the socialist world.

ROSTA's representations employ what was known as *tipazh*, a practice strongly encouraged in the field of propaganda in the 1920 and 1930s. It sought to shed a bright light on social categories, through strategies that imply the concentration or even the exaggeration of characteristic elements. As Victoria Bonnell explains, "In the Soviet Lexicon, the term *tipazh* implied a correct rendering of a particular social category. The essence of *tipazh* was not typicality but, rather, typecasting or typicalization."[21] In other words, *tipazh* was meant to translate into images (whether they be textual or visual) what was considered "the true essence" of things, beyond their strict everyday appearances. In his 1931 discussion of *tipazh*, Lunacharsky further insisted on the necessity to transform and exaggerate certain characteristic traits: "The artist should not be satisfied by what he sees. He must go beyond, in order to reveal tendencies that have not yet revealed themselves."[22] He believed that repetition of this deformed "true" image of the world could alter the very structure of social perceptions. Although *tipazh* could be positive as well as negative and was certainly not exclusive to the domain of caricature and satire, the concentration of signifying features into a single form lent itself well to the genres of laughter.

In a ROSTA window such as *The Frenzied Polish Gentry Pounced on Russia Arrogantly* by Vladimir Mayakovsky, *tipazh* is crucial to the understanding of the narrative. This representation corresponds to a news brief published in the newspaper *Izvestia* on 15 September 1921, which related that the French ambassador in Warsaw had sent a "note" to the Polish government advising that famine in Russia had created favourable conditions to exert pressure on the Soviet government. The Bolsheviks retorted without delay with a clear message: any negotiation would be bilateral, and would not be grounded in provocation or intimidation. In the series of twelve images that constitute the window, typecast figures of Polish officers prance around, portly in their green costumes decorated with gold trim and

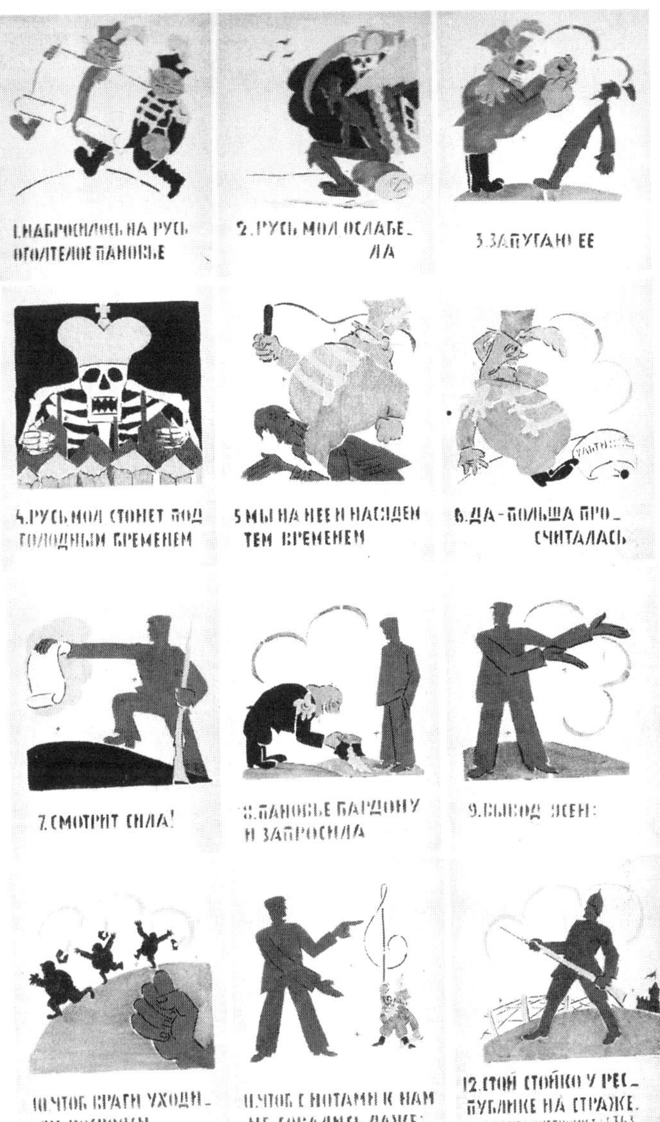

2.6 Vladimir Mayakovsky, *The Frenzied Polish Gentry Pounced on Russia Arrogantly*, 1921. The Israel Museum, Jerusalem. Photo © The Israel Museum, Jerusalem by Meidad Suchowolski.

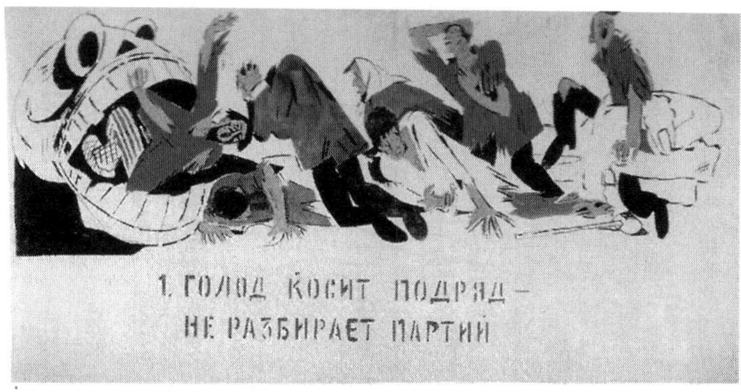

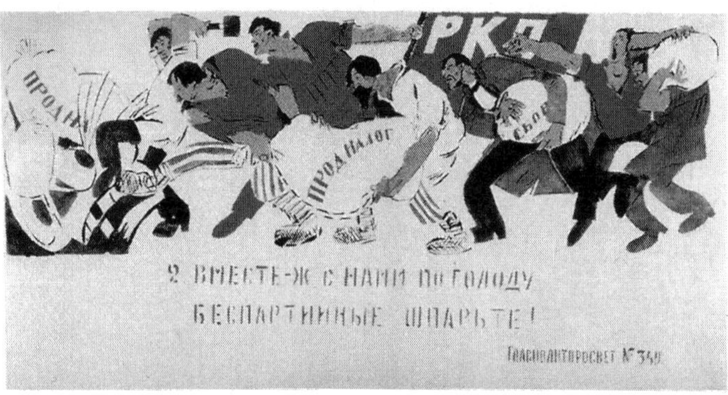

2.7 Vladimir Mayakovsky, *Famine Kills Mercilessly – Regardless of Party Membership*, 1921. The Israel Museum, Jerusalem. Photo © The Israel Museum, Jerusalem by Meidad Suchowolski.

epaulettes. Famine – which is more difficult to represent through exaggerated mimesis – appears as an enormous skeleton coiffed with the imperial crown, an image that reveals both its source and the interests it serves. In the following panels the Bolshevik worker and the Red Army soldier make an appearance. Each cuts an enormous red silhouette. They block the enemies of the regime in their stride. In the eleventh panel, a minuscule Polish general, radically diminished by the towering confidence shown by the worker, is sent back to Poland with his "note." In other examples, the enemy takes the form of an enormous emaciated skull, which deflates when confronted by the united front of workers (*Famine Kills Mercilessly – Regardless of Party Membership*); or of illness, here anthropomorphized, yellow from head to toe and covered with the suppurating pustules of smallpox (*Do We Need a Decree on Compulsory Smallpox Vaccination?*).

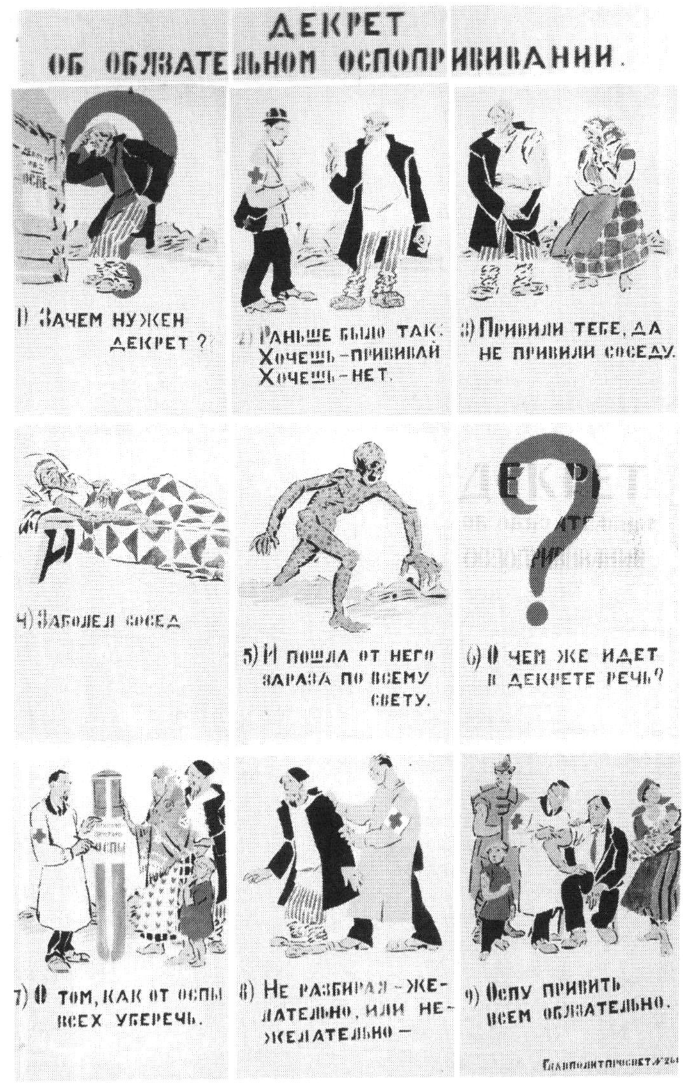

2.8 Vladimir Mayakovsky, *Do We Need a Decree on Compulsory Smallpox Vaccination?*, 1921. The Israel Museum, Jerusalem. Photo © The Israel Museum, Jerusalem by Meidad Suchowolski.

ROSTA windows constituted a world awash with menacing enemies, injustice, hunger, and illness. But, following Lunacharsky's reflections on the power of laughter, if the representations provoke strong affect by presenting frightful and galling enemies, it is only to swiftly undermine them, render them ridiculous, and defuse the threat. As the commissar explained, "The satirist anticipates victory. He says: let's laugh at our enemy. I assure you he is ignominious and that we are stronger than he."[23]

Posters produced during the Civil War at the offices of the Telegraph Agency would be expected to recognize, first and foremost, military threat and famine, but an important number of images also present internal threats: reactionary, antisocial, or criminal elements as well as residual tendencies inherited from the tsarist past that continue to evolve in Russia, in spite of the Revolution. *From Now On Riding on the Engine Will Not Be Permitted*, for example, accompanies a decree issued 15 April 1921 criminalizing illegal passage on locomotives. Towards the end of the Civil War, few locomotives were in service because of fuel shortages and scarcity of spare parts. It was therefore of outmost importance that trains that remained in functioning order not be damaged by careless stowaways. In panels nine to eleven of this window, an analogy is drawn that transforms the destructive nuisance into farce: "Imagine that someone hoisted himself onto your shoulders as you walked. You might be able to drag on for a bit. But you'll soon crumble into a breathless mass." Other internal targets of the windows were sabotage, prostitution, and alcoholism. In this satirical context, laughter served the purpose of shedding a comic light on deviations from the Bolshevik norm or on "an individual or collective imperfection which calls for an immediate corrective,"[24] to borrow, once again, from Bergson.

ROSTA windows were extremely popular yet short lived. They correspond exclusively to the period of the Russian Civil War. The form was, however, revived two decades later when the Soviet Union officially entered WWII. These were now produced by TASS (Telegraph Agency of the Soviet Union), which had gradually replaced ROSTA. Between 1941 and 1945, an estimated 1,250 individual windows were produced by over 130 artists and 100 poets. Just like their precursors, TASS windows were reproduced in great numbers and disseminated throughout Russia and abroad.[25] The overwhelming majority of the representations focused on external enemies of the Soviet Union, in particular Hitler's Germany. Hitler himself appears under various always unflattering and ridiculous guises, as a pig, a crow, or a raggedy busker.

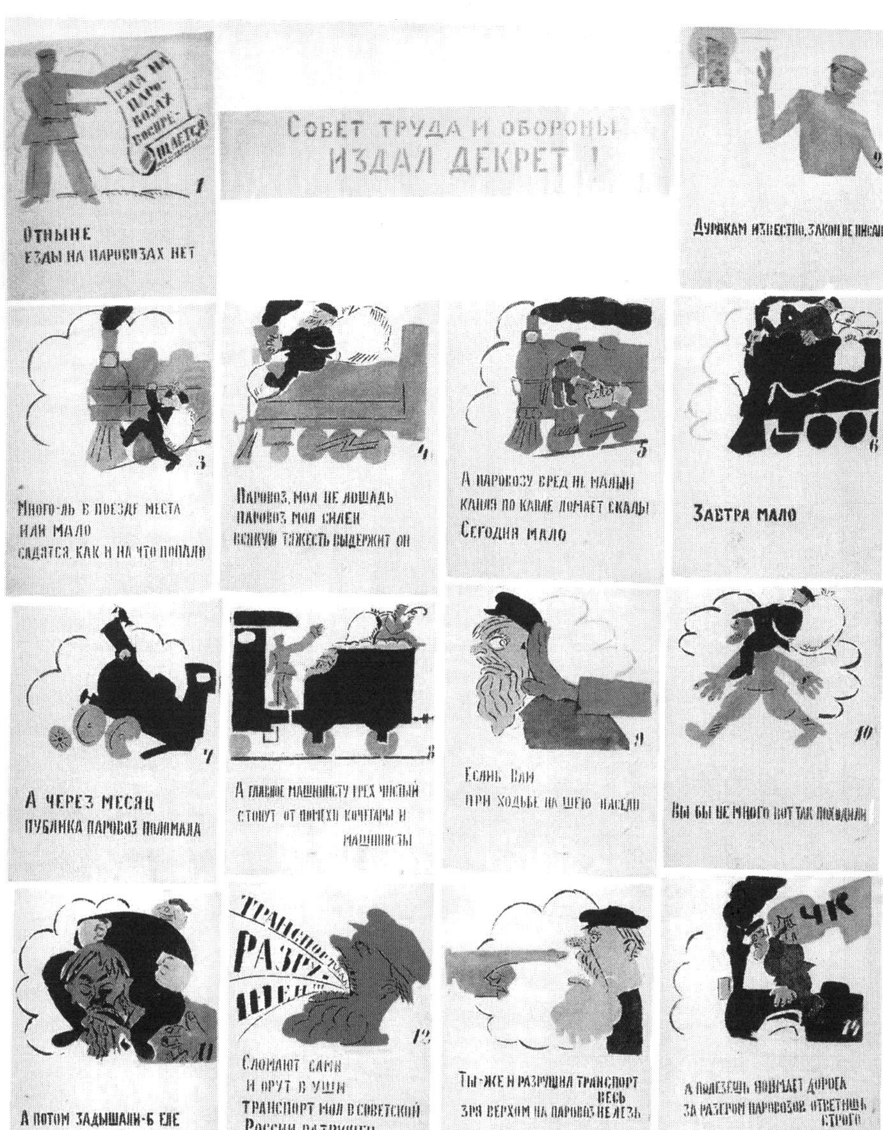

2.9 Vladimir Mayakovsky, *From Now On Riding on the Engine Will Not Be Permitted*, 1921. The Israel Museum, Jerusalem. Photo © The Israel Museum, Jerusalem by Meidad Suchowolski.

ROSTA windows, along with other posters published by state publishing agencies to support various campaigns, served to establish in early Soviet Russia both *tipazh* and satirical strategies as a means of propaganda in print culture. They opened the way for continuous use of laughter in print propaganda, until the collapse of the Soviet Union in 1991. Mayakovsky considered them "the ancestors of all Soviet satirical journals, ancestors from harder times, times when paper and machines were scarce and we worked by hand."[26]

Satirical Press in the Soviet Union

Except for the few exceptions mentioned in the first part of this chapter, there were no journals dedicated exclusively to satire in Russia before the period of the New Economic Policy (NEP, 1921–28) that followed the Civil War.[27] Graphic satire hence found itself most often relegated to illustrated supplements printed and distributed by Party papers. *Krasnaya kolokolnya* (*The Red Belfry*, 1918), for example, was a Sunday supplement distributed free of charge with the daily *Krasnaya gazeta* (*The Red Newspaper*, 1918). It served as an important forum for artistic and literary satirical creations from working-class, non-professional satirists. Similarly, *Krasnyi voron* (*The Red Crow*, 1922–23),[28] a publication known for its incisive tone, was published under the auspices of the daily *Krasnye ogni* (*Red Lights*, 1922–23), first as a free supplement and then, a few months later, as a paid publication more or less independent from the *Krasnye ogni* editorial board.

Since the Revolution, the majority of periodicals published by the state had been distributed for free. They focused mainly on theoretical issues and important social and political issues. These newspapers and journals have been criticized for the high level of literacy they required from their publics. Even free, they remained inaccessible to the average worker.[29] It is only with the NEP that periodicals started to be sold, either by street vendors, in kiosks, or, more often, by subscription. They were then subject to market laws[30] – even if the content of all periodicals needed to be approved by the party and their paper stock and ink were allotted by the state. The journals published during the NEP period thus became more specialized, targeting particular readers: peasants, urban workers, women, militants, soldier, even non-party citizens. In this matter, the satiric press was no exception. For example, *Mukhamor* (*The Fly Agaric*, 1922–23) was intended for Petrograd's non-party intelligentsia; *Krasnyi perets* (*The Red Pepper*, 1923–26) spoke to an educated,

Bolshevik readership interested in international politics, gender equality, party and bureaucracy reforms, and the like; *Komar* (*The Mosquito*, 1924–26) targeted Leninist youth; and *Bezbozhnik u stanka* (*Godless at the Workbench*, 1923–32)[31] was mainly dedicated to antireligious activism in urban centres. In spite of these new publishing opportunities, the satiric press remained, in the view of many, insufficient. Mayakovsky complained, in 1925, about the lack of organs publishing in the field. "I itch to write satirical pieces. It is not that anybody forbids them. We have so few satirical journals and they are filled to capacity. But in newspapers, not a single editor will print [satirical] poems. They find them altogether silly."[32]

Although the material challenges had been at least partially resolved, the lifespan of NEP-period satirical journals remained relatively short. According to Stykalin, the cause of these failures is not to be found exclusively in the conditions of production. The test lay rather in how journals were able to connect with broad readerships, in particular the workers, and address their concrete preoccupations. Throughout the 1920s, satirical publications often failed to reach the working class, resulting in limited print runs.[33] In turn, small editions precluded publishing houses from establishing a solid economic basis. In a system where the state considered the press as an important propaganda tool, this weakness did not go unnoticed.

Indeed, a moment that turned out to be pivotal in the development of Soviet satirical periodicals was the publication, by the Party's Central Committee, of the decree "On Humoristic-Satirical Presses" in April 1927. The decree constituted a severe critique addressed to the great majority of Soviet satirical journals. It expressly declared that they had not, in the past, sufficiently fulfilled their social and political role:

> The majority of satirical-humoristic journals have not achieved their goal of becoming the organs of a chastising satire, directed against negative elements that hinder the construction of our regime, against remnants of the old order, and against chauvinism, petit bourgeois attitudes and reactionary tendencies, which survive in certain segments of the working class. They must combat, on the one hand, class enemies, whether it be inside or outside the borders of the USSR and, on the other hand, ideologies hostile to the proletariat (in particular social democracy). If the journals do not target a mass readership, then they embark on a path that will inevitably lead them to espouse petit bourgeois interests.[34]

A clear mandate was then given them:

> The principal role of satirical-humoristic journals is to criticize and unmask
> negative influences that hinder the construction of communism; concep-
> tions, traditions and habits of the petit bourgeoisie, which reveal themselves
> in the everyday and in many aspects of social life; all corporatist tendencies,
> bureaucratic and chauvinist, which impede the interests and the duties of
> the proletariat in the construction of socialism; and all the enemies of the
> people, as well as those who support them, consciously or not.[35]

Finally, the decree ordered journals to better target their readership
and to use visual and textual strategies better adapted to the general
cultural and literacy levels. Five journals were then assigned specific
niche markets. First, *Krokodil* (*The Crocodile*, 1922–2000[36]) and *Begemot* (*The Hippopotamus*, 1924–28) were required to target a readership
mainly constituted of politically aware workers; *Buzoter* (*The Hellion*,
1924–27[37]), of professionals (and therefore a more educated public);
Smekhach (*The Wag*, 1924–28), of office workers; and *Lapot* (*The Bast Shoe*,
1924–33), of agricultural workers. The editorship of these publications
was strongly encouraged to consult members of their targeted public
and solicit opinions and feedback in order to best meet their mandate.
They were also helped in this by studies conducted about readers' likes
and desires.[38]
Then, swept by the wave of centralization of resources, effectives,
and organizations, which characterized the period of the First Five-
Year Plan (1928–32), all satirical journals were liquidated, except for
Krokodil and the antireligious illustrated satirical journal *Bezbozhnik u
stanka*, which held a special status. *Krokodil* hence reigned as the only
official satirical journal of Soviet Russia. Its print run shot up to 500,000
exemplars, in the 1970s reaching six million.[39] *Krokodil* preserved its
monopoly until the dissolution of the Soviet Union in 1991, in spite of
several attempts to create new journals that always tended to be topical and therefore short lived. For example, during the Second World
War, several satirical periodicals were created specifically to entertain
and inform soldiers stationed at the front, such as *Perekrestnym ognem*
(*Crossfires*, 1942), *Skvoznyak* (*The Draft*, 1942), and *Partizanskaya dubinka*
(*The Partisan Truncheon*, 1942–43). A number of important satirical journals, analogous to *Krokodil*, also appeared in the national languages of
the Soviet republics, for example *Perets dlya zapadnykh oblastei Ukrainy*
(*The West Ukraine Pepper*, 1944–49, published in Ukrainian), *Mush-
tum* (*The Fist*, 1951–present, published in Uzbek), *Ara* (*The Bumblebee*,

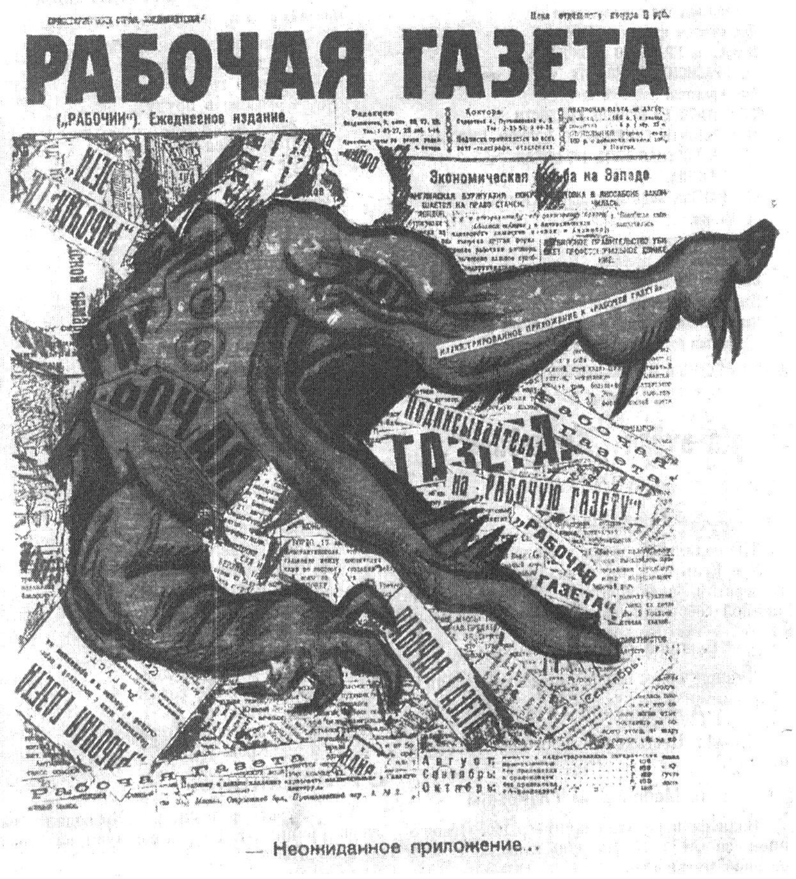

2.10 *Krokodil*, no. 1 (1922), cover. Part of the David King Collection. Presented to Tate Archive by David King 2016.

1956–present, published in Kazakh), and *Khorpushtak* (*The Hedgehog*, 1953–present, published in Tadjik).

Krokodil was the first journal to successfully capture the interest of the mass of Soviet workers. This allowed it to garner continuous state support for close to seventy years. Founded in 1922 by a decree of the Central Committee of the Communist Party of the Soviet Union, it was first produced under the supervision of *Rabochaya gazeta* (*The Workers' Newspaper*, 1922–32), and then, from 1932, by the daily paper *Pravda* (*The Truth*, 1918–91).

In its first years, *Krokodil* was more akin to a pamphlet than a journal. It was small (ten pages measuring roughly eight by six inches). It was issued once a month, printed in black and white on yellowish newsprint. From its very beginnings, its aims were openly ideological. Born in the first year of the New Economic Policy, it directed its venom specifically at NEPmen[40] and the international bourgeoisie. During the Second World War, the satirical journal became an instrument for patriotic mobilization, informing its readers on matters of international politics and ridiculing Russia's enemies, in particular Nazi Germany and Fascist Italy. In 1948, after the war, the Central Committee reviewed the journal's performance and determined that the propaganda effort waged during the war years in the pages of *Krokodil* had often been awkward, had had limited impact, or had missed its target altogether. In an official decree, it then ordered a revamping of the journal, which became more voluminous (twelve by twenty inches and about thirty pages). From a monthly periodical, it turned into a weekly, with a seriously augmented print run of five million copies. Most importantly, *Krokodil* editors were urged to improve the artistic quality of both graphic satires and texts. Furthermore, in peacetime, its mandate was once again adjusted: "The main task of the journal is to fight against vestiges of capitalism in popular consciousness. With the weapon of satire, the journal must unmask plunderers of socialist property, vandals and bureaucrats, as well as all occurrences of conceit, toadyism and banality; it must respond swiftly to international events, and carry out a critique of bourgeois culture in the West, revealing its insignificance and its degeneration."[41]

A similar message was sent once again in a resolution of the Central Committee taken on 28 September 1951. Here, the Central Committee accused *Krokodil* satirists of having a poor handle on politics: "*Krokodil* often prints tales and poems that are unrealistic and uninspiring, weak drawings and caricatures, which have no serious purpose, and are peppered with errors in their interpretation of questions of internal affairs or international events."[42] Editors were urged to fact-check and to ensure the level of political consciousness of their contributors. If nothing else has, this constant meddling of the Central Committee in both the form and content of *Krokodil* proves, once and for all, that in the Soviet Union satirical print culture was a serious affair.

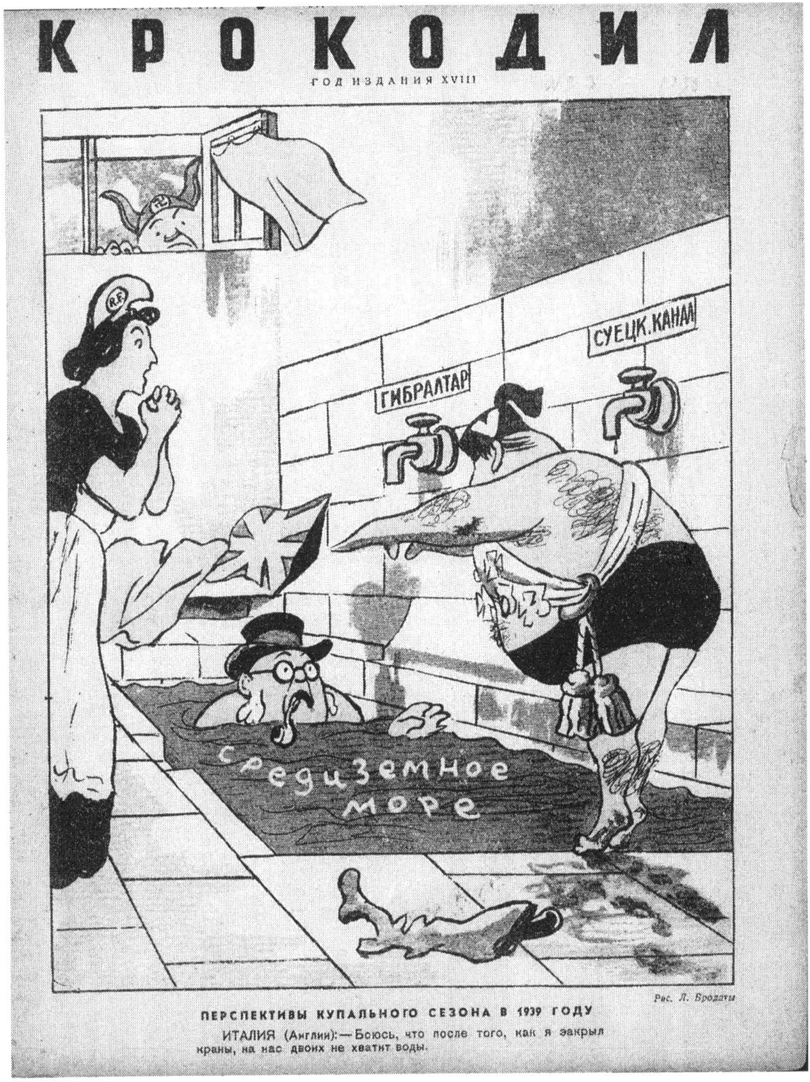

2.11 *Krokodil*, no. 3 (1939), cover. "Perspectives for the 1939 Swimming Season. Italy to England – I'm afraid there won't be enough water for both of us, since I've shut the tap." The image refers to the race to control of the Gibraltar and Suez canals. Part of the David King Collection. Presented to Tate Archive by David King 2016.

Soviet Scapegoats and Fall Guys

The targets chosen by Soviet satirical print media tell the story of the social and political preoccupations that characterize life in the USSR. They allow for taking of its pulse. Indeed, in spite of the specialization of the journals, starting in the 1920s, figures and themes circulate from one journal to another and recur from one issue to the next, fabricating more efficiently than any other medium could a brand new Soviet satirical iconography.

When in 1923, for example, a campaign for the promotion of aviation was launched, satirical journals (and all non-satirical journals, in fact) reacted rapidly by publishing myriad caricatures and satires featuring airplanes. In July 1923, at the height of the operation, *Krokodil* published a special issue entirely dedicated to airplanes and pilots. In this issue, stories, anecdotes, and images promoted aeronautics, all the while attacking the church, superstitions, and vestiges of preindustrial lifestyles. In fact, the satirical image that appears on its cover is of a squadron in flight, jostling and shoving from the sky angels, saints, and capitalists. Images that closely resemble this one are found that same month on the cover pages of several journals, including *Bezbozhnik u stanka*. The version published in this antireligious journal is especially interesting, since the opposition it plays on for comic effect, between the aeronautics/industrial world and religious obscurantism, is grounded as much in formal strategies as in the subject matter (Plate 4). Indeed, the configuration that places the Virgin Mary at the centre of the representation, surrounded by winged creatures, refers directly to the tradition of Russian orthodox icons.

The Soviet satirical press hence became a privileged site for popular information, as well as being a forum for debate. The breath of issues warranting discussion is dizzying: literacy, technical progress, education reforms, religion, alcoholism, hygiene, prostitution, and abortion, just to name a few. As in ROSTA windows, *tipazh* is called upon to create a range of caricatural figures, easy to interpret by the masses. The most prominent satirical character is the pot-bellied capitalist in his black dinner jacket and top hat, dragging along an enormous money sack. He keeps company with the NEPmenka, overly plump and rosy in her fashionable flapper dress, ridiculously adorned with feathers and jewellery; the priest, with his alcoholic's red nose and his thieving from peasants; and the scrawny bureaucrat, spectacles dangling from the tip of his nose, lazily scribbling on scraps of paper.

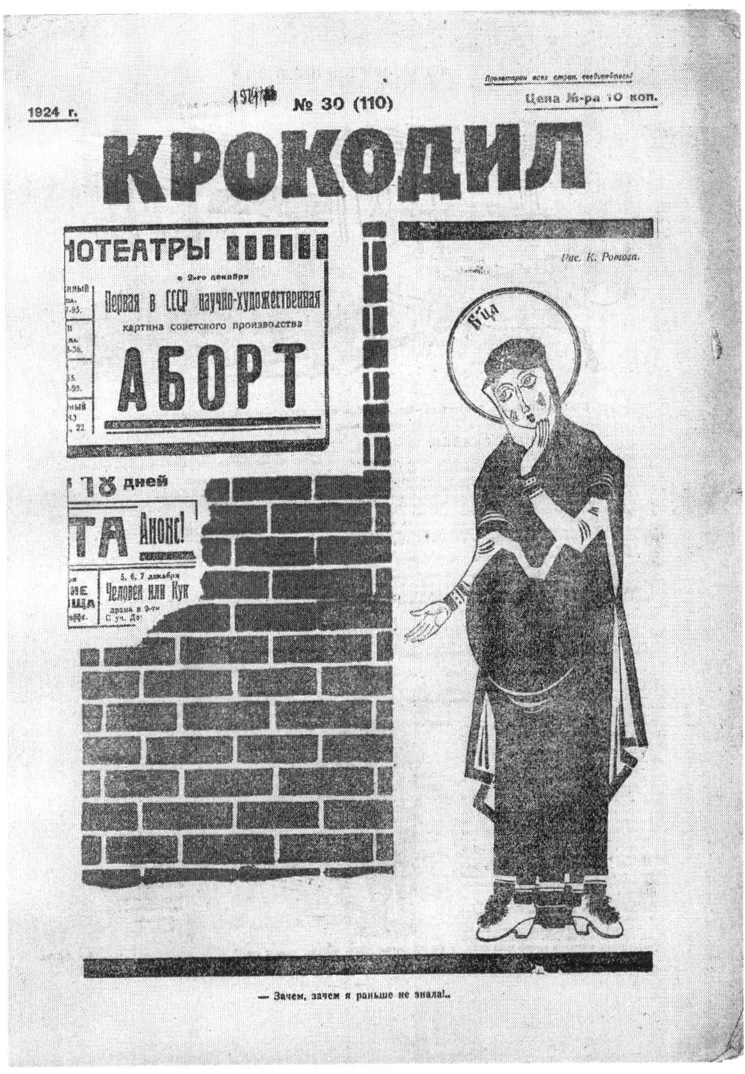

2.12 Cover of the journal *Krokodil*, no. 30 (1924). The Virgin Mary exclaims: "Why didn't I know about this?" The poster in the image advertises a film about the decriminalization of abortions in the USSR in 1924. Part of the David King Collection. Presented to Tate Archive by David King 2016.

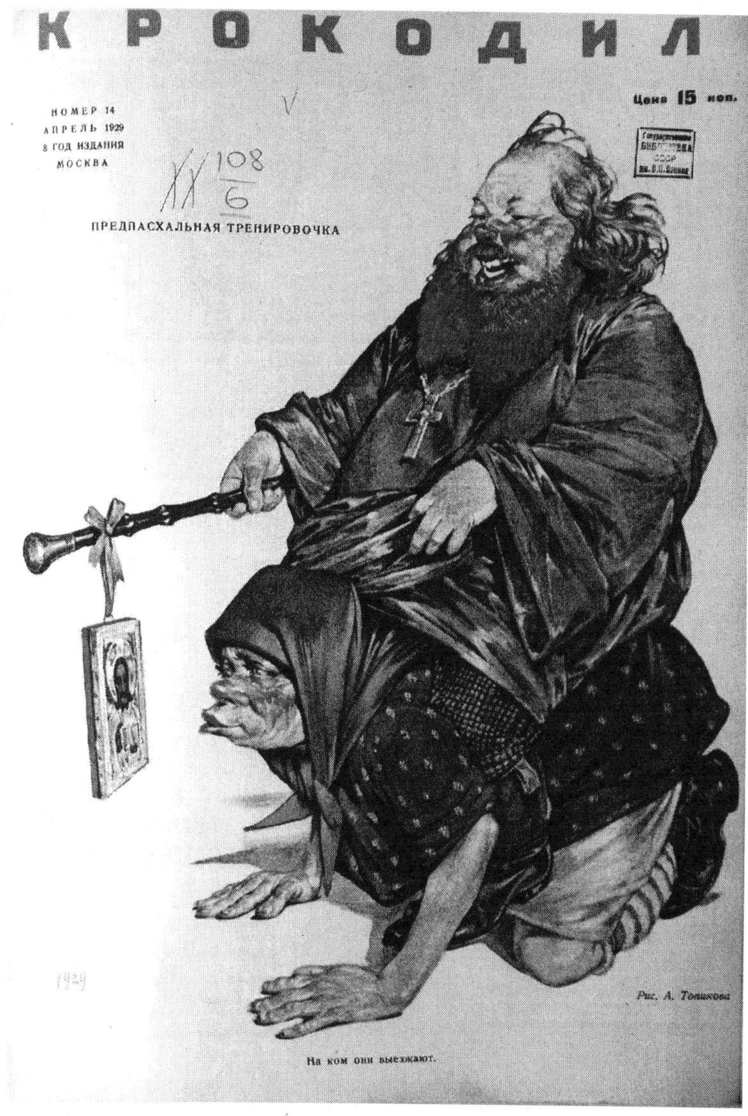

2.13 Cover of the journal *Krokodil,* no. 14 (1929). "Training for Easter." Part of the David King Collection. Presented to Tate Archive by David King 2016.

One of the most frequent themes exploited by satirical journals in the 1920s and 1930s – and the most surprising, from the point of view of the contemporary reader – is that of autocriticism (*samokritika*), in particular as it pertains to the bureaucracy and petit bourgeois attitudes. In the Soviet context, the concept of autocriticism assumed a particular meaning. As Alex Inkeles and Kent Geiger argue, its origin in the Soviet lexicon is to be found in *The 18th Brumaire of Louis Bonaparte*, an essay in which Karl Marx explains that the difference between a bourgeois and a proletarian revolution is that the latter adopts a relentlessly critical posture in relation to its own errors and weaknesses:[43] "proletarian revolutions … criticize themselves constantly, interrupt themselves continually in their own course, come back to the apparently accomplished in order to begin it afresh, deride with unmerciful thoroughness the inadequacies, weaknesses and paltrinesses of their first attempts."[44]

Lenin adopted this as a directive principle for the party, insisting that autocriticism was not to be understood in its individual sense, but rather as a social practice. *Samokritika* constituted a public act. It was a critique made in public – or in the media – of misconducts or structural vices of an enterprise, an organism, or a group, performed by a person who belonged to it or identified with it, even if only by his or her participation in the soviet world. For Lenin, autocriticism aimed to eliminate all the flaws and failings that could hinder the progress of communism. In a speech given in 1921 during the Second Congress of the Services of Political Education, he explained that to his mind "the three chief enemies that confront [Communist workers and educationalists] are the following: the first is communist conceit; the second – illiteracy, and the third – bribery." He added, a few months later, that one social category is exceptionally susceptible to those vices (in particular, self-conceit and vulnerability to bribery) and should conscientiously submit itself to autocriticism: "Our worst internal enemy is the bureaucrat."[45] Ten years later, Lunacharsky made explicit the role satire could occupy in this particular struggle: "the 'scorpions' of satire can be aimed at philistinism, narrowness of mind, and bureaucratism, which like dust in the air obstruct normal breathing in an otherwise vigorous organism."[46]

Following this prescription, in 1929 *Krokodil* featured on its cover a bureaucrat drowning in paperwork, while a worker attempts to save him, throwing him the lifeline of autocriticism. The figure recurs constantly over the next few years, always represented – according to *tipazh* – as inefficient, buried under a pile of documents, holding up by his laziness and inaction Soviet economic, political, and cultural activity. Ten years later, *Krokodil* illustrated the redundancy still perceived as endemic in Soviet bureaucracy by a truncated image suggesting the infinite multiplication of slumping bureaucrats seated at identical desks. The caption provides insight into the administrators' understanding of the situation: "We'll have to hire a few additional employees in order to evaluate if we have superfluous personnel." In *Bezbozhnik u stanka*, it is rather the endemic cause of the corruption of the bureaucracy that is at stake, treated in accordance with the journal's mandate of antireligious activism. An image such as "This is what is at the core of the party's inbred bureaucracy, moral corruption and decay" (Plate 5) renders explicit the deviation of which certain members of the party are accused. The *matryoshka* doll structure allows one, on the one hand, to visualize in pageant the cumbersome hierarchy of pencil pushers and, on the other hand, to trace back to its origins the source of party corruption: a kernel of religious spirit and of pre-revolutionary values. As the apparatchik-dolls are unpacked from the largest to the smallest – a caricatural figuration of God – gradual mutations become apparent. The overstuffed binder bursting with loose leaves transforms into a vodka bottle, and the party ID pinned to the lapel becomes the photograph of a woman revealing an ample *décolletage*.

Conclusion

In its social understanding, graphic satire is often associated with dissent and opposition. This was certainly the case of the Russian satire emerging from the crisis of 1905. However, the study of the Soviet context sheds a particular light on this practice. Regulated by the state, through a series of decrees that served to eliminate some journals, create others, and dictate their mandate, illustrated satirical press was mainly used to discredit enemies of the regime, organize knowledge, and consolidate Soviet culture and power. As Lunacharsky explained in 1931, Soviet laughter was a critical tool used for the self-discipline of a social class, allowing it also to exert pressure on other classes.[47] It also allowed, via the sharpened pen of experienced artists, the reorientation and legitimization of the party line, moving in sometimes contradictory or unexpected directions until 1991.

In the context of pervasive autocriticism described above, satirical journals therefore played an important role. In a self-reflexive gesture, *Krokodil* even submitted itself, ironically of course, to the exercise of autocriticism on several occasions. This practice, as Lunacharsky explained in the texts he penned in the late 1920s and early 1930s, was

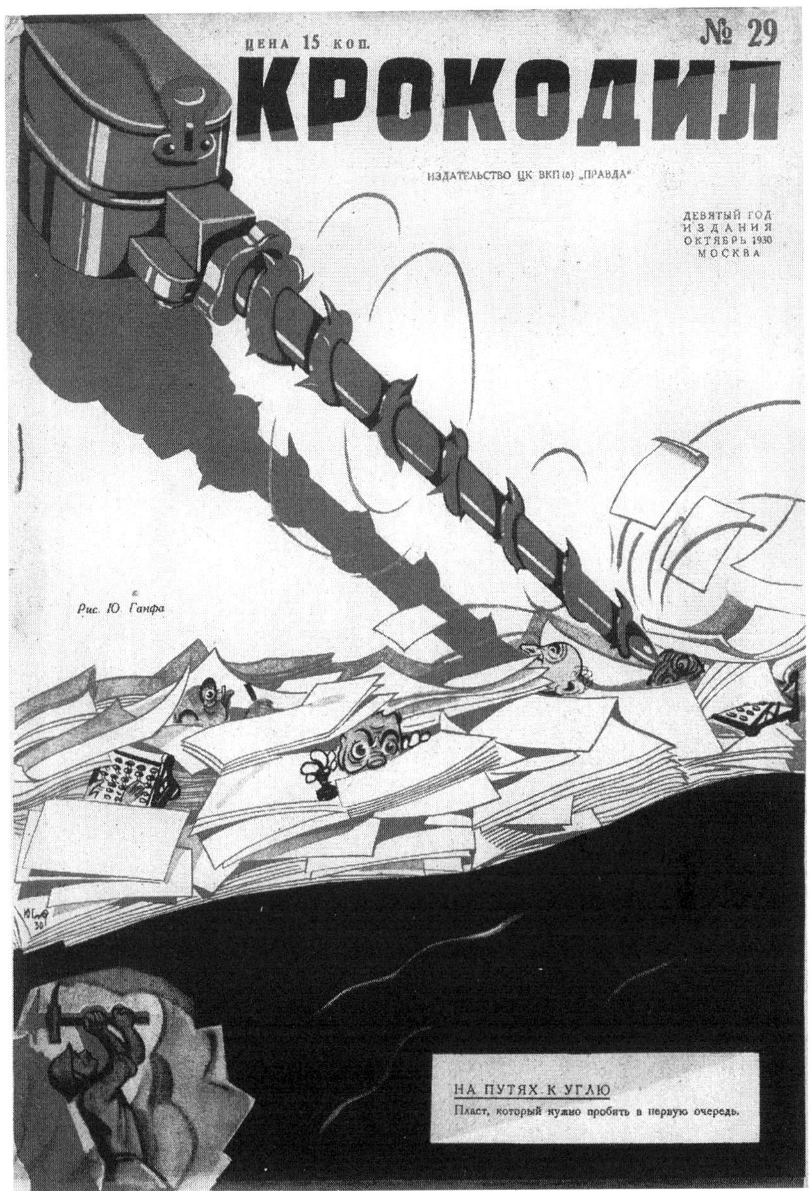

2.14 *Krokodil*, no. 29 (1930), cover. Part of the David King Collection.
Presented to Tate Archive by David King 2016.

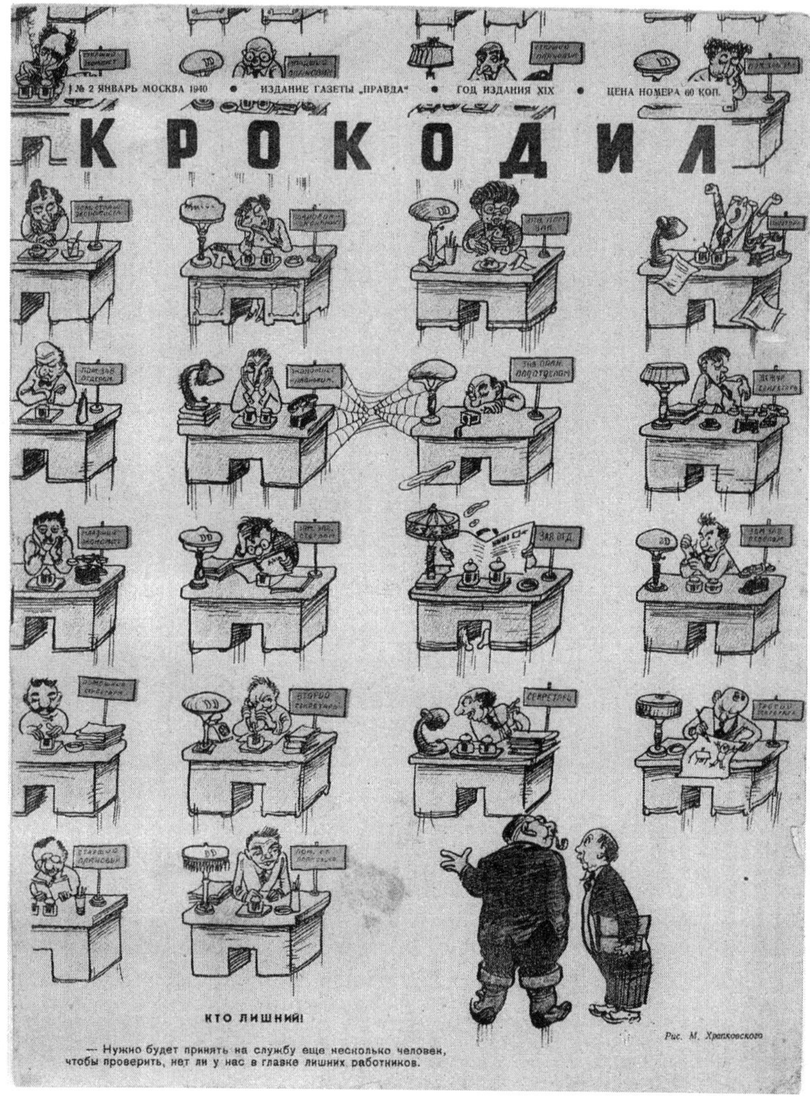

2.15 *Krokodil*, no. 2 (1940), cover. "We'll have to hire a few additional employees in order to evaluate if we have superfluous personnel." Part of the David King Collection. Presented to Tate Archive by David King 2016.

used to symbolically punish deviant behaviour by subjecting it to laughter, and thus to strengthen the mainstream ideology and social standard. But if we take into account the analysis of carnivalesque laughter that Mikhail Bakhtin produced during the same period,[48] laughter could also be thought to provide a momentary respite, like a valve that releases tensions generated by the stresses of everyday life. Furthermore, and especially in satires aimed at bureaucrats, it served to redirect public frustration from those who created policies to those who executed them.

Finally, satirical posters and journals, with their delivery of news, were for many an eye-catching alternative to the early Soviet press, which was particularly bland and poorly illustrated, and required a level of political literacy beyond that of many readers. In this way, one could argue that satirical journals became complementary to straight-forward political rhetorics.

Chapter Three

Laughter in the Ring, in the Street, and on Stage: The Emergence of a Satirical Scene

I often hear laughter. We live in a cold and hungry land, which recently was being torn to pieces. But I often hear laughter. I see laughing faces in the streets, I hear throngs of workers and soldiers laughing at entertaining shows and amusing films. I have heard the roaring of laughter even at the front, not far from where blood is being shed.

That shows we have a vast reserve of strength, for laughter is a sign of strength. In fact, it is not only a sign of strength, it is strength itself.

A.V. Lunacharsky[1]

A specific kind of deterritorialization is characteristic of early-twentieth-century art. The rejection of academies and traditionalist conservatories, the modernist thirst for experimentation, and the emergence of alternative art markets, exhibitions, and performance venues fostered new kinds of interdisciplinary practices. Not only did heterogeneous groups of artists start collaborating on the making of innovative *Gesamtkunst-werken* (total works of art, according to composer Richard Wagner's definition), individuals audaciously tried their hand at various media. Experiences drawn from the circus thus influenced theatre and film, avant-garde poetic practices affected the visual arts and industrial design, architectural concerns made their way into dance and music, and so on. Artists now circulated across artistic scenes[2] characterized by sociability and shared sensibilities, where protagonists seemed to have their fingers in every pie.

It becomes possible to observe an emerging Soviet satirical scene once we cut through disciplinary silos. This network, of course, was enmeshed within broader economic and ideological relations, and was supported (and eventually dispersed) by particular institutions.[3]

A number of factors contributed to the scene's development. The Narkompros, as mentioned above, was created in 1917 with the mandate to oversee all Soviet cultural production, along with education and propaganda. It did not always speak with a single voice, and often sent contradictory messages. But its influence and that of its commissar, Anatoly Lunacharsky, are nevertheless undeniable; and, as we have seen in chapter 1, Lunacharsky was keen on promoting the use of satire as a tool for social change. Furthermore, as early as 1918, processes for the nationalization of many cultural industries were launched. This responded to a double imperative: to purge influential cultural industries of anti-Bolshevik elements and to integrate propaganda goals into cultural production. Finally, if many pre-revolutionary artists were reluctant to support the new regime by lending their talents to its new institutions, some individuals showed a particular willingness to take full advantage of the clean slate that was created by the Revolution. The front-runner in this respect was certainly the poet Vladimir Mayakovsky. Aside from writing poetry that was often laced with satire and contributing to hundreds of the ROSTA windows discussed in chapter 2, he was actively involved in the Narkompros, where he integrated the fine arts section of the commissariat, IZO Narkompros. There he had the opportunity to rub shoulders with Lunacharsky, who included him as a contributor to *Iskusstvo kommuny* (*Art of the Commune*, 1918–19), its main periodical publication. Mayakovsky also wrote scripts for the circus, the theatre, and cinema and embraced a career as a silent-film star. Other prominent members of this scene included the clown Vitalii Lazarenko, suprematist painter Kazimir Malevich, constructivist artist Varvara Stepanova, theatre director Vsevolod Meyerhold, and film director Sergei Eisenstein, among many others.

This cultural syncretism fostered a certain unity of practice and stimulated the dynamic circulation of ideas within a specific geography and time frame, but also of the concrete building blocks of artworks: themes, iconography, and aesthetic strategies meant to convey satirical intent. It emerged in avant-garde circles in Petrograd on the eve of the Revolution, and moved to Moscow on the heels of the Narkompros, when the government relocated to the new Soviet capital in 1918. The scene also constantly radiated to the regions, disseminating works and influencing artists working outside the capital. Inversely, it drew to the centre the best talent and the finest ideas. By 1928, however, it was already breaking down due to pressures emanating from both the government and the cultural industries it intersected with. Then its most prominent members dispersed or retreated: in 1929 Lunacharsky left the Narkompros, Mayakovsky committed suicide in 1930, the campaign against formalism that reached its apex in the mid-1930s gradually marginalized, from the mid-1920s onwards, many of the artists and performers who constituted the Soviet satirical scene.

In the pages that follow, I focus on how this scene intersected with the circus and the theatre, always involving transdisciplinary practices. The defining aspects of satire that will be highlighted here are not mainly, however, literary or plot driven. In keeping with the objectives of this book, visual aspects of scenography, choreography, and costume and set design will be brought to the fore.

Soviet Circus, 1917–1929

It is Catherine the Great, unsurprisingly given her interest in graphic and literary satire, who introduced the circus into Russia. As Miriam Neirick explains, the monarch first encountered clownery and circus feats in 1790, when Charles Hughes, the manager of London's Royal circus, travelled to Saint Petersburg with a small group of performers and a stable of stud horses.[4] Hughes' troupe staged Russia's first circus, which immediately became popular. Catherine the Great herself fell in love with the comic spectacle and ordered amphitheatres to be built in Saint Petersburg and Moscow. Hughes spent three years in Russia. During this time his crew presented a great number of shows, but most importantly, he taught Russian performers the equestrian arts and other circus trades. When he left, his stable and students remained; a market had been created for the new cultural industry, to be taken over by local entrepreneurs. While it overwhelmingly resembled European circuses in form, Russian circus became different in one main aspect. Among the clowning, acrobatics, and animal tricks, it prominently featured comic pantomimes. These were simple stories, most often without words, acted out through the performer's feats. If the hero of the story set off on a long journey, for example, he might walk on a tightrope strung across the canopy, over the audience; if crossing the seas, he would get splashed by bucket-wielding clowns; if climbing a tree, he would farcically attempt to scale a greased-up pole.

In the days following the October Revolution, the Society of Russian Circus and Variety Performers was liquidated by the government, to be replaced by the Union of Stages and Rings, which ran fourteen amphitheatres. This move had the effect of centralizing energies around a few circus professionals who were in favour of the new regime. The following year, a "Circus Division" was created under TEO Narkompros, the Theatre Section of the People's Commissariat of Enlightenment. A few months later, two national theatres were founded in Moscow: the Salomonskii Circus became the First State Circus and the Nikitin Circus became the Second State Circus.[5] Then, in early 1919, Lunacharsky publicly turned his attention to circus arts in an article titled "Tasks for the Renewal of the Circus." In the commissar's view, the circus, like all art forms that had existed in the bourgeois period, could be revitalized if nationalized, directed by Soviet interests, and made to serve Soviet cultural objectives. He deplored the view of critics who considered the circus a "third-rate art, like an inferior kind of tobacco or cooking oil that may poison people."[6] He insisted that popular arts are an important means to reach soldiers, workers, peasants, and their children; they should therefore be seized from the bourgeoisie by the state and serve the cultural needs of the masses. Finally, in August 1919, Lenin signed the "Decree on the Unification of Theatrical Concerns" mandating the state appropriation of private theatres and circuses, recognized to be on the one hand profit-making enterprises and on the other profoundly democratic by virtue of the publics they attracted.[7]

From the onset, a number of circus artists integrated the concerns of Soviet edification into their work. In a comic pantomime performed in 1918, for example, Soviet clown and acrobat Vitalii Lazarenko enacted the "Revolutionary Leap," vaulting over a series of obstacles placed before him in the ring.[8] In 1919, Ivan Rukavishnikov presented a struggle between clowns personifying labour and capital that culminated with the "joyous celebration of the liberation of labour."[9] Then, in 1920, the ubiquitous Vladimir Mayakovsky, collaborating with his friend Lazarenko, wrote and staged the "Championship of the Universal Class Struggle." In this parodic wrestling match, the Bolshevik Revolution (incarnated by Lazarenko in red-headed clown regalia) took on scores of enemies in the ring: British prime minister Lloyd George, American president Woodrow Wilson, White Army general Pyotr Wrangel, Polish nationalist leader Joseph Pilsudski, and other warmongers and greedy capitalists all identifiable by their exaggerated, caricatural attributes. As František Deák remarks, the enemies showcased here are the same that populate the ROSTA windows produced concurrently by Mayakovsky.[10] Flipping each other dexterously in the ring, they fought for an oversized crown, a gigantic gold coin, and an enormous stuffed sack inscribed with the words "Profit of the Imperial War." The satirical performance concluded with an invitation extended to the public to join the Red Army and partake in the struggle.

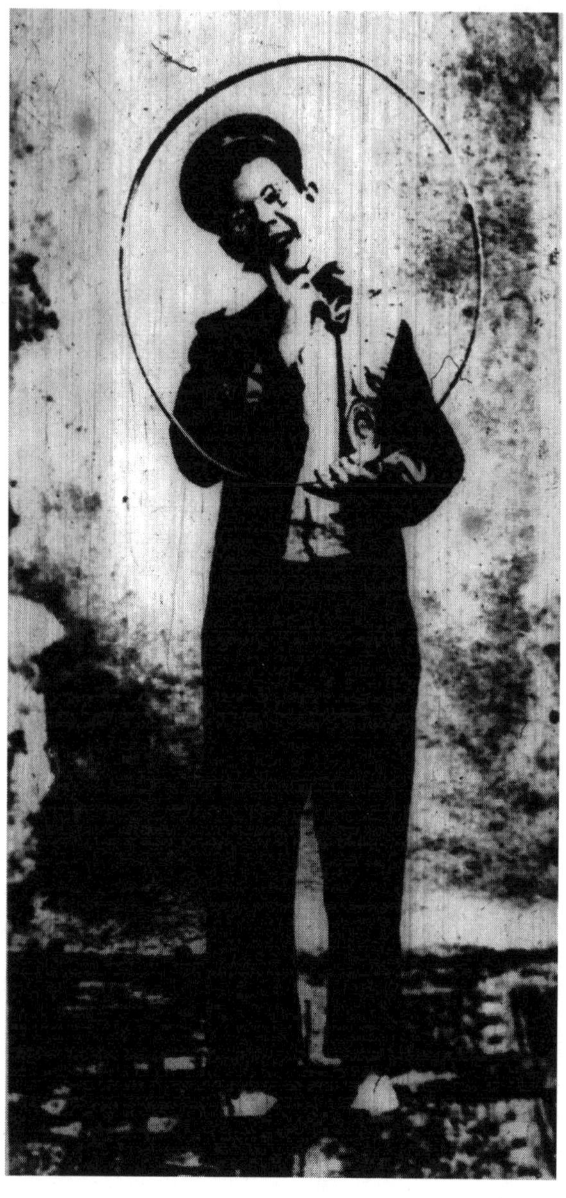

3.1 Soviet clown and acrobat Vitalii Lazarenko, circa 1915. Russian State Archive of Literature and Art.

Framed in satirical monologues and mocking barbs, comic equestrian shows that ridiculed the members of the upper classes and pantomimes that mirrored graphic satire in their use of *tipazh* to scoff at vulgar capitalists, infantile peasants, cowardly priests, and grotesque foreigners were popular in the first years of the Soviet circus. They constituted a world of extreme characterizations and outrageous gestures that, in the context of the Civil War, was thought to have the potential to dismantle the cultural tropes of the old regime and discredit enemies, using incredibly simple rhetorical means, and without demands for realism. At first glance, the circus therefore seems to be tailor-made for satirical propaganda. Yet Miriam Neirick suggests that the success of the circus in incorporating revolutionary discourse has to be viewed with a certain degree of scepticism:

> The topsy-turvy world of the circus could alert its observers to the frailty of the hierarchies that structured their world, or it could convince them that the social order suffered upheaval only in such extraordinary spaces as the circus.
>
> In other words, the circus meant so much because it meant almost nothing, or at least nothing to the exclusion of anything else. Does the acrobat's flip mean that gravity can be defied, or does the possibility of injury prove that the laws of nature remain a constant constraint? Do the aerialists' tricks convince viewers that with the proper persistence they too might fly, or do they provide a delightful spectacle of nearly inhuman achievement? Does a satirical barb inspire hatred or sympathy for its target?[11]

In spite of their indeterminacy, during the Civil War period the satirical pantomimes became the staple fare of circus goers. This phase, when equestrian feats and acrobatics became subjugated to storytelling, became known as that of "theatralization of the circus."[12]

But this movement was short lived. With the introduction of the NEP in 1921, the Soviet circus was required to turn a profit, and was then purged of its most didactic revolutionary content; its more recognizable, pre-revolutionary form was swiftly restored. Tried-and-true circus traditions of acrobatics, clownery, and equestrian displays now seemed devoid of their ideological content. This *volte-face* was applauded by avant-garde theatre director and circus enthusiast Vsevolod Meyerhold, whom Lunacharsky had appointed director of TEO Narkompros in September 1920, and who intensely deplored the theatralization of the circus. According to Meyerhold and other circus advocates, this tactical return to traditional circus forms did not, however, rob the genre of its revolutionary significance. "To their mind, it remained a modern, international, authentically proletarian, enlightening, antireligious, and, therefore, a properly socialist and naturally revolutionary form of art."[13]

Lunacharsky himself defended the reversal, claiming that children would be impressed by the strength and skill of acrobats; that athletic numbers instructed in the value of hard work and the potential to "achieve miracles by means of a tireless desire to attain perfection."[14] Variations on this argument included reflections on the work ethics of animal trainers; the pedagogic value of the exaggeration of movement and action; the community that it takes to create a show, considered a metaphor of socialist society; and the role that the amazement produced by magic tricks could play in the antireligious struggle, because such tricks showed that miracles can be engineered. All in all, proponents of the circus maintained that it was okay to be entertained by people who were good at their craft; it was entirely acceptable to be regaled by a wholesome performance.

In this period that spans roughly 1921 to 1929, the discourse surrounding the circus, rather than the show itself, was revolutionary, as official commentators maintained that even entirely conventional circus programs provided edifying demonstrations of physical strength, the disciplined will, a conscious attitude towards labour, and atheism. Detractors saw things differently. They accused the circus of being a mindless, conservative, bourgeois form of entertainment.[15]

In April 1928, one month after the introduction of the First Five-Year Plan, the annual production plan for the recently created Central Administration of State Circuses was circulated. It explained the relevance of the circus for the project of socialist construction, arguing that the most significant elements of the circus continued to be the demonstration of physical education and strength, the beauty of the human body, the mastering of techniques, and self-discipline.[16] After 1929, while remaining largely conventional, the Soviet circus focused on showcasing Soviet technology and increasingly difficult feats of athleticism, with performers defying the laws of nature for their public, showing the strength of the New Person. This is in fact the circus that was portrayed in 1936 in the musical film comedy *Circus* directed by Grigory Aleksandrov, which will be discussed in the next chapter.

If the circus interests us here, it is not simply because of Mayakovsky's collaboration and friendship with the clown Vitalii Lazarenko,

Lunacharsky and Meyerhold's involvement in championing the genre, or a few years of circus activity characterized by ROSTA-inspired satirical theatralization. It is rather because, as a popular form, just like the *lubok* and the *chastushka*, the circus had a remarkable impact on early Soviet cultural production, especially in avant-garde circles. As film director Lev Kuleshov put it in 1925:

> Theatre and film are having a love affair with the circus. In the past few years stage performances have come to include acrobatics, weightlifting, clownery. On the screen we see suspense films full of circus-like stunts and comedies with clownish characters like Chaplin. Left-wing directors have vividly demonstrated in their recent productions the extent to which circus culture has become incorporated in modern show business. Indeed, the links between the circus and all contemporary forms of entertainment are both undeniable and necessary.[17]

This love affair was grounded in the formal opportunities afforded by the circus, but also in long-standing friendships, affinities, and childhood memories. As film director Sergei Eisenstein recalled, "I have adored the clowns since I was in my cradle."[18]

The Origins of Soviet Theatre

Russian theatre boasts a long tradition, which can be traced to the medieval popular games and plays of peasant life. Performed by skilled entertainers, the *skomorokh*, early plays could involve a variety of forms of entertainment, including farces, mimes, puppetry, juggling, and music. They were often irreverent and constituted a vital component of carnivalesque culture, often condemned by clerics.[19] To create an alternative to these profane performances, in the sixteenth century church theatres began to showcase biblical stories. Then, in 1672, the first professional theatre in Russia opened at the court of Tsar Aleksei Mikhailovich. In 1702 Peter the Great ordered the building of a public theatre on Red Square in Moscow. Finally, in 1776 under Catherine the Great, Prince Pyotr Urusov and English entrepreneur Michael Medox opened in Moscow what was to become the Bolshoi Theatre, to stage operas and dramas. It exclusively presented productions imported from Europe.

The first important works of Russian drama were plays by Aleksandr Pushkin, Ivan Turgenev, Aleksandr Ostrovsky, Anton Chekov,

Aleksandr Griboyedov, and Nikolai Gogol, all penned during the nineteenth century. They borrowed from all the genres that were popular
in Europe, from tragedy to melodrama, from light comedy to biting
social satire. It is important to underscore the pre-eminence of satire as
a popular genre in nineteenth-century Russian theatre; as we have seen
in chapter 1, satire was viewed by Belinsky, Chernishevsky, Dobrolyubov, and other critics not only as marking the origins of Russian literary arts but also as a major progressive force and a weapon for social
and political reform.

On the eve of the October Revolution the theatre establishment was
under siege.[20] It was not challenged by the general public, who seemed
content with the time-honoured theatrical fare, but rather by the avant-
garde. Konstantin Rudnisky explains how

> from 1910 onward an antipathy among the Russian theatrical innovators
> to all "literature," including the classics – in fact against the written word
> in general, began to make itself felt. Theories were devised to justify the
> compulsion to rescue the actor from delivery of text of any kind. Word-
> less action was attractive because it created the possibility of proving the
> autonomy and intrinsic value of theatrical art, its complete independence
> from literature.[21]

Practice developed alongside theory: among others, Vsevolod Meyerhold and Aleksandr Tairov, both close friends of Anatoly Lunacharsky,
experimented with *commedia dell'arte*, mime, and clowning. Their interest lay in the creation of a stylized technique that actors could introduce
into their performance – away from naturalist forms. In Meyerhold's
practice, this would culminate a few years later in biomechanics, an
anti-naturalist acting method based on in-depth understanding of the
body's structure and articulations, and the expressive potential of exaggerated movements.[22] The circus also inspired the young directors
to rethink the spatial organization of theatre plays, and attempt the
destruction of the "fourth wall." They saw great possibilities in the
circular structure of bleachers organized around the circus ring. They
also admired the propensity of circus acts to spill out into the audience.
Both these features, they felt, provided democratic alternatives to the
traditional division between the audience and actors. In other words,
through their interest in the circus and other popular forms, Meyerhold and Tairov traced their steps back to the carnivalesque origins of

theatre, investigating more fluid relationships between performers and their publics.

Members of the Russian futurist group the Union of Youth[23] also set out to revolutionize theatre with their 1913 performance of the first two futurist plays: *Victory over the Sun* (a collaborative work by poets Aleksei Kruchenykh and Velimir Khlebnikov, composer Mikhail Matyushin, and painter Kazimir Malevich) and *Vladimir Mayakovsky: A Tragedy* (by Vladimir Mayakovsky), in a double bill at Saint Petersburg's Luna Park theatre. Both plays made liberal use of vernacular language, neologism, and archaisms, and both used biting satire to mock bourgeois world views as antiquated. They also showcased costumes and set decors that were stylized to the extreme. These were produced by avant-garde visual artists Kazimir Malevich, Pavel Filonov, and Ilya Shkolnik, and drew from cubism, futurism, and analytical realism. In *Vladimir Mayakovsky: A Tragedy*, except for Mayakovsky who had written the play and performed as the protagonist, characters took the shape of large-scale cardboard cut-outs, held by actors in white smocks. Futurist experimental theatre also integrated avant-garde music and poetry, and freely borrowed from the traditions of the circus and puppetry.

The Revolution gave theatrical innovators the opportunity to enter the establishment and transform it from within. The aforementioned creation of TEO Narkompros, the 1919 decree for the nationalization of private circuses and theatres, the 1920 nomination of Meyerhold as head of TEO, and the passionate involvement of Lunacharsky, a theatre critic and playwright in his own right,[24] all made for an exceptionally dynamic and pluralistic milieu. Indeed, the 1920s are characterized by great diversity in Soviet theatre – and consequently by momentous debates between traditionalists intent on preserving theatrical conventions and repertoire and avant-garde innovators who strove to revolutionize the stage on the basis of the above-mentioned pre-revolutionary developments. A third way also developed, drawing from minor genres: street demonstrations inspired by the carnival, open-air plays, mock trials, parodic processions, and satirical living newspapers.

Open-Air Theatre, Mock Trials, and Parodic Processions

Open-air theatre flourished in the years that followed the Revolution, sponsored by the Narkompros, trade unions, and other institutions.

Often large scale, didactic, and satirical, its most obvious characteristic was that it not only was appealing to the masses but was also accessible to them.

Mass spectacles were usually organized to coincide with the newly established "red holidays," and often celebrated particularly memorable events of the Russian Revolution.[25] Many hundred and sometimes many thousand people participated in these events. They were not only professional actors, but also soldiers, workers, peasants, who appeared in the productions as themselves while also constituting part of its public. In these collective works, rage and hatred against enemies of the Revolution and the former masters – the wealthy, factory owners, landowners, and merchants – were stoked and given expression. They were staged on city squares, the only conceivable sites that could accommodate such crowds, often stretching to adjacent streets, and involving as set and props surrounding architecture, street furniture, and tramways.

The *Storming of the Winter Palace*, directed by Nikolai Evreinov, testifies to the extravagance of mass spectacles and and the gigantic scale they could take. It was staged on the third anniversary of the Revolution (7 November 1920) and took place *in situ*, against the façade of the Winter Palace, decorated for the occasion by avant-garde artist Yurii Annenkov. Roughly eight thousand people participated in the historical re-enactment: workers, soldiers, and sailors participating as themselves. Elements of satire, clownery, and buffoonery served the purpose of caricaturing enemies of the people. These produced sharp contrasts with the blunt authenticity of the actual site and the genuine participants, polarizing the action. This clash of styles was an intentional strategy. It heightened both satirical and realist aspects of the spectacle, increasing the legibility of the work.

Mock trials were also often staged in the streets, with the audience serving as the jury. The defendants ranged from the murderers of Rosa Luxemburg played by actors, to grotesque and oversized straw puppets representing the clergy, to cardboard cut-out effigies of alcoholism or other social ills. The audience was encouraged to take sides, mock and ridicule the accused, yell out insults, and deliver a verdict. These spectacles that involved the masses in current controversies were hugely popular.

Satirical-parodic processions also periodically filled the streets. This was arguably the easiest form of mass performance to organize, since no strict scenario was needed. The form that aped pre-revolutionary

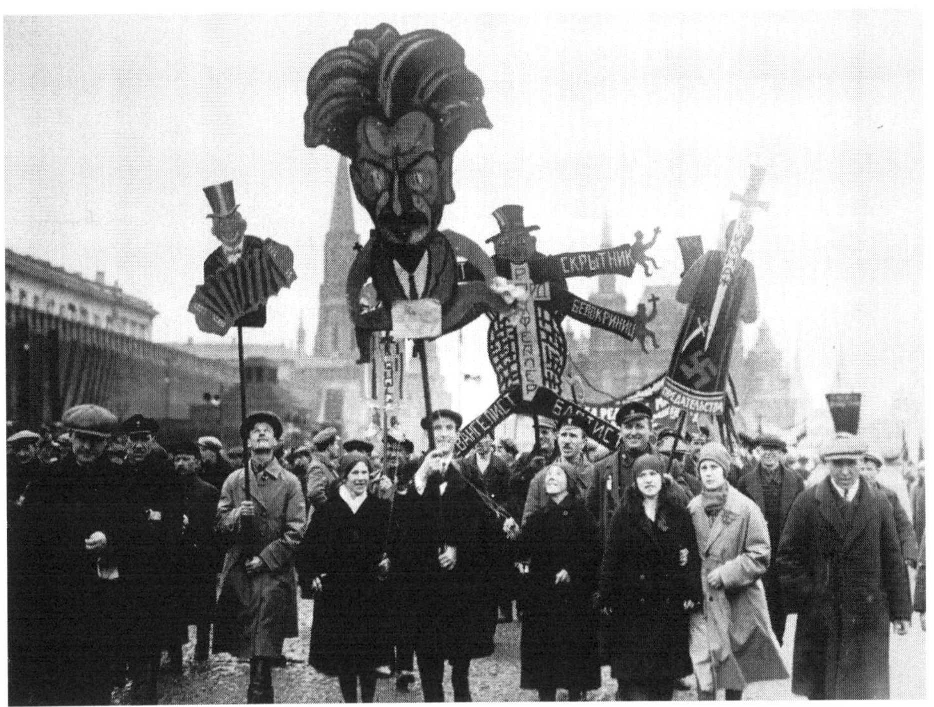

3.2 Anti-Trotsky, satirical demonstration in Moscow, 1930.
Part of the David King Collection. Presented to Tate Archive
by David King 2016.

Christian holiday ritual was well known by all. An example of this type of event is the Komsomol Christmas, orchestrated on 6 January 1923 by the Komsomol, the communist youth organization. The event consisted of a group mockery of the traditional holiday. It featured processions of students and young workers disguised as the gods and ecclesiastics of different world religions, cantering up and down streets and boulevards in cities across Russia. Parodying the procedures of the Christian Orthodox procession, the Komsomol sang the workers' anthem, the *Internationale*, while whipping and burning oversized and overstuffed effigies. In comparison to the open-air plays that were staged between 1919 and 1923, the trials and processions were minute in scale – but equally loved by the masses. Yet this type of street theatre became practically non-existent after 1929.

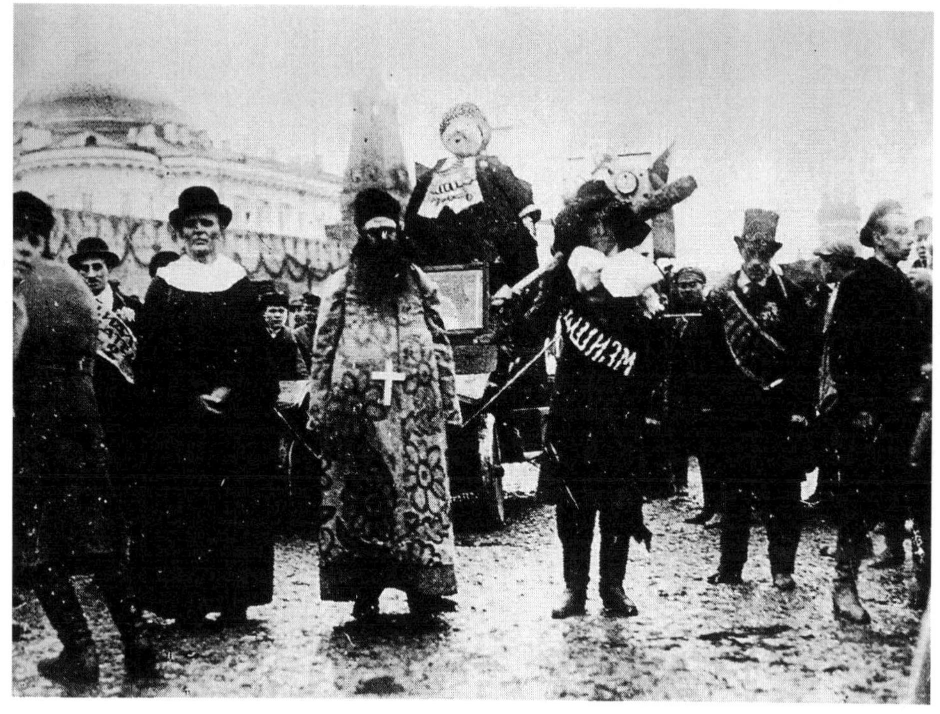

3.3 Antireligious satirical-parodic procession, the 1920s. Part of the
David King Collection. Presented to Tate Archive
by David King 2016.

The Satirical Living Newspaper

If satire was a staple of all the aforementioned popular forms, it flourished most freely in the so-called living newspaper. The Theatre of
Revolutionary Satire (Terevsat), which popularized the genre in Soviet
Russia, was imagined in 1919 by poet Mikhail Pustynin, friend and collaborator of Vladimir Mayakovsky, then director of the Vitebsk branch
of ROSTA.[26] His idea was to bring ROSTA windows to life by turning
them into staged sketches. Just like ROSTA windows, Terevsat's activities were mainly a means of spreading topical propaganda and news
from the Civil War fronts to the barely literate masses. Needless to say,
they also functioned as popular entertainment, causing "the roaring of
laughter even at the front, not far from where blood is being shed."[27]

During the first year of its activity, Terevsat toured up and down the front lines, giving over three hundred performances to some two hundred thousand spectators.[28] The format of the shows was similar to that of cabaret shows. Cabaret had reached Russia in 1908 when *Letuchaya mysh* (The Bat) opened in the basement of a Moscow mansion. It was followed a few months later in Petrograd by The Deforming Mirror (*Krivoe zerkalo*) and, in 1911, by the notorious Stray Dog (*Brodyachaya sobaka*),[29] where the futurists performed, dressed in bright colours and with their face decorated with graffiti, Mayakovsky wearing a painted wooden spoon or a radish in the buttonhole of his redingote.

Terevsat performances usually included a short address by a professional agitator on the current political situation. This speech, which was considered an integral component of the show, was meant to frame and aid in understanding of the topical sketches that were to follow. Then extravagantly dressed performers cleaned the stage with brooms, symbolically sweeping away the old to make way for songs, pantomimes, improvisations, and sketches as well as dramatization of current events or news. Because updates arriving from the Civil War front changed daily, actors often improvised to loose choreographies, and invited participation from the audience. Furthermore, as J.A.E. Curtis remarks, "just as *ROSTA* posters drew extensively on the folk tradition of [the *lubok*], so the repertoire of Terevsat relied heavily in the first year of its work on variations of popular theatrical forms: the names of items on the programme frequently invoked fairground forms, such as the balagan streetshows, the character Petrushka, the peepshow (*rayok*) and so on."[30] One of their signature numbers, the *tantomoresk*, consisted of life-size *lubok*-like cartoons, with cut-outs that allowed actors standing behind them to insert their heads and arms. Modernist painter Marc Chagall, who was then director of the Vitebsk Art Institute and of the local theatre, provided several costumes and backdrops for the sketches, as well as *tantomoresk* boards, as did his successor at the Art Institute, Kazimir Malevich.

In 1919, Terevsat performed for the first time in Moscow where, with the support of Lunacharsky and with TEO backing, they established a studio in April 1920. It included twenty-five actors and twenty-five students who were meant to grow the movement. They studied satirical forms in literature, theatre, and the circus, as well as improvisation. Satirical writers, among them Mayakovsky, wrote sketches for the troupe. That same year, encouraged by the commissar, Terevsat studios sprung up across the country, using the methods and repertoire of the original troupe. This effervescence was, however, short lived. In spite of their great popularity, most Terevsat studios had disappeared by the end of the year, affected by the winding down of the Civil War. The production of ROSTA windows ceased in 1921; designed as a topical weapon in the context of the Civil War, they were simply no longer necessary. Similarly, Terevsat was forced to examine its own relevance. In a document drafted by its artistic committee in December 1920, it summed up its dilemma:

> Terevsat … bore that name … because its main weapon was precisely satire, up until the end of 1920 … Its goals must now change, as the political situation has changed in the Republic … If, from its onset, the main task of the theatre was merciless criticism of the enemies of the Revolution and a call to battle with the enemy, now, in the context of the victory … the theatre should tackle new tasks. In other words, it should conduct agitational work aimed at consolidating the achievements of Soviet power.[31]

Terevsat survived a few more months. It changed its repertory from small topical sketches to larger-scale works and the tone became more earnest, more humoristic and less satirical. It finally stopped all activities in the summer of 1922, outliving the ROSTA windows by just a few months.

The living newspaper format had proven to be far too popular to expire. But it needed a new purpose. In a sense, NEP and the turmoil it induced saved satirical theatre. It provided new subjects; the internal enemy supplanted the external foes of the Civil War period. And with the realization that a brand new cohort of adversaries lay at bay, satirical theatre groups reappeared. From 1922 to 1929, the journal *Krokodil* periodically put on free admission shows in factories with a fixed stable of actors. Their main target was the clergy, bureaucrats, and the NEP bourgeoisie, echoing the themes satirized in the eponymous journal. The poster reproduced in figure 3.4 illustrates in the bottom-right corner the common targets of their mockery and reveals by an enumeration the adaptability of the repertoire: *Krokodil* report, sketches about daily life, political review, animated *lubok* (the equivalent of the Terevsat *tantomoresk*), and *chastushki* sung to the sound of the accordion. These were all adapted to current events and the crowd for whom they were performing on a given day. Date and venue were penned onto this all-purpose *Krokodil Evening* advert.

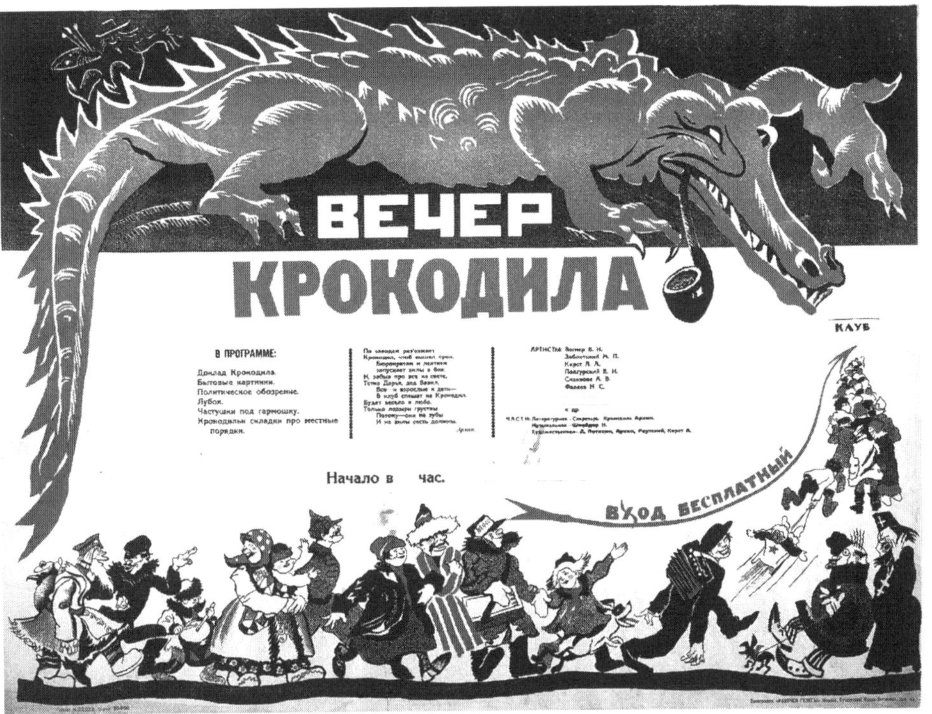

3.4 "Krokodil Evening," advertisement for a satirical propaganda show organized by the journal *Krokodil*, the 1920s, Collection of Annie Gérin.

The main protagonist of the NEP-period satirical movement was the troupe *Sinyaya bluza* (Blue Blouse), named after the standard blue uniform of factory workers, also used as *tipazh* for the "Unclean" characters in Meyerhold's production of Mayakovsky's play *Mystery-Bouffe*, discussed later in this chapter.[32] It was created in 1923 by journalism student and theatre enthusiast Boris Yuzhanin.[33] Initially, the troupe performed in worker's clubs and the tea shops of the Moscow Trade Union, borrowing the living newspaper techniques of Terevsat. They were so successful that, in a very short time, there were *Sinyaya bluza* collectives operating all over the country. By 1927, there were over four hundred groups performing across Russia.[34]

The *Sinyaya bluza* movement was mainly non-professional. Any newcomer could throw on a blue blouse, put up a sign, and climb onto a

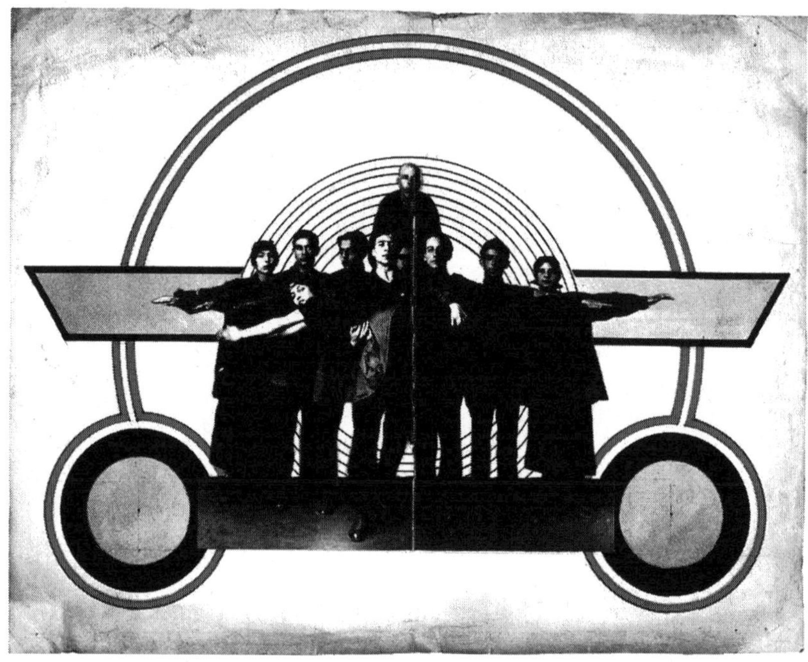

3.5 Gouache and collage artwork promoting one of the *Sinyaya bluza* troupes in the early 1920s. Part of the David King Collection. Presented to Tate Archive by David King 2016.

makeshift stage. In order to keep some coherence in the message and scenographic strategies employed by performers, Yuzhanin edited a bi-weekly journal, *Sinyaya bluza* (*Blue Blouse,* 1923–28), in which sketch scripts, scores, poems, complete production notes, and photographs of original productions were made available. Local groups could then virtually reproduce all aspects of an earlier production, including the costumes and set and stage design. The journal also included theoretical discussions on propaganda and detailed descriptions of the framework of stock characters that related clearly to earlier developed *tipazh*: kulaks, capitalists, fascists, home distillers, prostitutes, and so on.

The year 1927 marks the apogee and the demise of the *Sinyaya bluza*. Early in the year they toured Germany to great acclaim – the tour was so successful that it was extended twice and received overwhelming critical acclaim, particularly from the left press. Later that year, in a

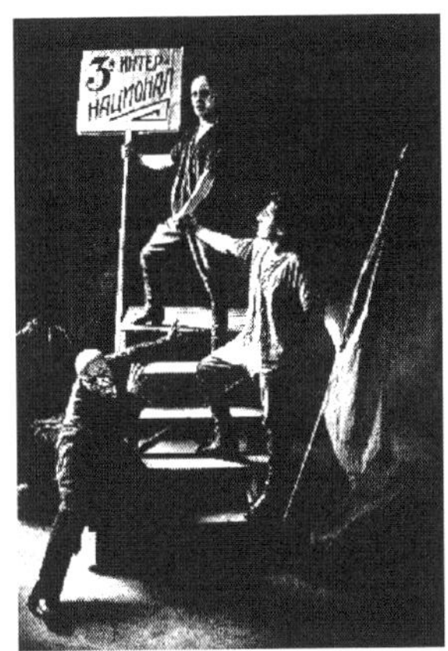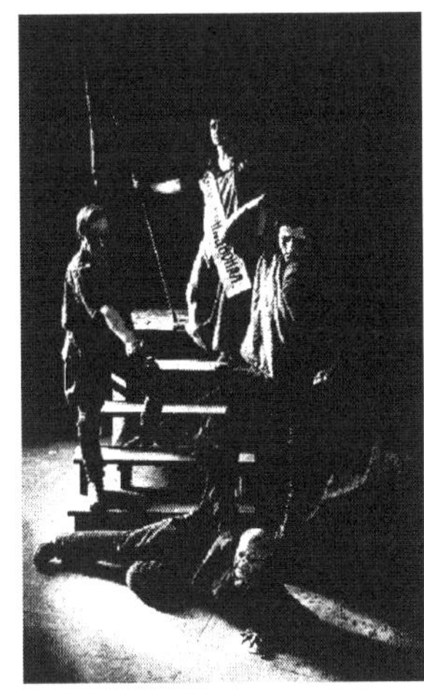

3.6 *Sinyaya bluza* sketch featuring the victory of the Third International over a very sinister capitalist. Part of the David King Collection. Presented to Tate Archive by David King 2016.

movement that parallels the tightening of control on satirical periodicals, the Communist Party instigated an inquiry into the *Sinyaya bluza* organization, to assess how it could best be used. This was not to stir up debate, as Robert Leach points out, but to further strategic goals determined by the party; this was the beginning of the period of the Five-Year Plans.[35] In 1928, the journal *Sinyaya bluza* was closed down and the troupes were ordered to strictly adhere to the party line.

In his memoirs of the early 1920s, writer Varlam Shalamov described the performances as incarnating the spirit of their time, innovating every day, experimental, optimistic, and satirical.[36] But with the early spirit of experimentation, collaboration, and self-motivation taken out of the equation in 1928, the groups simply disbanded and the *Sinyaya bluza* movement faded away.

In 1929, an article published in the newspaper *Literaturnaya gazeta* reported that since its foundation in 1923, the *Sinyaya bluza* had given 17,500 performances in Moscow alone, about 8,000 across the Soviet Union, and 200 abroad, reaching over fourteen and a half million spectators.[37] It had participated in every major campaign: for literacy, antireligious, against the Everyday and, since 1928, for "socialist emulation" and for the First Five-Year Plan.

Satire in the Theatre

Immediately after being appointed director of TEO Narkompros in 1920, Vsevolod Meyerhold proclaimed the "Theatrical October." The program, as its name suggests, assumed that a theatrical revolution should necessarily ensue from the political one. It not only declared war on apolitical theatre, it also sought to exterminate all plays, traditions, skills, and crafts characteristic of bourgeois, pre-revolutionary theatre. Lunacharsky, who overtly supported classical forms as well as the avant-garde, adopted a broader view and felt the need to intervene. As he put it, "I can charge Comrade Meyerhold with the destruction of what is old and bad or with the creation of the new and good. But I cannot entrust him with the preservation of what is old and good, even if it is alive and thriving in the revolutionary atmosphere."[38]

With the slogan "Return to Ostrovsky," Lunacharsky encouraged discriminate adaptation of the best nineteenth-century plays. This was in fact a necessary measure because of the lack of available "Soviet scripts." The commissar's intervention guaranteed a great diversity in theatre during the early Soviet period, in spite of the homogenizing efforts of Glavrepertkom, an organ created in 1923 and housed within the Narkompros, which was charged with approving all repertoire in the performing arts.

Vladimir Mayakovsky's *Mystery-Bouffe* was the first Soviet play to be performed; it was commissioned by the Narkompros and written during the first year of the Soviet regime. It reflected on the Revolution, and was entirely produced within Soviet institutions. For Mayakovsky, *Mystery-Bouffe* was a "Heroic, Epic and Satiric Portrayal of Our Epoch."[39] It premiered in Petrograd in November 1918 in a production staged by Meyerhold. The play parodies the biblical story of the Great Flood, and begins just after most of the earth has been swallowed by the seas. The survivors, the "Unclean" working class and the "Clean" bourgeoisie, seek refuge at the North Pole. The surviving "Tsar," who hoards scarce resources, is overthrown in what resembles a bourgeois revolution – an obvious reference to the Provisional Government that ruled Russia in the months that preceded October 1917. But soon the workers realize that little has changed for them under the new order. The "Unclean" defeat the "Clean" and create a workers' paradise on Earth.

Meyerhold organized the play as a series of circus and cabaret numbers announced by a sort of carnival barker or ringmaster. The innovations he had pioneered before the Revolution – the anti-naturalist acting method, the dialogical relationship between performers and audience, the adaptation of clownery, mime, and *commedia del'arte* references – came here into their own, now bathed in political purpose. In Mayakovsky's terms:

> The mystery is all that is great in revolution, and the *bouffe* is its comic aspect. The verse of *Mystery-Bouffe* consists of the slogans of mass meetings, shouts from the streets, and the language of newspapers. The action in *Mystery-Bouffe* is the movements of crowds, the conflict between classes and the struggle of ideas, it is a microcosm of the world within the walls of a circus.[40]

The play received a mixed reaction: some reviewers were outraged, others were ecstatic. Lunacharsky loved it. He called it "impassioned, audacious, high spirited and challenging." He considered the play "an excellent buffoonery, the first attempt and the prototype of a veritable revolutionary theatrical satire. And Meyerhold has perfectly captured and expressed its spirit."[41]

Meyerhold's next two creations were Aleksandr Sukhovo-Kobylin's comedy *The Death of Tarelkin* (1922) and Fernand Crommelynck's *The Magnanimous Cuckold* (1922). The director had, by then, resigned from the Narkompros to dedicate himself entirely to theatre. Working with constructivist artists Varvara Stepanova (for *The Death of Tarelkin*) and Lyubov Popova (for *The Magnanimous Cuckold)*, he imagined the stage as a dynamic yet completely nonsensical machine that encouraged and enabled the energetic clownery of his actors. In both cases, the stage construction was meant to be climbed upon, entrap actors, revolve and collapse at the opportune moment. Actors dressed in workers' uniforms performed without makeup, combining the exaggerated gestures of biomechanics with juggling, sham-boxing, and somersaults.

The Death of Tarelkin employed clowning techniques to satirize bureaucratic corruption and tsarist police methods. It was a great success. The *Magnanimous Cuckold*, however, slipped away from politically motivated satire to fall into gratuitous slapstick. This irritated Lunacharsky: "I felt ashamed for the audience who roared in animal laughter at the slaps, falls and salaciousness."[42] In his next production, Meyerhold was careful to realign himself more directly with the political goals of his own "Theatrical October."

With *The Earth in Turmoil* (1923), Meyerhold chose to work with Sergei Tretyakov's adaptation of French socialist playwright Marcel Martinet's

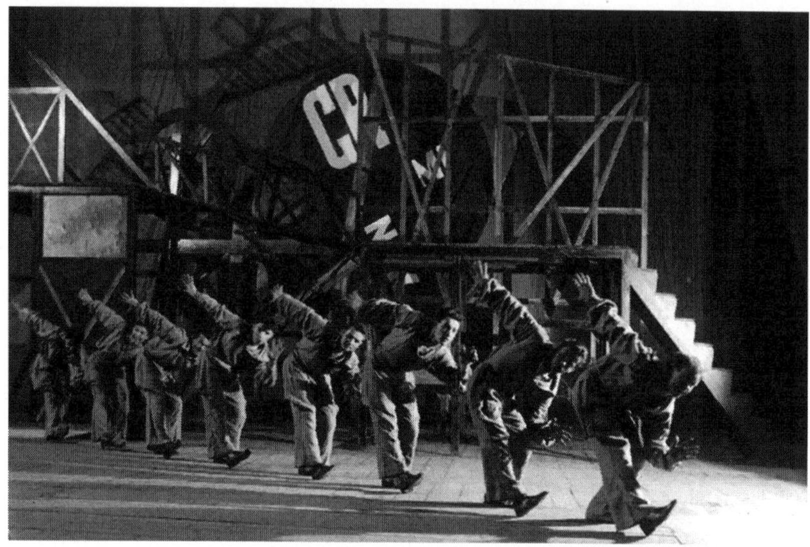

3.7 Vsevolod Meyerhold's 1922 performance of *The Magnanimous Cuckold*, set design by Lyubov Popova. Part of the David King Collection. Presented to Tate Archive by David King 2016.

La Nuit, originally penned in 1921. This was a political revue dedicated to Trotsky and the Red Army, a serious topic unexpectedly peppered with satire and played in the style of farce and buffoonery. Once again, he collaborated with a constructivist artist, who provided innovative costume and set design, structurally suited for the satirical genre. "Lyubov Popova's Constructivist set," as Konstantin Rudnitsky observed, "was partially reminiscent of a collage: beneath red wooden supports which imitated the mechanism of a crane, authentic items of a military environment appeared – carts, hospital stretchers, rifles, machine-guns, motorcycles."[43] This collage structure is precisely what brings together heterogeneous elements and creates the cognitive clashes that are often at the root of the laughter reaction, as described by Lunacharsky in his theoretical work (see chapter 1).

With these plays, Meyerhold established himself as the master of avant-garde, experimental satire in the theatre; better than any other he managed to harness scenographic strategies to intensify mockery and wit. He also influenced a whole generation of young directors, among them Grigory Kozintsev and Leonid Trauberg, who in 1922 co-founded

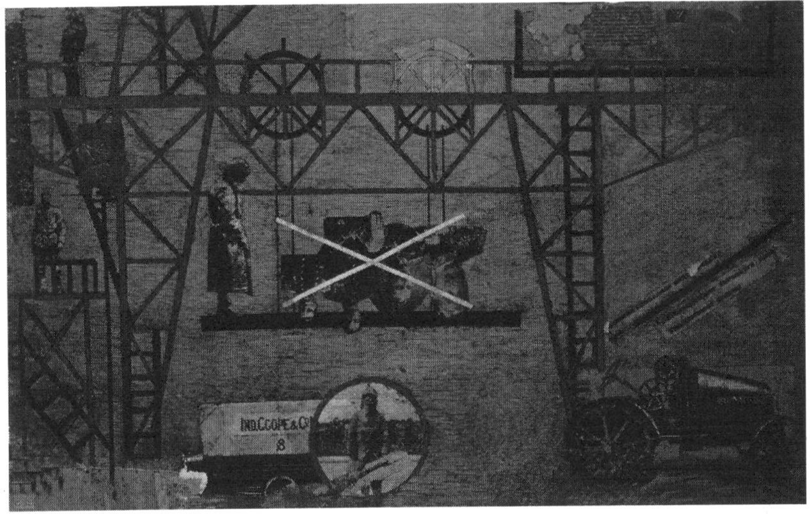

3.8 Collage produced by Lyubov Popova as a set design sketch for
Vsevolod Meyerhold's *The Earth in Turmoil*, 1923. Part of the David King
Collection. Presented to Tate Archive by David King 2016.

the Factory of the Eccentric Actor (FEKS); Ukrainian theatre director
Les Kurbas; and future film director Sergei Eisestein.[44]

Eisenstein had worked as Meyerhold's laboratory assistant in *The
Death of Tarelkin*. His own first production for the Moscow Proletkult
Theatre[45] showed that he was profoundly influenced by his mentor
and the exploitation of the popular arts of the circus and the cabaret
Meyerhold encouraged. *The Mexican* (1921), which Eisenstein directed,
was an adaptation of a 1911 short story by American writer Jack London. It centred on a fighting match staged by rival boxing promoters.
Eisenstein organized the action in a ring, the public sitting all around.
The match was staged with arresting realism. The punches, panting,
and sweat were entirely believable – while the rest of the play took
on an almost surrealist atmosphere, once again borrowing from circus and stylized acting. This contrast between realism and buffoonery
entirely disregarded narrative unity and foreshadowed strategies developed later in Eisenstein's films. Indeed, in *The Mexican* he put into
practice the techniques and theoretical framework that he revealed in
1923 in a well-known manifesto titled "Montage of Attraction."[46] Here,

Eisenstein proposed that theatre should move away from narrative forms in order to become more dynamic. Spectators should be exposed to strong, contrasting theatrical effects that would cause definite emotional shocks and force the viewer to play with meaning in ways that resemble the deciphering of a collage work, of a pun or a joke. In other words, the viewer is elevated to the role of participant, if not of co-creator. She is asked to partake actively in the creation of meaning, filling in the details and reaching conclusions suggested – but not given – by the cues presented on stage. This technique, which Eisenstein carried through to his cinema production, can be found in certain satirical moments in films such as *The Strike* (1925) and *The General Line* (1929).

In 1923, the Party Conference on Theatre Affairs declared that current Soviet theatre repertory was hit and miss. Not enough political plays had been written, and their quality was often poor. The preference of the public was obviously for easier plays, but these were not necessarily helpful in terms of propaganda, and could even be considered counterproductive. The party decreed that "It is necessary to pose the question of how theatre can be used for systematic mass propaganda in the spirit of the struggle for communism."[47] This is what prompted the creation of the aforementioned Glavrepertkom and the gradual homogenization of Soviet theatre repertoire.

Meyerhold's last great satires of the period were Mayakovsky's *The Bed Bug* (1929) and *The Bath House* (1930). They featured set designs and costumes by constructivist artist Aleksandr Rodchenko and the trio Kukryniksy, who were becoming famous as graphic satirists.[48] Instead of mocking former enemies of the regime or NEPmen, these plays focused on those whom the revolution had anointed: bureaucrats of "impeccable proletarian origin." This was a theme that had gained currency in graphic satire during the NEP period and, in the spirit of autocriticism, was still commonly exploited at the beginning of the First Five-Year Plan. Here again, visual contrast and *tipazh* constitute the triggers of satire, contributing to the overall meaning of the works. In *The Bed Bug*, these are enhanced by the play's temporal structure: the first act is cast in a realist present peppered with caricatural exaggerations (by the Kukryniksy) that highlight the protagonist's petit bourgeois inclinations. The satirical affect is only truly launched by contrast, when the second act opens to a futurist world (designed by Rodchenko) where half-human, half-robot characters attempt to protect themselves from petit bourgeois contagion in a world that has become eerily clinical. In *The Bath House* a bumbling Soviet bureaucrat in exaggeratedly drab and old-fashioned suit and tie is revealed as ridiculous and incapable of thinking in truly progressive ways, in particular through his encounter with a stylish phosphorescent woman from the year 2030, sent by the future Institute for the Study of the History of Communism.

Both plays were performed to full houses, but received mixed reviews. Appreciated by the general public, they were condemned by the activists of the Russian Association of Proletarian Writers (RAPP), established in 1925, who would form the hard core of the socialist realist movement a few years later. RAPP stood against satire in principle. It was especially hostile to the comic treatment of Soviet society. In this specific case, they accused Mayakosvky and Meyerhold of "artificial magnification" of the phenomena they observed and of unjustified intent to portray exceptional cases as something typical.[49] This critique was tantamount to accusing them of anti-Bolshevik activity.

RAPP members dominated Glavrepertkom and some of them had been attempting to steer repertoire in the direction of earnest realism since 1923. In a letter dated 1929, theatre director Vladimir Nemirovich-Danchenko deplored how the ideologically conservative organization had put the hatchet in anything that didn't follow RAPP's narrow understanding of realism: "it bans a play when it considers it counter-revolutionary, or when it isn't Soviet enough, or when there's a tsar (*Snow Maiden*) or a figure of authority (*The Governor*) or when the past is beautiful or there's a church (*The Nest of the Gentry*) or whatever."[50]

Lunacharsky had intervened in favour of writers and directors on numerous occasions, defending diversity in theatre and attempting to open up the term "realism" to broader interpretations. In a 1927 article published in the newspaper *Krasnaya gazeta,* he wrote:

Extraordinarily precise realism – that is an extremely good thing ... But that kind of thing has little to do with theatre ... Theatre should not simply portray nor should it simply caricature, it should rather provide stylized sketches of what lies before it. These sketches are close to caricature specifically in how they are not limited to resemblance; instead they preserve some likeness in spite of substantial deformations, drawing out characteristic traits of its subject. Waggish, evocative satire goes beyond caricature; it then acquires a full range of critical possibility – from the sharpest mockery to the whimsical.[51]

But by 1929, Lunacharsky was being marginalized in his own commissariat, from which he resigned that year. The influences behind

Glavrepertkom gained an even stronger hold on theatre, sanctioned in a declaration by the Agitprop section of the Central Committee: "Under the dictatorship of the proletariat, when theatres are the property of the Soviet government ... when we hold the means to regulate and direct their activities, such as state subsidies and the *Glavrepertkom*, all theatres ... can move more or less quickly in a socialist direction, they can and must undergo a period of ideological and political reconstruction."[52]

The main attack fell on the avant-garde, which was charged with formalism. Practices that borrowed from the circus were condemned as merely entertaining; and satirical plays – especially those that examined contemporary failings of the system – were swiftly suspected of relaying anti-Bolshevik views. In the early 1930s, remakes of satirical pre-revolutionary works continued to be staged, by Vladimir Nemirov-Danchenko, Konstantin Stanislavsky, Vladimir Soloviev, and others – but much less often. Nikolai Gogol's *Dead Souls*, for example, a satirical novel first published in 1842 about Russia's failing social system in the years following the war of 1812, was adapted as a play by Mikhail Bulgakov in 1932. It met with a very hostile critical reaction. It is only after a decade or so that it became a favourite at the Moscow Art Theatre.

The fate of satire is strangely exemplified by that of Moscow's Teatr satiry (Satire Theatre), created in 1924. There, ironically, satire increasingly came under attack throughout the second half of the 1920s. In its early days, the "current affair sketch" dominated its repertoire. It was in fact closely related to the Terevsat movement, working from scripts developed by its former participants. But, in 1929, it was reorganized and redirected towards optimistic comedy, a humorous genre that usually contains a happy resolution of the thematic conflict, unlike satire, which aims at discredit and symbolic destruction. Meyerhold deplored this state of affairs and recommended that Teatr satiry endeavour to regain its health by an urgent study of great satirical classics, such as the works of Molière, Nikolai Gogol, and Mikhail Saltykov-Shchedrin.[53]

By 1934, when the All-Union Congress of Writers took place, the Soviet satirical scene was already dispersed. The same can be said about a number of different scenes that cut across the worlds of theatre, visual arts, cinema, and the like and that were structured around different communities of interest. While this retreat had started in the mid-1920s, it was achieved in 1932, when the Central Committee published a "Decree on the Reconstruction of Literary and Artistic Organizations."[54]

The declarations aimed at harnessing in much more organized ways creative forces in all the arts to promote the objectives of the five-year plans. It also attempted to push artists back into disciplinary silos. If satire did not entirely disappear in the performing arts, it was nevertheless largely replaced with optimistic comedy, a shift that also affected cinema. But in the latter medium, dependant on international trade and involving much more investment and infrastructure than the theatre or the circus ever did, the pressures took on different shapes, as we will see in the following chapter.

Chapter Four

Laughter on the Silver Screen: From Satire to Optimistic Comedy

Many of our people do not understand that our film production must stimulate the public appetite, that if the public is not interested in a picture that we produce, it will become boring agitation and we shall become boring agitators. But it is well-known that boring agitation is counter-agitation.

A.V. Lunacharsky[1]

"Of all the arts, for us the most important is cinema." This sentence, purportedly uttered by Lenin and reported by Lunacharsky in 1922, frames Soviet understandings and uses of the seventh art.[2] Over the years, and particularly at the 1928 Party Conference on Cinema Affairs, it was used to support Soviet cultural policy with regard to film, a medium that was seen as having many advantages over printed matter and the performing arts as a vehicle for propaganda. Movies could, for instance, be watched simultaneously by a large group of individuals and hence become a lively instigator of discussion. Furthermore, their reproducibility allowed for a great number of copies to circulate at any given time, potentially reaching the remotest confines of the country. Finally, because of their indexical nature, they were considered to be the medium most intelligible to Russia's poorly educated population. Their promise for mass education was clearly underscored in the Narkompros' first cinema manifesto published in 1918, where cinema is compared to a "book for the illiterate."[3]

In spite of this early framing of film as a vehicle for propaganda, cinema was never fully subjugated to enlightenment. Its pre-revolutionary history, the dependence of the Soviet film industry on foreign materials and trade, and public taste and demands always made it oscillate between two poles; more than any other art, cinema became the site of debates between high and low culture or, more precisely, between enlightenment and entertainment.

In these debates, laughter became a strategic terrain where, Lunacharsky argued, the aims of the proponents of both ideals could converge. But if satire made recurrent appearances on the silver screen throughout the 1920s, it was mainly "dispersed in the guise of satirical elements found in various genres of films."[4] To the chagrin of the commissar, very few Soviet films could qualify as fully fledged satires. And by the 1930s, the rhetorical mode that Lunacharsky had championed for its potential to reveal internal threats to the system and chastise antagonists was rapidly being replaced on the silver screen by ideologically laden optimistic comedy lacking any critical edge.

Enlightenment versus Entertainment

Debates opposing high culture to entertainment were not unique to Soviet Russia. They also raged across Europe and North America, where mass culture was understood by a certain cultural elite, at least since the nineteenth century, as representing intellectual degradation and societal decline. In Soviet Russia, detractors of cinema were well versed in the theories of mass culture "as social decay."[5] But they added an additional line of reasoning to their critique. Their rejection of cinema was also rooted in the denunciation of "art for art's sake," a theme that was developed in the writings of the aforementioned intellectuals Belinsky, Chernychevsky, and Dobrolyubov, who applied social and utilitarian criteria to their analysis of art, and promoted art as a tool for social change. While intellectuals such as Lenin understood cinema's potential role as a propaganda tool, it could also be condemned on two counts: as an unworthy product of cultural industries, or as the site for elitist formal experimentation.

After the Revolution, the debate took on both ideological and concrete dimensions. If the cinema could serve the purposes of propaganda, film-makers needed to proceed with great caution. Indeed, as Richard Stites explains, entertainment could be seen by the political apparatus as a dangerous bearer of reactionary or bourgeois values, or of much loathed Americanism.

The Bolsheviks associated commercial popular culture with the old regime. The spectacle of private profit in the midst of suffering and deprivation, the continuing celebration of "bourgeois" values in song, story, and film, the perceived immorality and triviality of their themes, and the fear of the cultural power of their styles – all coalesced in the decision, taken after about two years of haggling, to shut down private entertainment, kill the market mechanism, and nationalize film companies, publishers, sheet music houses, recording studios, music halls, theatres, and dance halls.[6]

Furthermore, as noted above, in the days that followed October 1917 resources were nationalized. This was a process that transformed the government into the main patron of the arts and chief producer of mass culture. In addition, during the Civil War shortages in paper, film stock, ink, and paint as well as restrictions on fuel and electricity forced the government to cherry-pick where resources would be best allocated. In this context, "entertainment for entertainment's sake," just like "art for art's sake," could seem frivolous. As a result, many journals were shut, several theatres closed down, and film production was reduced.

The debate over how cinema could function in the early days of the Soviet Union is extremely complex. For the purpose of this discussion, it can be schematized as a continuum stretching between two extreme positions. On one end of the scale, the Central Committee for Political Education (Glavpolitprosvet) stood firmly. Glavpolitprosvet was established on the basis of the Extramural Education Department by a decree of the Council of People's Commissars on 12 November 1920. Its mandate was to develop adult education programs within the Narkompros. Its permanent chairwoman was Nadezhda Krupskaya, Lenin's wife. Active in print culture, theatre, and cinema affairs throughout the 1920s, Glavpolitprosvet organized campaigns for the "cinefication" of the countryside and sponsored film and theatre agitation. Its members also indefatigably attacked avant-garde practices as being elitist and hermetic, and entertainment as incompatible with the aims of socialist edification.

On the other end of the spectrum, a heterogeneous group of artists, theatre heads, and film studio administrators considered it their mandate to keep cultural industries solvent and the publics interested. Some went as far as defending the autonomy of art. Their voice became most important after the beginning of the NEP period, when state-run circuses, theatres, cinemas, and production studios were expected to compete with private cultural institutions and yield a profit. They felt artists and the entertainment industries should focus on what they did best: entertain the masses.

Between these two poles a range of positions existed, occupied by artists and critics of all creeds as well as several prominent Bolsheviks. Many believed the often bitter pill of propaganda could be sweetened with a bit of drama or laughter, that "People love to laugh, and they'll buy a pound of laughter more readily than a pound of serious emotions."[7] They understood that because mass culture had in the past served the purposes of obscurantism and exploitation, careful planning and direction were crucial to foster revolutionary arts and new forms of ideologically sound entertainment. But they also recognized that a light touch was needed in this regard, or else laughter would suffocate. Adopting this view, in 1923 Leon Trotsky wrote: "The longing for amusement, distraction, sight-seeing, and laughter is the most legitimate desire of human nature. We are able, and indeed obliged, to give the satisfaction of this desire a higher artistic quality, at the same time making amusement a weapon of collective education, freed from the guardianship of the pedagogue and the tiresome habit of moralizing."[8]

Lunacharsky also adhered to this position, even though this stance put him at odds with members of his own commissariat, in particular Nadezhda Krupskaya. As he put it:

> The proletariat is entitled to all artistic methods that lead it to its objectives, in spite of what pedants believe. The proletariat is therefore free to enjoy whimsy. And we indeed often use it: every issue of *Krokodil* is replete with caricature. It is not only possible, but also fully legitimate in literature, theatre and cinema. In order for it not to turn into simple mockery, it only needs to communicate some valued concept.[9]

Lunacharsky was certainly as committed to cinema as to literature, the visual arts, the circus, and theatre. He wrote a number of film scenarios, among them *The Bear's Wedding*, 1926, a satirical horror film about tsarist-era peerage; *Locksmith and Chancellor*, 1923, a revolutionary themed drama set in imaginary Norlandia; and *Salamander*, 1928, a fictional biography about the Austrian biologist Paul Kammerer, who studied and advocated for the now largely abandoned Lamarckian theory of inheritance. He also happily performed cameos as himself in a number of films (most notably in *Salamander*), and was married to actress Natalya Rozenel. She performed both in the theatre and in cinema, in a number of comedies and dramas, including *The Bear's Wedding* (1926), *Miss Mend* (1926), and *Salamander* (1928). They both participated, with Vladimir Mayakovsky,[10] Sergei Esisenstein, Lev Kuleshov, Aleksandr

Medvedkin, Grigory Aleksandrov, and others, in the satirical scene, as it intersected with the film cinematic industry. Indeed, Lunacharsky's intervention quoted above brings us back to the use of satire and humour in Soviet cultural practices. Because of satire's ability to make people laugh, and because of its critical edge, Lunacharsky saw it as a genre that could kill two birds with one stone: properly employed, laughter could entertain *and* enlighten.

This tug of war between enlighteners and entertainers was cut short around 1928, the period that marks the beginning of the First Five-Year Plan, of the Cultural Revolution, of the Stalinist period, and Lunacharsky's retirement from the Narkompros. Neither side won the struggle. Opponents were realigned in the 1930s, forced to rethink their position by, among other things, the introduction of sound in cinema, institutional changes, and the establishment of the doctrine of socialist realism. And satire-laced comedy was abruptly replaced by optimistic comedy.

Early Soviet Cinema

The cinematograph was introduced in Russia in 1896, just one year after the French public famously witnessed the brothers Lumière's short

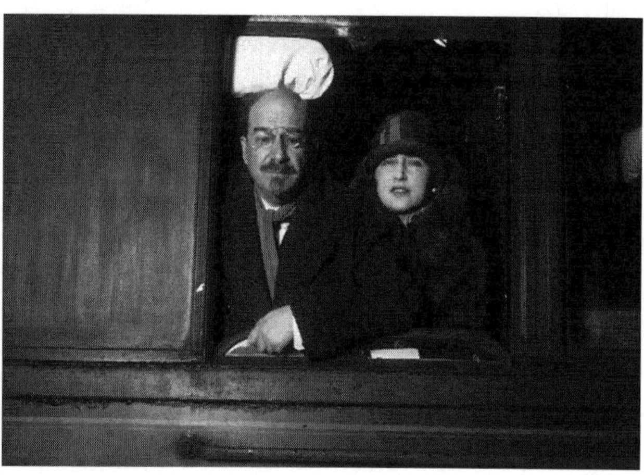

4.1 Anatoly Lunacharsky and his second wife, silent film star Natalya Rozenel, in a train, 1930. Part of the David King Collection. Presented to Tate Archive by David King 2016.

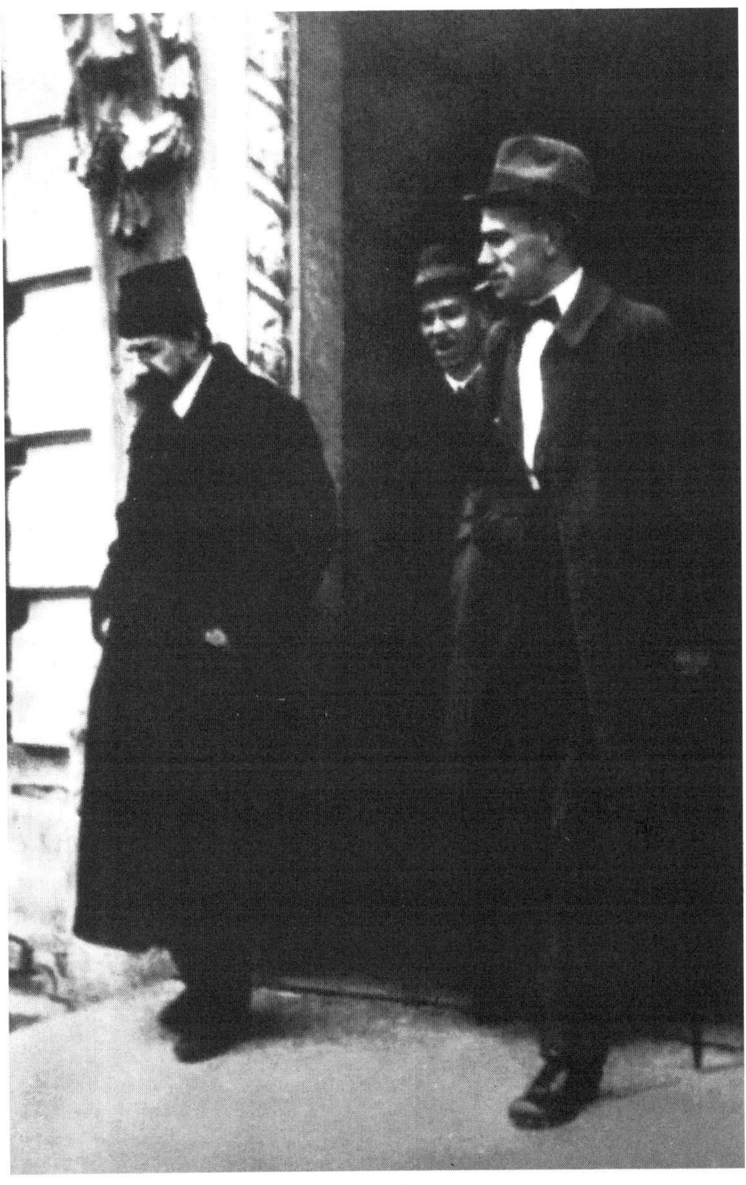

4.2 Lunacharsky and Mayakovsky exiting the offices of the Narkompros cinema subsection in 1918. Collection of Annie Gérin.

film of a train arriving at a station, which allegedly struck fear in the audience. It rapidly gained popularity, providing cheap entertainment across Russia's immense territory. At first, cinema houses in Moscow and Petrograd exclusively showed foreign films, but a young industry gradually developed in Russia. The first professional film studios opened in 1907, releasing documentary films and features. The most popular genres were melodramas, historical films, and romantic comedies; as in the other arts, censorship under the tsarist regime limited the topics that could be featured.

The history of early Soviet cinema mirrors that of the printing industry. The 1917 February Revolution temporarily loosened the grip of censorship and allowed film-makers to exploit themes that had previously been forbidden, such as the tsar, religion, and the like. Film workers formed trade unions, which began to organize strikes. After the October Revolution, unionized film workers refused to collaborate with private studios, several of which closed down or moved from Russia. In 1918, the closure of cinemas was prohibited by the Soviet government in order to prevent the disappearance of equipment and the complete eradication of the Russian film industry. But this rule could not, by itself, have the effect of reviving film production. Indeed, film stock and cameras, commodities that were not produced in Russia at the time, had become rare since trade relations with Western countries had been interrupted. The film stock crisis lasted through the Civil War, until trade with Germany was resumed in 1922. As Birgit Beumers argues, "It was largely the government's inability to find a way of ensuring the support and collaboration of private enterprises that led to the ultimate nationalization of the film industry."[11]

The nationalization took shape gradually. In 1918, a movie subsection was organized within the Extramural Education Department of the Narkompros. Its main focus was to produce educational shorts with a strong visual message. These became known as *agitki*. Some of the most famous *agitki* were made on agitational trains (*agitpoezda*) by the likes of Dziga Vertov and Lev Kuleshov, who worked together producing newsreels and documentary footage as they travelled across the land, and of Aleksandr Medvedkin, who created satirical shorts inspired by ROSTA windows and Terevsat sketches.[12] The remaining private film studios managed to produce very small numbers of feature films, plummeting as the Civil War progressed. A meagre sixteen feature films were produced between 1918 and 1921. The number remained low in the early 1920s and picked up only around 1926, when the NEP was well under way.[13] To satisfy the appetites of Russian movie-goers, recycled pre-revolutionary films were dusted off, and a few dated foreign films began to appear. As with print media, censorship was by no means heavy handed at that time. It only came down heavily on explicitly anti-Soviet films.

In December 1922, the Council of People's Commissars established a new state cinema enterprise called Goskino (Central State Film and Photo Enterprise). Its main mandate was to distribute films. It was replaced two years later by Sovkino (All-Russian Photo-Cinematic Stock Company) "with the aim of unifying throughout the entire territory of the federation both the capital of cinema organisations and their operations in the fields of production, distribution and import-export."[14] Sovkino was a joint stock company held by the Commissariat of Trade (Narkomtorg), the Commissariat of Enlightenment (Narkompros), the Leningrad and Moscow Soviets, and the Supreme Council of the National Economy (VSNKh). In 1926, Sovkino reviewed the viability of Russian studios and ordered unprofitable studios to close. This left three studios in operation: the Moscow and Leningrad branches of Sovkino and Mezhrabprom-Rus, a quasi-independent studio that received support from the German International Worker's relief fund. Both Sovkino studios and Mezhrabprom-Rus were determined to remain viable and launched into the production of big-budget entertainment films. Some of the profits earned from these would then be channelled into the production of less sustainable ventures, avant-garde films, and propaganda works that were less likely to appeal to the taste of the public, as well as animated propaganda shorts that were meant to be viewed before features.[15] All the while, the Narkompros continued to produce *agitki*, satirical or otherwise, through its Extramural Education Department and its Central Committee for Political Education.

Paradoxically, as the nationalization of the industry was progressing, the NEP period was in full swing, and most of the movie theatres were still run by private entrepreneurs. In these venues, the overwhelming majority of films that were screened were foreign imports, brought into Russia by Sovkino. In fact, in 1924 approximately 95 per cent of the films shown in Soviet theatres were foreign.[16] The public loved them, in particular melodramas, adventure films, and comedies featuring Douglas Fairbanks, Mary Pickford, Harold Lloyd, and Charlie Chaplin. As film-maker Lev Kuleshov noted in 1922, "Anyone who, from 1914 to the present day, has visited cinemas, watched all the films that have been released by both Russian and foreign film studios, and observed which films most effectively force the public to react to cinema action, will have no difficulty in stating that: *Foreign-made films are more popular than Russian ones.*"[17] Most critics, on the other hand, condemned imports systematically as petit bourgeois and stupid.[18]

The Public's Taste

There was a clear divergence of opinion among those involved in the industry about what kinds of films should be made and shown in Soviet Russia. A wide gap also separated critics' perceptions and the taste of the public. In this sense, contemporary scholarship on Soviet cinema that highlights innovative practices to the detriment of viewing habits can be misleading. As Denise Youngblood points out, "the public's reaction to the films of Eisenstein, Dovzhenko, Vertov, and Kozintsev and Trauberg is well documented and unambiguous. Films 'without scripts' or with a battleship as a hero generally did not appeal to the ordinary movie-goer, however much they appealed to the critics."[19] There were, of course, a few notable exceptions that managed to create consensus among various publics. For example, Eisenstein's *The Strike* (1925), one of Eisenstein two attempts at satirical comedy (along with *The General Line,* originally titled *Old and New,*1929), garnered both critical and popular acclaim, running in theatres for over a month. It produced satirical effects through montage and meaningful juxtapositions, what Eisenstein termed "montage of attraction."[20] Sequences showing strikers hunted by militia, for example, are spliced with those of cattle being led to the slaughter house, and outlandish bourgeois management dining scenes are abruptly juxtaposed with views of a bustling pigpen.

Until the creation of Sovkino in 1924, Soviet cinema was generally not perceived by the public to be entertaining. Ilya Trainin, a Sovkino administrator and one of the main proponents of entertainment films, characterized the reaction of the public to Soviet propaganda cinema in a speech given to the Moscow Art Worker's Union in 1924: "With agit-films, they expect pretentious films in which the agitational side predominates, in which numerous intertitles abound, often very revolutionary, but at the same time very boring."[21] He proposed that melodramas and comedies, the genres loved by the public, could draw attention to Soviet messages, and that some of the profits earned through the commercial production could be channelled to the production of films less likely to be commercial successes: Dziga Vertov's documentaries, for example, or Sergei Eisenstein's historical recreations. As Denise Youngblood remarks, "For the first time, a state film executive had acknowledged that entertainment might have an official role in Soviet cinema, if only to 'agitate.'"[22] Lunacharsky, who was a member of the organizational bureau of Sovkino, supported Trainin's views. He argued that "there is one area in which we must imitate the bourgeoisie: we must wherever possible avoid tendentious films – that

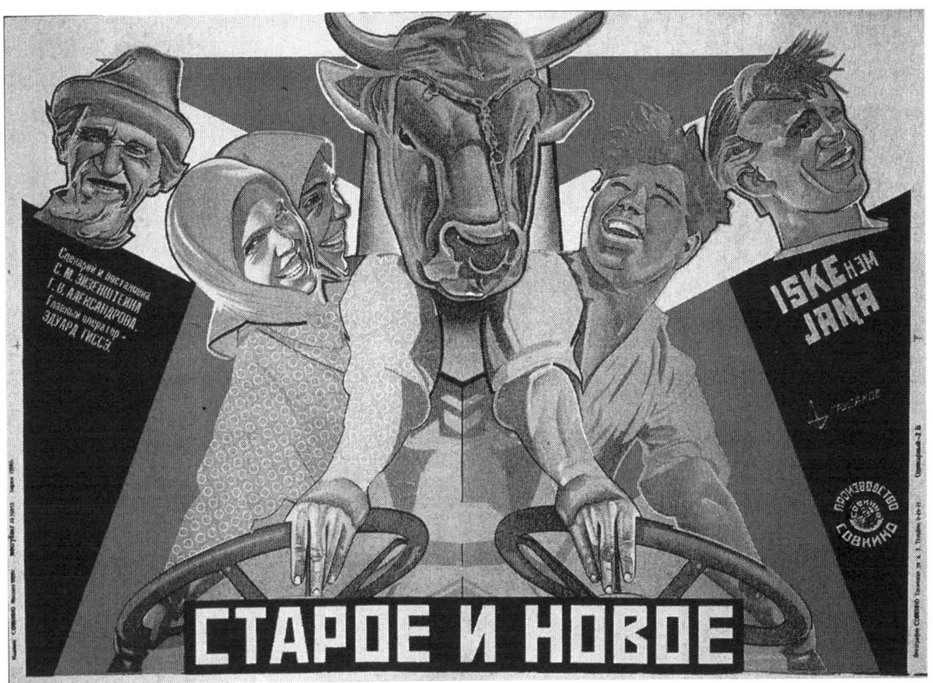

4.3 Poster for *The General Line* (originally titled *Old and New*) by Sergei Eisenstein, 1929. Part of the David King Collection. Presented to Tate Archive by David King 2016.

is, large scale films in which a didactic theme is unravelled rather obviously. Our films must be just as entertaining as bourgeois films."[23]

This direction, adopted by both branches of Sovkino and Mezhrabprom-Rus, had a tremendous impact on the film industry, which recovered by 1926. A number of home-grown box office successes, hyped in the popular press, appeared. Audience surveys similar to those used in all cultural industries at that time confirmed the preference of audience for Soviet films such as *The Extraordinary Adventures of Mr. West in the Land of the Bolsheviks* (Lev Kuleshov, 1924), *The Girl with the Hatbox* (Boris Barnet, 1927), *The House on Trubnaya* (Boris Barnet, 1928), and *The Kiss of Mary Pickford* (Sergei Komarov, 1927), four comedies peppered with satirical elements, and boasting a sardonic outlook. What did these productions have in common? Although they exploited Soviet content (but not enough, according to some critics), they were entertaining and they resembled American films.

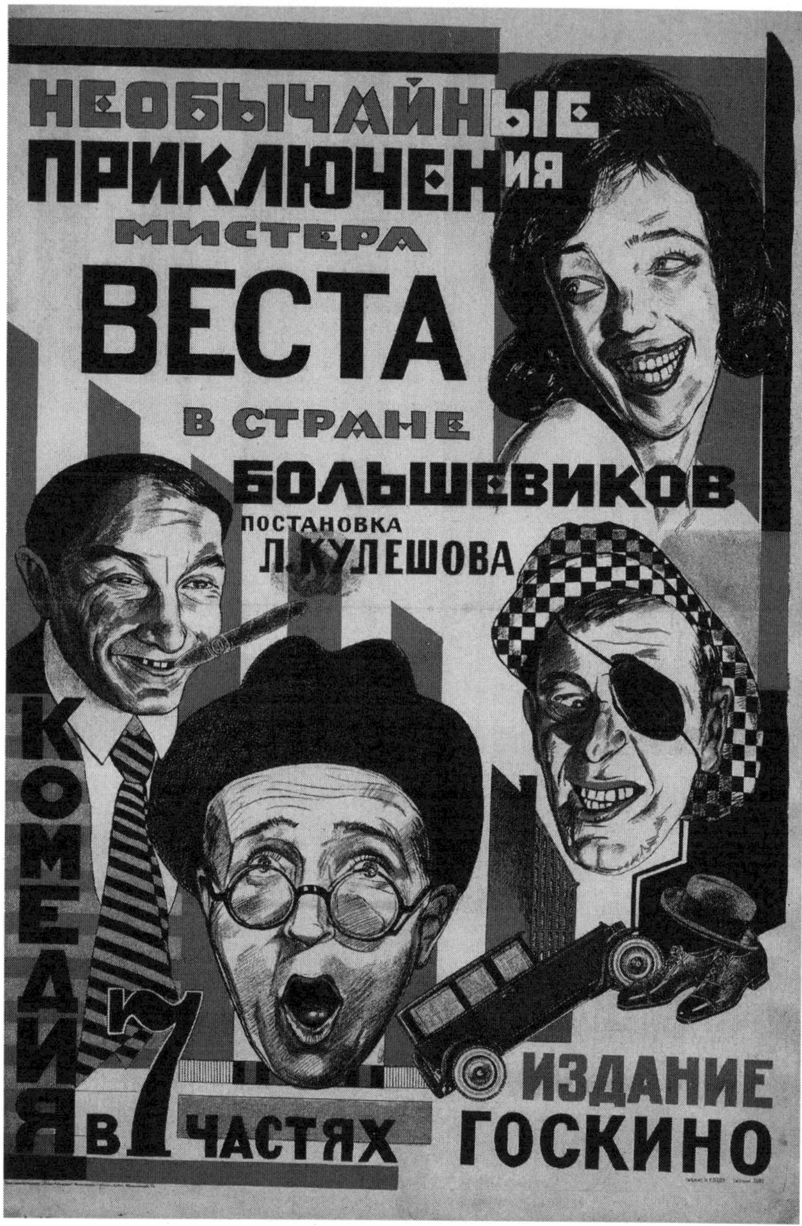

4.4 Poster for *The Extraordinary Adventures of Mr. West in the Land of the Bolsheviks* by Lev Kuleshov, 1924. The Alexander Dobrovinsky Collection.

The Extraordinary Adventures of Mr. West in the Land of the Bolsheviks is a satirical, action-packed comedy about American gullibility and willingness to believe anti-Soviet propaganda. Ironically, it loosely mimics the American Western genre, but also draws from theatre practices developed in Meyerhold's circle, including clowning techniques. Because cinema in the 1920s was still silent, it relied largely on visual strategies to create effect and affect, in particular *tipazh* produced with the use of clothing or prostheses, parody, meaningful juxtapositions, and exaggerated gestures or facial expressions. This is one of the many reasons why, as *Mr. West*'s director Lev Kuleshov put it in 1925, "Theatre and film are having a love affair with the circus."[24]

Mr. West, a Harold Lloyd lookalike, is a naive American who happens to be the YMCA president. At the beginning of the movie, he plans a trip to the newly founded Soviet Union, where he hopes to introduce the idea of the Christian youth organization. A few days before his departure, Mr. West receives unsolicited advice from an anonymous "friend," who sends him American magazines depicting brutish Bolsheviks wearing ratty furs and walking around holding oversized hammers and sickles. Encouraged by his fearful wife, he decides to take along as a bodyguard his friend, the rambunctious cowboy Jeddie, played by film director Boris Barnet, who happened to be a boxer and had training in clowning techniques. Upon his arrival in Moscow, Mr. West's briefcase is stolen. He then immediately gets separated from the cartoonish Jeddie and falls into the hands of a group of thieves and counter-revolutionaries. These "anti-social" elements, these "parasites," play on West's fears; they concoct his abduction by petty crooks dressed up as caricatures inspired by the same magazines the victim had brought along in his luggage. Extorting thousands of dollars from Mr. West, they fake his rescue from the phony communist riff-raff. It is only after he is liberated by the real Bolshevik police and reunited with Jeddie that the American finally gets to tour Moscow. He then realizes that the Soviet government had not destroyed all cultural landmarks, such as Moscow University and the Bolshoi Theater; the magazines and his abductors had been spreading lies. Understanding that American views of the Soviet Union are profoundly erroneous and that Bolsheviks are in fact outstanding people, he promptly telegraphs his wife. He asks her to hang a portrait of Lenin in his office.

Boris Barnet, while he acted in action films such as *Mr. West, Miss Mend* (by Boris Barnet and Fedor Otsep, 1926), and Vsevolod Pudovkin's *Storm over Asia* (1929), also specialized in the making of sweet romantic comedies with a satirical edge. *The Girl with the Hatbox* (1927) centres on the theme of housing shortage. It features a young, free-spirited milliner from the countryside who travels regularly to Moscow to sell her wares. On one of her trips she meets a student who is rendered homeless by the scarcity of available dwellings; he cannot find a corner to rent. In order to help him out, the milliner marries him and moves him into the Moscow room registered to her name, above the shop where her hats are sold. The supercilious shopkeepers are hence forced to share their roof with the girl's new husband. A comedy of errors ensues, grounded in a love triangle and turmoil over a winning lottery tickets. Shades of satire colour the comedic storyline. Through the use of *tipazh*, slapstick, and comical misunderstandings that highlight the disparity between proletarian and bourgeois lifestyles and values, the film takes aim mainly at the grotesquely portrayed NEPmen, their entrenchment in petit bourgeois luxury, and the outdated institution of marriage.

The House on Trubnaya (1928), also by Boris Barnet, focuses on the difficulty certain young people experience in adapting to Soviet society. The protagonist is a young, naive girl from the countryside who moves to Moscow. She finds employment as a maid with a pompous hairdresser and his indolent wife in an apartment building on Trubnaya Street, an environment rich in caricatural characters and evocative objects. Exploited by her petit-bourgeois employers, she becomes a member of the domestic workers' union and gradually affirms her proletarian rights. The comedy hinges on clever camera tricks, clowning techniques, and the visual representation of a house that operates like a hectic machine – no doubt inspired by the set designs produced by Lyubov Popova and Varvara Stepanova for Meyerhold's theatre works. While the film appears generally humorous – making light of inadequate infrastructures and the coexistence of Bolsheviks and NEPmen in a shared house – element of satire strongly infuse the narrative. Its venom is directed, once again, at NEPmen. But it also serves an autocritical purpose, aimed at the naiveté and lack of vigilance of young provincial workers.

The most popular satirical comedy of the period is perhaps *The Kiss of Mary Pickford* (1927), a film that pokes fun at the Soviet public's love for American movies and movie stars, based on an original idea by Lunacharsky.[25] *The Kiss* features a cameo by the popular American film couple Mary Pickford and Douglas Fairbanks. The original footage was shot during their visit to the USSR in 1926, the pair apparently participating knowingly as a gesture to the Soviet film industry.[26] The story revolves around a movie theatre usher, Goga, in love with a young undiscovered actress with laughable petit bourgeois aspirations. She has a crush on Douglas Fairbanks and aspires to date someone equally famous. In order to improve his standing, Goga submits himself to a battery of tests conducted at the Laboratory of Experimental Studies, where he is poked and prodded and made to perform ridiculous physical feats. As a result, he is certified as a "cinema professional of the highest level." As Peter Christensen remarks, the lab scenes are most likely a parodic barb at biomechanics and the blooming interest in reflexology in Soviet avant-garde film and theatre circles.[27] Finally, a fortuitous encounter, leading to a kiss on the cheek from Mary Pickford, transforms the protagonist into a local celebrity. Throngs of women farcically chase him throughout Moscow streets; the usher's newfound popularity makes his beloved jealous, and she finally falls for him.

If these movies were very popular with the public, they were also sharply criticized by the professional film press, which mainly represented the interests of the Narkompros and of avant-garde directors. Lunacharsky was also critical. Although he supported popular genres, he nevertheless found that the time-proven recipe of romance, action, drama, laughter, and happy endings was not always used to its fullest potential in these films. "I wouldn't say that we haven't done anything in the field of film comedy," he wrote. "A few very good films were produced by some of our most famous filmmakers. But, for example, a film like *The Girl with the Hatbox* can't really count as a Soviet comedy: it is simply a little farce, aimed at securing a viewership base. This is all very good – but does not constitute a true comedy."[28]

He believed that while internal enemies of the regime were still roaming about, the satirical elements of comedy needed to be ramped up.

Humorous mockery can be good-hearted or self-critical. Autocriticism is an instrument of class struggle. When we criticize each other in a small revolutionary circle (small not because we are few – two and a half communists – but small in the sense of a close-knit group), autocriticism that is conducted in humorous journals, through jokes and comedies, can only be good-hearted. Having said this, if the object of mockery is degeneration, then there is no place for good-heatedness. The fouler, the more dangerous the circumstance, the nastier humour must become, and it must soon turn into satire.[29]

As Sovkino started to develop export markets for Soviet films, the debates around Soviet comedy became increasingly complex. A new question needed to be seriously examined: How would autocriticism, whether it be light-hearted or all-out satirical, be understood by foreign publics? Lunacharsky himself, who had always been a fervent defender of the satirical mode, acknowledged that autocritical laughter could be perceived as straightforward criticism in the eyes of the enemy.

> Sometimes, in our literature, theatre, and cinema, comedies and satires are made about which one could say: they shouldn't be shown here, and it would be a crime to show them in the West because they disparage our life. Every artist arming himself with laughter must address these concerns. He must always bear in mind one important rule: never exploit satire without opposing to what is ridiculed what we hold dear and good. A play focusing exclusively on a negative angle, and presenting in each act only what is negative, reserving only for the end something happier, will produce on foreigners the impression of a symbolic representation of the USSR that is close to those produced by the White movement.[30]

In spite of these reservations, Lunacharsky continued to champion the importance of satirical cinema into the 1930s. In a text dated 1931, for example, he defended Aleksandr Medvedkin, whose work had been criticized for being too ambiguous.

> We can't be afraid of mistakes, because this attitude will lead art into a dead end. We can't let comradely critique scare artists so that they refuse to work. … I am certain that our comrades working on satirical works will find the courage to continue their work, in spite of its difficulty, and that we will find the strength to support them until the end. Cinema comedy and satire is a field boundlessly rich and fruitful. But it has been insufficiently developed and it now requires from us particular attention.[31]

Among Soviet productions, if comedy was not a dominant genre, it certainly held a respectable position, second only to melodramas and revolutionary dramas. In 1922–3, 14 per cent of films were comedies; in 1924–5, 19 per cent; in 1926–7, 15 per cent; in 1928–9, 13 per cent. This number dropped to 9 per cent for the following five years.[32] Why did the genre of satirical comedy start waning significantly after 1928? For the most part, it became increasingly difficult to make entertainment films – not because they could not be made technically, but because of cultural policy, redrawn according to the logic of the First Five-Year Plan at the 1928 conference on cinema. The political climate was changing during this period, and the targets of Civil War satire ·or those of the NEP period no longer seemed appropriate as Soviet society reoriented itself towards the collective reconstruction of the country. Furthermore, just as increasing suspicion was being directed to foreign movies and plays, Soviet films were also being more closely scrutinized. Accordingly, there was a new push to create works that would show Soviet life in an unambiguously positive light. Fear of potential reprisal began to be felt in creative circles, and particularly across the Soviet satirical scene. As writer and critic Osip Brik put it laconically in an article published in 1927, "Without Laughter, comedy is impossible. But it is difficult to make a Soviet Comedy because we don't know what to laugh at."[33]

The 1928 Conference on Cinema

By the beginning of the First Five-Year Plan, it looked as if the film industry had recovered from the Civil War. The quality of Soviet films had improved greatly, and it seemed that viewers liked what they saw. In spite of this apparent success, one important problem remained. If the film industry had started to liberate itself from its dependence on foreign films, it was still entirely reliant on the importation of film stock and foreign-made equipment. To further complicate things, sound had made its appearance in cinema; the Soviet industry was in grave danger of swiftly falling behind. In the context of the First Five-Year Plan, when limited resources were all redirected towards a concerted process of industrialization, spending hard currency on film stock and the overhauling of the industry was problematic, to say the least.

The Party Conference on Cinema Affairs that took place in March 1928 was to evaluate the state of the industry and set new goals for Soviet cinema. It followed a series of conferences aimed at looking at all media, the first of which had examined theatre in 1923. More concretely, it called for cinema to embark upon the spirit of the First Five-Year Plan and take part in socialist construction and the Cultural Revolution. As one critic noted, Soviet cinema under Sovkino had become "90% commerce – 10% ideology."[34] The balance needed to be redressed. Accordingly, bourgeois vestiges would have to be eradicated from the industry and its production, and it would need to strengthen itself economically, but most importantly, politically and ideologically. The conference's first resolution was unambiguous. Quoting Lenin via Lunacharsky, it stated:

Cinema, the "most important of all arts," can and must play a large part in the Cultural Revolution as a medium for broad educational work and communist propaganda, for the organisation and education of the masses around the slogans and tasks of the Party, their artistic education and their wholesome relaxation and entertainment.

Cinema, like every other art, cannot be apolitical. Cinema must be a weapon of the proletariat in its struggle for hegemony, leadership and influence in relation to the other classes, it should be, in the hands of the Party, the most powerful medium of communist enlightenment and education.[35]

Reforms followed swiftly: in February 1930 Sovkino was liquidated, to be replaced by Soyuzkino (All-Union Photo-Cinematic Association), headed by Boris Shumyatsky, a party functionary with no previous film experience, who became the de facto executive producer for the Soviet film monopoly from 1930 to 1937. Foreign imports dropped and film libraries were purged of foreign movies, as well as Soviet features that were considered bourgeois in content. Yet Soviet film production did not manage to compensate; its own numbers went into rapid decline, from 147 films made in 1930 to 35 in 1933.[36]

Furthermore, rigorous thematic planning ordered the logic of film production, corresponding – in the spirit of the Five-Year Plans – to government imperatives and various campaigns that were under way. Therefore, the small number of satirical comedies that were made during the period are the product of thematic planning. Yakov Protazanov's two comedies *Don Diego and Pelagia* (1928) and *St Jorgen's Day* (1930), for example, are finely tuned satires on religiosity and explicitly contribute to the antireligious campaigns, which had been under way since 1918. *Happiness* (1935) by Aleksandr Medvedkin, a blunt condemnation of the "left-behind peasants" who still survived after the drive for collectivization, is one of a number of movies commissioned by the Soviet government to serve the campaign for the collectivization of the countryside.

Happiness can be considered the last of early Soviet satires; it also still bears experimental qualities that were characteristic of post-revolutionary attempts in satirical propaganda. Indeed, it borrows liberally from ROSTA windows, Terevsat living theatre, and Medvedkin's own Civil War–time *agitki*, which all drew on Russian folklore and medieval laughter for inspiration. The first half of the movie depicts the circumstances of a peasant in the pre-revolutionary era. The protagonist, surnamed the "loser," is a poor peasant whose exaggeratedly tattered

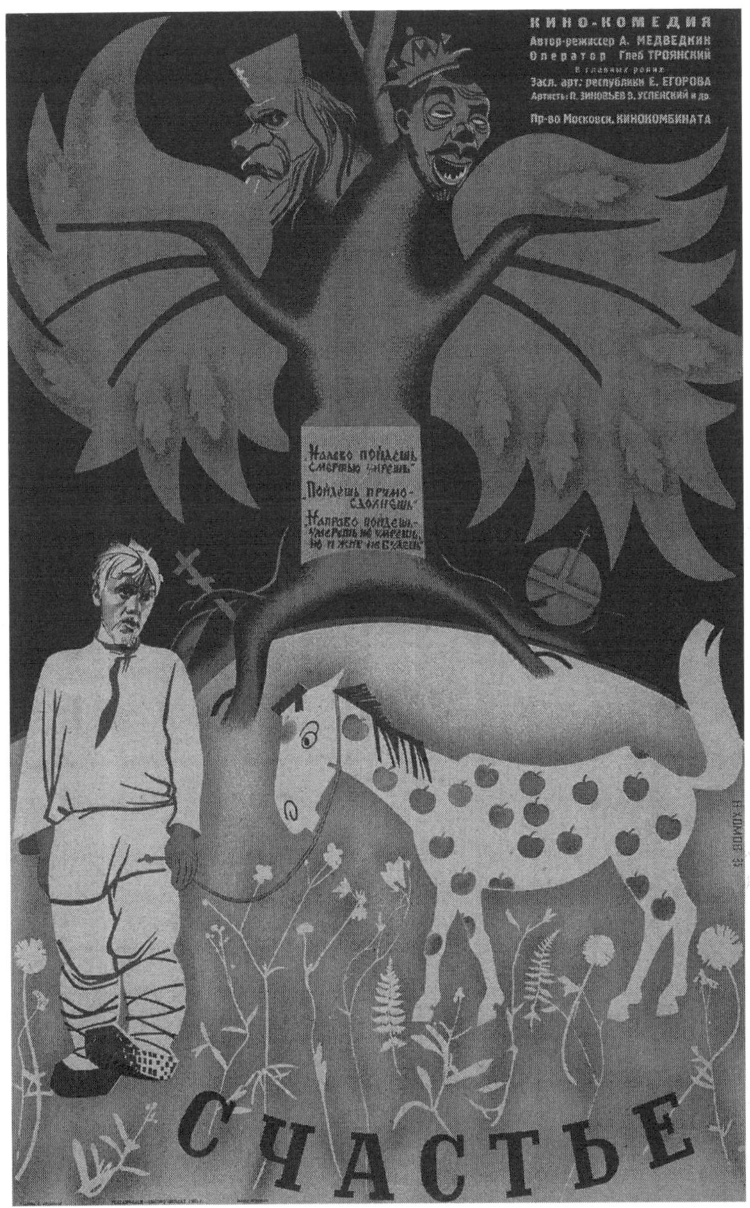

4.5 Poster for *Happiness* by Aleksandr Medvedkin, 1935.
Russian State Library.

clothing and derelict house reveal him as having nothing. Venturing out into the world to seek happiness, he comes across an enormous wallet fat with money. He and his wife buy a polka-dotted horse, farm their land, and for once reap a good harvest. But happiness does not ensue. No sooner have they celebrated their good fortune than caricatural figures of social parasites appear, each more ridiculous than the previous: fat priests and nuns – bare-breasted in see-through cassocks – beg for donations, tax collectors and mask-wearing soldiers pile bags of grain in their trucks, while their neighbours plainly steal from them. The peasant is once again left with nothing. In the second part of the film, the same cast of characters has been transported to the Soviet era and to a collective farm. The broken man, feeble and drunk, is unable to contribute. Even worse, he serves as a point of entry into the farm for saboteurs and other misfits. Again, they are represented in caricatural ways, in outmoded rags, hump-backed and hooked-nosed; they exhibit crooked fingers and toes on their unnaturally elongated hands and feet created by prostheses. In contrast, the collective farms workers are tall, healthy looking, and beam white-toothed smiles. In the end the "loser" finally adapts to Soviet life and the collective farm. He is suddenly transfigured: dressed in modern clothing, beard shaved, sporting a clean haircut and standing straight. But he comically has much trouble getting rid of his bast shoes and rags, symbols of his now shunned backwardness. They keep being brought back to him by various characters. When he finally throws them in a barren field, the cast of social parasites scurry like rodents and fight for the spoils. The satirical intent of this silent movie, embodied in *tipazh* and gesture, could not be clearer.

Medvedkin's film had been greatly anticipated. But, as Emma Widdis explains, its timing was unfortunate.

> At the end of 1934 the debate on comedy, always complex, took a new turn. *Happiness* was released shortly after Alexandrov's musical comedy *The Happy Fellows* (*Veselye rebyata*, 1934), which was hailed by the influential administrator Boris Shumyatsky as a solution to the sticky problem of Soviet comedy. The film united the three qualities that Shumyatsky proclaimed as essential in the new cinema of the 1930s (ideology [*ideinost*], joy [*radost*] and merriness [*bodrost*]), encouraging in the spectator a joyful appreciation of the Soviet world.[37]

Shumyatsky was a pragmatist. He understood that for Soviet cinema to be successful, it needed to be adapted to the taste of the public, whatever professional critics though. "Why [do critics] think that in the epoch of proletarian revolution the proletariat does not need poetry, laughter and love? Neither the revolution nor the defence of our socialist fatherland are a tragedy for the proletariat. We have always gone into battle, and we shall go into battle again in the future singing and, at times, laughing."[38] But he also understood the potential of laughter differently than Lunacharsky had. While the commissar, who was by then deceased, had favoured satire for its potential as a social corrective and tool for autocriticism, Shumyatsky was much more interested in humour, a sort of laughter that had the potential to alleviate conflict, gloss over contradictions internal to the regime, and encourage optimism.

Shumyatsky's report titled "A Cinema for the Million," published in 1935, was in fact his adaptation of the doctrine of socialist realism, proclaimed by Andrei Zhdanov and others at the 1934 Writer's Congress. It declared that the main goal of art in general, and of cinema in particular, was to provide viewers with vivid images of what Socialist Russia could be. In other words, the critical edge of satire not only needed to be dulled; it needed to be replaced by a different kind of ideological tool.

For Shumyatsky, Grigory Aleksandrov's musical *The Happy Fellows*, a 1934 box-office success, was the first true Soviet comedy and a model to emulate. It told the story of a shepherd mistaken for an international concert star. In a cascade of comic musical numbers he becomes the leader of a jazz band and gives a series of hilarious shows that take him from his native Odessa to Moscow. This Soviet-style rags to riches story rapidly became the basic script of 1930s optimistic comedies. As Shumyatsky put it, "*The Happy Guys* was a good start for a new genre: the Soviet film comedy. *The Happy Guys* played this part successfully. We have an optimistic film sprinkled with joy, laughter and merriment. The film is a marvellous relaxation and audiences that have seen *The Happy Guys* will find it easier to work afterwards."[39]

A number of optimistic comedies, musical or otherwise, that followed this basic script were produced in the 1930s, mainly by Grigory Aleksandrov and Ivan Pyryev. Both directors had been active members of the Soviet satirical scene in the 1920s, as they cut their teeth in the performing arts as actors in plays by Meyerhold and Eisenstein. They had then collaborated on the latter's early film works. However, in the 1930s, adjusting to the ideological climate, their work avoided the critical edge of satire and espoused the forced earnestness and optimism of

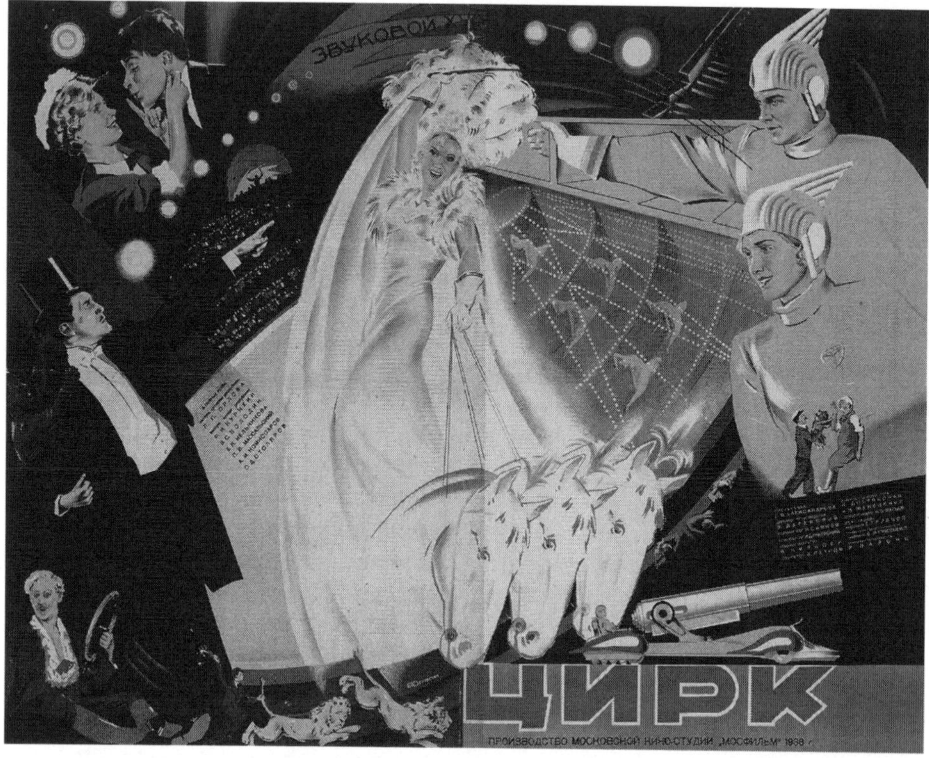

4.6 Poster for *Circus* by Grigory Aleksandrov, 1936. Russian State Library.

the Five-Year Plans. Their films surprise today's cinema enthusiasts, because they challenge stereotypes of grimness often associated with the Stalinist period. They most famously include *The Shining Path* (Aleksandrov, 1940), a Cinderella story about a textile worker who becomes a shock worker and is eventually elected member of the Supreme Soviet; *Tractor Drivers* (Pyryev, 1939,) about a demobilized tank driver who finds love and purpose as a tractor driver on a collective farm; and *Volga Volga* (Aleksandrov, 1938), often claimed to have been Stalin's favourite Soviet comedy. *Volga Volga* is a musical centred on a group of amateur performers on their way to the Soviet capital to take part in a talent contest called the Moscow Musical Olympiad. Most of the action, singing, dancing, and romance unfolds on a steamboat travelling downstream on the Volga River.

The most celebrated of the Stalin-era comedies is undoubtedly *Circus* (1936). In this film, the clowning and exaggerated grimaces that had so well served avant-garde satirical theatre and cinema since the early days of the Revolution are put back in what could be considered their rightful place – the representation of circus life and extraordinary physical feats. If there is some derisive *tipazh*, it is straightforwardly directed at satirizing Nazi and American conceptions of race, and it is used to provide context. The overall narrative, however, is clearly and unambiguously an optimistic representation of the Soviet world, and humour is here used to make light of inevitable incongruities and gloss over contradictions internal to Soviet society. The story, based on a play by Ilf and Petrov, follows Marion, an American vaudeville dancer on tour in Russia. Her act includes being shot from a cannon into the canopy, where she grabs onto a trapeze. The Soviet circus master, impressed with the feat, decides to adapt this act for the USSR. In dialogue with the developments happening in the circus ring in the early 1930s, he improves greatly on the original's technological complexity and required athleticism. He also adds futuristic flair to the performance, introducing shiny art deco costumes and machinery. As Marion falls in love with a Soviet acrobat, she also succumbs to the blackmail of her manager, who threatens to reveal her dark secret: she is mother to a coloured child, the reason why she left racist and intolerant America. The film ends with Marion's secret being revealed in the middle of a performance staged for delegates representing all the republics of the Soviet Union. Without skipping a beat, in a cascade of their native languages, they sing the baby a lullaby; in this socialist realist version of the USSR, racism is simply not an issue.[40]

Just as they had enjoyed the satirical comedies of the 1920s, the movie-going public largely gave themselves over to optimistic comedies of the Five-Year Plans period. In contrast with earlier silent movies, these were loud, fun, colourful, and extravagant. Who could resist? But as always in the field of Soviet culture, the tension between entertainment and enlightenment remained. About *Happy Fellows*, critic A. Surkov wrote that it was the result of "lemonade ideology," that "the film is the apotheosis of vulgarity," and that it will stoop to anything "for the sake of making people laugh at all costs."[41]

Laughter and the Cultural Revolution

The tug of war described above between enlightenment an entertainment, and between satire and optimistic propaganda, is characteristic of the so-called Cultural Revolution (1928–32), a movement that had a tremendous effect on the arts. It was mainly driven by young proletarians, the generation that had grown up with the Revolution.

The Cultural Revolution can be understood as a grass-roots movement, lead mainly by agitprop activists and members of the Communist Youth Association (Komsomol), the Communist Academy, and RAPP, the Association of Proletarian Writers, who had come to dominate Glavrepertkom in the field of the performing arts. It directed its actions principally against the establishment's alliance with the intelligentsia. It was seen by contemporaries as analogous or complementary to the rapid industrialization, the total collectivization, and the uncompromising thrust towards communism that characterizes the First Five-Year Plan. And it was often righteous, violent, and could be destructive – of institutions, careers, and practices. Sheila Fitzpatrick described it best: "The Cultural Revolution was somewhere between class war and class war game: the young proletarians shot words not bullets at the fleeing bureaucrats and wavering intellectuals, but they were words which carried a real threat of deprivation of livelihood, loss of employment and employability."[42]

Concretely, the Cultural Revolution meant the proletarianization of culture or, in other words, the explicit politicization of culture, more stringent party control, and a bias for explicitly proletarian concerns, publics, or artists. It involved breaking away from the pluralism and the liberalism of the NEP period. It also destroyed the climate of experimentation and of collaboration with fellow travellers, avant-garde artists, and bourgeois intellectuals that Lunacharsky had fostered and defended throughout his career as People's Commissar of Enlightenment. Because of this, it is also the cause of the dispersal of various artistic scenes, such as the one that brought together Lunacharsky, Mayakovsky, Meyerhold, Eisenstein, and their fellow practitioners and advocates of satire.

In the arts, experimentation in particular became suspect. This is because experimental practices could not always be straightforwardly understood, but also because they might fail. The indeterminacy of circus feats, the double-entendre of visual parody and irony, reversals of expectations, montage of attraction, and any strategy that required viewers to meet artists halfway in the co-construction of meaning were also branded potentially dangerous and therefore chastised.

Furthermore, arguing that socialism had already been achieved in the Soviet Union, proponents of the Cultural Revolution rejected a role for critical art. They felt enemies from the tsarist period or the Civil War no longer needed to be invoked since they no longer constituted a meaningful threat to be scorned and defused. And, as we have seen in chapter 3 with the case of Meyerhold and Mayakovsky's *The Bed Bug* and *The Bath House,* their last two satirical plays that mocked Soviet bureaucracy, autocriticsm in the performing arts as in the cinema was starting to be considered dangerously interpretable; it could too easily collapse into outright criticism.

The Cultural Revolution movement was short lived. Between 1932 and 1936, many of the policies it had generated were reversed, and the term came into disuse. What remained, however, is the broad instrumentalization of culture and the repudiation of diversity. Through all this, however, laughter did not disappear. But in Soviet films it largely changed in nature: from satire to humour. To be more precise, it is not merely that laughter in the cinema came to *lack* a critical edge, as I wrote earlier in this chapter. Rather, the *refusal* to be critical became understood as a means to pave the way for optimistic representations of socialism. It is this complex process that is encapsulated in Boris Shumyatsky's 1935 deceptively simple call for a new kind of optimistic cinema: "The victorious class wants to laugh with joy. That is right, and Soviet cinema must provide the audience with this joyful Soviet laughter."[43]

Chapter Five

The Strategies and Targets of Satire

In order to be funny, the plot must be constructed on contrasts, unexpected courses of action leading us to surprise and astonishment.

A.V. Lunacharsky[1]

In an article written in 1923, Vladimir Mayakovsky poses the question of how one becomes a satirist. He argues that if some subject matter, such as saboteurs, counter-revolutionaries, or parasites, is easy to ridicule and seems to generate the comic in and of itself, the best satire arises when the form of the work contributes to creating comic effects: for example, the unusual treatment of rhyme or rhythm in a poem, or the incongruous use of a traditional genre such as the *lubok*.[2] He concludes his article by stating that "laughter is in the making and there are rules to the production of laughter. Therefore, satirists are not born, they learn their trade. It takes a deliberate method to create spontaneous laughter."[3]

This chapter follows Mayakovsky's lead in identifying the various strategies developed and adopted by Soviet satirists in the visual arts, including the visual aspects of theatre and cinema. These strategies can be grouped into four broad categories: caricature, collage, parody, and irony. Here, they are defined with an eye to how each functions pragmatically. The chapter also introduces three case studies chosen from the most important early Soviet propaganda campaigns. They are examined through the combined lens of their historical significance and their reliance on satirical propaganda techniques. The discussion highlights the type of subject matter most fertile for satire, and the broader goals artists aimed at through their sardonic treatment of a given theme. Bearing in mind that Soviet laughter was understood by its producers as an implement of battle, it is considered in terms of its rhetorical potential, as deliberate and conscious communication rife with impelling qualities. In other words, intentionality and anticipated response are presented here as crucial to the decoding of satire in Soviet cultural production.

The Mechanisms of Laughter Production

A broader reflection on the mechanisms of laughter production can provide some initial insight. In 1991, Salvatore Attardo and Victor Raskin developed the General Theory of Verbal Humour (GTVH) for the analysis of jokes and short humorous texts. What is particularly compelling about the GTVH is that, while it grounds itself in semantic analysis, it is also open to broader narratological, aesthetic, and social concerns, foregrounding the transtextual[4] nature and the cultural specificity of laughter.

The GTVH is based on the *incongruity/resolution* model. Incongruity theories (or theories of inconsistency, contradiction, or bisociation) go back to Aristotle's discussion of metaphors and puns in *Rhetoric*.[5] Grounded in cognitive processes, incongruity theories claim that the comic results from the perception of a disparity between a set of expectations and what is observed, or a mismatch between things that are simultaneously perceived. There is an ongoing debate about whether incongruity stands on its own or is always part of the incongruity/resolution dyad.[6] Christian Hempelmann and Andrea Samson speak of a spectrum of resolvability. They explain that "resolution [is] always partial, as the logic that enables it is always playful, or faulty. Thus, incongruity-resolution humor should be considered one extreme, namely one closest to but distinct from full resolution, while nonsense humor takes up the opposite extreme, closest to no resolution but at least pretending to have one."[7]

Because incongruity points to cognitive mechanisms, as Attardo argues, "linguistic analysis has tended to side (largely unwittingly) with this kind of theory."[8] For the same reason, the incongruity theory seems like a convenient basis on which to establish analytical models for the investigation of comic genres in visual practices. But, as Arvo Krikmann points out, "most of the humor theories ever proposed are actually mixed theories, and many contemporary researchers believe that humor in its totality is too huge and multiform a phenomenon to be incorporated into a single integrated theory."[9] It is therefore possible that readings of works based on incongruity theory in the first instance might also draw from other prevalent theories of laughter, such as *hostility* and *relief.* Hostility theories and relief theories shed light on the function of the comic rather than focusing on cognitive mechanisms. Indeed, hostility theories claim that laughter is lodged in a feeling of superiority over what is ridiculed or considered deviant from the norm; according to Paul de Man, this might even apply to self-irony.[10] Relief theories, on the other hand, propose that the comic is meant to release tensions, frustrations, desires, or other forms of psychic energy. While Lunacharsky never refers to these categories by their current terms, we saw in chapter 1 that the conception of laughter he developed over the years combined all three. Furthermore, just like Mayakovsky, the commissar understood that a trigger or an effect deliberately created by the satirist is necessary to spark spontaneous laughter. This catalyst, generally resulting from incongruity or a mismatch between expectation and what is observed, is what provokes surprise and the ensuing psychophysiological reaction he described, basing his understanding of this phenomenon on the work of Herbert Spencer. But the actual intent of the work, and its social role, go beyond making people laugh; it is intended to attack, shame, or chastise (as in hostility theories) or to provide an outlet for fear or hatred (as in relief theories).

The GTVH uses, for the purpose of analysis, the following six "knowledge resources":[11] *script opposition* (the incongruity between two or more overlapping narratives or scripts that serves as a trigger for the comic); *logical mechanism* (the resolution phase of the incongruity/resolution model); *situation* (the elements, often non-humoristic, that ground the joke or the humorous statements in a context or recognizable circumstances); *target* (the butt of the joke); *narrative strategy* (the genre or type of the joke or comic statement); and *language* (the actual lexical, syntactic, phonological, and all other choices made at the linguistic level). For Attardo and Raskin, a close analysis of a joke using this model allows the researcher to find out not only how (structurally, semantically, phonetically, etc.) it manages to be funny, but also why (in which broad cultural context, and in relation to what other "texts"). While it was developed for the study of short verbal humoristic pieces, it can be transposed with some adaptations to longer or more complex texts: novels, short stories, theatre plays, and films scenarios.[12] With careful attention to formal devices and compositional strategies, it can also be adapted to the study of graphic arts and other visual practices.

Indeed, it is crucial to remember that the comic, in the visual as in language, rarely emanates solely from the subject matter. Form, colour, technique, medium, scale, kinetic properties, mismatch between the subject matter and the way it is represented or between an image and its caption, are what provoke a laughter response, or encourage a second-degree interpretation of the representation.[13] They constitute the trigger, or script opposition in the GTVH model, which animates a visual manifestation.

Caricature

In its most common meaning, a caricature is a representation that exaggerates or overly simplifies certain features of a face, body, object, or situation. It does so in order to highlight these aspects, give them a disproportionate importance, reduce the target's stature to isolated traits, or reveal some hidden character symbolized by the overblown feature. Caricatures of Leon Trotsky produced after his banishment from the Soviet Union in 1929, for example, exaggerate his nose and pointy ears. In a context of growing anti-Semitism under Stalin, these caricatural traits function to demonize him and highlight his hidden Jewish roots (Trotsky was the revolutionary surname of Leon Bronstein).

Sometimes, entire groups or classes of people are caricatured. Since there are no individual traits the artists can draw from, they often then resort to *tipazh*, which, as we have seen in chapter 2, served the purpose of typecasting, or creating ensembles of physical and moral characteristics, translating the essence of a given group detached from society in order to be better observed. The red-nosed priest, the potbellied capitalist, the ditsy NEPmenka, and the corpulent kulak garbed in a traditional Russian shirt, a cap on his head, are hence not caricatures of individuals, but of whole groups. A 1933 cover of the satirical journal *Krokodil* is surprisingly self-reflexive in how it makes light of the practice of caricature and the inescapable inconsistency between the caricatural use of *tipazh* and its actual referent. In this image, a skinny man in an overcoat watches from afar an artist painting a picture of a kulak immediately recognizable by his emblematic attributes. "Let him go on representing me that way," he says. "It hasn't occurred to him that I've slimmed down."

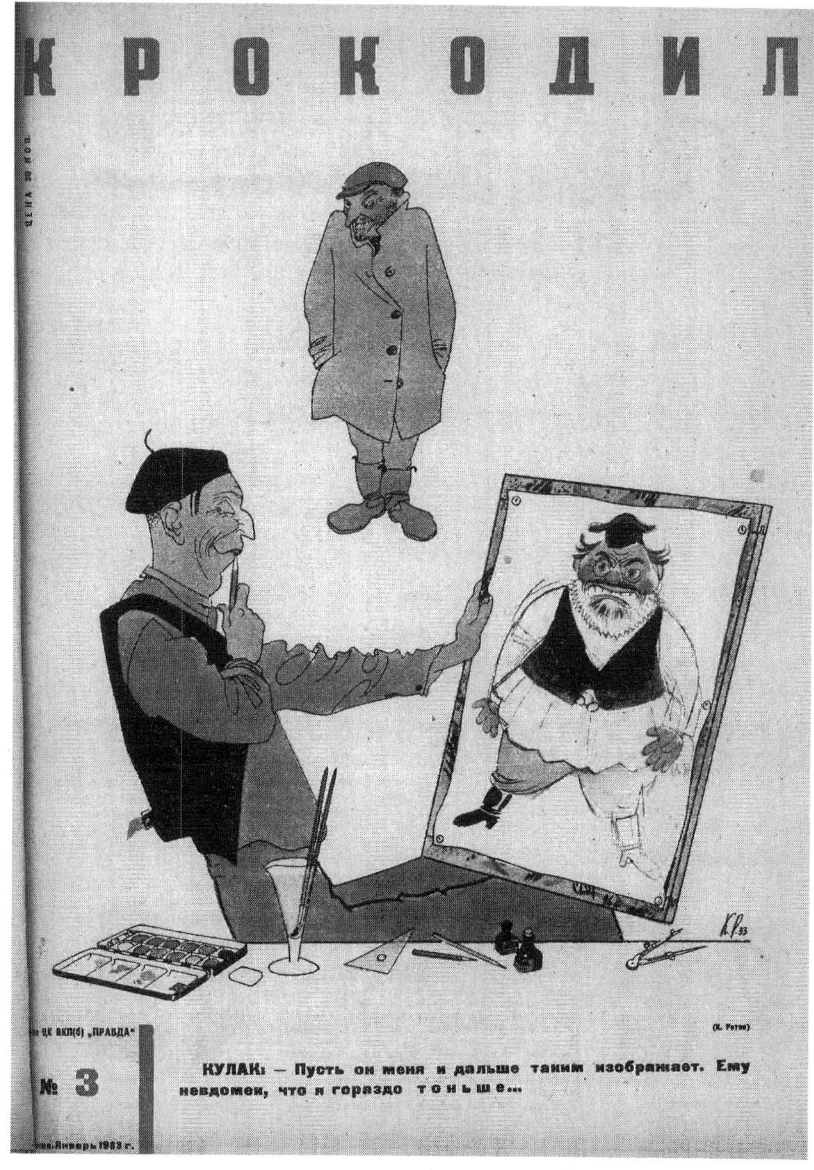

5.1 *Krokodil* 3 (1933), cover. "Let him go on representing me that way. It hasn't occurred to him that I've slimmed down." Part of the David King Collection. Presented to Tate Archive by David King 2016.

For caricature to be effective, it needs to be grounded in some degree of reality or experience. More precisely, it must oscillate incessantly between fiction and reality. It is only then that it can fulfil two critical conditions: it should be easily linked to its mark, and it needs to mock it, by deforming it.

Historically, it seems appropriate to associate the introduction of caricature with that of illustrated satirical journals in the eighteenth century. However, caricature's roots run much deeper: in medieval grotesque, carnivalesque figuration, and in the wearing of masks.

Collage

Collage is structurally linked with incongruity. Strictly speaking, the technique consists in the combination on a surface of heterogeneous elements in order to create a new whole. It is the cubists Georges Braque and Pablo Picasso who coined the term in 1912 to describe works in which they juxtaposed elements drawn from the empirical world (as opposed to the world of art): scraps of newspaper or wallpaper, oil-cloth, rope, nails, buttons, or sand.[14] The technique was rapidly imported into Russia where it most famously found expression in Vladimir Tatlin's wood and metal reliefs, Olga Rozanova's geometric paper abstractions, and Aleksandr Rodchenko's photomontages illustrating Mayavovsky's poems, where outsized images lifted from print advertising acquire a grotesque quality. But it also moved beyond the technique of pasting, and penetrated art production in a broader, more conceptual way. If *An Englishman in Moscow* (1914), Kazimir Malevich's cubo-futurist painting, is not a collage in the strictest sense, it nevertheless borrows its structure, highlighting the associative aspect of the representation. The juxtaposition of religious symbols (the fish, the candle, the church, and the cross); images of tools and weapons such as the saw, scissors, and sword; a figure in modern attire; and scattered scraps of language produce the effect of a collage. As in early futurist plays, such as *Victory over the Sun* (1912), the allogism and the clash of elements produce a liberating sort of laughter. It incarnates a certain state of mind that is grounded in rupture, disturbance, and creative association.

The strategy of collage also became a staple in Soviet theatre and cinema. Meyerhold used it in, among other instances, his scenography for Vladimir Mayakovsky's *Mystery-bouffe*, which juxtaposes circus, street theatre, and visual propaganda elements; Sergei Eisenstein theorized it as a theatre device that was later to inform his cinematic work in his 1923 manifesto "Montage of Attraction"; and Aleksandr Medvedkin

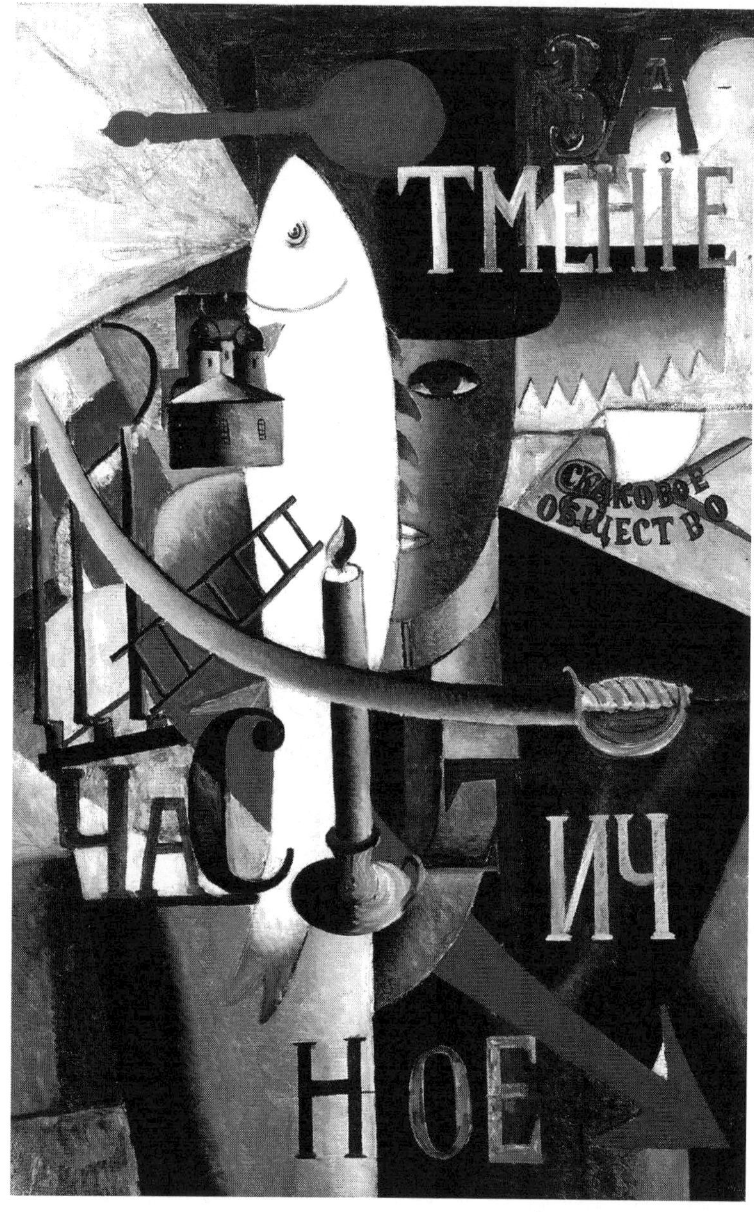

5.2 Kazimir Malevich, *An Englishman in Moscow*, 1914. Collection Stedelijk Museum Amsterdam.

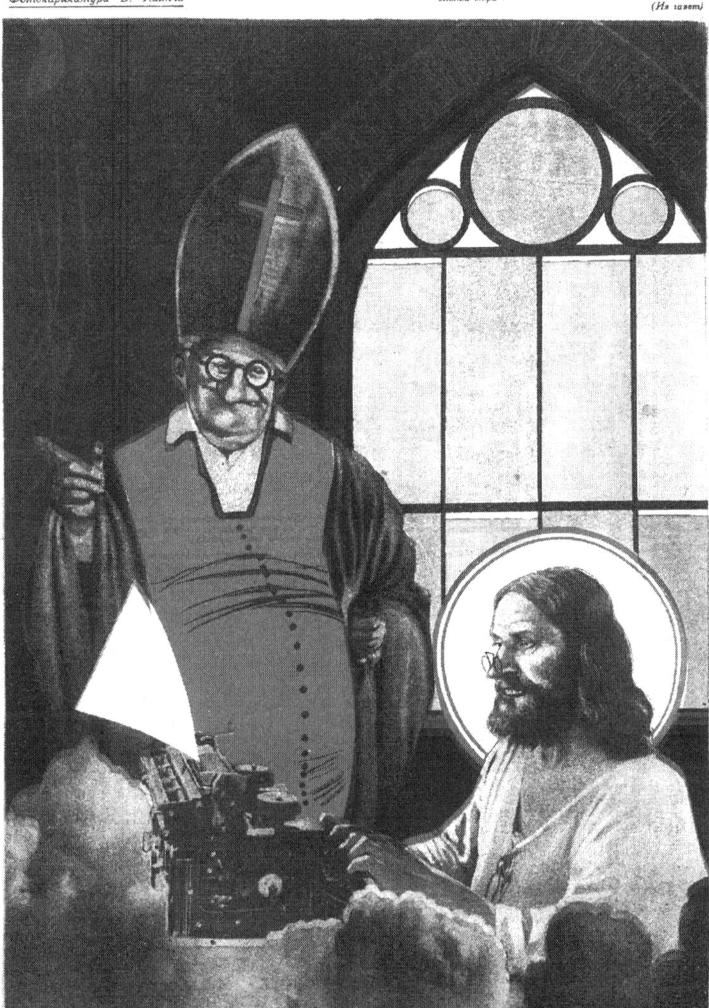

5.3 *Krokodil* 9 (1932), p. 3. The pope dictates answers to prayers as Jesus Christ types. The faces and the typewriter are drawn from photographs. Photomontage is one of the many techniques that allows the commingling of concrete elements and fictional ones. Part of the David King Collection. Presented to Tate Archive by David King 2016.

used it to structure his film *Happiness* and highlight the discrepancy between old and new. Collage allows creators to play with contrasting imagery, with the objective of increasing the viewers' intellectual involvement in the construction of meaning and affect. If collage is not always funny, one could argue that the comic is most often rooted in the practice of collage, of some type or another – as incongruity theories of laughter and the GTVH propose.

Parody

As opposed to caricature and collage, which are woven into the formal structure of a visual work, parody is essentially transtextual, that is to say, it necessarily refers to another, pre-extant work. A parody is a productive imitation created to comment on, mock, or trivialize its original source, often but not always leading to satire. It resembles its referent, but also exhibits differences and thence plays with the expectations of the viewer, which it challenges to a certain degree. For parody, as a transtextual form, to be efficient, its source needs to be well known by its public. Because of this, it is often ambivalent, at once affirming the cultural importance of the source and mocking it or ridiculing practices that are contiguous to it. In the early Soviet context, the most common instances of satirical parody lie in comic repurposing of the traditional forms of the *lubok,* of the orthodox icon, and of religious mass celebrations, particularly in street theatre. The parodies of icons, especially in satirical images targeting religion, always aim at challenging the credibility of their source and exposing the seductive and propagandistic aspects of religious art.

Other parodies are kinder to their referent and could even be considered homage. Vassilii Vereshchagin's *The Apotheosis of War* (1871) is an example of a painting that became a preferred source and a staple in Soviet visual parody. The work is not linked to a specific historical event. It represents a monumental pyramid of skulls amidst burnt desert, vultures circling above, and the ruins of a city appearing in the distance. On the frame the painter wrote an ironic dedication, "To all conquerors, who were, who are, and who will be," that constitutes a powerful condemnation of war. In fact, in 1874 the painting was censored by the tsarist government because it became understood as a covert critique of Russian military and imperialist politicy.

In the 1920s, *The Apotheosis of War* could be seen at the Tretyakov Gallery. It was extremely popular and, during that decade, it made its

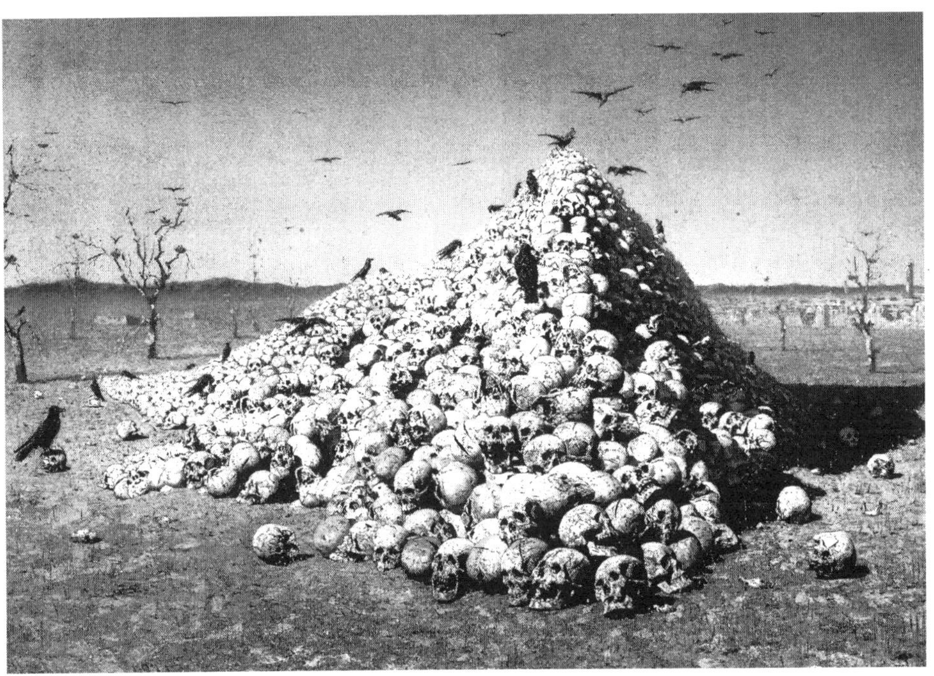

5.4 Vassilii Vereshchagin, *The Apotheosis of War*, 1871. The State
Tretyakov Gallery.

way into dozens of satirical works through the device of parody. Here
is a small sampling: on a 1924 *Krasnyi perets* cover, the gigantic heap of
skulls overshadows a fictional city that collages elements of New York,
Paris, and London. It becomes, as the title claims, a "Monument to Imperialism." Then, on the cover of the journal *Smekhach* (no. 9, 1926), cri-
tiquing an absurd production-planning decision, the skulls are replaced
by superfluous chamber pots. They also become empty bottles in the
context of the campaign against alcoholism in a *Krokodil* issue (no. 35,
1928, p. 5). The original meaning of the painting is reactivated during
the Second World War in a poster by Viktor Deni to evoke the massacre
of nearly two million people that took place during the 199-day siege
of Stalingrad. Finally, in a striking photograph taken in May 1945 to
commemorate the Battle for Berlin, which all but marked the end of the
Second World War in Europe, the skulls are replaced by Nazi helmets
rendered useless by the occupation of the city by the Red Army.

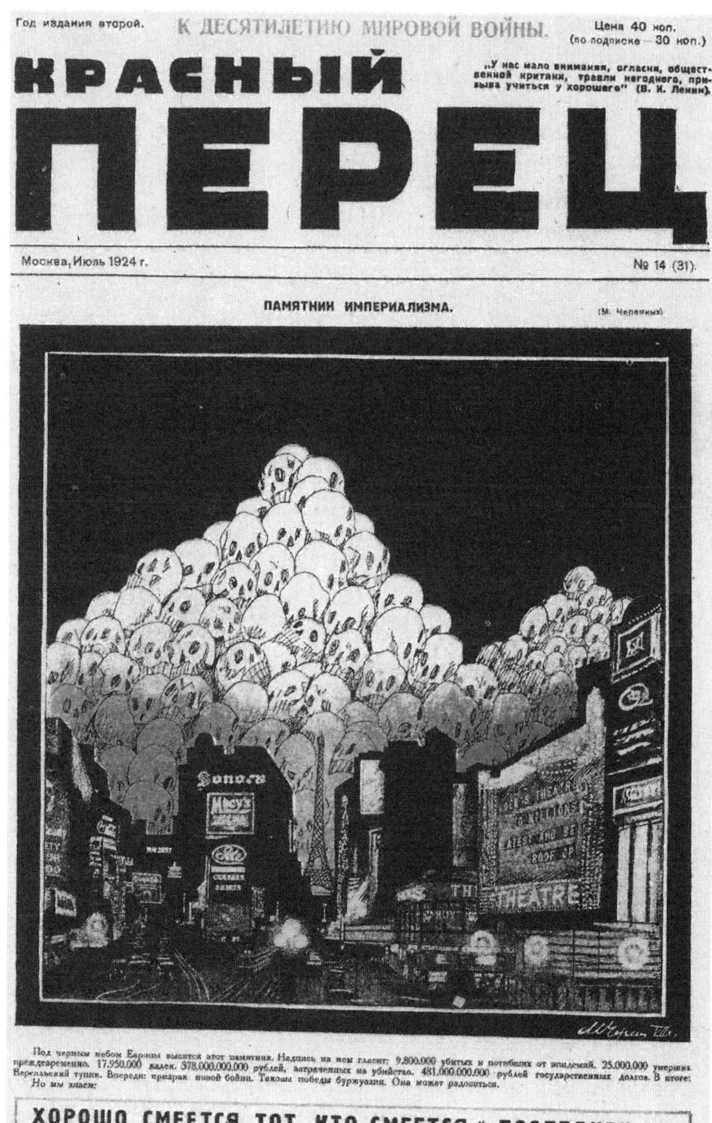

5.5 *Krasnyi perets*, no. 14 (1924) cover, "Monument to Imperialism."
Collection of Annie Gérin.

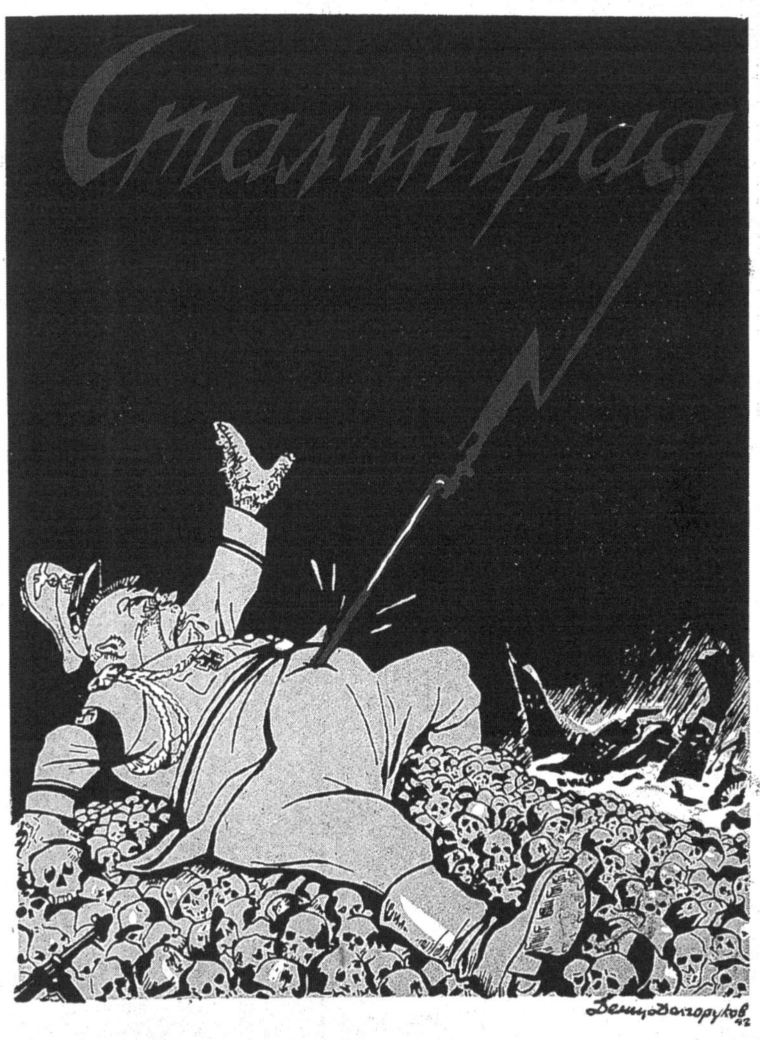

5.6 "Stalingrad," poster by Viktor Deni, 1942. Part of the David King Collection. Presented to Tate Archive by David King 2016.

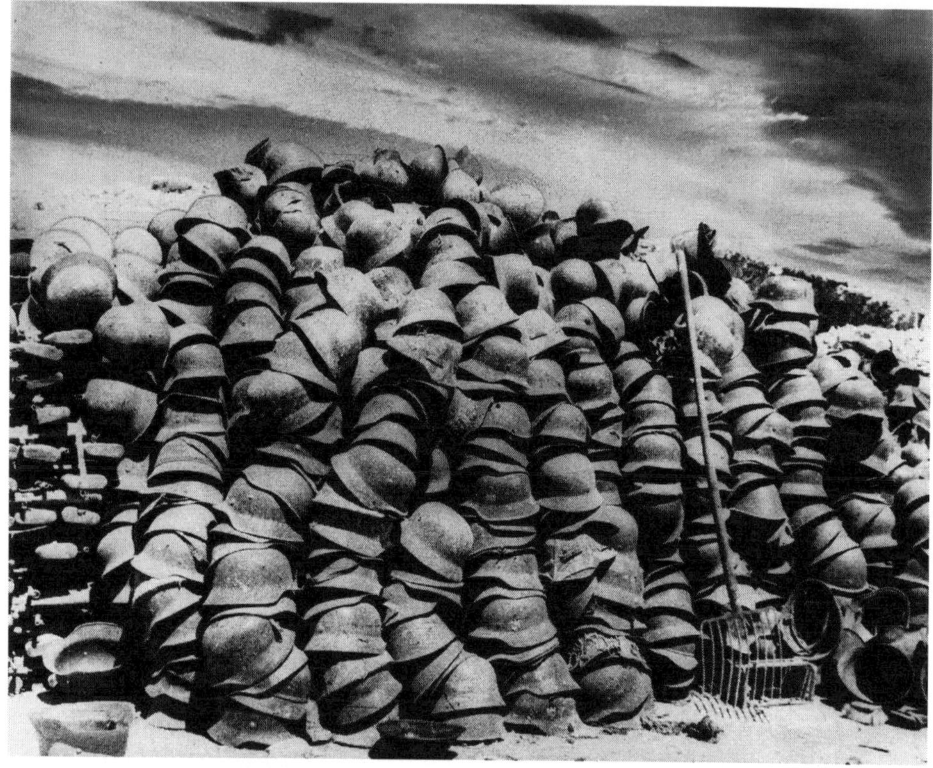

5.7 Evgenii Khaldei, "Nazi Helmets of No Further Use," 1945. Part of
the David King Collection. Presented to Tate Archive
by David King 2016.

This doubling of meaning in one image does more than play with
semblance/difference. The parodic image, when disseminated in various contexts, can eventually destabilize, redirect, or even rewrite the
meaning of its source, to the point where the meaning of the original
could become lost. In fact, this is often the ultimate goal of satirical
parody, which aims at acculturation.

Irony

The ironic work says something different than what it really means,
sometimes even the opposite. This structural gap between representation

and meaning inevitably complicates its interpretation. Indeed, if parody demands from its viewer knowledge of the cultural form that is appropriated to serve as its source, irony entails another type of understanding. It requires the viewer to already be "in the know" with regard to the situation that irony serves or attempts to highlight. So while it may produce laughter, it also garners another, perhaps more important, effect. It includes the laughing subject within a community of laughers, while excluding those who do not grasp the irony's displaced meaning.

Irony most often presents itself as a positive or even laudatory statement, implying on the contrary a negative judgment, as in *Novyi satirikon*'s 1918 disingenuous praise of the Bolsheviks described in chapter 2. While it could serve to foil censorship or to fuel covert protest (since it can only be understood by those in the know), it can also be used in the context of satire as a tool to challenge the authority of its object and, as we will see below in the discussion of antireligious satire, to even contest the very existence of what it represents, or signal its absence. Finally, it asks that the viewer develop a sceptical attitude with regard to representations, training her to look at all images as always potentially duplicitous.

Three Case Studies

The Campaign against the Everyday

The Campaign against the Everyday was undoubtedly the most broad-ranging of the early Soviet propaganda crusades. Indeed, if the Revolution first took shape through the seizure of political power and industry, for it to endure it demanded nothing less than the transformation of everyday practices. These were understood as broadly as the relationship of men to women and the organization of family life, and encompassed concerns such as hygiene, nutrition, education, and proper social etiquette.

The question of the everyday (*byt*) entered the sphere of Soviet propaganda in 1923, immediately after the publication of a series of essays by Leon Trotsky in the newspaper *Pravda;* these were collected that same year in a book titled *Voprosy byta* (*Questions of Everyday Life*). The essays were based on a series of three ten-to-twelve-hour-long meetings during which Trotsky conversed with Communist Party activists. The exchanges revealed that some of the population's most pressing concerns were not to do with party doctrine or economic issues, but with various aspects of workers' basic conditions of existence. This was indeed a period of rapid change, of great transition, and many had difficulty finding their footing in the emerging Soviet world. This subject of "old and new" became from then on a central theme in the arts and propaganda, most vividly portrayed in satire-laced film comedies such as Boris Barnet's *The Girl with the Hatbox* (1927) and *The House on Trubnaya* (1928) where backward bourgeois and enlightened Soviet practices uneasily coexist, especially in domestic settings. But the question was: how can change be fostered on such a broad scale? And, as Trotsky asked, "How to begin? ... We have never thrashed out these questions concretely as, at different times, we have thrashed out the question of wages, fines, the length of the working day, police persecution, the constitution of the state, the ownership of land, and so on. We have as yet done nothing of the kind in regard to the family and the private life of the individual worker generally."[15]

Originally, *byt* simply referred to everyday existence or a way of life shared in a community. It was opposed to *bytie*, the spiritual sphere. In *Common Places: Mythologies of Everyday Life in Russia,* Svetlana Boym traces the evolution of the term and its emergence as a social concern in the nineteenth century, when it gained increasingly negative connotations. Under the influence of the symbolists, the intelligentsia, including early revolutionaries, infused it with connotations of banality, "stagnation and routine, of daily transience without transcendence, whether spiritual, artistic or revolutionary. *Byt,* the ordinary way of life, began to be seen as the order of chaos and contingency that precludes any illumination."[16]

Trotsky also understood *byt* as a negative force that could hamper social progress, and even potentially bring down the cultural level of a population. In his series of essays, however, he introduced a new term that broke the traditional and seemingly inescapable duality between *byt* and *bytie.* Trotsky contrasted the soul-destroying, conservative (even atavistic) everyday to a *novyi* (new) *byt,* a utopian new quotidian where daily life could provide the conditions of possibility to evolve a new Soviet citizen in a dialectical relationship with political and economic progress. Throughout his essays, Trotsky identified a number of targets that needed to be addressed for a positive reconstruction of *byt:* the liberation of women from domestic slavery; the reformulation of social relations, including the observance of rules of politeness; the removal of swear words from everyday conversations; and the shifting of spare-time interests from alcohol consumption and religion to better socialist pastimes. As he observed, with the development of the film industry, the acculturation process had already started: "In attracting and amusing, the cinema already rivals the beer-hall and the tavern."[17]

Among these varied objectives, the liberation of women and the restructuring of the family was key. Indeed, women were seen as both the main victims of an oppressive *byt* and the guardians of outmoded values and practices that contributed to enslave them. As Trosky explained:

> To institute the political equality of men and women in the Soviet state was one problem and the simplest. A much more difficult one was the next – that of instituting the industrial equality of men and women workers in factories, the mills, and the trade unions, and of doing it in such a way that the men should not put the women to disadvantage. But to achieve the actual equality of man and woman within the family is an infinitely more arduous problem. Our domestic habits must be revolutionized before that can happen. And yet it is quite obvious that unless there is actual equality of husband and wife in the family, in a normal sense as well as in the conditions of life, we cannot speak seriously of their equality in social work or even in politics. As long as woman is chained to her house work, the care of the family, the cooking and sewing, all her chances of participation in social and political life are cut down in the extreme.[18]

In Marxist thought, the oppression of women is understood to be an effect of capitalist conditions of exploitation, and in particular women being seen as their father's or husband's property.[19] Upon seizing power, the Bolsheviks had passed sweeping legislation proclaiming women's equality. But it immediately became clear that decrees were not enough to instate a new order based on a form of equality that few could even imagine. A complex process of acculturation needed to be put in place. This is what led to the creation, in 1919, of the Zhenotdel (the Women's Section of the Secretariat of the Central Committee of the Communist Party). Led by the Bolshevik feminist Aleksandra Kollontai, its mandate was to propagandize socialism to women and to educate them politically. It also took on the role of "lobbyist" on behalf of women, repeatedly calling for state intervention into women's *byt*.[20] Often faced with indifference, particularly in the context of the Civil War, the Zhenotdel frequently took matters into its own hands, organizing in factories and dormitories daycare centres, public laundries, and cafeterias to alleviate the domestic burden in the most concrete way. This attempt to circumvent the party led to the accusation of "feminist deviationism" and to Zhenotdel being stripped of any real power.[21] According to Elizabeth Wood, "*Zhenotdel* activists expressed consternation that their persistent attention to the issue of daily life had brought little fruit, yet Trotsky's [1923] articles now opened up an avalanche of public discussion."[22]

The propaganda images that attempt to influence the role of women in the context of the creation of a *novyi byt* often exhibit a binary structure that presents old and new ways of being in an anti-naturalist composition that has the benefit of being overtly didactic and immediately legible in its intent. It is featured in the 1930 poster "In Our Collective Farm, there is no Room for Priests and Kulaks," a poster that is meant to be "read" from top to bottom. Here, the protagonist, wearing her headscarf tied at the nape of her neck as emancipated factory workers did (at least in the world of *tipazh*), rejects the old in order to establish the new. Both realities – that can also be read as different temporalities in the historical process leading to the establishment of socialism – are represented in frames collaged into the overall composition. The old *byt*, at the bottom, on a black background, offers caricatures of a priest, a kulak, and a drunken husband. The *novyi byt*, set against golden fields and blue skies, reveals a much brighter picture where women are strong, and free to participate fully in the construction of a socialist society.

This strategy of juxtaposing divergent realities in a single composition almost becomes cliché in the campaigns for *novyi byt*. It allows a work to contrast and compare, to mock atavistic practices by the means of caricature, while indicating more positive alternatives. But why appeal to this collage structure? Why not just present the new without the old?

In the essay "Habit and Custom," Trotsky insists on the necessity for a critical analysis of current problems. He argues that "it is therefore necessary first to know what already exists, and in what manner its change of form is proceeding, if we are to cooperate in the recreation of morals. We must first see what is really going on in the factory, among the workers, in the cooperative, the club, the school, the tavern and the street. All this we have to understand; that is[,] we must recognize the remnants of the past and the seeds of the future."[23] This quote reveals, perhaps in an exemplary manner, the destructive role that satire was expected to play during the first decades of the Soviet regime; it was meant to address critically outdated practices and values that persisted in the present, opening up a space to imagine and enact the new.

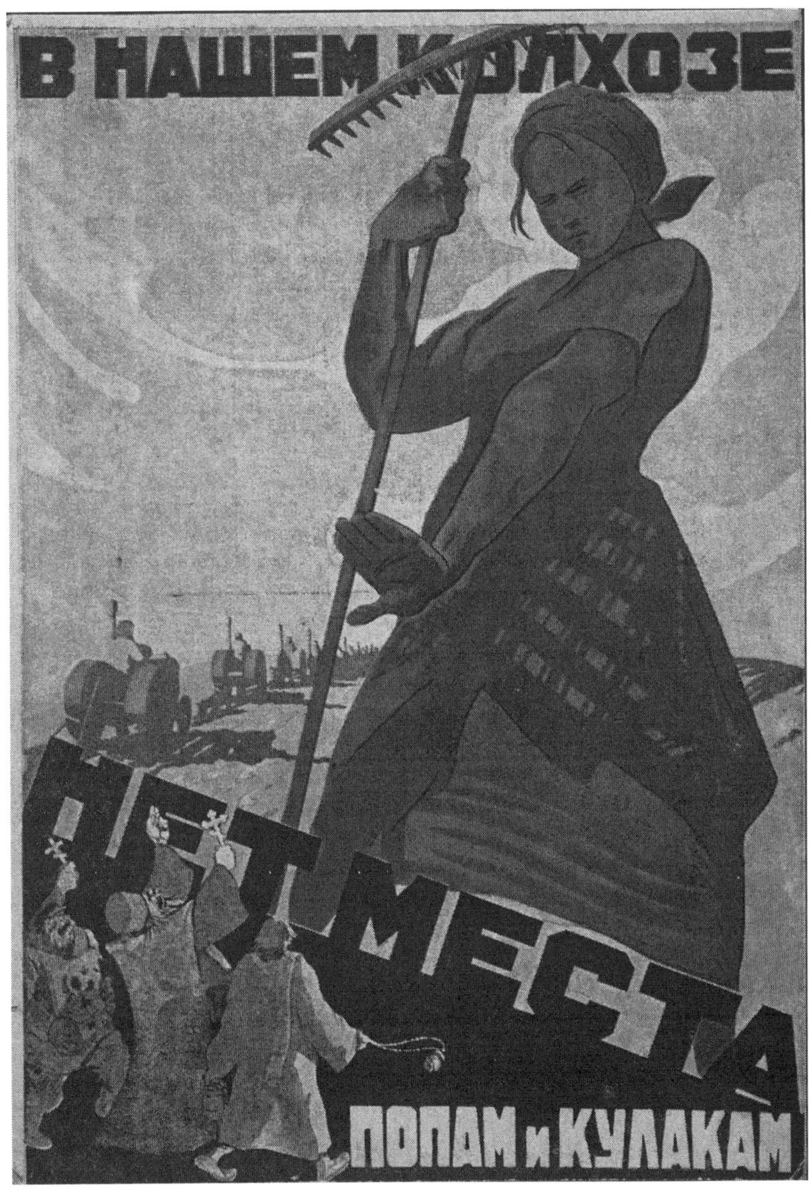

5.8 "In Our Collective Farm, There Is No Room for Priests and Kulaks," poster by Nikolai Mikailov, 1930. Part of the David King Collection. Presented to Tate Archive by David King 2016.

In some propaganda images, the collage structure is more subtle than in the poster discussed above; the old and new have merged into one cohesive composition. On the cover of a 1926 issue of *Krokodil*, for example, a red-kerchiefed woman grabs her teenage daughter by the hand and brashly leaves a hovel. The scene is chaotic: a bric-a-brac of dirty dishes, bottles, icons, a drunken husband, a crying child, and a wood-burning stove spewing black smoke. As in many satirical works, clutter and disorder here suggest moral or ideological chaos, or simply *byt*. The caption reads "Woman! There is no going back. Find your path into the light." Following this advice, she marches towards an open door, leading to a bright and uncluttered future. In a similar representation published in 1923 in *Krasnyi perets* a woman is stuck in an outrageous heap of domestic junk: pots and pans, a sewing machine and scissors, even a caged canary, a pet often used as a symbol of petit bourgeois materialism. She seems to be sinking into *byt* as in quicksand. This caricatural representation contrasts with the light of communism towards which the woman's outstretched hand reaches.

In the context of the NEP, with the re-emergence of private enterprise and the luxury goods market, the Campaign against the Everyday took on an expanded meaning, particularly under the pen of Lunacharsky and the left-wing critics associated with LEF (1923–25), the journal of the Left Front of Art, directed and edited by Vladimir Mayakovsky.[24] In its inaugural issue, the poet and art theorist Sergei Tretyakov published a polemical piece titled "Where From, Where To?" Contrary to Trotsky's position, which called for state intervention in daily life, Tretyakov's piece focuses on the role that artists should assume in creating new forms and objects that would contribute to the "inevitable battle against *byt*"[25] by providing the material conditions for new social relations.[26] He was of course referring to the constructivists Vladimir Tatlin, Varvara Stepanova, Lyubov Popova, Aleksandr Rodchenko, and others, who in the early 1920s were abandoning easel painting and sculpture to devote themselves to the production of textile and everyday objects, while also contributing to print culture, theatre, and film. In this context, *byt* pushed beyond banality. Paired with another concept, *meshchanstvo* (petit bourgeois sensibility or philistinism), *byt* became a reactionary force that enslaved people, even true communists, to things through the mechanisms of what Marx had termed "commodity fetishism." For Tretyakov, "*Byt* is a deeply reactionary force, which in pivotal moments of social change prevents a class from organizing its forces and plotting critical assaults. It is comfort for comfort's sake

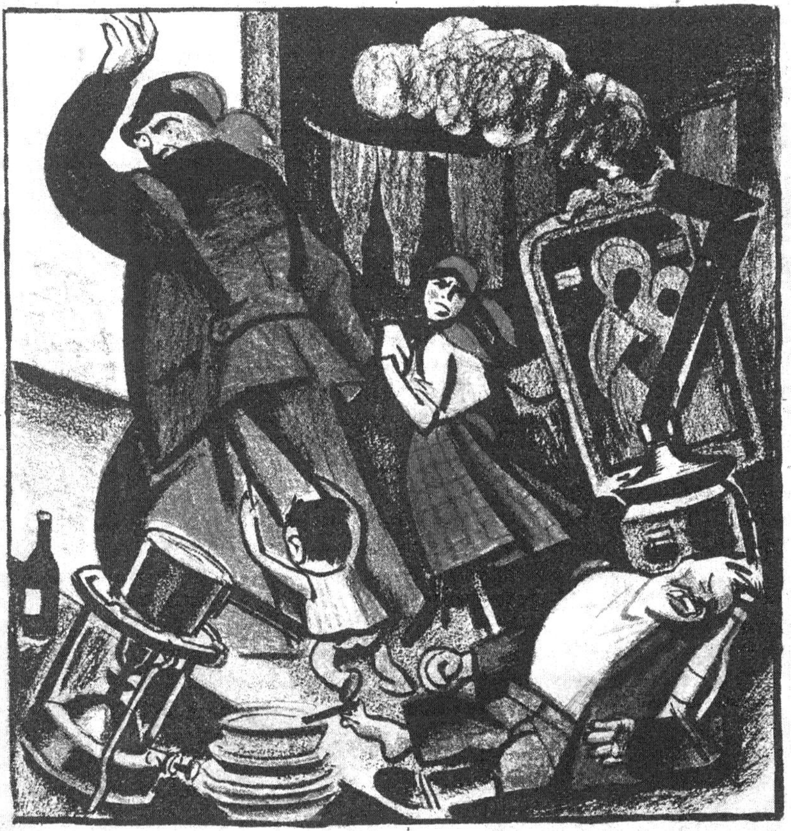

5.9 "A Thorny Path," *Krokodil*, no. 8 (1926), cover. Collection of Annie Gérin.

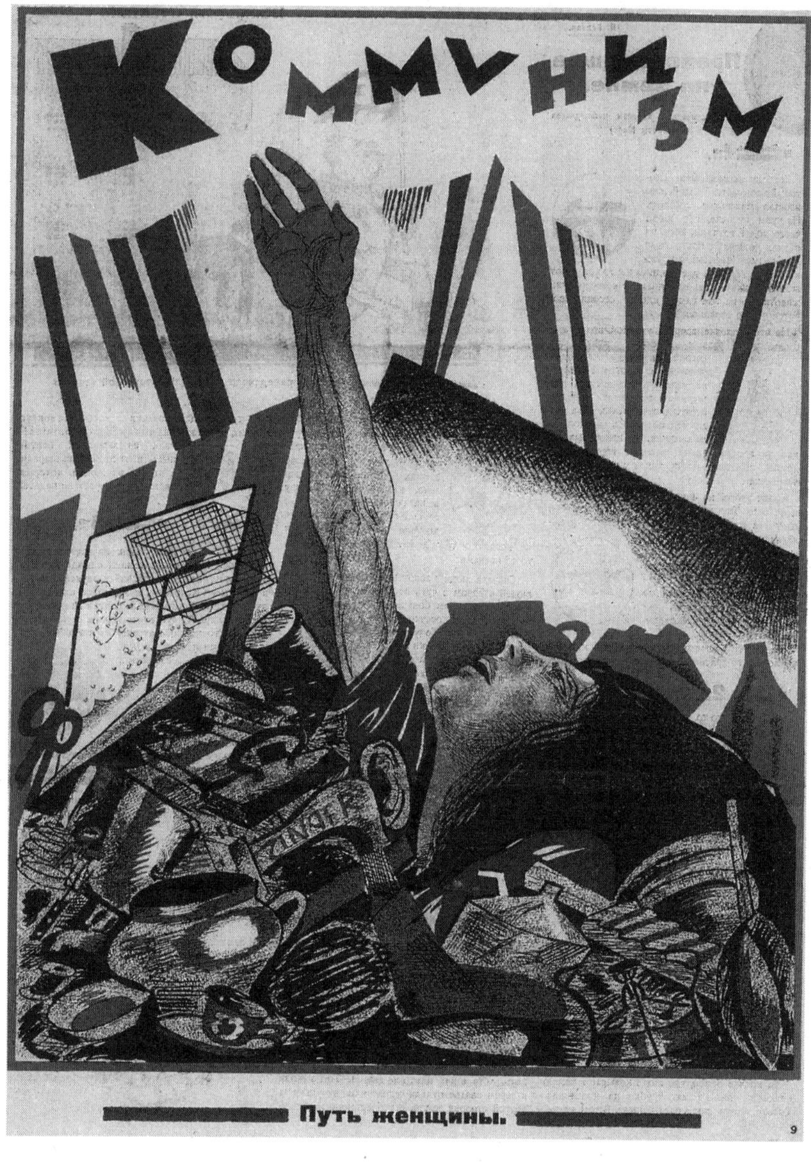

5.10 "The Path of Women," *Krasnyi perets*, no. 14 (1923), p. 9. The woman's arm stretches towards the word "Communism." Part of the David King Collection. Presented to Tate Archive by David King 2016.

and coziness as an end in and of itself; it is the chains of tradition and the worship of objects that have lost their practical meaning, beginning with the necktie and ending with religious fetishes."[27]

In the poem *About This* (1923), dedicated to his lover Lily Brik, Mayakovsky explored how *byt* is a force that destroys not only political consciousness but also love. The series of collages produced by Aleksandr Rodchenko to illustrate the poem mock and warn against the finely chiselled silver and the carved furniture, which have grown so big as to suffocate (Plate 6). Here, the strategy of collage allows for an image that is at once fanciful and indexical, and that opposes in one single composition petit bourgeois sensibilities and new Bolshevik attitudes to the everyday. Mayakovsky's sustained hatred of *byt* is most evocatively conveyed in his 1930 suicide note, in which he wrote "*Lyubovnaya lodka razbilas o byt*" (The boat of love crashed against the daily grind).[28]

For Lunacharsky, the Campaign against the Everyday needed to most fiercely address petit bourgeois sensibilities. Because of its insidious and enduring nature, *meshchanstvo* had to be exposed and fought with all available weapons. Exploring this idea, he wrote in a text penned in 1928 that

> the struggle between old and new continues ... We must bear in mind that, alongside bourgeois currents that are overtly and deliberately hostile, there is another element that may be more dangerous and perhaps more difficult to destroy: petit bourgeois attitudes to the everyday. This current has insinuated itself deeply, like a worm, in the daily habits of the proletariat, and even of communists. This explains why class struggle, at the stage of the construction of a new life bearing the imprint of the socialist aspirations of the proletariat, doesn't subside. On the contrary, class struggle takes on more profound and more subtle forms. It is these current conditions that grant the arts ... extreme importance.[29]

This enslavement by bourgeois comfort is the target of a satirical image also published in 1928, in the satirical journal *Begemot*. Here, the juxtaposition of a bourgeois interior with another filled with objects referencing Bolshevik engagement (red flags, hammer and sickle wallpaper, busts and photographs of Marxist ideologues, etc.) renders visible the persistence of *meshchanstvo*, even with card-holding communists. The objects that populate the home are different, but the overall ambience remains the same. *Krokodil* presented an analogous critique that same year. A portrait of Karl Marx, ironically framed as a gaudy work of art, is hung from an equally showy wallpapered partition (Plate 7). The interior betrays the outdated bourgeois taste of its occupants, and reveals traces of a recent feast and a card game. Confronted with the petit bourgeois attitudes of Soviet citizens, Marx breaks out of the frame and spits in disgust. For Lunacharsky, the caricatural exaggeration found in these representations was necessary to render visible the insidious problem. "It is more difficult than ever to portray *meshchanstvo* ... but its all-around analysis will reveal where the old and the new world meet, a mixture of which is the main means of self-preservation of the old world. We must reveal *meshchanstvo* where it hides, and not just where it lies in plain sight."[30]

For writer Marietta Shaginian, who authored satirical novels and film scripts under the pseudonym Jim Dollar, this kind of "collision" of old and new was a productive strategy for artists to develop in revolutionary times. She felt the dissonant juxtaposition of meaning and form not only brought excitement to the representation, but also encouraged the brain to play and create new meaningful associations.[31] Just like her colleagues Lunacharsky, Mayakovsky, Meyerhold, and Eisenstein, she believed that collage could render visible the struggle between old and new. As she astutely remarked in *The New Everyday and Art* (*Novyi byt i iskusstvo*), published in 1926, "The battle for a worldview is a battle between two epochs, between two cultures."[32]

The rhetorical strategy that opposes old and new, and uses the means of collage to do so, is omnipresent in the visual culture of the Campaign against the Everyday. The lack of temporal stability manifest in its representations, whether they be pictural, theatrical, or cinematographic, requires that the viewer choose between two different realities, one established as positive, the other represented as laughable by means of iconography, caricature, colour, or composition.

According to Umberto Eco, humour functions as the breaking of rules, but only for a public who knows these rules. And indeed, the juxtaposition of pre-revolutionary and post-revolutionary practices allows the artist to state the frame of the broken rule while also asserting the appropriate frame of reception. This strategy assists the targeted viewer in her understanding of the satire and of the broader stakes it serves. This didactic temporalization also provides the viewer with a means of dissociation, so that she can laugh at her old self, and feel proud of her new enlightened state; so that she can grasp the value of her newly acquired membership in socialist society and *novyi byt*.

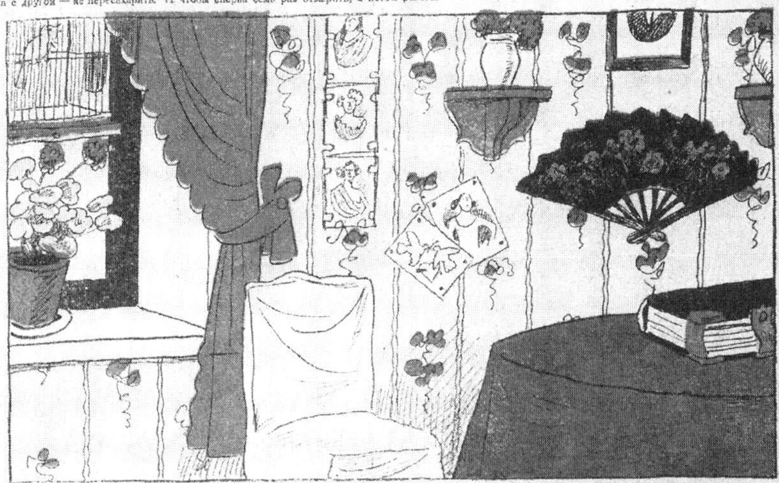

Вот, многие думают, что вопиющее мещанство в канарейке сидит.

И на цветочки тоже кивают. Дескать, герань в горшке на окошке — это форменная ягодка мещанства. И если мебель мягкая, то это — гнусная мещанская база. И карточки разных мамаш и папаш на стенках и в альбоме, и обои с цветочками, и всевозможные вязочки с бессмертниками, и прочая хурда-мурда — все это, дескать, позор мещанства, которое нужно вырвать с корнем на черную доску; все это нужно срочно заменить созвучными эпохе предметами пролетарской роскоши.

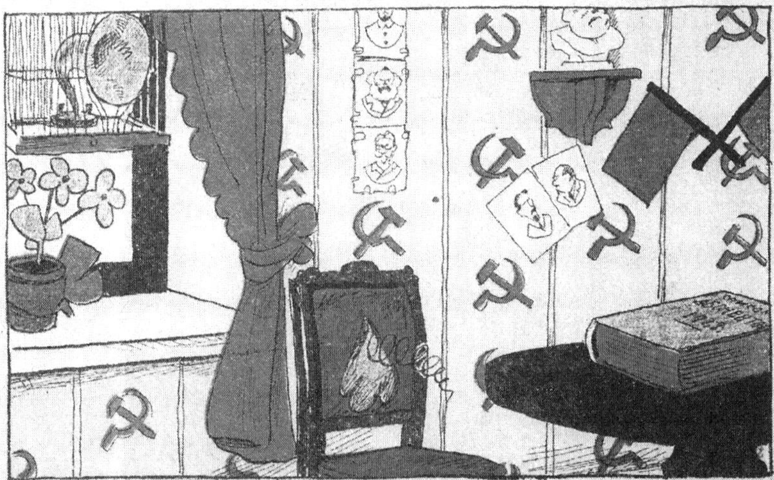

5.11 "*Meshchanstvo* Then and Now," *Begemot*, no. 4 (1928), back cover.
Collection of Annie Gérin.

The Antireligious Campaign[33]

The Antireligious Campaign went hand in hand with the Campaign against the Everyday. Indeed, antireligious propaganda always coupled religious exploitation and belief with common concerns such as the oppression of women, alcoholism, illiteracy, and the like. And while it also often used collage strategies to oppose old and new practices and worldviews, it also harnessed satire for two other main purposes. Through the parody of religious images, it attempted to subvert and reframe them; and through the mechanisms of irony, it served the very difficult purpose of representing a world void of deities.

Religion became one of the main targets of Soviet propaganda very early on. This came about as Russian society was exposed and criticized by Bolsheviks as a culture that had been essentially guided by Orthodox Catholic principles since the days of Saint Vladimir, a thousand years in the past. Indeed, Russia had been a theocracy since one of its princes had converted it to Christianity in 988. Following the tradition of the Byzantine emperors, Prince Vladimir had positioned himself as the imperial head of the Russian Orthodox Church. This close bond with the state had naturally freed the church from overt political activity. But its inherent political nature was revealed when, with the Revolution, it lost the support of the government.

Rejecting the combined influence of the tsars and the church, the Soviet regime viewed as popular deception the promise of an afterlife to those who had suffered through their earthly journey in compliance with the teachings of the church. They considered the assurance of a blissful hereafter a powerful myth that had convinced the population to allow itself to be enslaved by perennial poverty, capitalist exploitation, patriarchal dominance, and ignorance of the law and of sciences. This was what Marx had evocatively described as "the opium of the people."[34] For socialism to take root in Russia, the orthodox spiritual framework that had been used to justify the exploitation of the majority by the few needed to be replaced by a different value system. The ethics associated with socialist labour, scientific progress, civic rights, and education would replace religious faith and spirituality. The demystification of religions – Christian, Judaic, Muslim, Buddhist, all regarded as illusionary forms of human fulfilment – was therefore at the core of socialist practice.

The cultural roots of religion extended to language, as well as social and political practices. For example, Russian peasants had traditionally referred to themselves as *krestianin*, from the word Christian (*Khristianin*), and a person's religious identity was marked on their

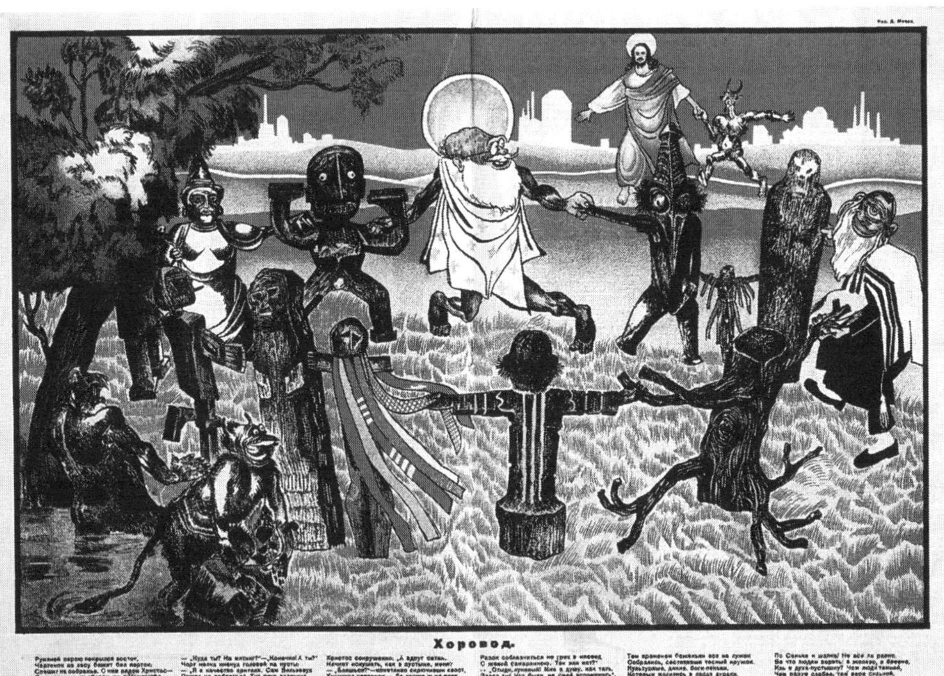

5.12 "The Round Dance of Faith," *Bezbozhnik u stanka*, no. 1 (1924), centrefold by Dmitrii Moor. Part of the David King Collection. Presented to Tate Archive by David King 2016.

work papers and passport until 1917. This hinging of Russian identity to religion by language and bureaucracy was condemned by the Soviet regime as the basis for anti-Semitism and other forms of social exclusion.[35] Following the Revolution, peasants were encouraged to think of themselves as farmworkers rather than *krestianin,* and references to religious affiliation were removed from all official documents.

The ongoing denunciation of outward forms of organized religion extended to pagan convictions and symbols, which included a sophisticated demonology believed by a segment of the population to influence all aspects of life. These moody and mischievous demons had survived the import of Christianity and still thrived in the early part of the twentieth century. Indeed, *dvoeverie* (double-faith), the concurrent belief in Slavic deities and a Christian or Judaic god, was common and generally not considered a paradox. This allowed the *domovoi* (house spirit) to go on occupying peasant abodes, most often dwelling in the wood-burning stove. The *leshii* (spirit of the forests) continued watching over wooded areas and their fauna, while the *vodyanoi* (water spirit) oversaw all aquatic activity. These small demons adapted surprisingly well to urban life during Russia's industrial revolution. When peasants migrated from the country to the city, it was not unheard of for a *domovoi* to take up residence in a communal apartment, or for a *vodyanoi* to immerse itself in tap water.

Soviet ideologues such as Lenin, Trotsky, Lunacharsky, and Bogdanov all understood that belief systems that had survived hundreds of years would not easily be uprooted. Therefore, the government resolved to tread carefully and to initially protect freedom of religion as a basic human right – at least on paper. On this topic, chapter five, article thirteen of the 1918 Constitution of the Russian Socialist Federal Soviet Republic (RSFSR) is unambiguous: "In order to ensure genuine freedom of conscience of the working people, the Church is separate from the State, and the school from the Church: and freedom of religious and antireligious propaganda is recognized for all citizens."[36]

This article of law was composed in order to satisfy three objectives: first, to secularize political, social, and cultural institutions; second, to appease religious practitioners and include them in a debate about liberty of thought and social freedom; third, to prevent extremists from causing irreparable damage to pro-Soviet public opinion by persecuting the clergy, a group that had been at the core of all social activity and ritual. Yet, as Lewis Siegelbaum remarks, the general administrative disorganization that plagued Russia in the years that followed the Revolution ensured that if Moscow's wishes were known at all in the provinces, they were ignored with impunity. Persecutions and killings of priests as well as looting and desecration of churches and monasteries were very much part of the Civil War.[37]

Furthermore, although the 1918 constitution "secured" freedom of belief, the church was intentionally undermined by the gradual confiscation of its resources and the loss of its privileges. By 1922, all state assistance to the church had been withdrawn and it was forbidden to hold collections. Expropriation of church-owned land and buildings followed whenever the need arose for food storage or for Red Army barracks. By the late 1920s, numerous monasteries, churches, and chapels had been transformed into factories, movie theatres, museums, candy shops, and artist studios.

This first phase of Soviet antireligious activity is characterized by the legislative dismemberment of the church and the expropriation of its assets. A second phase, which started around 1922, represents a shift from the disenfranchisement of religious institution to a focus on the systematic eradication of popular religious beliefs and practices,[38] marked by the deployment of mass propaganda techniques, in particular in print culture.

Cheaply printed and widely circulated antireligious newspapers and journals started to appear: *Bezbozhnik* (*Godless;* the newspaper was published in 1922–34 and 1938–41 and the journal in 1925–41), *Antireligioznik* (*The Antireligious,* 1926–41), *Derevenskii bezbozhnik* (*The Godless Peasant,* 1928–32), *Yunie bebozhniki* (*The Young Godless,* 1928–34), *Bezbozhnyi krokodil* (*The Godless Crocodile,* 1925), and *Bezbozhnik u stanka* (*Godless at the Workbench,* 1923–32).[39] These journals, which all benefited from state support, were run by independent militant associations. They were meant to compensate for the lack of skilled propagandists.

The most stiking antireligious journal, *Bezbozhnik u stanka,* was created by the most radical group of activists, whose biting strategies based on visual satire were called by its detractors *popoedstvo* – clergy eating. The monthly illustrated journal was published between 1923 and 1931, its print run ranging from thirty-five to sixty thousand copies per edition. Rather than discussing the historical construction of religion, *Bezbozhnik u stanka* concentrated almost exclusively on contemporary issues, many relating to *byt*: hygiene, literacy, alcoholism, hooliganism, women's work and conjugal violence. It also welcomed testimonies of conversions from religious devotion to atheism and solicited jokes, poems, riddles, songs, and games from its readers.

Many images published in the journal targeted women, as responsible for propagating faith in the family unit through *byt*. In "My poor dear, they have poisoned your soul and now you poison our children ...," a worker with a saddened gaze, wrench peering from his pocket, stares at a barefoot woman dressed as a peasant. She lies on her back, surrounded by her children. Five colourful figures – the holy family accompanied by two angels – lean towards the group. They thrust in front of the vacant eyes of the woman and her eldest the heavy volumes of the "Divine Law." A more sustained examination of the image reveals the fabricated character of God's envoys, whose modernist and caricatural treatment contrasts with the naturalism used to represent the other figures. Upon scrutiny, another sign of the ideological farce appears; the "poisoners of souls" are hanging from the heavens as simple marionettes, tied with red ribbons and bows. It is an image that, in fact, seems to allude to Henry Bergson's writings on the comical treatment of bodies: "The attitudes, gestures and movements of the human body are laughable in exact proportion as that body reminds us of a mere machine ..., a jointed puppet."[40]

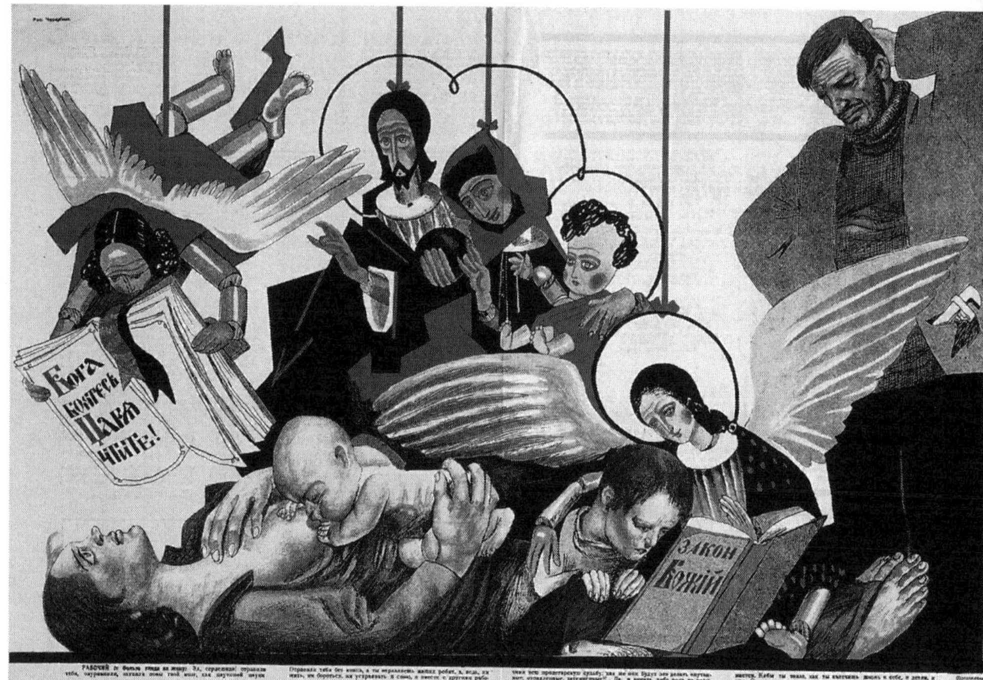

5.13 "My poor dear, they have poisoned your soul and now you poison our children …" *Bezbozhnik u stanka*, no. 6 (1923), centrefold by Mikhail Cheremnykh. Part of the David King Collection. Presented to Tate Archive by David King 2016.

Several examples of visual satire published in *Bezbozhnik u stanka* not only mock religion and religiosity but also parody the formal tradition of icons. *The Sermon on the Mountain* and *Vessel of the Devil* borrow their composition from a particularly popular category of devotional images dedicated to biblical verses or to the lives of saints. This type of icon features a holy man or woman, generally depicted at the centre of the composition, framed on all sides by moments of his or her life organized in chronological order. In *Vessel of the Devil,* the satirical parody imitates the familiar configuration to tell the story of the devout peasant woman (derogatorily called a *baba*), whose stylized, vessel-like figure occupies the heart of the image. The narrative unfolds as follows: the Devil creates the *baba* in the image of a milk jug. God provides her with arms like handles and a soul like a cauldron. She then fritters her life away,

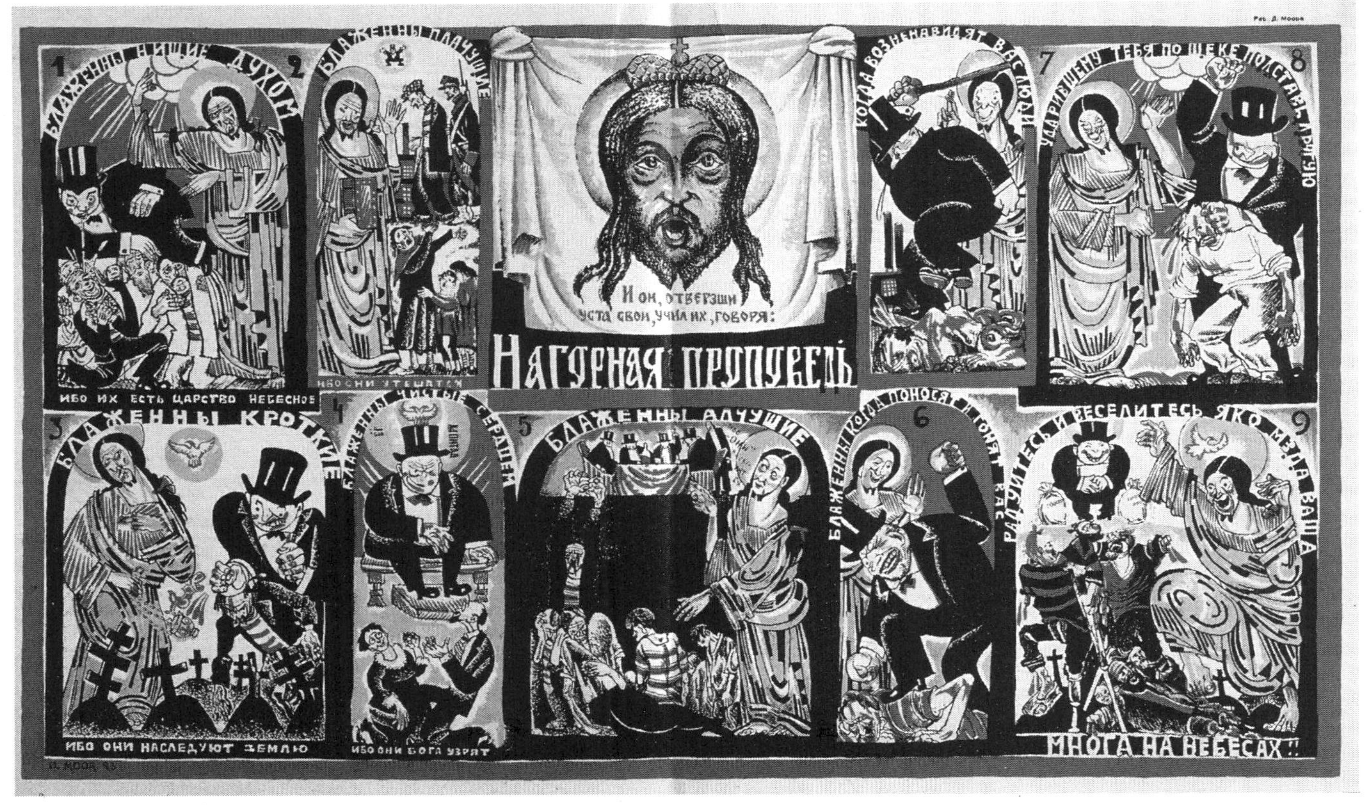

5.14 "The Sermon on the Mountain," *Bezbozhnik u stanka*, no. 3 (1923), centrefold by Dmitrii Moor. Part of the David King Collection. Presented to Tate Archive by David King 2016.

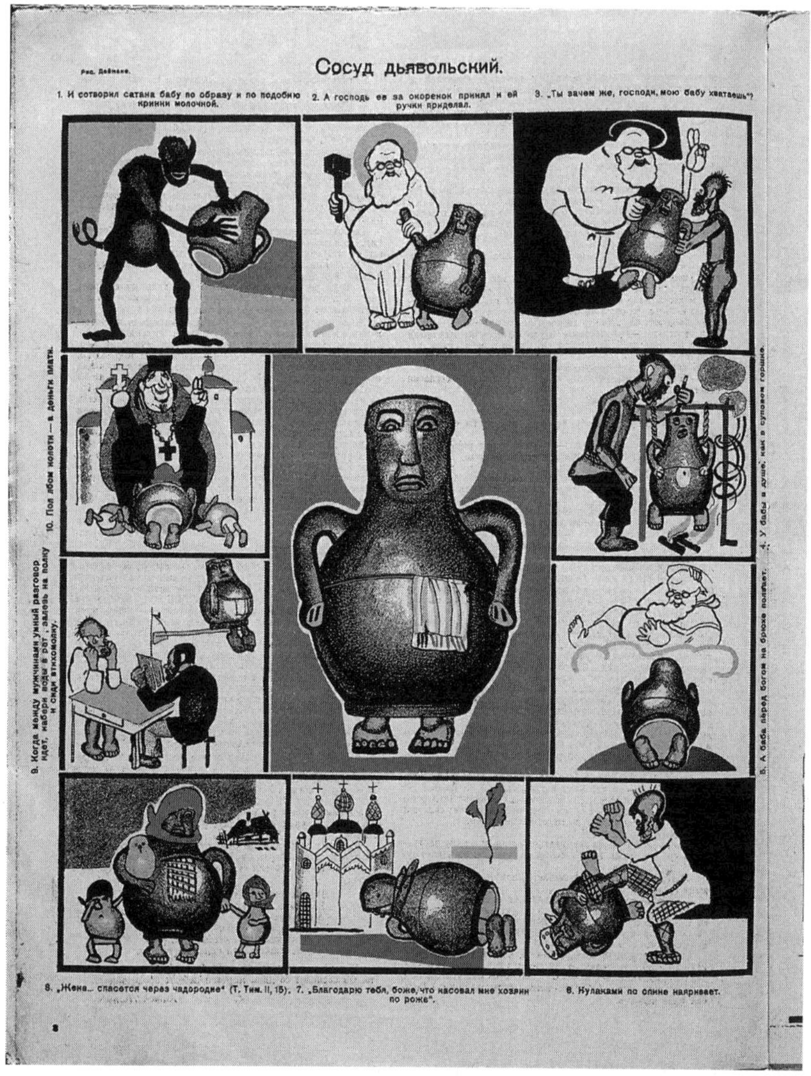

5.15　"Vessel of the Devil," *Bezbozhnik u stanka*, no. 1 (1924), page 8, by Aleksandr Deineka. Part of the David King Collection. Presented to Tate Archive by David King 2016.

bowing to her husband, her children, the kulak, and the priest, thanking the latter for enslaving her by paying him a tithe.

The strategy of parody used in *Vessel of the Devil* serves to mock religiosity and shame the devout. But there is an additional, more subtle level of critique that informs the reading of this image. The parodic infringement on the genre of icon painting exposes sacred arts as propaganda tools devised by organized religions to indoctrinate the people. Indeed, historian Nicholas Timasheff has described the aesthetic quality of religious art and architecture and the crucial role they occupied in Russia over centuries as "the strongest attraction to the Russian Orthodox Church."[41] According to Timasheff, the elaborate decorations, excess of gold leaf, semi-precious stones, luxury textiles, and sumptuous iconography offered a respite from the harshness of the everyday.

Satirist Dmitrii Moor, in his position as artistic director of *Bezbozhnik u stanka*, recommended that the artists employed at the journal study religious art, emulate it, and make use of its features in their propaganda work. The parody of recognizable forms would appeal to the mind, while also exerting a fascination rooted in the population's resilient cultural heritage. But it had as well the potential of redefining familiar configurations by imparting them with new meaning, especially through repetitive parodic use. As he explained, "you have to study your enemy. You have to fight religion with its own tools."[42]

This prescription was also taken up by practitioners of antireligious street theatre, who often borrowed the form of religious processions, well known by the public. This practice had the advantage of allowing semi-spontaneous propaganda events to occur, since all participants knew exactly how to behave. And just like the images published in *Bezbozhnik u stanka*, street theatre could rob traditional ceremonial forms of their established significance and assign them new purposes, infusing them with revolutionary meaning.

One of the key challenges faced by artists involved in creating antireligious propaganda was the creation of a vocabulary and iconography to deal with the topic of religion in an atheist state. Print media, as we have seen in chapter 2, permitted artists to experiment with visual and narrative *tipazh*, the heart of which was not to reveal typicality, but to typecast, or forge new motifs by creating widely circulated stereotypes, codes, symbols, and categories that could be used to interpret the emerging Soviet world.

But the concept of a culture creating an iconography divorced from previous social codes (in this case those of pre-revolutionary Russia) is quite problematic. Indeed, iconography is generally based on traditional use of visual forms. It is the cumulative use of an image through history that permits the viewer to understand its meaning and cultural function. Yet this was a time of rapid change, and the types of objects available for modern representation, such as aeroplanes, automobiles, factories, or skilled female workers, had no tradition in the history of art. Artists were therefore deprived of the traditional iconographic model. This question becomes even more complex with the willed creation of an antireligious iconography, which could not be satisfied with creating new types, but also had to represent the *absence* of religion and superstitions previously accepted as underlying every aspect of the material world.

The tactic chosen by antireligious illustrators was most often irony, a rhetorical mode that says black when it means white. *People Live* …, published in *Bezbozhnik u stanka*, is a perfect example of this strategy. The scene, unfolding in an urban dwelling, depicts two workers going about their daily activities, while pre-Christian demons take over their space. The caption reads: "People live, they drink, eat, go to work, but they don't see what really goes on around them. And this is what *really* goes on: the water spirit showers in the tap, the house demon lives in the stove, and the light fairy plays with the lamp shade. All this happens in broad daylight but nobody notices. This is the *true* essence of things."

The irony of this comment is obviously lodged in the mismatch between two worldviews; a past ensconced in a superstitious peasant lifestyle, and a present or future firmly entrenched in urban materialism. Of course, no self-respecting Soviet industrial worker would share her residence with all these pagan manifestation. Because the conception of the world the artist sought to depict is void of gods and demons, in order to express the absence of superstition, he had to resort to a rhetorical mode that says something very different from what it means.

In the *Old Man's Riddle*, the intrusion of the Christian god into a Soviet textile factory was meant to highlight the absurdity of such an occurrence. *Bezbozhnik u stanka*'s signature satirical image of God exclaims in puzzlement: "So many *baba*s and not a single one praying. Where the heck am I?" Here, Soviet women are depicted as skilled urban workers, as opposed to the devout peasant women implied by the derogatory term *baba*. As well as mocking religiosity among *baba*s, this representation sought to encourage Russian women to join the ranks of the remunerated proletariat, a step that would break the shackles of economic dependency, patriarchy, illiteracy, and the clergy, all seen as interdependent evils. This quadruple liberation would answer Nadezhda Krupskaya's famous 1918 call to educate, employ, and empower women, and thereby "give Soviet society a new member."[43]

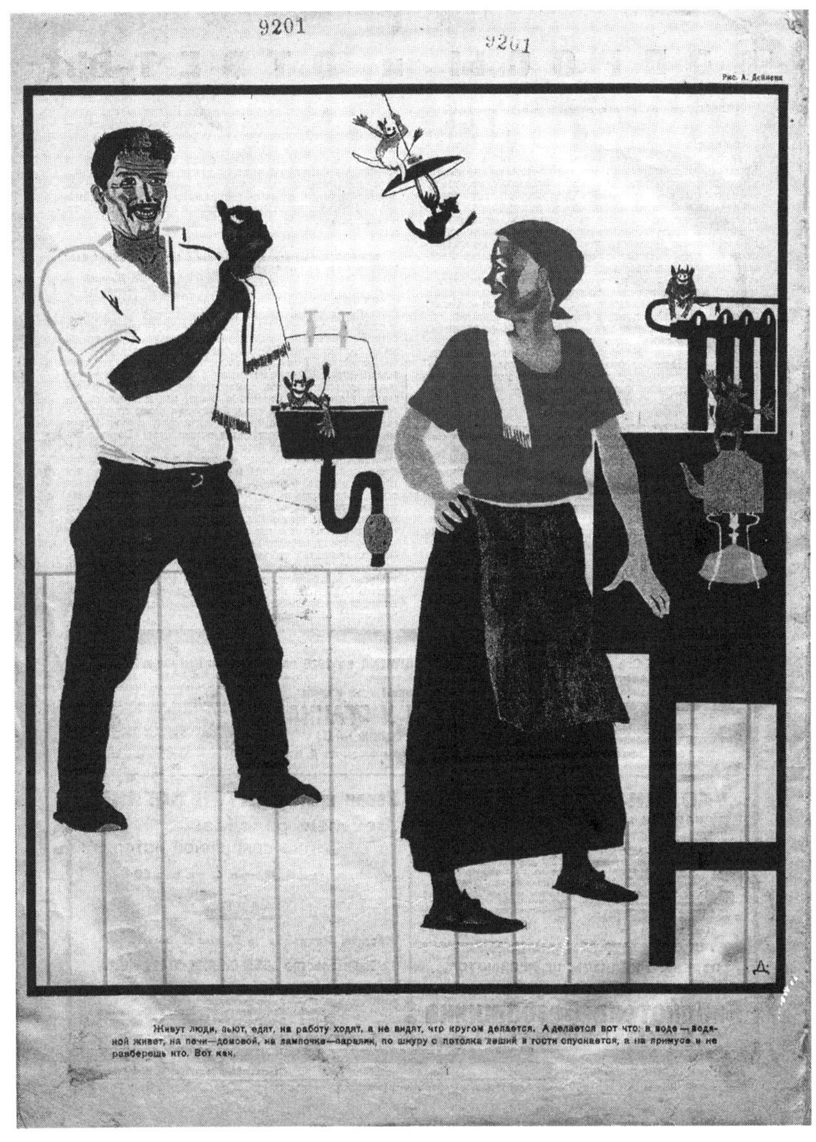

5.16 "People Live …" *Bezbozhnik u stanka*, no. 6 (1925), page 4, by Aleksandr Deineka. Part of the David King Collection. Presented to Tate Archive by David King 2016.

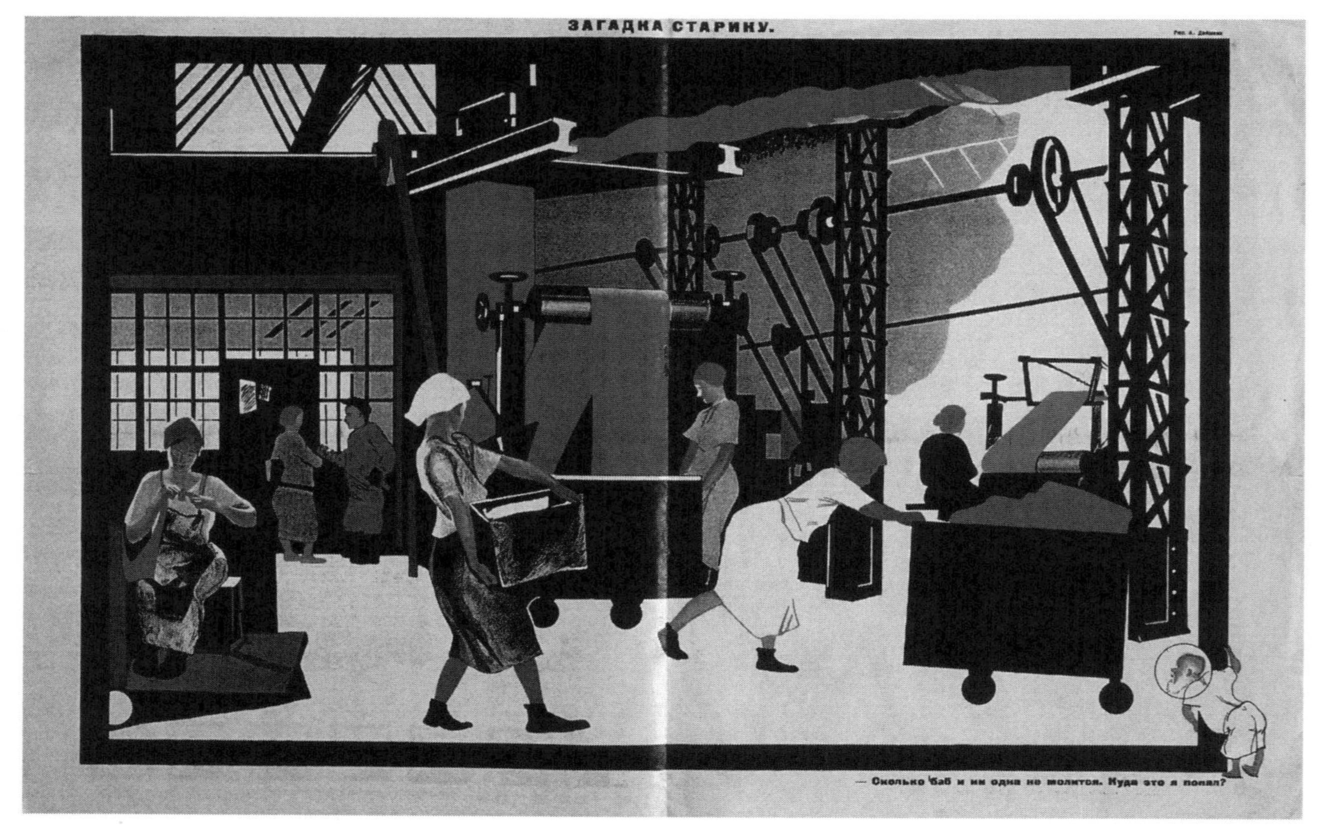

5.17 "Old Man's Riddle," *Bezbozhnik u stanka*, no. 2 (1926), centrefold by Aleksandr Deineka. Part of the David King Collection. Presented to Tate Archive by David King 2016.

The popularity of *Bezbozhnik u stanka,* mainly attributed to its specific brand of illustrated propaganda, permitted the journal to reach publics that had traditionally not been courted by antireligious periodical publications. In order to expand this supporter base to even broader circles, in 1924 *Bezbozhnik u stanka* encouraged workers to tear out satirical illustrations from the journal and use them as posters, exhibiting them in public places. That same year, it published a brochure titled *How to Build a Godless Corner.*[44] The concept of godless corners, which appeared roughly at the same time that Lenin corners emerged as a popular form,[45] was drawn directly from the Russian Orthodox tradition. It parodied the common holy corners used for everyday devotion that were set up in the kitchens of pious homes, displaying icons, candles, prayer books, and other religious artefacts. For the modest sum of two rubles and eighty kopecks (which was roughly a worker's hourly wage in 1924), the Godless Corner Kit could be ordered from *Bezbozhnik u stanka.* The set of antireligious paraphernalia contained the following articles: a godless corner banner, slogans, large and brightly coloured satirical posters, and back issues of *Bezbozhnik u stanka* from which to extract centrefolds and additional images. Visual instructions on how to assemble the corner in an alluringly symmetrical composition were provided. The brochure also recommended that current antireligious literature be made accessible to supplement the imagery and slogans affixed to the factory walls. Whenever possible, activists were encouraged to spend time at the corner and interact with workers, introducing them to the antireligious material on display.

Through the journals, godless corners, street theatre, and all the other manifestations that supported it throughout the 1920s and early 1930s,[46] antireligious propaganda became omnipresent in Soviet visual culture. But, most importantly, it did something that other representational modes simply could not do. It established a visible *absence* – the absence of religion depicted through the rhetorics of satirical irony.

The Campaign against Trotskyism

The Campaign against Trotskyism had two main objectives. After Lenin's death in 1924, and in the context of the reorganization of the government that eventually led to Stalin's rise to power, it served to discredit the ideas and leadership of one of the main and most

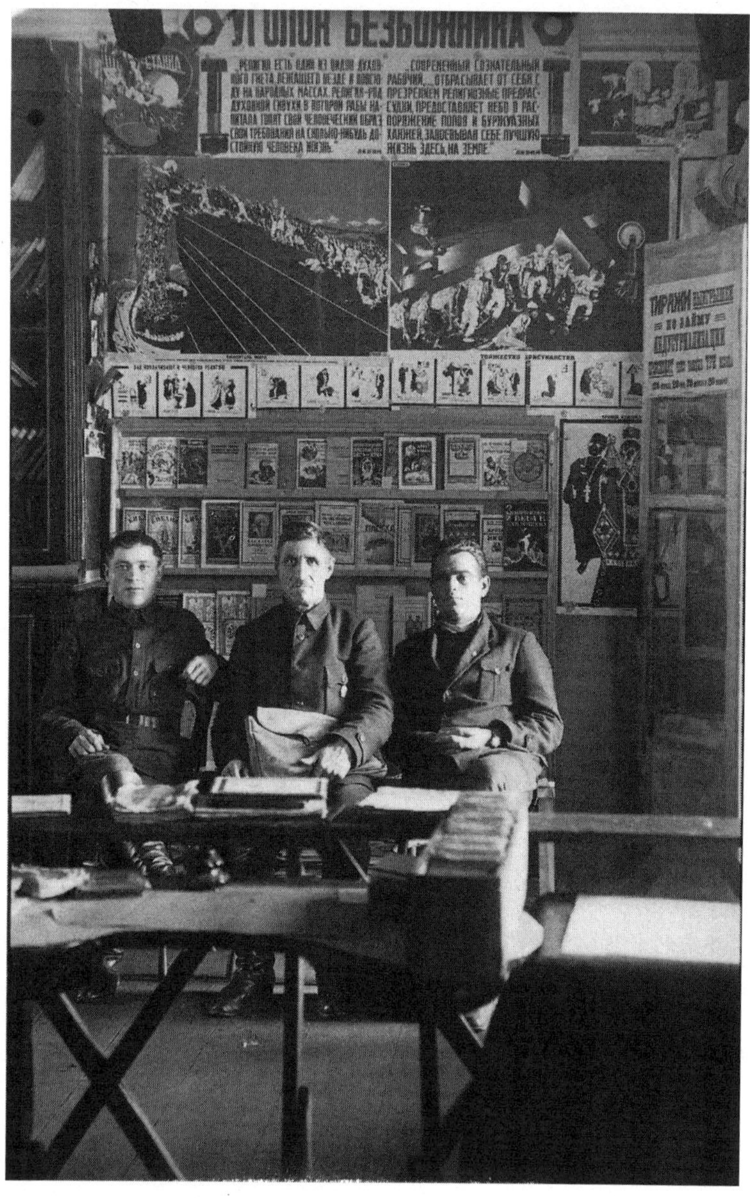

5.18 Godless corner, the 1920s. Collection of Annie Gérin.

popular ideologues of early Soviet Russia, and to perform character assassination.

Leon Trostky met Lenin in London in 1902. He had just escaped from Siberian exile, where he had been sent for subversive activities. He was twenty-three years old. Lenin was immediately impressed by the intelligence, the energy, and the oratory skills of the young revolutionary and invited him to join the editorial committee of the newspaper *Iskra* (*The Spark,* 1900–1903), the official organ of the Russian Social Democratic Labour Party (RSDLP). From then on, in spite of sporadic divergences, Trotsky became one of Lenin's closest and most trusted collaborators. In October 1917, as president of the Leningrad Soviet, he organized the insurrection that lead to the seizure of the Winter Palace and the October Revolution. A few days later, on 6 November 1917, Stalin saluted Trotsky's momentous contribution to the Revolution in an article he published in the newspaper *Pravda*.

During the early days of the Soviet regime, Trotsky served as People's Commissar for Foreign Affairs. In 1918, he founded the Red Army and became its first commander as People's Commissar of Military and Naval Affairs. His pivotal role in the Bolshevik victory in the Russian Civil War made him the subject (and the target) of both Bolshevik and anti-Bolshevik propaganda. In a Bolshevik poster from 1918, he is depicted as a heroic modern-day Saint George slaying a dragon wearing a top hat. The beast, the caricatural target of this satirical work, is branded with the word "counter-revolution." The image that likens the People's Commissar to the patron saint of Moscow is an unambiguous homage. In a White Army propaganda poster probably produced that same year, however, Trotsky is transformed into a malignant creature to be slain: the ogre of the Kremlin (Plate 8). The chauvinistic image makes full use of anti-Semitic stereotypical elements to depict Trotsky, who is accompanied by Asian Bolshevik supporters depicted as mass murderers sitting on a pile of skulls, referring explicitly to Vereshchagin's 1871 *Apotheosis of War*. The ironic caption reads, "Peace and Liberty in Sovdepiya," a derogative term invented by the Whites to describe the new regime, ruled by soviets and deputies.

With the defeat of the Whites in 1920, the Soviet government's emphasis shifted to the economy, and later to questions of the everyday. In 1921, following economic collapse and social uprisings, Lenin launched the New Economic Policy, a measure to boost the economy that had been advocated for by Trotsky for at least a year. Soon after, in late 1921, Lenin's

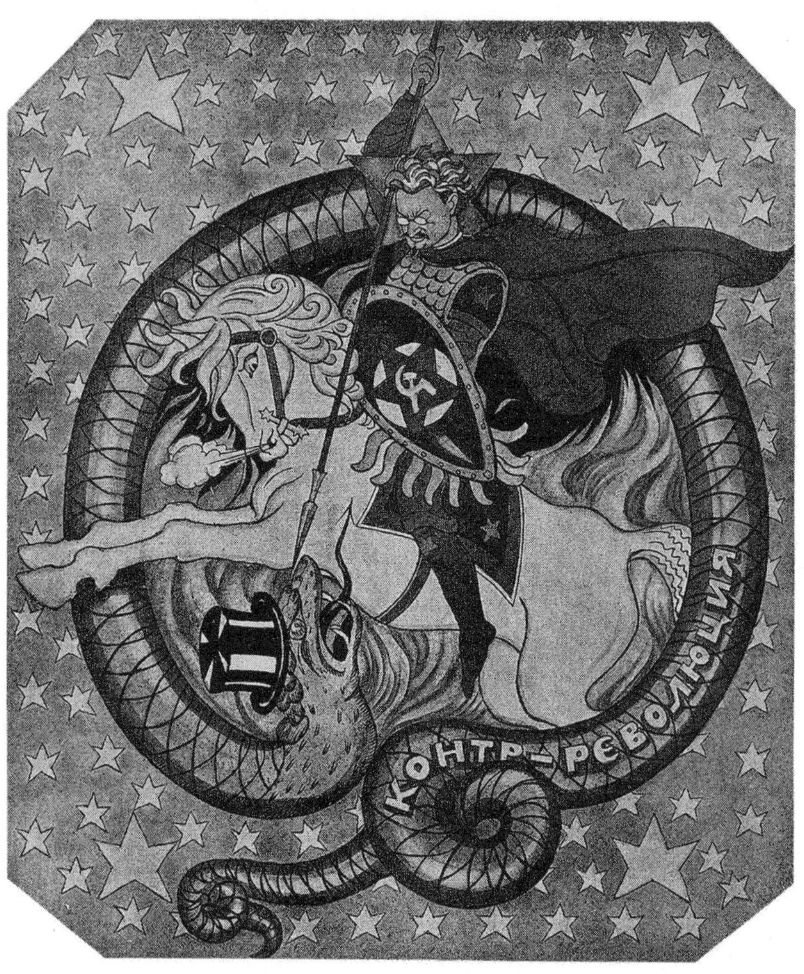

5.19 "Trotsky Slaying the Dragon of Counter-revolution," poster by Viktor Deni, 1920. Part of the David King Collection. Presented to Tate Archive by David King 2016.

health deteriorated. He became increasingly absent from Moscow and eventually suffered a series of strokes, which caused paralysis, loss of speech, and finally death on 21 January 1924. With Lenin increasingly sidelined, a power struggle within the party leadership started to take shape. Joseph Stalin had been elevated to the newly created position of the Central Committee General Secretary earlier in the year. This was a strategic position within the party bureaucracy. He joined with Grigorii Zinoviev and Lev Kamenev to form a triumvirate to ensure that Trotsky, Lenin's right-hand man and heir apparent, would not succeed him.

Trotsky formed the Left Opposition to fight the rise of Stalin, oppose the policies and principles he developped (in particular the doctrine of "socialism in one country"), and denounce the increasing role of bureaucracy in the Soviet Union. As Stalin secured his hold on power, Trotsky was successively removed from the Politburo (1927), expelled from the Communist Party (1927), exiled to Kazakhstan (1928), and finally deported from the Soviet Union in 1929.

The systematic removal of Trotsky from political life found an eerie correspondence in Soviet print culture. Throughout the late 1920s and the early 1930s, images of Trotsky were taken down in public places, removed from circulation, and cut out from library books. In historical photographs, such as that of a 1919 May Day celebration, the former hero's figure suddenly vanished, replaced by a telling blur.[47] But if the figure of the former People's Commissar of war needed to be obliterated from past publications, it became omnipresent in the satirical print culture of the period.

In an article titled "The Work of Representation," Stuart Hall explains that "*physical* things and *actions exist* independently of discourse, but they only take on meaning and become *objects* of knowledge within discourse."[48] In other words, what is understood as reality is constructed by representation, oral, textual, visual, or otherwise. Images of the Revolution therefore mattered in that they constituted its shared understanding. And Trotsky had been omnipresent as a positive figure in revolutionary imagery since its earliest days. The masses remembered Trotsky slaying the dragon of the counter-revolution, they recalled him dressed in Red Army military garb, protecting the country from sea to sea, crushing bug-sized enemies underfoot. It was therefore not enough to erase and physically destroy these images; they remained etched in peoples' minds. As Stuart Hall would argue, it was necessary to open up the existing representations, deconstruct them, delegitimize them, and reinvest them with alternative significations.

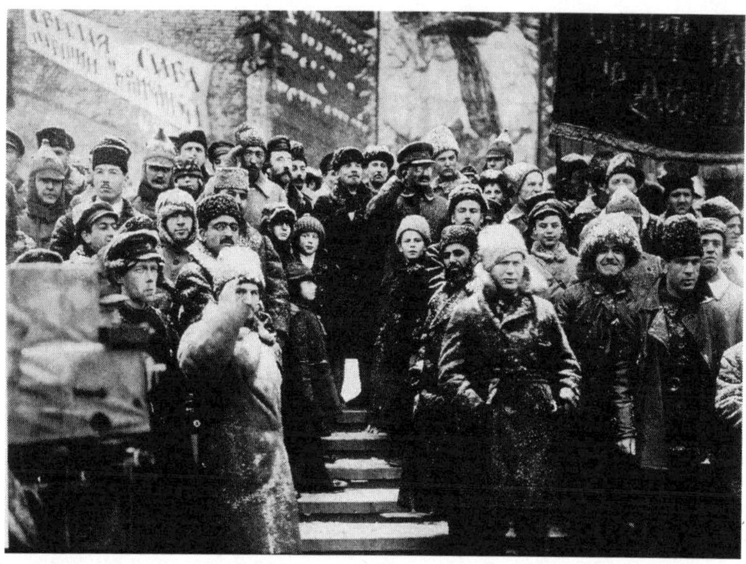

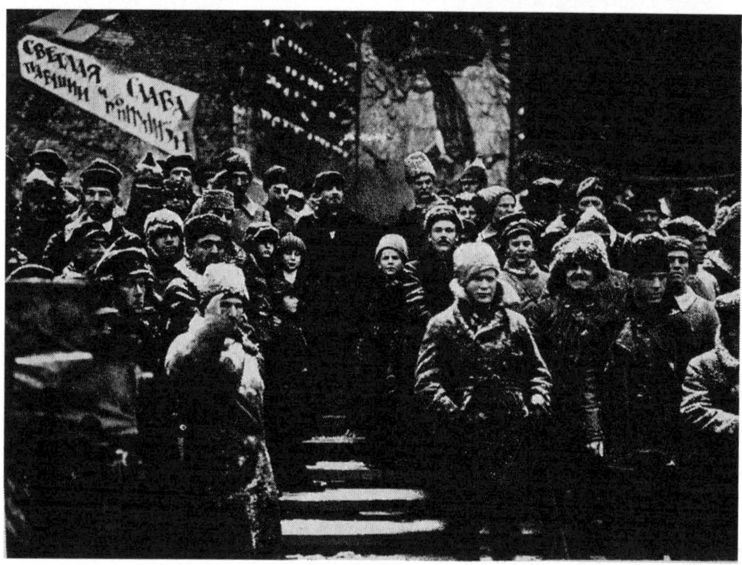

5.20 May Day celebration, 1919. In the image at the top of this page, Trotsky is standing to the right of Lenin. The doctored image below shows a blur where Trotsky was standing. Part of the David King Collection. Presented to Tate Archive by David King 2016.

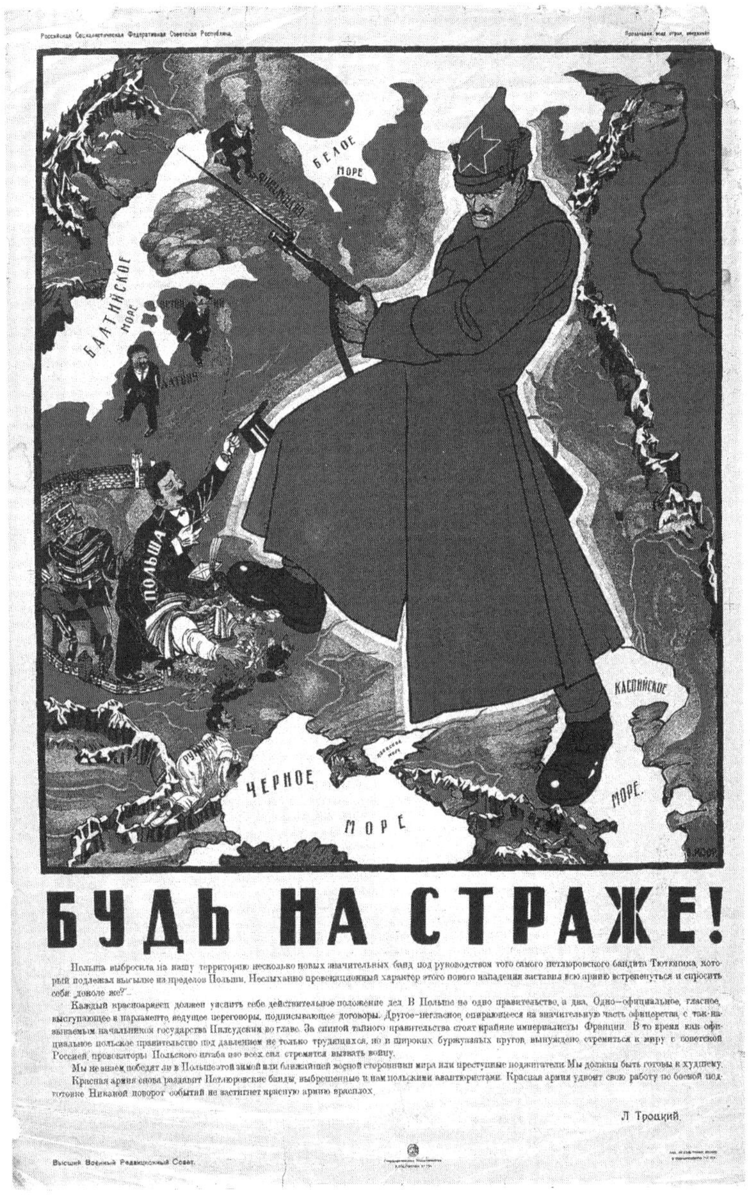

5.21 "Be on Guard!," poster by Dmitrii Moor, 1921. Part of the David King Collection. Presented to Tate Archive by David King 2016.

In satirical images published from 1926 on, Trotsky is hence depicted by his enemies in a less than heroic light. On the cover of a *Krokodil* issue from 1927, for example, he is represented as a Jewish street performer, along with Zinoviev dressed as a gipsy and Kamenev turned into a parrot. (In 1926, Zinoviev and Kamenev had broken with Stalin to join the Left Opposition.) The caption reads: "We play, we play, but no one comes to hear." The caricature transforms the Left Opposition into marginal characters, old-fashioned street musicians and their pet. On another *Krokodil* cover, also from 1927, the ostracism of Trotsky is further apparent. In the background of the image, a celebration takes place. Hundreds of people are gathered, holding red banners. In the foreground, a forlorn Trotsky sits on a chair, hunched over. The caption reads: "Lenin is dead, but his deeds live on. Trotsky is alive, but his deed is dead." On a 1929 *Lapot* cover (no. 7), Trotsky is portrayed in a room cluttered with icons; he is once and for all relegated to the realm of reactionary bric-a-brac.

Then, with the Second World War looming, the rhetoric against Trotsky hardened. He who would oppose Stalin's 1939 non-agression pact with Hitler moved from being a marginalized deviant to an outright enemy and fascist collaborator. A *Krokodil* cover from 1938 shows Trotsky as the dirty-handed waiter proposing Ukraine, Belorussia, Uzbekistan, and other mouth-watering dishes listed on the menu pinned to the wall to Hitler, Hirohito, and Mussolini. In "Fatherland," a 1938 caricature by Boris Efimov, he is transformed into a pig gorging himself from the trough of the German *Vaterland*.

After waging battle from Turkey, France, and Norway, Trotsky continued to oppose the Stalinist bureaucracy while in exile in Mexico. In May 1940, a first assassination attempt against Trotsky was led by Mexican muralist painter and Stalinist sympathizer David Alfaro Siqueiros. A second attempt on Trotsky's life came in August of the same year. Trotsky was struck a fatal blow with an ice-pick by Ramón Mercader, a Spanish-born agent sent to Mexico by Stalin's secret police. With Trotsky gone, the satirical character assassination became less necessary and rapidly ceased.

Conclusion

Other Soviet propaganda campaigns made ample use of satirical strategies in the visual culture they produced: the campaigns against alcoholism, against illiteracy, and the de-kulakization of the countryside,

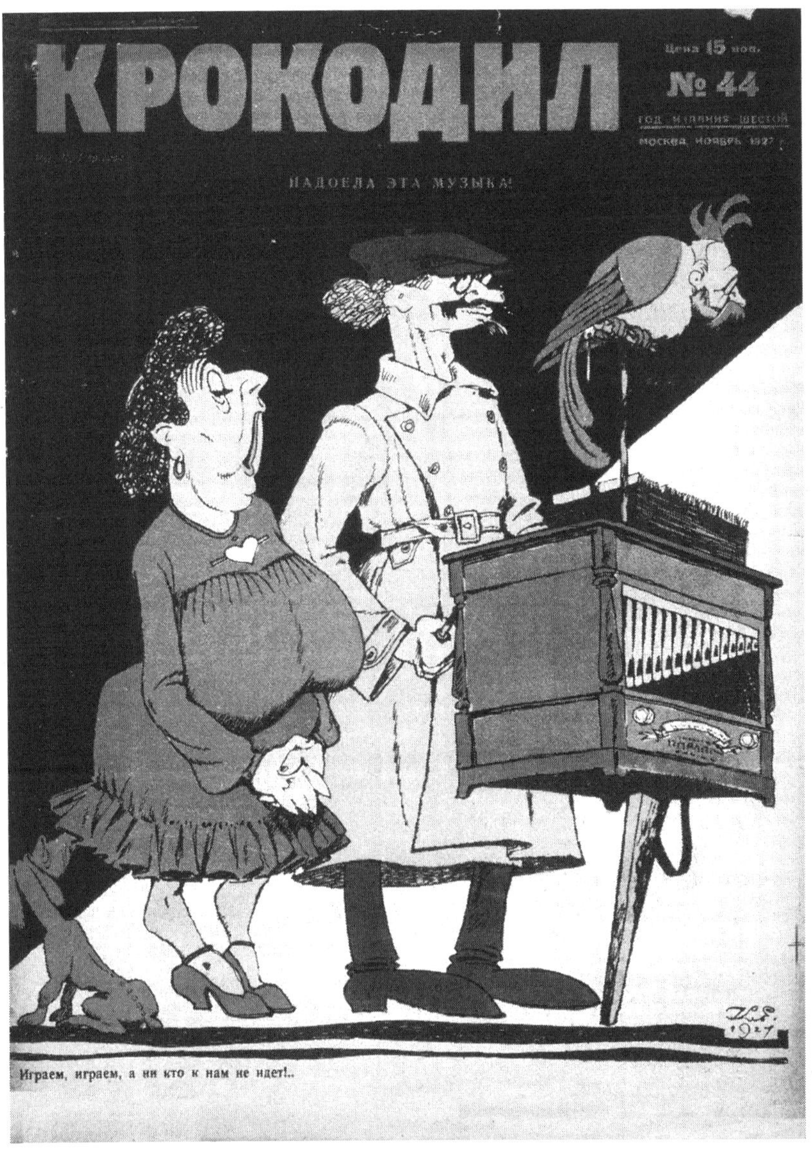

5.22 "We play, we play, but no one comes to hear." *Krokodil*, no. 44 (1927), cover. Part of the David King Collection. Presented to Tate Archive by David King 2016.

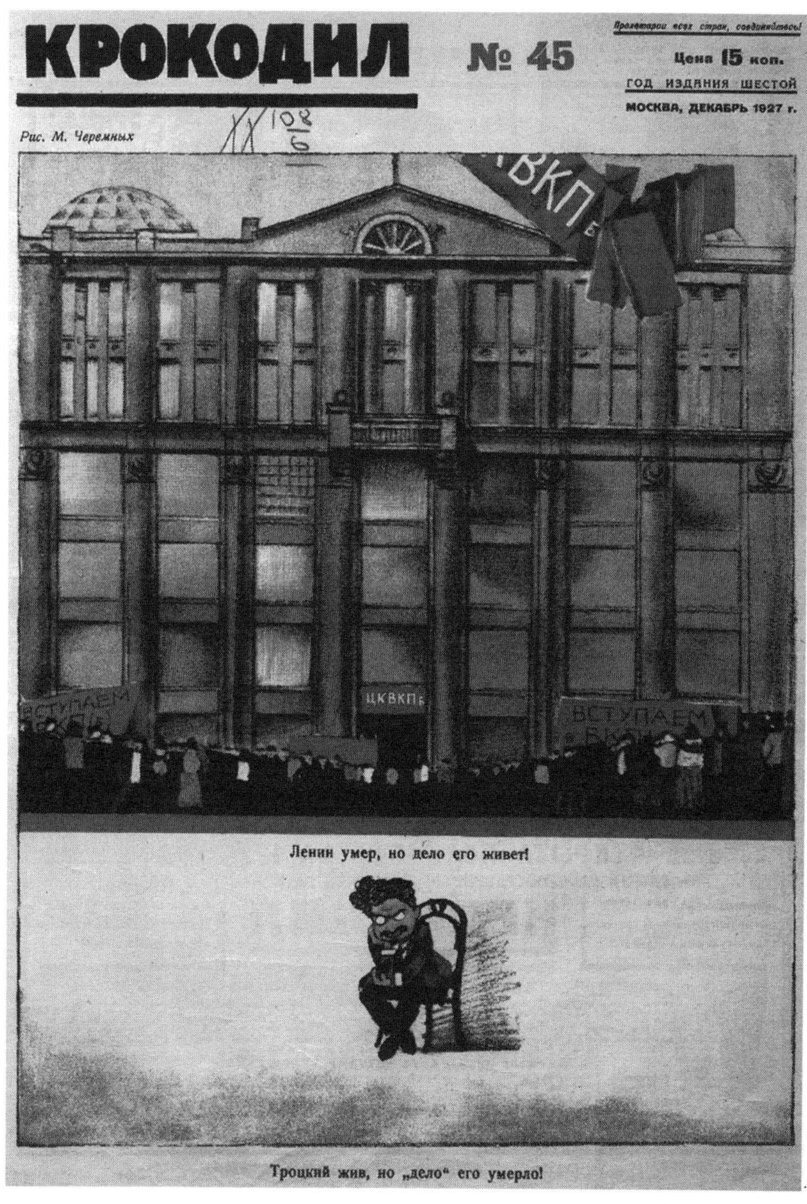

5.23 "Lenin is dead, but his deeds live on. Trotsky is alive, but his deed is dead." *Krokodil*, no. 45 (1927), cover. Part of the David King Collection. Presented to Tate Archive by David King 2016.

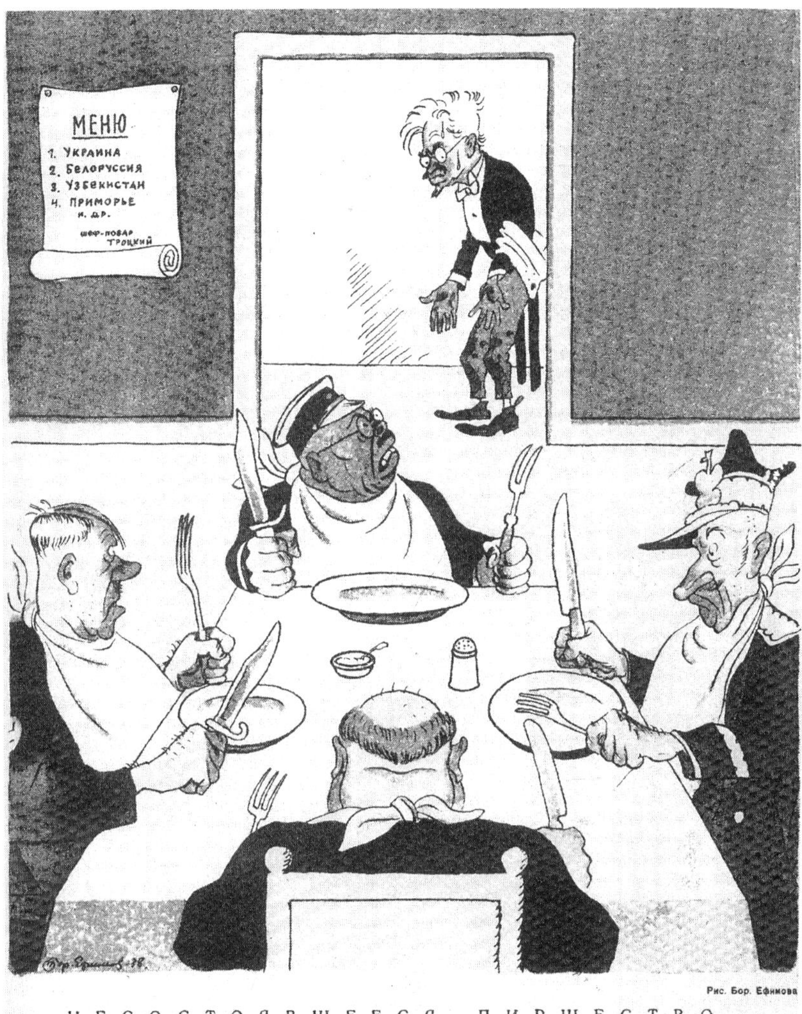

5.24 "Unsatisfying Banquet." *Krokodil*, no. 7 (1938), cover. Part of the David King Collection. Presented to Tate Archive by David King 2016.

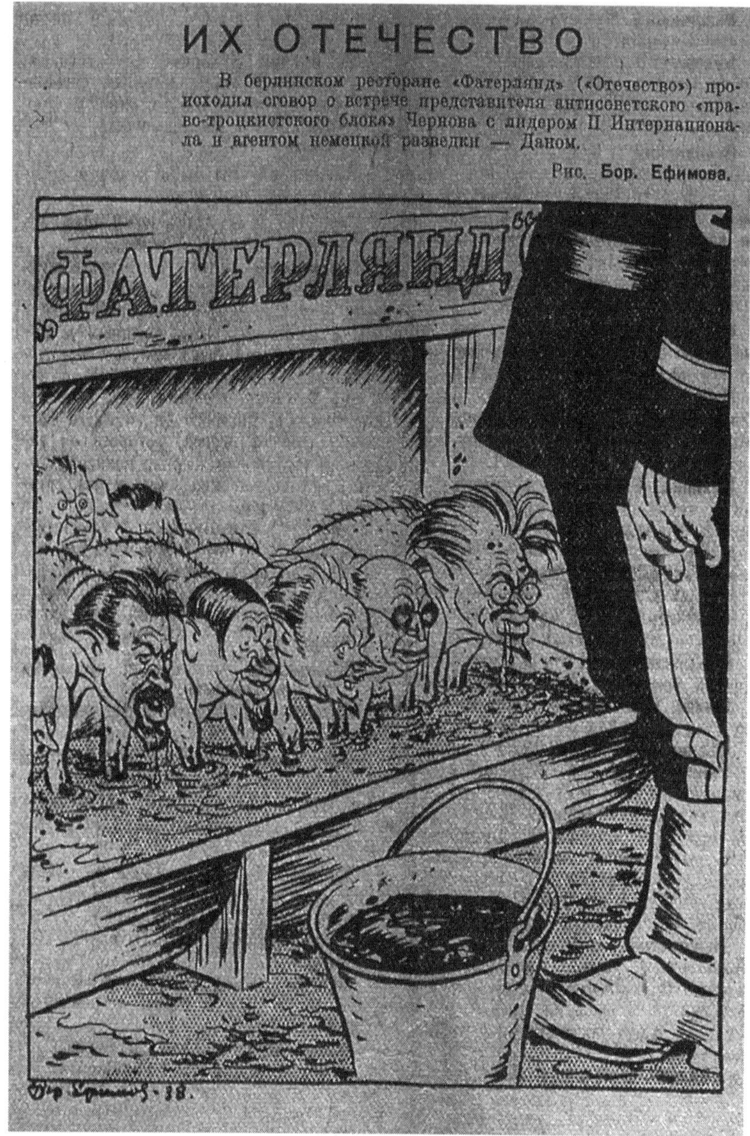

5.25 "Fatherland" by Boris Efimov, *Izvestiya*, 5 March 1938. Part of the David King Collection. Presented to Tate Archive by David King 2016.

among many others. These all addressed pressing, current issues. But unlike campaigns that could be considered "positive" in their intent (*for* the electrification of the country, *for* the collectivization of the countryside, *for* the Five-Year Plans), they were rooted in a kind of institutionalized hatred, what philosopher Philippe Saltel describes as anger that has crystallized, and that focuses on an object that has become emblematic of an affect too large for any individual to grasp. Hatred is an emotion that pushes those who hate to desire the disappearance or the outright devastation of the object of their scorn. As Saltel explains, "the subject believes the hated object to be bad in and of itself, and opposes to it the utopia of a world that has been rid or freed of that evil incarnate."[49]

In this sense, satirical campaigns served a very specific rhetorical purpose, that of symbolic destruction. They were therefore complementary to other forms of propaganda that aimed to establish certain practices as positive, or to project optimistic and utopian visions of a bright future.

Chapter Six

The Rhetorics of Satire and Socialist Realism

"Laughter is especially powerful when linked to artistic realism."

A.V. Lunacharsky[1]

The preceding chapters have traced the rise and decline of Soviet satire in the visual arts, cinema, circus, and theatre during the fifteen years that followed the October Revolution. The first movement was driven by a revolutionary artistic scene, rooted in the avant-garde and working closely with emerging Soviet institutions, most notably with the Narkompros and its various offices. The subsequent waning of satire is linked to concrete ideological and institutional changes that occurred throughout the 1920s: the formation of the Association of Artists of Revolutionary Russia (AKhRR) in 1922 and of the Russian Association of Proletarian Writers (RAPP) in 1925, the 1927 Central Committee decree "On humoristic-satirical presses," the 1928 Party Conference on Cinema Affairs, Lunacharsky's retirement in 1929 from his leadership position at the People's Commissariat for Enlightenment,[2] the beginning of the Cultural Revolution, and so on.

These events ushered in a new, aesthetically conservative cultural elite that would vociferously defend its own interpretations of what socialist art could be, what its social and political function should be, and how it might be used to achieve certain goals. As writer Ilya Ehrenburg recalled in his memoires, in the late 1920s and early 1930s "loudest of all were the voices of the RAPP group. The exhibitions were crowded with huge paintings of the AKhRR. The days of experiments and eccentricities had been left behind."[3]

This decline is what has led many authors to declare that, with the beginning of the First Five-Year Plan, satire disappeared from the art world, retreating underground to the realm of illicit political *anekdoty* (jokes). And indeed, Nadezhda Mandelstam and others have commented on how, in the 1930s, *anekdoty* served as a coping mechanism and the only legitimate response to the senselessness of the Stalinist repression and of faceless bureaucracy.[4] But Soviet satire did survive; it adapted to socio-political changes and found its way among the realist artistic trends that became the hallmark of Soviet art under Stalin and beyond. Ehrenburg even takes note of it in his retrospective description of early Stalinist art: "The style that was to prevail for a quarter of a century was coming into being: the style of ornamented architecture, of those metro stations crammed with statues, of incessant panegyrics, and of satire modestly pillorying the careless house-manager or the tipsy music-hall artist."[5]

In the late 1920s and early 1930s, as what would become known as socialist realism was coming into being, satire gradually broke its ties with the avant-garde and once again adjusted its targets. It became more controlled and certainly less experimental in terms of its form, but no less biting. It also came under attack in spirited debates. Its detractors felt it was a counterproductive artistic strategy that could interfere with revolutionary efforts. But a number of intellectuals and artists, Lunacharsky among them, understood satire as one of the many possible forms socialist realism could adopt, and as a rhetorical tool that could complement optimistic representations.

The *Literaturnaya gazeta* Debate on Satire

From April 1929 to January 1930, a debate around the relevance and usefulness of Soviet satire was waged. Chiefly, it took place at the Polytechnic Museum in Moscow and in the pages of *Literaturnaya gazeta*, which was arguably the most influential cultural periodical of the time. The debate was foregrounded by an earlier article titled "The Line of Least Resistance" published in 1925 by Vladimir Blum, a theatre critic who had been an enthusiastic supporter of Meyerhold's work in the early days of the Revolution, and who would become satire's most virulent detractor by the mid-1920s. Here, he wrote that the young communist system was too fragile to bear the brunt of satirical criticism: "To mock the proletarian state through the use of old satirical devices and thereby to shake its foundations, to laugh at the first steps – albeit uncertain and clumsy – of the new Soviet society is at the very least unwise and ill considered."[6] This is an argument that was to be widely used during the mid-1920s in debates concerning satirical cinema and theatre; their arsenals, it was feared, could turn against the Soviet state if viewed by non-sympathizing publics, in particular those of foreign countries.

By 1929, however, the arguments against satire were changing, following transformations that were also shaping the Soviet metanarrative.[7] The earliest conceptions of the Soviet state had been moulded by the revolutionary impulse as well as continued conflict and class hatred throughout the Civil War; the state was commonly perceived as a "citadel of socialism surrounded by the hostile capitalist world."[8] This view of a socialist state encircled by enemies, which found its way into images such as the cover of a 1929 issue of *Bezbozhnik u stanka* and was supported by repeated declarations by Lenin and other Soviet leaders that "the socialist fatherland is in danger,"[9] was the fuel that nourished early Soviet satire. But the ideological shift that marked the conclusion of the Civil War and the launch of the NEP in 1921 occasioned a major reorientation of the metanarrative and of the images that were used to shape it in mass culture.

The NEP was initiated as a temporary measure. It was justified in terms of the need for a provisional settlement with the peasantry, to preserve and nurture the achievements produced by the October Revolution in Russia until the outbreak of the World Revolution. The targets of satire, as we saw in the previous chapters, changed from external enemies of the Revolution and of the state to internal enemies: saboteurs, parasites, NEPmen, and the atavistic pre-revolutionary practices that became their attributes. In the arts and in propaganda in general, strategies increasingly shifted from criticism to laudatory forms. It is in this context that Blum first appealed to his contemporaries to dispense with satire, to avoid any blow that could compromise the foundations of the fragile state.

When Lenin died in 1924, the temporary compromise of the NEP was transformed into a new status quo. This is the point at which the revolutionary period can be said to have definitely concluded. Ambiguity was nevertheless maintained about whether full and final victory of socialism could be achieved without world revolution. A new, optimistic construction phase was inaugurated, most successfully captured by Joseph Stalin's catchy slogan of 1924: "Socialism in one country."[10] By the late 1920s, residual petit bourgeois sensibilities as well as the constant

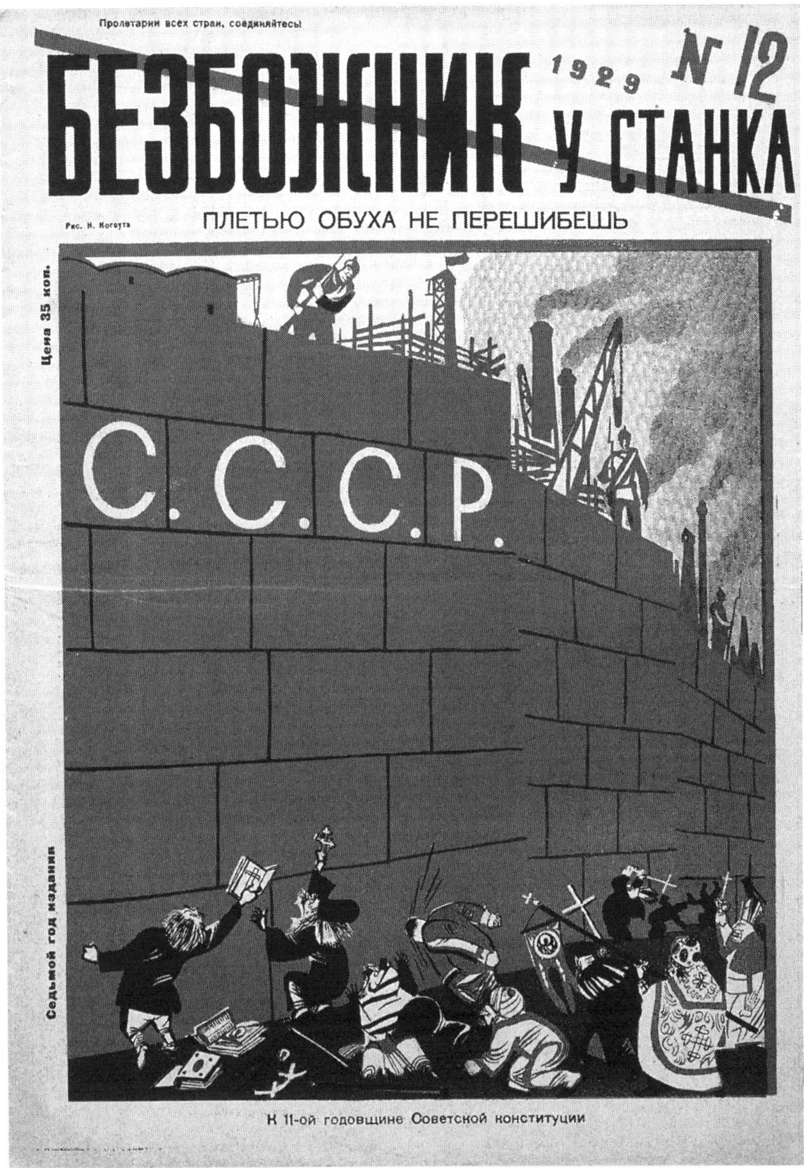

6.1 "You can't strike us down." *Bezbozhnik u stanka*, no. 12 (1929), cover by Nikolai Kogout. Part of the David King Collection. Presented to Tate Archive by David King 2016.

threat of philistine infection of the bureaucratic apparatus seemed to dominate satirical discourse, highlighting the fact that social anxiety had decidedly shifted inward the boundaries of the state. This popular fear was enacted most publicly during the Shakhty affair and the party trials of 1928 and 1930, events that depicted intellectuals and bourgeois specialists as potential saboteurs defending their own class interests.[11]

Paradoxically, the myth of internal enemies – and their purge from the heart of the party – laid the groundwork for another ideological shift: socialism was being successfully built through industrialization, social reforms, and the elimination of antagonist elements through the purges. This new conception became the hallmark of the first two Five-Year Plans (1928–32 and 1933–37). It even found its way into the 1936 Soviet Constitution, where it was declared that socialism had actually been achieved.[12] It is in this context, when the idea of triumphant social-ism was starting to take hold in popular imagination, that the 1929–30 *Liternaturnaya gazeta* debate occurred.

The first of the series of six articles, "On the Path towards a Revival of Satire," was written by prominent literary critic Abram Lezhnev, under the pen name Abram Gorelik. Under the pretext of a favour-able critique of Andrei Novikov's satirical novel about bureaucracy, *The Causes and Origins of Nebulosity* (1929), which Lezhnev described as a fine example attesting to a renaissance of the genre, he laid the grounds for the debate. In his opinion, Soviet society's critical impulse was, at that point in history, consumed by autocriticism, public tri-als of saboteurs, and public denunciations published in newspapers. The power of these events was grounded in their ability to straight-forwardly name and describe the culprits to be shamed or punished. This effervescence of public accusations was to blame, according to Lezhnev, for a decline in artistic satire, now relegated to specialized publications, in particular satirical journals. If the need for satirical art was still very present, he concluded, it needed to be treated more than ever with an expert's touch, focusing on the right targets, using forms that would truly resonate with its intended publics. Indeed, for Lezhnev, the context of autocriticism and the trials did not in any way mean that artistic satire had lost its social relevance and potency. "Firstly," he wrote, "satirical energy has grown more vibrant than ever. Second, the struggle against individual or concrete 'evil' does not pre-clude – on the contrary – a more general comprehension of 'evil.' Ar-tistic satire can present a powerful means to achieve precisely this kind of broad understanding."[13]

Roughly a month later, a response to Lezhnev's article appeared under the title "Is There Really a Revival of Satire?" This one was penned by the aforementioned Vladimir Blum. In a nutshell, the answer to the question posed in the title was: No, there is not, should not, and will not be a revival of satire. According to Blum, satirical artworks had never really been effective, and only the naive were still calling for laughter as a tool fit for the struggle towards socialism. "It is strange," he wrote, "that satirists (with all the communists, Marxists and materialists among us) don't notice how idealistic their hopes for satire are. It seems they genuinely believe that predators, absentee workers, bureaucrats, and other scapegoats of satire – as soon as they see their image reflected in the 'mirror of art,' will immediately be shamed into changing their ways. They think that through laughter they can correct mores. This theory is absolutely antiquated."[14] Furthermore, he explained, satire was *no longer needed* in the Soviet state. This is the most trenchant part of Blum's argument, and would become the foundation of all his later interventions in the press and in public debates. According to him, before 1917 satire had always been used as a weapon directed against the state. But since the Revolution had ushered in the rule of the proletariat and peasants, the state had ceased to be the enemy. In the context of the successful construction of "socialism in one country," why would the people aim the arrows of satire against themselves? This would clearly amount to counter-revolutionary behaviour.

A third article came as a reply to Blum in early July 1929, this one by Georgii Yakubovsky.[15] "Satire," the author wrote, "sheds light on harmful social practices that have endured through time, and are still deeply rooted in our society. V. Blum shows himself to be naive when he states that those who produce satire, those who generalize, are striking blows against the Soviet state. The satirist who exposes bureaucrats, thoughtlessness, the exuberance of vulgarity, and the narrowness of the petit bourgeois spirit, does not strike against the Soviet state, but rather against the legacy of the past." For Yakubovsky, satire was an indispensable tool for collective autocriticism, and therefore a judicious, even necessary mode of artistic expression. In other words, if Soviet art was to aspire to be social in character and pursue political goals, it needed to draw on satire.

Two more articles appeared in defence of satire over the following weeks. In "About the Paths of Soviet Satire" the unidentified author also took issue with Blum. "The creation of a truly Soviet form of satire is the question of the day. We have many responses to give to V. Blum's articles (no. 6), which insists on the inoperability of satire under current conditions. Most of these point to opposite conclusions: the ongoing necessity, and the inevitable development of Soviet satire."[16] Reflecting on the current interest of the public and of critics, the author further argued that Soviet satirists would need to develop their craft to serve a public that was becoming increasingly sophisticated and demanding. It would also need to distinguish itself from simple comedy, a genre now growing in importance in the late 1920s, in particular in the cinema and the theatre. "We must insist that simple funniness, joking, laughter for laughter's sake, all of this has nothing to do with Soviet satire. Soviet satire will necessarily distinguish itself by its dynamism, its energy, and its tone, which must be without precedents. It must open the way for clearer understandings and perceptions of the world, serving the global reconstruction. Satire must precipitate the decline and the demise of religion, nationalism, cowardice, duplicitousness, idleness, and all remaining decay and abominations."[17]

In a fifth contribution to the debate, M. Rogi's "The Paths of Soviet Satire (About the Claims of Comrade V. Blum)" took Blum's argument apart, section by section. He concluded, as others had, that if art could be useful at all in the construction of socialism, then artistic satire was definitely needed. His main contribution to the debate has to do with how he highlighted the rhetorical properties of satire, as complementary to optimistic art forms and discourse.

> Stumbling upon the particularities of the Soviet system, comrade Blum involuntarily offers protection to all kinds of bureaucrats, ruffians, saboteurs, and obvious enemies. With what delight they will hold on to their false kinship with the Soviet system; and in chorus they will scream at the satirists, the writers, and all members of the press: "So! You're trying to build the Soviet world. Who do you think you are!"
>
> What is comrade Blum afraid of? That satirists speak of saboteurs? Good, so they should, comrade Blum. This won't mess up anything, "on the contrary," comrade Blum, it will help the Party, the unions, and the volunteers' associations. Satire arms workers and peasants with class anger, revealing to them the secret pathways and the nests where enemies hide.
>
> Comrade Blum is right about one thing. Satire should not attack the foundations, sever the roots, or snatch the fruit of the Soviet system. Nor of the Party, the unions, or the volunteers' associations. Satire, if it is truly Soviet, cannot bypass all these organizations, it cannot avoid taking into

consideration the positive role they play in the struggle against the remnants of our loathsome past. Otherwise a one-sided satire will ensue, leading to misapprehension, disorientation, and unwarranted panic.[18]

One last article, "Do We Need Satire?," brought the final word to the debate. Here, Efim Zozulya presented an account of the public debate on the future of Soviet satire that took place at the Polytechnic Museum in Moscow on 8 January 1930, at which were present, among others, Vladimir Blum, Anatoly Lunacharsky, Vladimir Mayakovsky, and Mikhail Koltsov, the editor of the satirical journal *Krokodil*.[19] Zozulya recounted Blum's intervention, which can be summed up by a clever declaration by the detractor: "The notion of 'Soviet satire' is a contradiction in itself. It is just as absurd as the notion of 'Soviet banker' or of 'Soviet landlord.'"[20] But the crowd of satirists and other interested parties gathered at the event seem to have unanimously turned against Blum. "They weren't only defending satire in its literary and formal sense, but rather the right to laugh."[21]

For all intents and purposes, and even if several articles on the topic of satire followed in *Literaturnaya gazeta* and elsewhere,[22] the debate was then closed. Soviet satire had been saved and once again legitimized.

Then, on 6 March 1931, a short communiqué appeared in the pages of *Literaturnaya gazeta*.[23] Penned by Anatoly Lunacharsky, it announced the launch of a governmental commission for the study of satirical genres in art and literature, working under the auspices of the Social Sciences Division of the Soviet Academy of Sciences. It was headed by the now retired People's Commissar of Enlightenment, who had been appointed Member to the Academy in 1930. Satire would become a field of study within the highest scientific level of authority in the nation.

Several things can be gleaned from the 1929–30 *Literaturnaya gazeta* debate on satire. First, satire was considered a literary/artistic genre significant enough to warrant discussion in one of the most important cultural journals of the period. Second, in spite of the rejection of the satirical mode by members of the new artistic elite, its fate had not been sealed. Finally, the debate reveals that, by the late 1920s, the intelligentsia had assimilated Lunacharsky's arguments on satire (some sentences found in the texts defending satire seem to have been directly lifted from the commissar's prose), and that the destructive forces of satire were increasingly being understood as complementarity to the optimistic rhetoric of the Five-Year Plans. In other words, the creation of a new world needed to be accompanied by the destruction of remnants of the past. This dual task (deconstruction/construction) was to occasion much debate in the fields of art production in the years to follow, as would the question of what to do about the often embarrassing coexistence in the present of the lingering old and the emerging new.

Realism in the 1920s and 1930s

In a speech he gave in Moscow in 1934, at the first All-Union Congress of Soviet Writers, Ilya Ehrenburg summed up the complexity of the period. "The frontiers of our country," he said, "are not only travelling through space, they are also travelling through time. Our foreign guests are now taking a trip in a time machine. They see the country of the future. Together with remnants from our past, with our deep-rooted backwardness, they see the foundations of a new world."[24]

The foreign communist sympathizers, fellow-travellers such as André Malraux, Louis Aragon, Jean-Richard Bloch, Martin Andersen Nexö, and Theodor Plivier who had travelled to Moscow to attend the event, were in fact witnessing in the very speeches of Soviet writers and ideologues a collage of utopian visions and stark reality. Furthermore, at that very moment, in various parts of the union, modernist skyscrapers were being erected in provincial towns where sewers would not be installed for many years, streets stayed unpaved, and sidewalks were nonexistent. In print and in other media, images circulated of state-of-the-art automobiles, farming equipment, and communications technology; but these remained an extreme rarity in the empirical world, where technological backwardness was still the norm. In a similar way, in spite of measures taken to educate and empower women, most were still struggling with the oppression of *byt*, and very few had actually become specialized industrial workers or political activists.

Two years later, Stalin used the launch of the 1936 Soviet Constitution as the occasion to redesign the Soviet government and to declare that socialism in the USSR had been achieved. This rhetorical move was the logical conclusion of the theory of "socialism is one country" he had put forth a decade earlier. For Stalin, this proclamation was meant not only to consolidate the gains of the first two Five-Year Plans, but also to impose a worldview that would focus on socialist achievements rather than on inconvenient residues inherited from the past. But the empirical world, as Ehrenburg had remarked, was unmistakeably lagging behind political discourse.

The main strategy artists developed to address the mismatch between rhetoric and reality was socialist realism, declared the official doctrine for Soviet arts in 1934 at the aforementioned congress. Over the next few years, grounded in the principles of *ideinost, partiinost,* and *narodnost,*[25] it came to favour the projection of a socialist ideal from which residual or backward elements were simply excised. The future-oriented form of socialist realism was elaborated through trial and error, gaining a certain amount of coherence after 1941, when the creation of the Stalin Prize provided artists with concrete models to emulate. Although today socialist realism is often understood as a monolithic and formulaic construct, in the 1920s and early 1930s the concept of realism, and even that of socialist realism, was understood much more broadly.[26]

In his seminal *Metahistory,* Hayden White astutely remarked that, throughout the history of representation, realism has been approached in divergent ways, revealing ideological, epistemological, and ethical underpinnings.[27] In the context of early Soviet Russia, starting in the early 1920s, the term became the focus of much debate, highlighting the polyphony of political and aesthetic positions. In a text written in 1923, for example, Leon Trotsky described realism as "a feeling for life as it is, in an artistic acceptance of reality, and not in a shrinking from it, in an active interest in the concrete stability and mobility of life. It is a striving either to picture life as it is or to idealize it, either to justify or to condemn it."[28] If critics such as Aleksei Fedorov-Davydov believed that the basic tendency in Soviet painting was a striving towards realism, they recognized that definitions needed to be opened up to include new artistic tendencies. Fedorov-Davydov proposed, as a case in point, that non-objective constructivist works in which "iron is precisely that, iron, and rope is rope," could also claim to be realistic.[29] Other conceptions, such as the one developed by members of the Society of Easel Painters (OST), focused on the dialectical conditions that characterize historical processes. For them, this meant producing paintings based on "revolutionary contemporaneity" and the illustration of conflict: the old and the new, the bourgeois and the proletarian, accompanied perhaps by an indication of the resolution of such conflict.[30] These artists drew from primitivism, cubism, and futurism, and sometimes resorted to satirical devices such as caricature and collage to establish their strategies for the representation of class struggle (Plate 9). The eclectic Four Arts Society of Artists, for their part, defended under the term "painterly realism" the right to artistic freedom and formal exploration.[31] The Association of Artists of Revolutionary Russia (AKhRR), on the other hand, denounced such bourgeois-modernist deviations. Founded in 1922, the group called for a kind of realism that would concentrate on Soviet life's most positive elements: a kind of "optimistic" or "heroic" realism, recording "artistically and documentarily, the revolutionary impulse of this great moment of history."[32] Finally, the October group, also adhering to the notion of realism, firmly rejected "the vulgar realism of imitators," an unmistakable reference to the work of the AKhRR. They proposed a dynamic realism, "showing life in movement, in action, revealing systematically the perspectives of life, a realism that rationally reconstructs the old life."[33]

But if realism was never exhaustively defined during the 1920s, if consensus around its meaning was never reached, one of its essential components became clear in all interpretations. Realism required artists to display class consciousness and to participate actively in the class struggle.[34]

By the end of the decade, the necessity of realism was recognized by all. The futurist poet Vladimir Mayakovsky even declared on 26 September 1928, in front of a crowd of artists, writers, and critics gathered at the Polytechnic Museum, "I amnesty Rembrandt!"[35] Yet that same year, the Left Front spokesman Viktor Pertsov complained that "no one really knows what realism, and in particular proletarian realism, is in art."[36] Three years later, in a speech titled "The Creative Method of Proletarian Artists," art critic Ivan Matsa denounced realism as an "abstract slogan." "There is no realism in general," he said. "Realism is always a certain class-based understanding of actuality and transmission of this actuality."[37] He also suggested it was high time to put an end to the practice of adding epithets to the term, to create meaningless phrases such as "heroic realism," "optimistic realism," "compositional realism," "naive realism," "dynamic realism," "constructivist realism," "political realism," "dialectical realism," and so on.

The term "socialist realism" is the handle that was eventually settled on collectively. It made its first public appearance 17 May 1932 in a speech given by Ivan Gronsky, president of the Organizational Committee of the newly formed Union of Soviet Writers.[38] Then, on 23 May 1932, it found its way into print in the pages of *Literaturnaya gazeta*, not as a discrete neologism but as a call for the "honesty and truthfulness of revolutionary art."[39] Its principles are said to have been put forward as the foundation of all future artistic and literary production during a secret meeting between Stalin and a select group of Soviet writers in Maxim Gorky's apartment in the late hours of 26 October 1932. But the

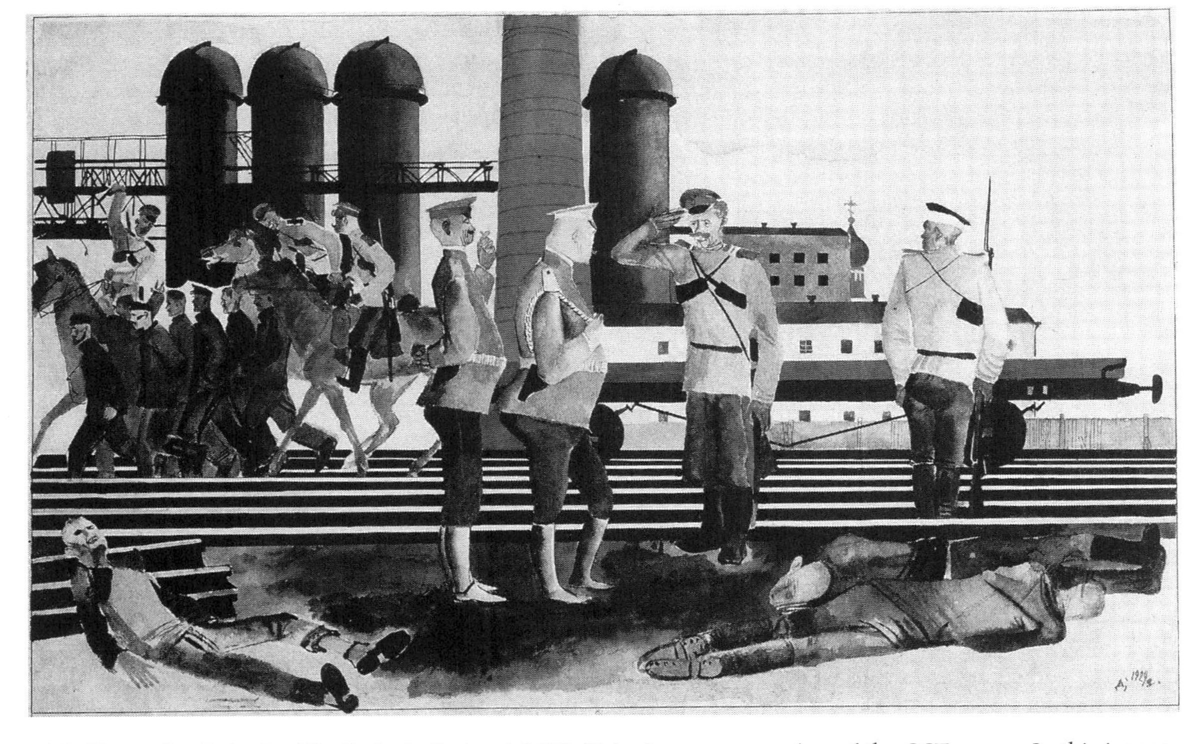

6.2 Alexandre Deineka, *The Order Is Restored*, 1929. Deineka was a member of the OST group. In this image of peace reached at the expense of human life, the artist shows the irony of war. The State Tretyakov Gallery.

term remained polyphonic for at least several months. In a speech titled
"Socialist Realism," delivered in 1933 to the same Organizational Committee over which Ivan Gronsky presided, Lunacharsky explained that
"Socialist Realism is an extensive programme: it includes many different methods – those we already possess and those we are still acquir-
ing."[40] The speech mentions myriad strategies to be adopted by creators
of all genres, including satire, sarcasm, and caricature. Lunacharsky returned to the theme of the relationship between satire and socialist realism several more times in his writings of 1933, explaining that

> in endeavouring, for instance, to synthesise the gigantic collective re-
> sources of his class in monumental images the Socialist Realist is not
> obliged to stick to the limits of realism in the sense of verisimilitude. The
> creation of the image of a proletarian Prometheus is by no means the fruit
> of a thirst for illusion, but is merely the fruit of a thirst for the artistic em-
> bodiment of infinite resources that cannot be transformed into a concrete
> image, employing a real human person. In just the same way, in his strug-
> gle with negative phenomena, the Socialist Realist may of course resort to
> all sorts of hyperbole, caricature and utterly improbable comparisons – not
> to conceal reality but, through stylisation, to reveal it.[41]

Socialist realism received its more definitive formulation at the first
All-Union Congress of Soviet Writers of August 1934, in an often-
repeated speech by Andrei Zhdanov, a member of Joseph Stalin's inner
circle. Zhdanov presented the doctrine as a commentary on the wise
instructions of Stalin.

> Comrade Stalin has called our writers engineers of human souls. What
> does this mean? What duties does the title confer upon us?
> In the first place, it means knowing life so as to depict it truthfully in
> works of art, not to depict it in a dead, scholastic way, not simply as "objec-
> tive reality," but to depict reality in its revolutionary development.
> In addition to this, the truthfulness and historical concreteness of artistic
> portrayal should be combined with the ideological remoulding and educa-
> tion of the toiling people in the spirit of socialism. This method in belles
> lettres and literary criticism is what we call the method of Socialist Realism.[42]

In the context of the 1934 Congress, realism and satire were not
seen as divergent approaches to literature and art. Indeed, Zhdanov

proposed an open method, one that was not anchored in any way in a set of rethorical strategies or a definite stylistic vocabulary. And the various literary figures who spoke at the event adapted the notion of socialist realism to their own practice, whether it be children's literature, epic poetry, documentary journalism, or satire.

Lunacharsky was not there to defend and promote the satirical genre; he had passed away a few months earlier, in December 1933 in Menton, France, on his way to Madrid to take up a position as Soviet ambassador to Spain. But others took up the baton. Playwright and critic Boris Romashov, for example, presented an address on the role of satire and laughter in the theatre, arguing that "vivacity and the laughter of the victor are most familiar to our optimistic spectator, whose favourite genre is [satirical] comedy."[43] Mikhail Koltsov also gave an impassioned speech in favour of the continued use of satire as an ideological weapon in the USSR. Koltsov was one of the leading journalists of the day, a member of *Pravda*'s editorial board. He was also the founding editor of the illustrated satirical journal *Krokodil*, which was, as mentioned above, created by governmental decree in 1922 with the explicit mandate to attack the enemies, internal and external, of the Soviet Union.[44] In his plea for satire, Koltsov argued that the genre provided a type of realism that was complementary to optimistic or heroic realism. Referring to the 1929 *Literaturnaya gazeta* debate, he explained:

> Many a time has the thesis of the unnecessary nature of satire, of its duplicitous role, and even of its senselessness in our current situation crept into our discussions and into our print media.
>
> This thesis can be summed up as follows: since the beginning of time and throughout the history of literature, satire has always been an accusatory, oppositional genre, aiming to overthrow the political and social establishment. All famous satirists of world literature were opponents of the government and social order of their time. Opposition and hatred of the ruling circles was the main source of inspiration for satirists. It fed their temperament, it stoked the fire of their pens ... But in a Soviet country, in a socialist country where the working class and the Bolshevik party are in power, does it make sense for proletarian writers, for Bolshevik writers to engage with satire?
>
> Whom will they criticize and denounce? Whom will they ridicule? Themselves?

What good can come out of that? It is from this reasoning that comes the assertion that during socialist construction, in the context of the dictatorship of the proletariat, satire is senseless and unnecessary ...

In this country, roots and stubs, leftovers from capitalism were left behind. We must continue to struggle with them, because they endure, whispering their old songs to parts of the working and peasant classes. Even the party is vulnerable to petit bourgeois contamination. It is cleaned up at regular intervals, but each time a small quantity nevertheless remains. And isn't it possible that in ourselves, in those who sincerely consider themselves new people, devout Bolsheviks, the conscious and devoted builders of a classless society – isn't it possible that some old, petit bourgeois poison remains, impossible to burn off with a red-hot iron, that nevertheless needs to be somehow leached out?

Under these conditions to deny the existence and indispensability of Soviet satire would be analogous to negating the need for autocriticism for the dictatorship of the proletariat.[45]

Along with satire, however, other forms of laughter were discussed as part of the emerging canon of socialist realism. In his speech, Koltsov also reflected on the growing importance of humour in the cultural production of the period of the Stalinist Five-Year Plans. "But now, comrades," he said, "since the working class has won, since it feels its strength accruing, the bilious, mournful notes of its laughter are starting to disappear. They are giving way to new notes: notes of strength and power, along with notes of severe anger and superiority over their enemy. Over the past few years we have seen humour blossom alongside satire, often intertwined with it."[46]

Indeed, in the early 1930s humour was becoming omnipresent as a favourite genre in cinema and theatre. Sometimes peppered with satire, it could also be entirely joyful and optimistic. Humour also gradually made it into the pages of the satirical journal *Krokodil*, which it nevertheless continued to share with its more biting counterpart. But, as Lunacharsky had pointed out on numerous occasions, including in his "What Is Humour?," satire and humour are fundamentally different rhetorical genres; their objectives diverge greatly.[47] Satire denounces, shames, or carries out symbolic destruction; humour on the contrary attempts to make light of a difficult or embarrassing situation. In the Soviet context, it could also serve to attenuate the disorienting (and for some distressing) effect of rapid social and technological changes, as well as the widening gap between party rhetoric and empirical reality.

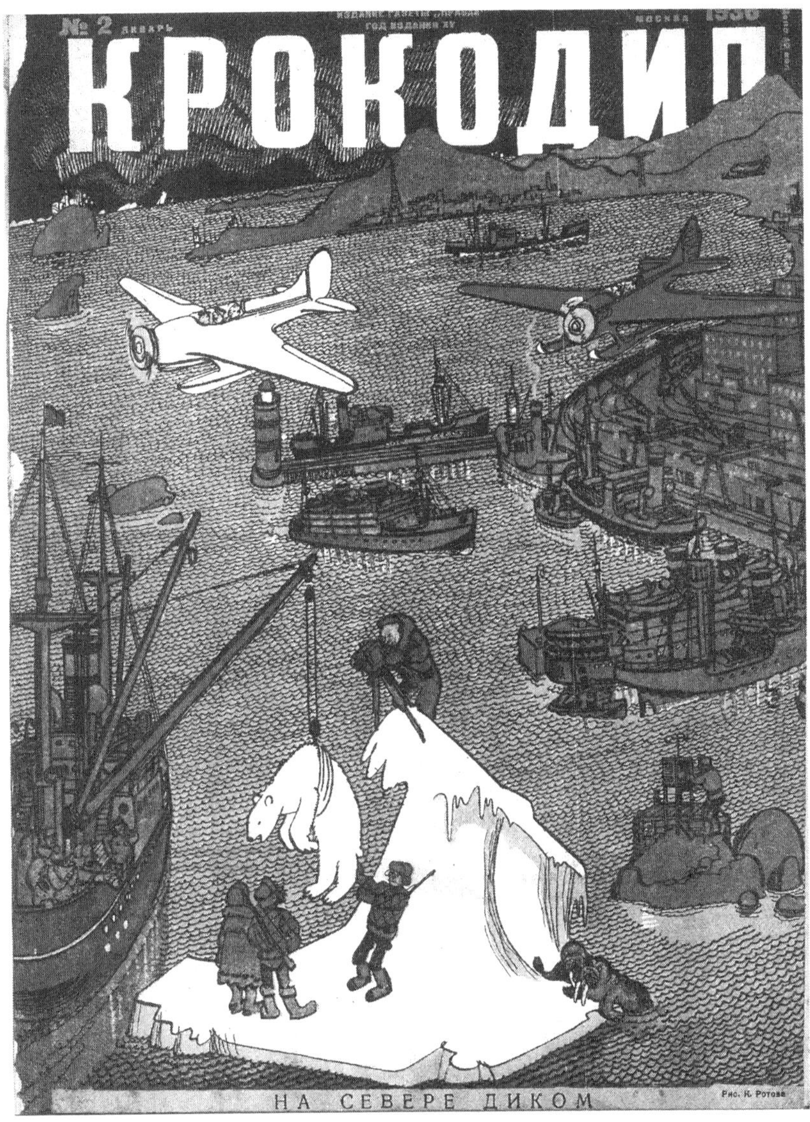

6.3 "In the Northern Wilderness," *Krokodil*, no. 2 (1936), cover. The humoristic image refers to the Arctic exploration program organized by Glavsevmorput (1932–36), the "Commissariat of Ice," and the fascination as well as the fears it generated in popular imagination. Part of the David King Collection. Presented to Tate Archive by David King 2016.

Conclusion: Rhetorics and Temporality

In the fifteen years that followed the October Revolution, satirical practices in the arts established themselves as valued implements of battle against the enemies of the regime, whether external or internal to its geographical borders. But as the Soviet Union gradually took shape and political discourse evolved through a succession of important metanarrative shifts, in particular with the rise of Stalinism in the late 1920s, the critical genre came under attack.

Aside from the arguments given above in the *Literaturnaya gazeta* debate, other reasons for the anxiety that satirical representations caused among certain groups can be gleaned. As the regime shifted from a revolutionary one under Lenin's governance to a conservative one under Stalin, the main purpose of arts and propaganda also changed: from a constant attack against the previous order to the consolidation of recent accomplishments. State-sponsored satire then had to adjust its targets, and satirists increasingly took risks when gauging the boundaries of what could be ridiculed and what could not. Indeed, especially in the context of the purges, laughing at the expense of the wrong scapegoat could be a perilous affair, and equally so refraining from mocking the right one. Furthermore, the transtextual nature of satirical devices such as irony and parody and their semantic instability made some creators and members of the public nervous. Satirical representations, it was understood, could speak on a different level to those "in the know." They therefore had the power to exclude from communal laughter and a sense of belonging or membership in Soviet society those who did not possess the cultural codes or the political savvy to understand the charge. Worse – the failure to understand satire could expose them as philistines or enemies of the regime.

In spite of these fears and the heated debates of the late 1920s and early 1930s, satire nevertheless continued to be produced in artistic circles, as an established form that could coexist with other strategies under the broad umbrella term of socialist realism. In fact, several artists, such as Sergei Eisenstein, Aleksandr Rodchenko, Aleksandr Deineka, Yurii Pimenov, and the trio Kukryniksy worked simultaneously in satirical and what could be called "earnest" genres, depending on the aims of the artworks they were producing. While optimistic trends were certainly more prominent than satire and occupied centre stage in critical writing and scholarship on the arts, satire continued to be present until the collapse of the Soviet Union in 1991, as a necessary supplement.

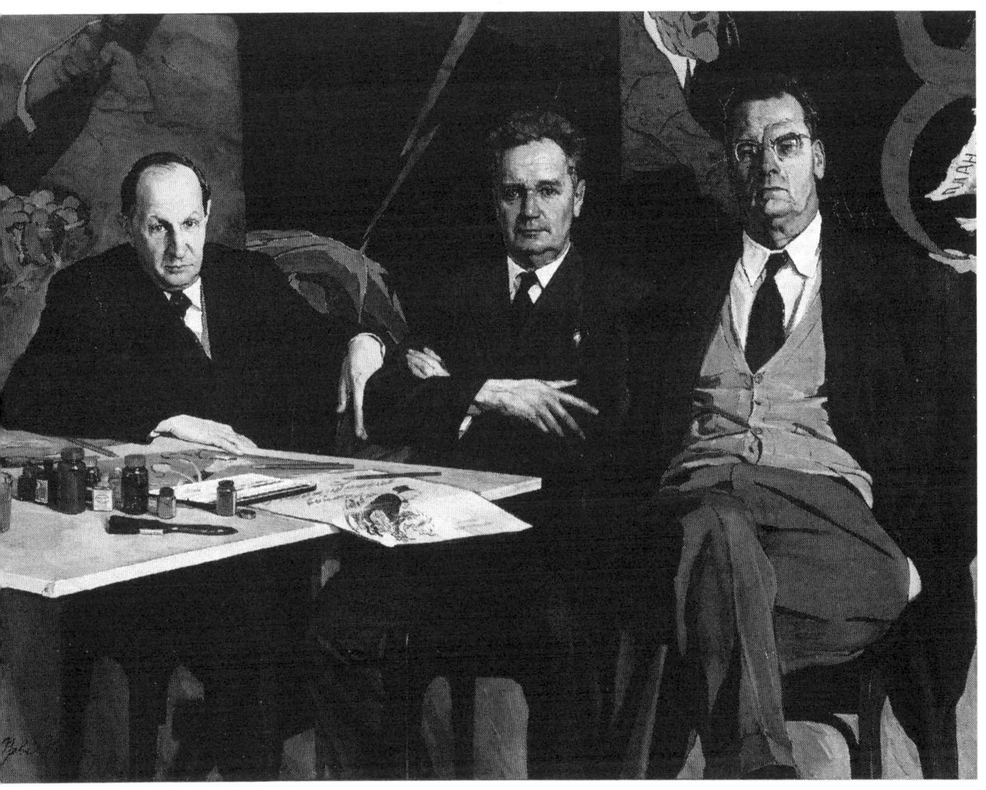

6.4 Pavel Korin, *Portrait of the Kukryniksy*, 1957. The trio, made up of Mikhail
Kuprianov, Porfiri Krylov, and Nikolai Sokolov, formed in 1924. They
regularly contributed graphic satire to the journal *Krokodil* and established
the TASS windows during the Second World War. They concurrently
produced a number of socialist realist paintings on historical themes.
The State Tretyakov Gallery.

Optimistic trends *needed* satire as a companion, to deal with the rhet-
oric/reality gap. Indeed, avant-garde movements of the 1910s–1920s
were profoundly positive and utopian. The futurists, suprematists,
constructivists, and productivists all created fantasies of worlds to
come and the non-objective shapes that could either populate these
or allow their publics to imagine the new. Optimistic realist currents
that emerged in the 1920s were also, in a sense, future oriented.[48] They

aimed at projecting into the present the fiction of achieved socialism, relieved from remnants of the past. Neither the avant-garde nor optimistic realist trends were equipped, however, with rhetorical tools that could serve to address present concerns. This is precisely why satirical practices remained necessary. Through the strategies of caricature, collage, parody, and irony, they afforded artists the means to examine critically subjects and ways of being in the contemporary world, or vestiges of the past that survived therein. In this sense, the key to understanding the enduring need for Soviet satire, whether it be in the context of the avant-garde or of socialist realism, is rooted in questions of rhetorics and temporality.

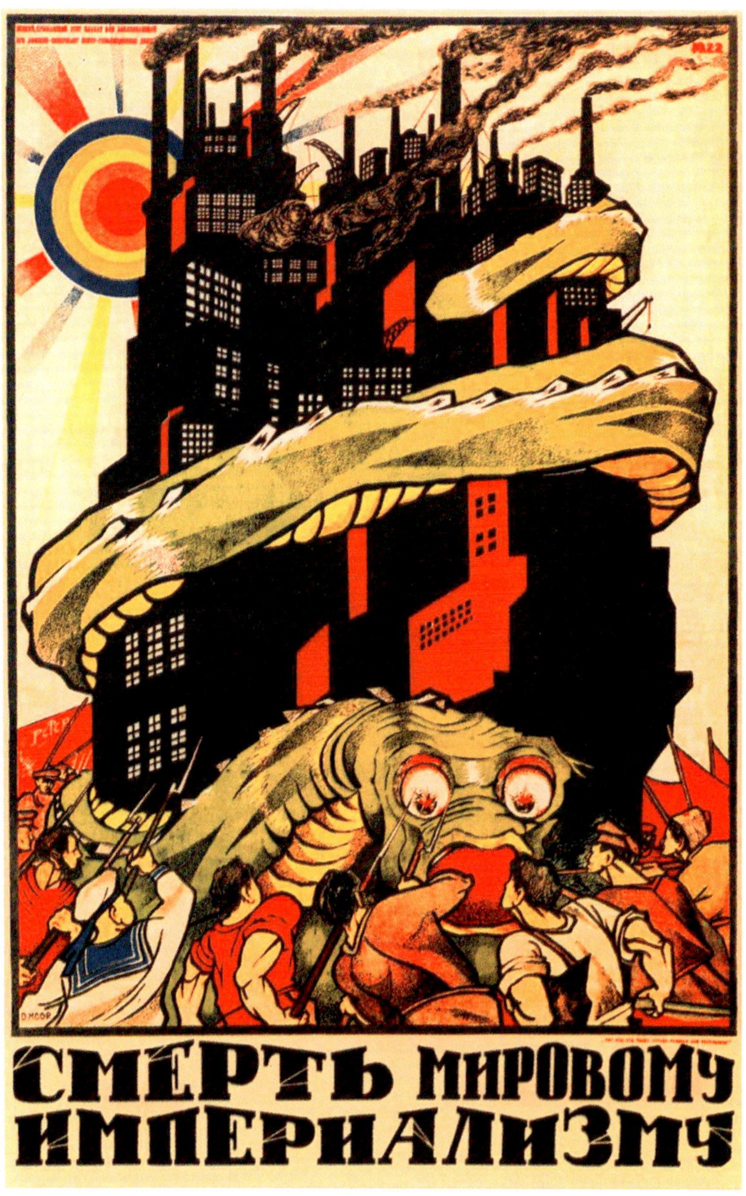

Plate 1 "Death to World Imperialism," poster by Dmitrii Moor, 1919. Part of the David King Collection. Presented to Tate Archive by David King 2016.

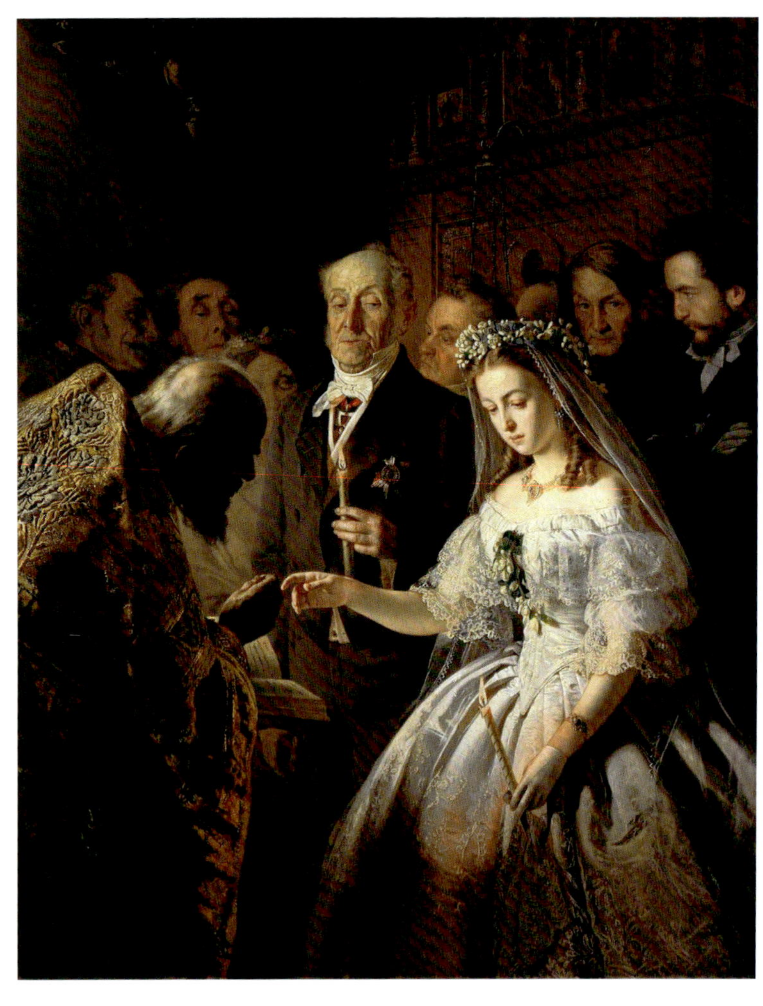

Plate 2 Vasily Pukirev, *The Unequal Marriage*, 1862.
The State Tretyakov Gallery.

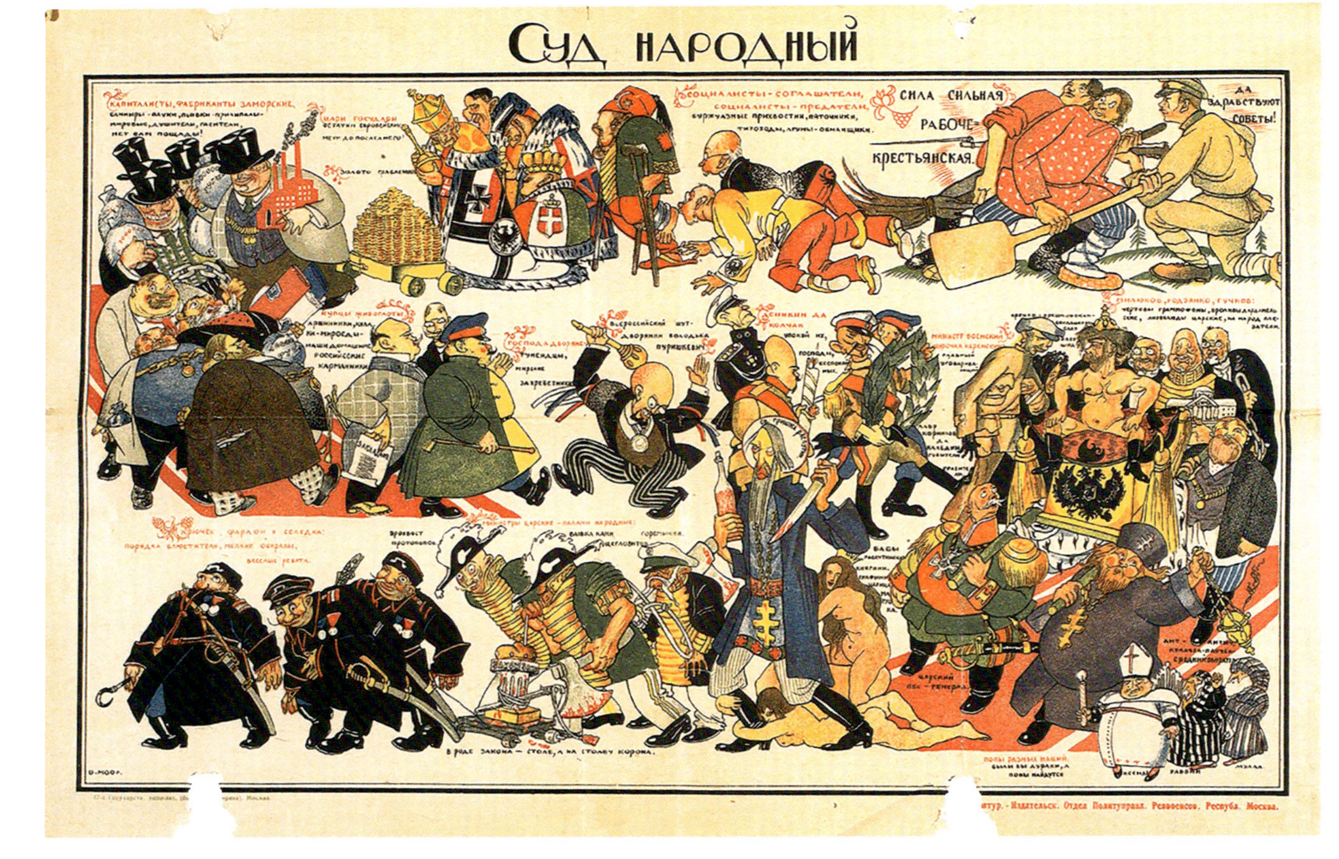

Plate 3 Dmitrii Moor, *The People's Court*, 1919. A soldier, an industrial worker, and a peasant team up to sweep away past and present foes. Collection of Annie Gérin.

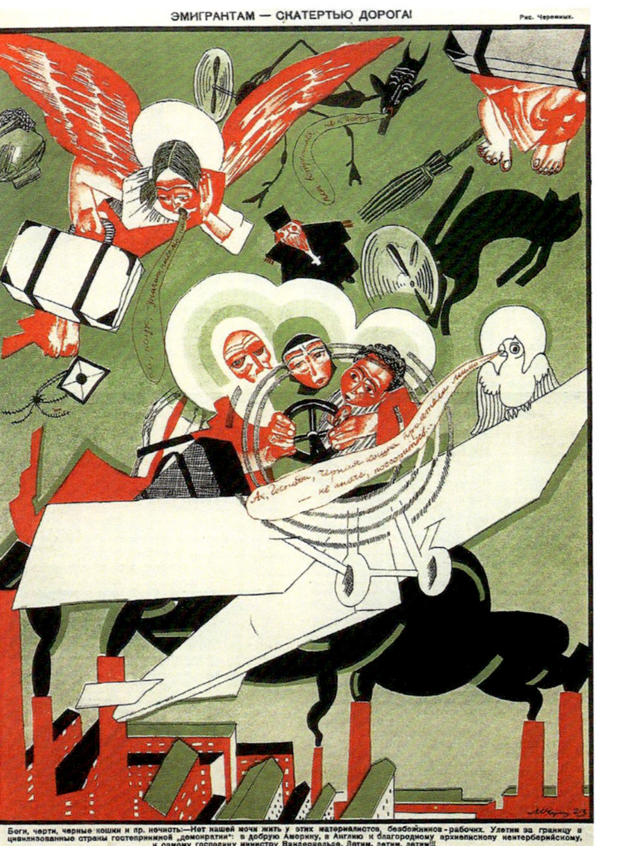

Plate 4 Back cover of the journal *Bezbozhnik u stanka*, no. 5 (1923), "Emigrants – good riddance!" Part of the David King Collection. Presented to Tate Archive by David King 2016

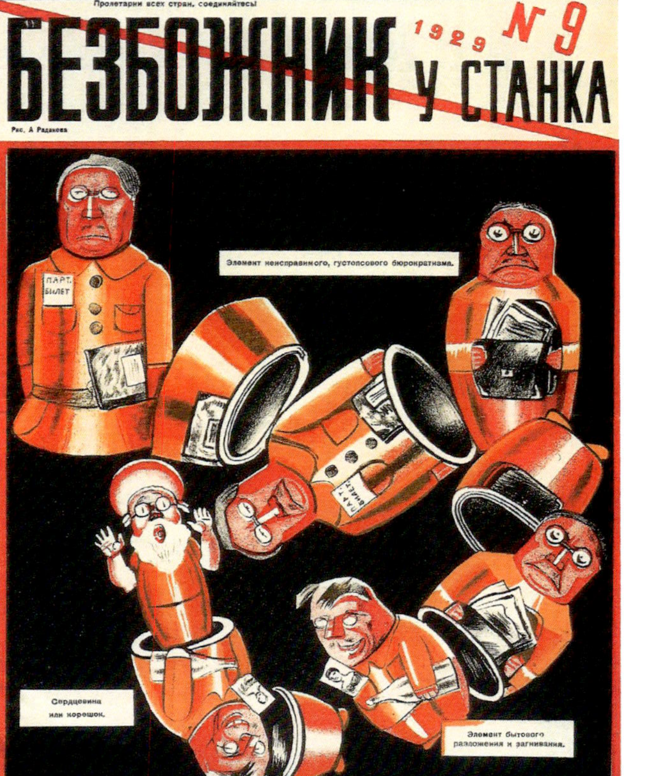

Plate 5 *Bezbozhnik u stanka*, no. 9 (1929), cover, "This is what is at the core of the Party's inbred bureaucracy, moral corruption and decay." Part of the David King Collection. Presented to Tate Archive by David King 2016

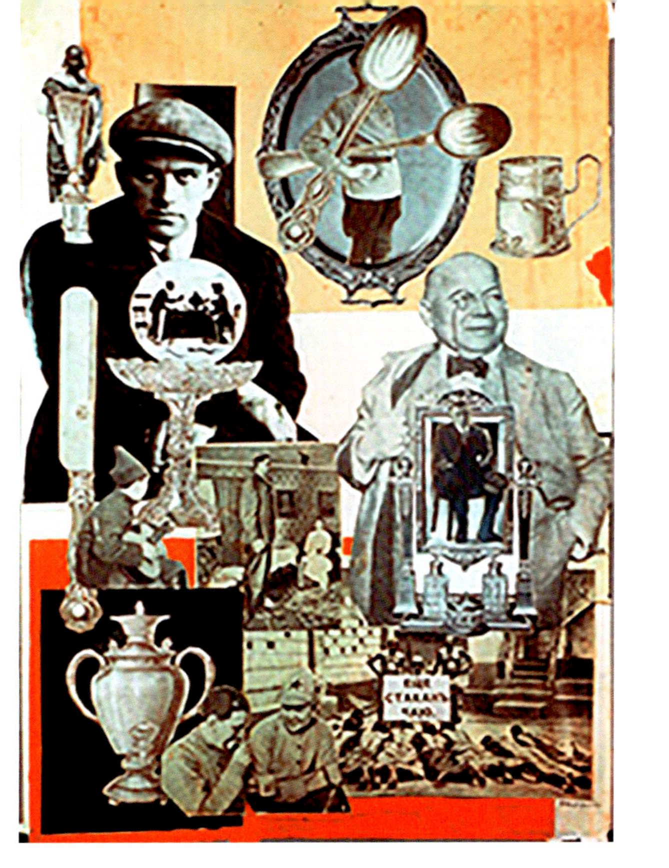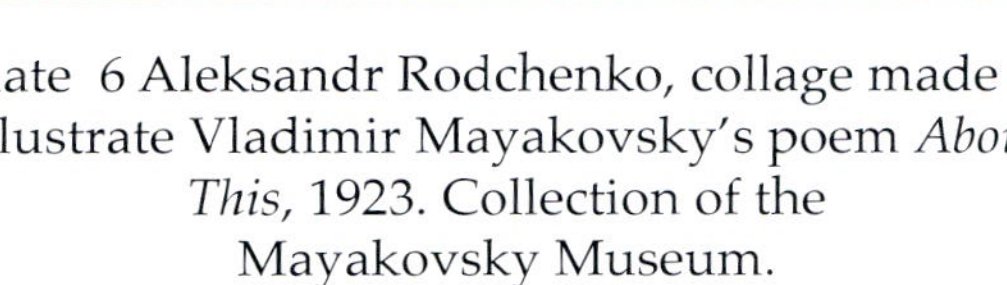

Plate 6 Aleksandr Rodchenko, collage made to illustrate Vladimir Mayakovsky's poem *About This*, 1923. Collection of the Mayakovsky Museum.

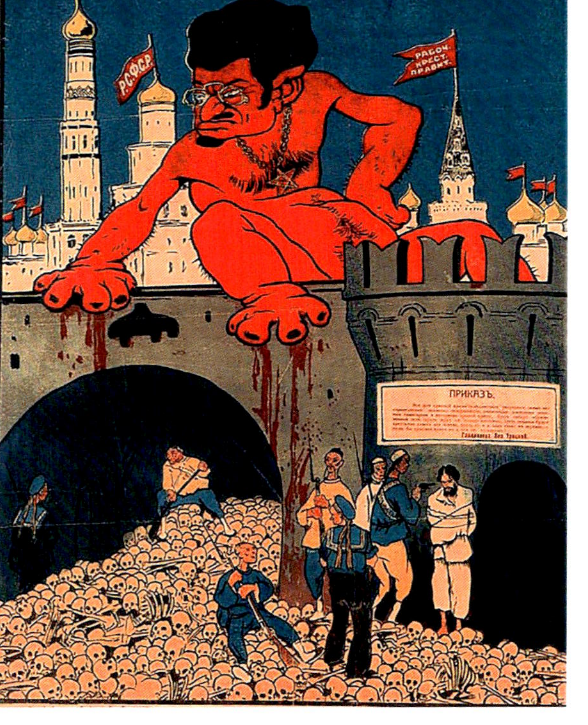

Plate 7 "Peace and Liberty in Sovdepiya," circa 1919. White Army propaganda poster. "Sovdepiya" is the derisive name anti-Bolsheviks coined for the nascent regime ruled by soviets and deputies. Part of the David King Collection. Presented to Tate Archive by David King 2016.

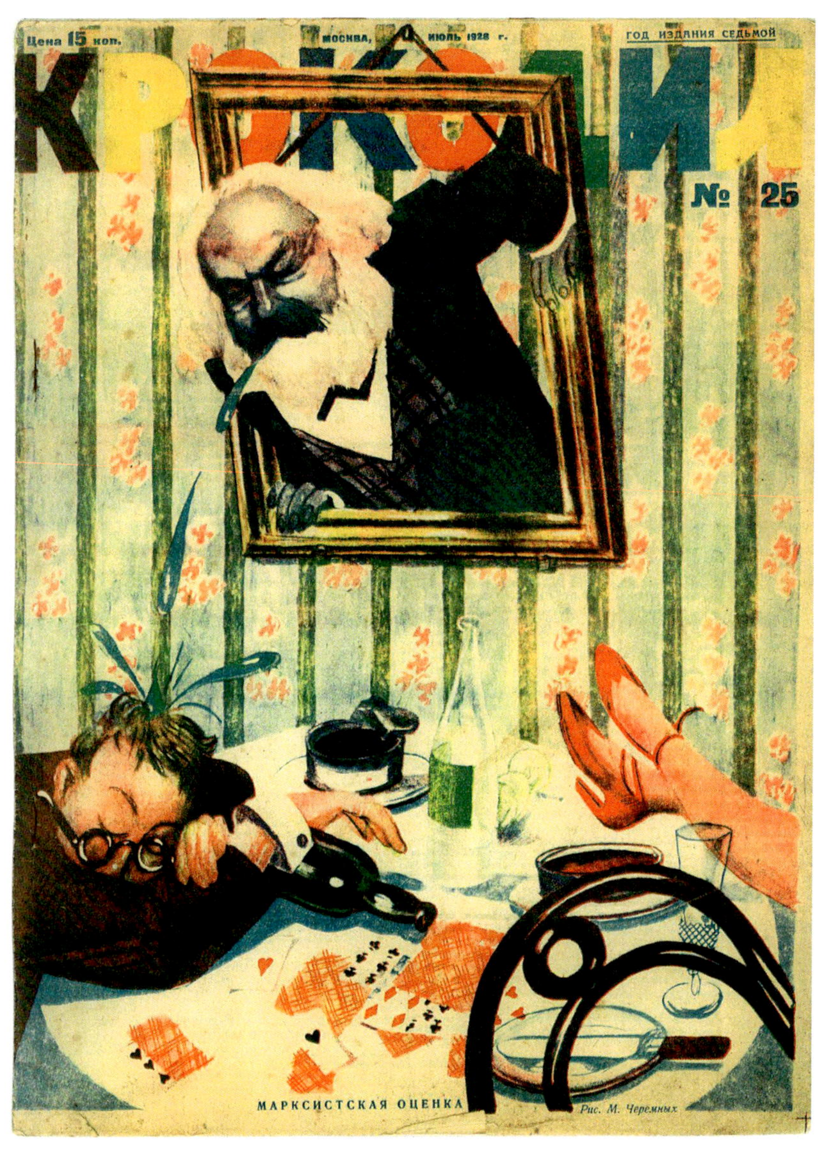

Plate 8 "Marxist Evaluation," *Krokodil*, no. 5 (1928), cover. Part of the David King Collection. Presented to Tate Archive by David King 2016.

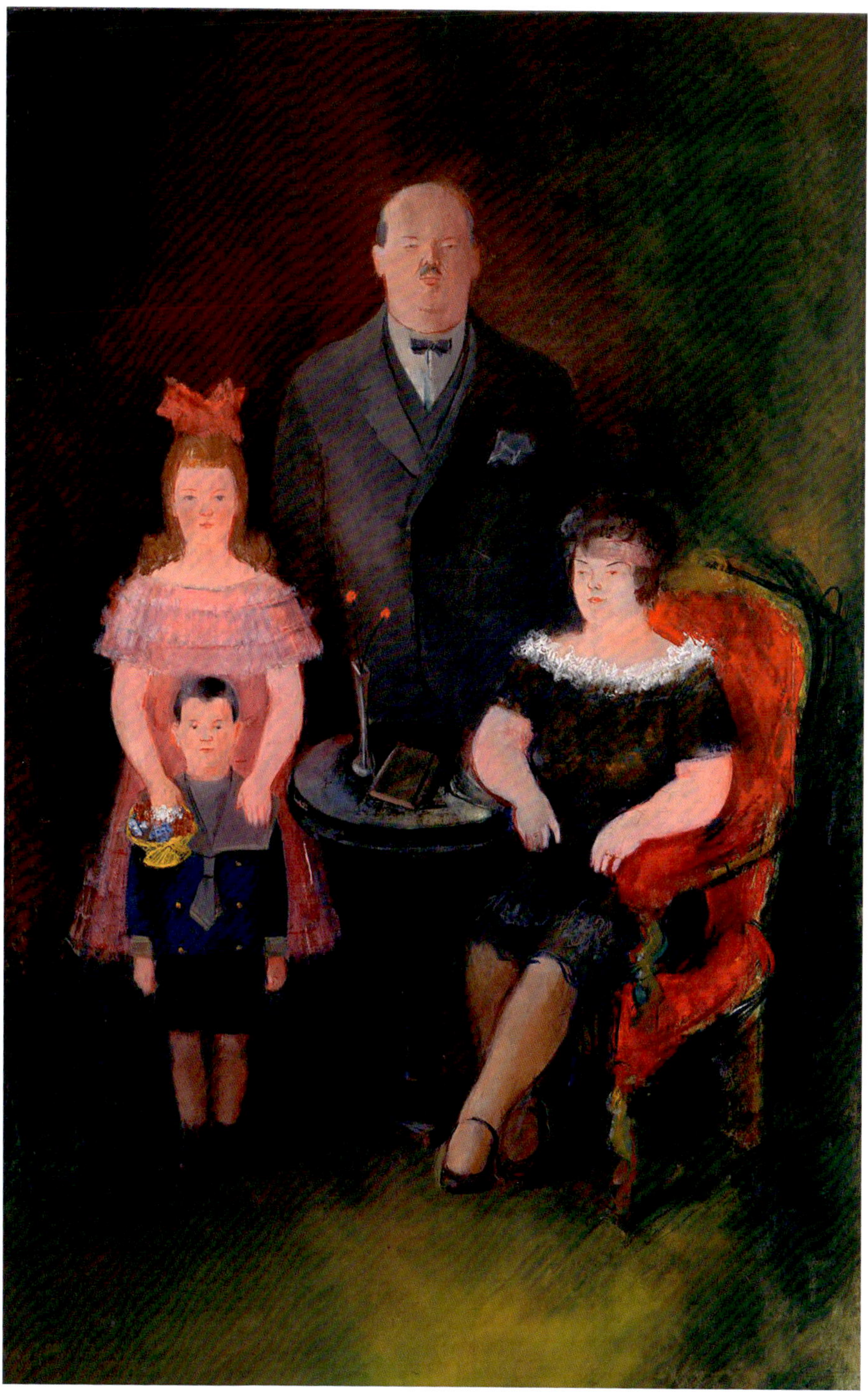

Plate 9 Nikolai Denisovsky, *Petit Bourgeois Portrait*, 1928. Denisovsky was a member of the Society of Easel Painters (OST). During the NEP period, he produced a series of paintings mocking NEPmen and their petit bourgeois values. The State Tretyakov Gallery.

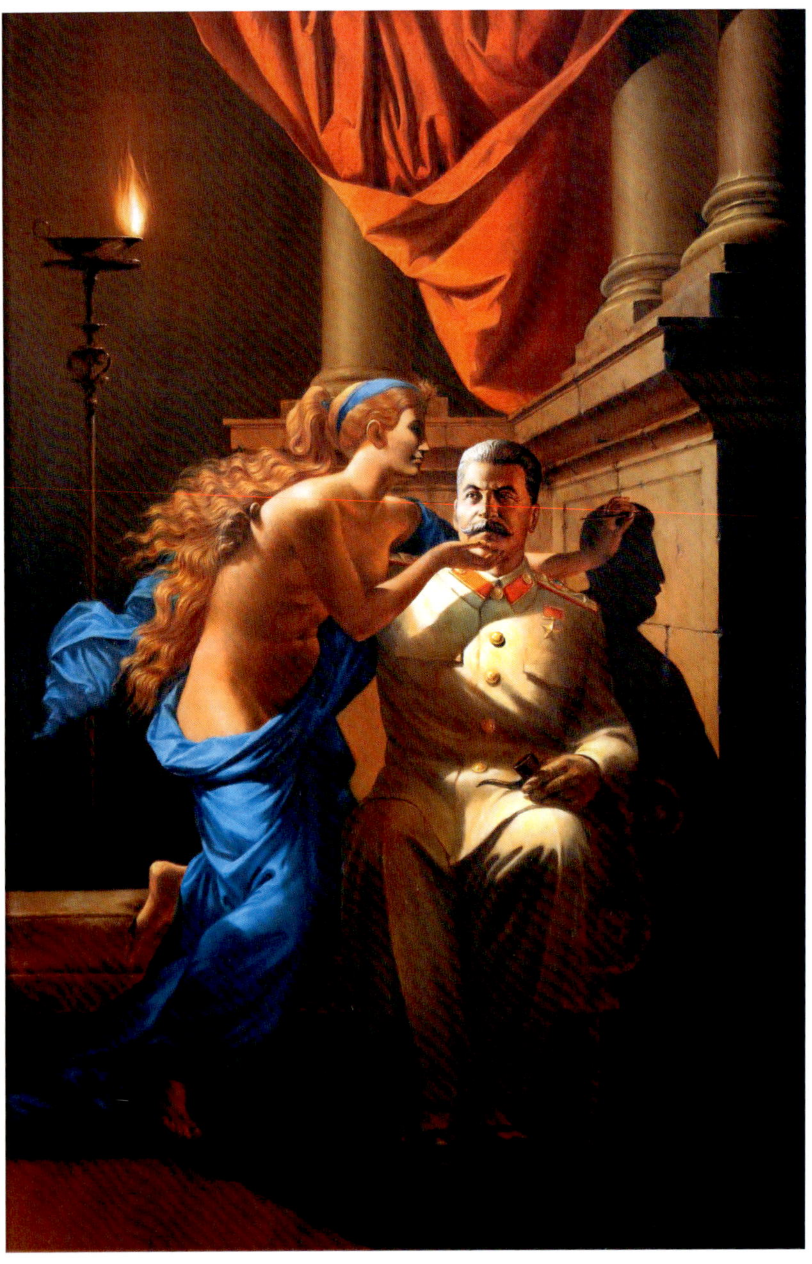

Plate 10 Vitaly Komar and Alexander Melamid, *The Origins of Socialist Realism*, from the series *Nostalgic Socialist Realism*, 1982–1983. Tempera and oil on canvas 183.5 × 122 cm (72 1/4 × 48 1/16 in.) Collection Zimmerli Art Museum at Rutgers University, Norton and Nancy Dodge Collection of Nonconformist Art from the Soviet Union. 2001.0415/17463. Photo by Peter Jacobs.

Conclusion

The opposition between mockery and seriousness is crucial to the understanding of the social function of laughter.

A.V. Lunacharsky[1]

Laughter's greatest power is its ability to create critical distance between the subject and the object of mirth. For theorists such as Lunacharsky, Bergson, Freud, Lipps, Spencer, and others, this detachment is necessary if the affect immediately caused by a perceived incongruity or threat is to evolve into a laughter response, affording emotional release or a sudden feeling of superiority over the mocked target. It is also through this separation between subject and object that laughter can be articulated in relation to seriousness. This is where it becomes more than amusement or a laughter-reflex, but a rhetorical tool.

Depending on the objectives of those who generate it, laughter takes on different shades. It can be temperate and generous, bridging the gap between apparently irreconcilable realities; it can provide respite or escape from a tense situation; it can also be incendiary, filled with scorn and venom, chastising or discrediting its target, vilified through satirical impulse. All depends on who laughs at whom, and why.

This is where the uniqueness of the body of satirical works explored in this book stands out. As Lunacharsky has observed in a number of essays dedicated to world satire, throughout history satirists have almost always stood in opposition to power and official discourse. But in the early Soviet context, members of Moscow's satirical scene worked hand in hand with the regime (many even integrated within the Narkompros workforce) and produced satire that complemented and supported serious or optimistic discourse. By addressing a laughter-inducing critique of practices past and present that were incompatible with the emerging Soviet world view, they created the distance necessary for autocriticism and allowed the future-oriented avant-garde and socialist realism to fully develop their utopian visions. They also afforded a means to bridge the growing gap between rhetoric and reality, especially as empirical reality increasingly – and visibly – started to lag behind political discourse by the late 1920s. In other words, in early Soviet Russia, along with optimistic art forms, destructive laughter became part of a singular dialectical movement fueling praxis.

Two issues remain to be briefly addressed. The first concerns the quasi-absence of satire in disciplinary histories of art, cinema, and theatre. The second has to do with the role of laughter in late Soviet and post-Soviet art.

On Satire and Modernism

The type of satirical laughter described in this book was born of the Enlightenment. It was introduced into Russia mainly by Catherine the Great and her entourage, and provided a break with the carnivalesque laughter that had periodically punctuated the medieval world, providing communal reprieve from its harshness and austerity. Although satirical forms have always been seen as peripheral to histories of art and visual culture, they should nevertheless be considered an intrinsic part of the modernist project. Indeed, the essence of modernism is a self-conscious break with the past, in a movement characterized by self-questioning, critical thinking, and suspicion with regard to established values as well as continuities fashioned by tradition.

In the visual arts, modernism is generally understood according to two main conceptual frameworks. The first is organized as a progression of self-critical gestures that draws art away from popular culture and traditions of representation towards overwhelmingly formalist concerns – eventually reaching abstraction. American critic Clement Greenberg described the modernist impulse as "the use of characteristic methods of a discipline to criticize the discipline itself, not in order to subvert it but in order to entrench it more firmly in its area of competence."[2] According to this teleological formula, the Russian avant-garde produced some of the most progressive artworks of the early part of the twentieth century, bringing art to its "degree zero," to borrow Malevich's 1915 description of suprematism.[3] Monochrome paintings, non-objective constructions, sound art eschewing harmony, films without scripts, and performances from which naturalistic artifice has been banished and the actor's body becomes the main vector for affect all follow this formalist logic.

An alternative interpretation of artistic modernism endows art with agency; it recognizes its wilful participation in social processes. This conception encompasses critical forms of realism, futurist and Dadaist iconoclasm, and rejections of tradition and bourgeois values, as well as utopian design and architecture projects that aim straightforwardly at changing the world. In the Soviet context, several artists abandoned traditional media in the 1920s and shifted their practice to productivism, a radical offshoot of constructivism. They created textiles and clothing prototypes optimized for industrial labour, they designed workers' clubs and elaborate theatre sets, and they produced propaganda films, posters, advertisements, and magazine layouts. The utopian impulse of the Russian avant-garde, which attempted to shape the environment to afford new, revolutionary ways of being in the world, was often articulated with formal innovations. But not always.

In his provocative essay *The Total Art of Stalinism*, Boris Groys argues that socialist realism completed and even radicalized the project of the Russian avant-garde. Through the repetition of normalized subject matter and conventions it gradually discredited representation itself. Furthermore, socialist realism managed to collapse into one another artistic creation and the Soviet political project; art became synonymous with propaganda, and the emerging socialist world was constructed as a complex *Gesamtkunstwerk* under the watchful eye of Stalin, the great creator. As Groys puts it, "The Stalin era satisfied the fundamental avant-garde demand that art cease representing life and begin transforming it by means of a total aesthetic-political project."[4]

Groys' point of view challenges mainstream understandings of modernist artistic production that have condemned socialist realism, whether in the visual arts, theatre, or film, as a retreat from the avant-garde or an aberration in the teleological history of art. His view is particularly compelling in that it allows for a focus on socialist realism's social-optimistic function in the Soviet context, and manages to entirely avoid the conception of modernism as a series of recognizable movements and styles.

Modernist art historiography has similarly shown little interest in Soviet satirical practices, precisely because of their obstinate reliance on figuration and overtly didactic strategies, as well as their instrumentalization by the Soviet state. Indeed, if modernist art can be understood as participating in crafting the modern world, its relationship with political regimes is paradoxically almost always disavowed.

In his *Introduction to Modernity*, Henry Lefebvre defines the mechanisms of critical laughter as a "truer way of thinking than modernism's enthusiastic (triumphant and triumphalist) consciousness."[5] Satirical practices should then be construed as iconoclastic in spirit, and akin to futurist and Dadaist sensibilities. The numerous manifestos produced by Russian futurists display their suspicion with regard to established values, artistic traditions, and the apparent continuities of historical time. Plays such as *Victory over the Sun* make ample usage of satirical devices to discredit the past and wreak havoc on reason and bourgeois taste. The same can be said of avant-garde collages that fracture accepted worldviews, parodies that subvert the meaning of traditional forms such as *lubki* and icons, and caricatures that shock viewers into seeing past the world of appearances. Russian futurism was profoundly satirical, and early Soviet satire made full use of its avant-garde techniques of collage, distortion, parody, and irony. This dynamic back and forth between modernist and satirical practices should in no way surprise, since producers of satirical works often *were* avant-garde poets, painters, cinematographers, and playwrights. For them, destruction and utopianism were part of a single aesthetic-political project.

Soviet satire is hence not anomalous to the period that brought it forth. It embodies in its own way the critical spirit of modernism, which revealed itself in Russia according to a series of conditions that were ushered in by the Revolution. These include, of course, state support of modernist trends and the participation of artists in the political process through propaganda work, but also a dynamic artistic scene centred in Moscow that permitted collaboration and the immediate circulation of iconography and strategies across traditional disciplinary boundaries, here rendered extremely porous.

On Post-Utopian Soviet and Post-Soviet Laughter

Soviet satire survived the Stalinist period. Although history was to prove him wrong about an ultimate world revolution, *Krokodil* editor-in-Chief Mikhail Koltsov announced in 1934 that laughter was part of the socialist project's destiny in Russia and around the world: "The working class is already laughing in our country, and it will soon laugh all over the world ... In the history of class struggle, the working class will have the last laugh."[6] But from the late 1930s on, satire was never again as prominent as it had been in the first fifteen years of the Soviet regime. It was revived periodically when it was needed as a rhetorical weapon, during periods of world conflict or internal crises; but it no longer garnered much critical attention or became, as it had been in the late 1920s, the topic of heated debates. Soviet satire simply had its place as part of a complex propaganda arsenal, alongside socialist realism, optimistic comedies, and a few other genres.

In parallel (and particularly after the death of Stalin in 1953), unofficial types of laughter started to thrive. *Anekdoty,*[7] for example, gained unprecedented importance as part of collective ritual in the 1960s and 1970s. "In those years," Alexei Yurchak recounts, "it was almost impossible to go through a single day without hearing and telling *anekdoty.*"[8] At the same time, laughter invaded the production of a number of unofficial artists, who in the initial days showed their works only to restricted groups of friends behind the closed doors of private apartments. Their efforts ranged from Oskar Rabin's social grotesque that borders on the aestheticization of misery, to Ilya Kabakov's ironic installations narrating the lives of assorted dwellers of overcrowded communal apartments, to Sots Art, a movement exemplified by works of the duo Vitalii Komar and Alexandr Melamid, Eric Bulatov, Leonid Sokov, and Aleksandr Kosolapov.

Sots Art appeared on the international art scene in February 1976. After two years of negotiations that led to a series of artworks being sent clandestinely across borders, the first exhibition of Soviet unofficial art to take place in the West opened its doors at the Ronald Feldman Gallery in New York. The works Komar and Melamid presented played on the concepts of socialist realism and pop art, a movement that at once exalted and critiqued consumer culture by representing banal retail products, using the techniques of advertising and mass culture. Sots Art's originality rested on a witty feature. While in Europe and North America the art scene could afford to be critical of over-production and over-consumption, Soviet artists were confronted with very different circumstances. In the 1970s, under Brezhnev, queues for food and other necessities were the norm in cities across the USSR. What the Soviet Union over-produced was not consumer goods, but ideology (Plate 10).

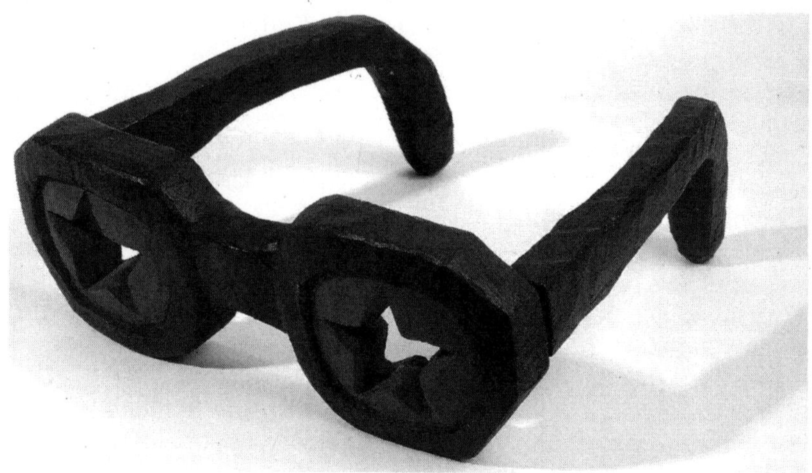

7.1 Leonid Sokov, *Project to Construct Glasses for Every Soviet Citizen*, 1976.
Painted wood 11.3 × 33.3 × 31 cm (4 7/16 × 13 1/8 × 12 3/16 in.). Collection
Zimmerli Art Museum at Rutgers University, Norton and Nancy Dodge
Collection of Nonconformist Art from the Soviet Union (1991.0873/07809).
Photo by Jack Abraham.

With the collapse of the Soviet Union in 1991, Russian art took a
nostalgic turn. Timur Novikov, for example, in a series titled *Lost Ideals of a Happy Childhood* (2000), presented large red velvet banners that
served as frames for retouched photographs documenting sculptures
of pioneers; Aleksei Morosov's work mimicked playfully socialist realist portraiture in *Young Woman Wearing a Tank Helmet* (2004); with
Kitchen Suprematism, the Blue Nose Group recovered the avant-garde
formal vocabulary, transposing it in black bread, cheese, and salami;
and Yevgeniy Fiks brought out astonishing historical ironies in *A Gift
to Birobidzhan* (2009), a work that draws its inspiration from the history
of the Jewish autonomous region established in the late 1920s on the
Trans-Siberian railway in the Far East near the Chinese border, and in
The Lenin Museum (2014), a large-scale installation that proposes that,
between the 1940s and 1980s, the public toilets in the basement of the
Central V.I. Lenin Museum in Moscow were covertly used for anonymous gay sex.

These post-utopian works, to borrow Boris Groys' term,[9] evoke ironic, humorous, or nostalgic laughter as a means to question and understand the optimistic codes that have shaped the consciousness of those Alexei Yurchak has called "the last Soviet generation." They further serve to make sense of a world that transformed rapidly and irremediably. Indeed, as Yurchak explains, "although the system's collapse had been unimaginable before it began, it appeared unsurprising when it happened."[10] The works hence help one to reflect on, and provide a historical "shape" to, the very unique phenomenon that constituted the USSR and its collapse. And they tend to do so while displaying a generosity unfathomable in the years that immediately followed the October Revolution, when satire was used to urgently discredit and destroy pre-revolutionary practices and worldviews.

This generous approach that makes ample room for historical ironies has provided a template of sorts for this book. It has allowed me to address in one fell swoop the shaping and reshaping of the Soviet world through often contradictory representations, without shying away from acknowledging mistakes, hesitations, and changes of heart on the part of this book's protagonists. It has also afforded a means to understand the interrelatedness of optimism, devastation, and laughter as they unfolded in art practices as well as in the empirical world. Finally, it has motivated me to steer clear of Cold War assumptions and moralizing impulses that have glorified certain modernist artistic practices to the detriment of others.

As I was writing this book, bluntly satirical works – which had been conspicuously absent in late Soviet and post-Soviet art – suddenly reappeared. The most publicized one was a performance by the punk-feminist collective Pussy Riot that took place in late February 2012, a few days before the March 4th Russian presidential election. A handful of anonymous performers clad in colourful hand-knitted balaclavas invaded Moscow's Christ the Saviour Cathedral, the seat of the Russian orthodox patriarchate. In a surprising collage of prayers and mock chants they belted out in a ferociously ironic tone, they appealed to the Virgin Mary to remove Vladimir Putin from the presidential race.[11] Less than two weeks later, on 3 March, two women from the group were arrested in conformity with article 213 of the Russian criminal code. A third was apprehended on 16

March. Convicted of "hooliganism motivated by religious hatred," each spent up to twenty-one months in Russian penal colonies. This sad conclusion recalls the 1934 arrest and exile of Osip Mandelstam, who was condemned for composing an epigram that poked fun at Stalin. Satire is evidently still considered a redoubtable weapon by today's Russian leaders.

Appendix

The following speech was given by Anatoly Lunacharsky on 30 January 1931 during the inaugural meeting of the Commission for the Study of Satirical Genres at the Academy of Sciences of the USSR in Moscow. It was published for the first time in April 1935 in the journal *Literaturnyi kritik*. This translation is based on the 1967 reprint of this text, in Lunacharsky's collected works.[1]

On Laughter

Comrades, when I suggested that the Academy of Sciences organize a commission for the study of satirical genres, I was first and foremost guided by considerations that have to do with the rapid development of research on the history of literature conducted according to a Marxist method, that is to say dialectical materialism. While pondering on what area of literature would allow trying out this method with greatest ease, and yield prompt results – so that Marxist research in all areas of literature can use this experience as a basis – I reached the conclusion that satire is the type of literature that should be first considered.

What do we mean by Marxist research?

Before all else, we consider each literary phenomenon we study as performing a social function. We search for concrete historical manifestations of class relations, as reflected in a given literary form or a given literary work. We confer great value on this genetic point of view, but it does not, however, prevent us from looking for the actual meaning of a literary work. We believe that in many cases literary works are quite intentionally written by their author to make a certain impression on their world, the social class they belong to, other classes, their targeted publics, as well as the more casual publics they might reach. Whether or not it is possible to prove that the author of a literary work had any outright intention to propagate certain views, we have to consider that such intent may be unconscious, but it is nevertheless undoubtedly present.

The aspiration of certain critics to direct the attention of our contemporaries towards an absolutely "pure" work of art (one that would maintain maximal distance from social issues) is a long-standing trend that values above all else the "extra-social." But in essence, even such a work of art fulfils a social function and, furthermore, it reflects class consciousness, which stems from its social situation at a given time.

In instances when a work of art undertakes outwardly and formally to produce the laughable – *das Lächerliche* (it is the widest term available to designate our field of inquiry), then, more than ever, the particular features of social trends become evident. It is true, we could single out grotesque-comical phenomena that seemingly pursue no other goal than entertainment. But the aspiration to "simply make people laugh," regardless of any social tendencies, is already in itself a social tendency. There is much discussion about artistic periods when laughter had no other purpose than to entertain, but these can and should be explained by Marxist literary history.

The class consciousness of an individual writer or of the masses that create this or that satirical object is always fairly clear; it is much easier in satire to distinguish the threads of social fabric that construct it, than in sentimental or highly emotional lyric poetry, or in an apparently objective epic work.

Very often, guided by certain characteristics of satire, we can learn how to distinguish the specific social tendency that informs works produced in analogous genres.

What immediate theoretical problems does our commission face, and which concrete historical questions have moved to the foreground?

Obviously, we absolutely cannot avoid considering the general question of what laughter is.

As is well known, laughter is innate only to humans. There have been attempts to observe in pets something resembling a smile – Turgenev, in particular, made such attempts – but the word "smile" can only be used here in its allegorical sense. This fact in itself tells us that laughter is not simply a biological phenomenon, accompanied by a particular irritation of the nervous system, rapid exhalation, etc.; laughter supposes, obviously, some other cause, and can only occur at a very high level of development.

I will not attempt to put forward a single theory of laughter, mine or anybody else's. I will only say that, in my opinion, at the present there is no absolutely satisfactory account. The most interesting theory is Herbert Spencer's, which has been widely accepted as a basis for physiological and psychophysiological research.

However, even the most rigorous psychophysiological analysis, establishing under what circumstances laughter occurs and what it means in biological terms, cannot resolve the problem of the social and historical character of laughter (even if psychobiological analysis can shed light on this problem).

That is why I proposed to organize a commission for the study not of laughter and the laughable in general, but namely of satirical genres in art; where the social character and value of this phenomenon is clearest.

Laughter is a tool, I would even dare to say a critical tool, which can either serve the objectives of auto-discipline for a social class; or alternatively, that can allow this class to exert pressure on other classes.

With the exception, of course, of direct confrontations in the guise of national wars or class struggles, expressed through civil war or other organized forms, the core and principal tools used to exert class pressure are religious and state laws, which establish what is allowed by either deities or the state. For a long time, state law was considered given by god; during some periods this assumption weakened to some degree, though bourgeois society never fully emancipated itself from it. When a deviation from the norm occurs – a crime, for example – then the law, which orders social norms, intervenes and casts punishment on the perpetrator, whether it be an individual or a whole social group.

But outside the law, there is another force of social disciplining that punishes violations – this force is public opinion. Public opinion, working outside the legal system, punishes through social means. It does not impose penalties on individuals, groups, or a whole class through courts, executioners, or prison. It nevertheless imposes penalties of a sensitive nature, through different forms of boycott. Among these, laughter plays an enormous role. Yet, even though this phenomenon has been identified as such by researchers, and there are clear instructions on how to use laughter as a weapon in class struggle, laughter has not been thoroughly studied from this point of view. In bourgeois literature, only hints relating to this phenomenon appear here and there (e.g., in Bergson's theory of laughter), but it is never analysed in detail, nor rigorously confirmed. Meanwhile, as we know through ethnographic material dating from the prehistoric period, history has provided us since time immemorial with a multitude of striking monuments dedicated to the social role of laughter.

We have all heard the expression: "People will laugh you down." It means that the behaviour of a given individual merits public condemnation, which is expressed through laughter and sneers.

"Public opinion" is a tool of class struggle. Indeed, the dominating class uses it in order to exert discipline. Other, oppositional classes also aspire to generate forms of public opinion according to their world-view. The need for a class to discipline its own members becomes particularly evident when its discipline has not fully developed or risks collapse. The need for discipline becomes most tangible when a class emerges, when not all its members have achieved class consciousness, and when these members act in ways that reveal their cultural backwardness, manifest their egoism, or betray their pitiful imitation of the ways of the higher classes, against which they must struggle. In order to understand the value of laughter for this class problem, it should be enough to say that in its time, the emerging bourgeoisie had a lot to learn from those who were called "Gentlemen of the King's Bedchamber." In fact, in his plays, Molière has created a magnificent school of self-discipline; one could argue that three quarters of Molière's comedies are meant to teach the bourgeoisie self-knowledge and self-respect.

Look closely at the early period of formation of the bourgeoisie as a class. You will be surprised by that amazing number of great, sometimes brilliant efforts deployed by bourgeois writers in order to force the most backward elements of a class into rank and to call individuals to order, not by legal means but with the help of laughter.

I will point out a few more phenomena, which concern our area of interest and call for attention. Ethnography teaches us that even at a rather primitive cultural stage organized laughter existed, which expressed itself during times of clan or tribal conflict: two tribes would challenge each other to a laughter tournament. This custom of mutual mockery between neighbours endures to this day; this form of laughter exists now in many places. People gather, stand across from each other, sometimes wearing masks. Then in one or another rhythmic fashion, they think up and spew out sarcastic insults, astonishing their opponents. They might say, for example, that there are no beautiful girls in such or such a settlement, that the workers are neither skilful nor strong, etc. The opposing side waits until the explosion of caustic words stops. It is then their turn to engage in battle, using the same weapon.

It is particularly interesting to think of laughter as a way to mark the distance that constitutes the specificity of various neighbourhoods of cities and villages. Legend says that long ago, before any kind of literary comedy was ever produced, peasants gathered with the sole purpose of making fun of townspeople, at their features and manners, which seemed alien and ridiculous to the peasants. But we could say that the city repaid them generously: the country bumpkin, seen as a person to be kept at a certain distance, and in relation to whom one can freely feel superior, is represented in masses in the comic genres. Here, of course, class divisions already establish themselves between "city slickers" and "country bumpkins"; however, this simple categorization is far from accurate, for the population of cities and villages may consist – and consisted during the early development phase of cities – of several classes.

We will examine later various cases of present-day class-based conflicts that express themselves through mockery.

Carnival is a custom that goes back to the depth of history in Babylon and continues today. Carnival played an important role in Roman and Dorian cultures. Magical practices were integrated in its form, as well as transmutations of an even more ancient custom – human sacrifice – a cultural phenomenon of enormous importance. This transformation is not simply a matter of replacing a valuable victim by a less valuable one. Anciently, the victim was chosen by the aristocracy, in carnival it is chosen by the people. Furthermore, carnival provided the ruling classes with a kind of safety valve, since during carnival the oppressed classes were temporarily allowed certain social liberties. In ordinary times the lowest classes could only laugh at the higher ones covertly. But during carnival time, the possibility of unconcealed laughter opened up. On the one hand, for the carnival organizers, this type of laughter allowed the discharge of built-up class discontent. On the other hand, this release was considered frivolous, simply not serious.

The opposition between mockery and seriousness is crucial to the understanding of the social function of laughter.

He who laughs has established his superiority in relation those he subjects to mockery; he attempts to reveal his opponent's weaker traits, and to reveal weakness can be an important manoeuver in social interactions.

I have already said that laughter is opposed to seriousness. In situations when an individual abnormality reaches such an extent that it becomes impossible not to take it seriously, then laughter fades. Let's say you encounter a particularly ugly person. If his physical deformation is serious, then you will experience feelings of compassion, or horror perhaps. It may happen that during the first moments of this encounter the ugliness frightens or startles you. But if at second glance you realize that the abnormality is in fact not so serious, that it is harmless and not of great consequence – then you may burst out laughing; the energy you mobilized to defend yourself against the threat of abnormality is released, as its importance diminishes.

Similarly, in social struggle laughter arises when the enemy is suddenly perceived as insignificant. Laughter inflicts wounding blows to the enemy, causing him to lose confidence in his own strength, and exposing for all to see the powerlessness of the enemy. If you say: "It is useless to argue with you. You'd make chickens laugh," you underline the negligibility of the arguments presented by your enemy. A sharply directed mockery can sometimes bring a bigger victory than a serious debate with your enemy.

Satirical genres vary, and they have different purposes. If you say of something: "This is just funny," it means that it is not necessary to take drastic measures, to struggle against a given social evil, it can be easily neutralized; it is enough to laugh about it. You can evaluate the phenomenon and let it go. There is no need to continue thinking about it. In other cases, a smile can smooth over an irregularity, an unpleasant situation, and resolve it. But sometimes it is impossible to get rid of your troubles so easily. Writers in particular, as spokespeople of a given class or a particular worldview, may find it difficult to ignore their personal feelings and overlook irritants. In such cases the artist resorts to a fairly difficult operation, by way of which he draws out what is ridiculous in a given abnormality. But he goes further than this, he also highlights the traits that cause pity or other strong reactions. In this process, laughter plays a dominant role. Caricature is a very malleable form, it can be soft or rigid; it can include shades of compassion or of indignation. But laughter is always at its core.

When satire is the purpose the author has set for himself, then laughter can be lethal. Sarcasm consists in humiliating the enemy by way of making insignificant what he considers important, what he considers sacred. It turns the positive into a negative.

For laughter to be effective, the laugher himself must first and foremost be convinced of the insignificance of his enemy. Second, laughter should attack the self-esteem of its target. Third, in the eyes of its witnesses, mockery should be convincing; it should attract sympathy for the satirist's attempt to break his enemy.

Satire can be taken to extremely high degrees of malevolence, which makes laughter poisonous, biting. So, while laughter remains laughter, while it testifies to how you consider yourself pounding and defeating your enemy, your laughter also proves that you consider the evil that you mock so deep and harmful that you cannot hide your irritation and animosity. This sarcastic laughter is particularly powerful when it attacks the principles your enemy holds dearest, from which he draws his authority. When such a Voltairian type of laughter is directed towards something that was praised to the skies, the effect of laughter is so strong that no other polemical weapon can compare to it. This sarcastic laughter not only negates the beliefs of the enemy, but it also weakens the authority of what he considered sacred; and this is something that can only be achieved with scornful laughter. When it acquires a contemptuous purpose, laughter becomes like a steel weapon, inflicting particularly deep and incurable wounds.

Let's imagine the following situation. The intelligentsia of an emerging class has been, for a long time, recognizing the internal emptiness, the absurdity and the cultural dysfunctionality of the ruling class. It considers its claims for ruling over society fundamentally unjustified and ridiculous. If this group were powerful enough, it would establish a new social order; but it cannot do it. Its members often have to mask their laughter, for fear of being punished by those against whom they direct their mockery. Furthermore, when the satirist is unsure of how his laughter will be perceived by his own class, and what its chances are of victory (such a situation is often connected with a recognition of the political or material supremacy of the enemy), this paradox is reflected in the satirist's work as a shade of deep grief. This is mournful laughter, "weeping laughter," which we often encounter in the work of great satirists.

The study of the history of art will reveal that laughter was never abandoned as a weapon for class struggle. Studying particularly dark figures, such as Swift, Gogol, and Saltykov-Schedrin, will allow us to see that their attitude and satirical practice were the inevitable form of laughter under the social conditions that were theirs.

It is possible to say that in the ancient days of the East, Greece, and Rome, that in the life of the Middle Ages and the Renaissance, of the seventeenth and eighteenth centuries, that for people who lived under capitalism – all of history has unfolded, agitated as the sea, and on the crests of its waves, laughter has always shimmered. Throughout history laughter resounds. It may be a roaring cannonade or an original music, accompanied by the clanking of little bells.

Laughter has always been an important element in social processes. The role of laughter is as important as ever in our struggle, the last struggle for the emancipation of human beings.

We will therefore be happy and proud if we succeed in defining and analysing the historical development of laughter through concrete examples, and thereby fashion sharp tools for our humorists and our satirists.

Extraordinarily captivated by the task that lies ahead, its relevancy from the point of view of literary history and of our contemporary struggle, the Commission for the Study of Satirical Genres joyfully sets about its work.

Notes

Introduction: Devastation and Laughter

1 Anatoly V. Lunacharsky, "O smekhe" [1931], in *Sobranie sochinenii v 8 tomakh*, vol. 8 (Moscow: Khudozhestvennaya literatura, 1964), 538.
2 Dmitrii S. Moor, "Moskovskie mastera satiry" [1938], in *"Ya – bolshevik!" Sbornik statei* (Moscow: Sovetskii khudozhnik, 1967), 88. This text was first published in the journal *Iskusstvo*, no. 2 (1938).
3 The poem, titled "The Kremlin Highlander" (1933), was not originally written down but recited to a small group of friends. Osip Mandelstam, *Complete Poetry of Osip Emilevich Mandelstam*, trans. Burton Raffel and Alla Burago (Albany: State University of New York Press, 1973), 98–9. Mandelstam died in a transit camp on his way to Siberia in 1938, a few months after his second arrest.
4 Nadezhda Mandelstam, *Hope Abandoned* [1974], trans. Max Hayward (New York: Athenum, 1981), 121.
5 Lunacharsky, "Budem smeyatsya" [1920], in *Sobranie sochinenii*, vol. 3, 76.
6 Umberto Eco, "The Frames of Comic Freedom," in *Carnival!*, ed. Umberto Eco, V.V. Ivanov, and Monica Rector (Berlin: Mouton de Gruyter, 1984), 6.
7 For a broad overview of humour research, see Victor Raskin, ed., *The Primer of Humor Research* (Berlin: Mouton de Gruyter, 2008).
8 Aristotle, *Poetics*, trans. Gerald F. Else (Ann Arbour: University of Michigan Press, 1967), 23–4.
9 Thomas Hobbes, *Leviathan, or the Matter, Forme & Power of a Common-wealth Ecclesiaticall and Civill* [1651], ed. Richard Tuck (Cambridge: Cambridge University Press, 1996), 42.
10 Henri Bergson, *Laughter: An Essay on the Meaning of the Comic* [1900], trans. Cloudesley Brereton and Fred Rothwell (New York: Macmillan, 1911), 198.

11 Herbert Spencer, "The Physiology of Laughter," in *Essays: Scientific, Political, and Speculative* (London: Williams and Norgate, 1863), 115–16.

12 Sigmund Freud, *The Joke and Its Relation to the Unconscious* [1905], trans. Joyce Crick (New York: Penguin Classics, 2003).

13 An often-used model drawing on this approach is the General Theory of Verbal Humor (GTVH). See Willibald Ruch, Salvatore Attardo, and Victor Raskin, "Towards an Empirical Verification of the General Theory of Verbal Humor," *Humor: International Journal of Humor Research* 6, no. 2 (1993): 123–36.

14 Arthur Schopenhauer, *The World as Will and Representation*, vol. 2, trans. E.F.J. Payne (New York: Dover, 1966), 91.

15 Joseph Polimeni and Jeffrey Reiss, "The First Joke: Exploring the Evolutionary Origins of Humor," *Evolutionary Psychology* 4 (2006): 347–66.

16 Michael Billig, *Laughter and Ridicule: Towards a Social Critique of Humour* (London: Sage, 2005), 225–8.

17 Vladimir Propp, *On the Comic and Laughter,* ed. and trans. Jean-Patrick Debbèche and Paul Perron (Toronto: Toronto University Press, 2009).

18 Quintilian, *The Institutio Oratoria* [95 CE], vol. 2, trans. H.E. Butler (Cambridge, MA: Harvard University Press, 1977), 439.

19 Simon O'Sullivan, "The Aesthetics of Affect: Thinking Art beyond Representation," *Angelaki: Journal of Theoretical Humanities* 6, no. 3 (2001): 126. See also Brian Massumi, "The Autonomy of Affect," *Cultural Critique,* no. 31 (1995): 83–109.

20 See Ruth Leys, "The Turn to Affect: A Critique," *Critical Inquiry* 37, no. 3 (2011): 434–72.

21 Hillary Fink, *Bergson and Russian Modernism 1900–1930* (Evanston: Northwestern University Press, 1999). For Bergson on affect, see in particular *The Creative Mind: An Introduction to Metaphysics*, trans. Mabelle L. Audison (New York: Philosophical Library, 1946); and *Matter and Memory*, trans. N.M. Paul and W.S. Palmer (New York: Zone, 1988).

22 Gilles Deleuze and Félix Gattari, *A Thousand Plateaus: Capitalism and Schizophrenia*, trans. Brian Massumi (Minneapolis: University of Minnesota Press, 1987), 400.

23 Deleuze and Gattari, *A Thousand Plateaus,* 395.

24 See Vladimir Dal, ed., *Tolkovyi slovar zhivogo velikorusskogo yazyka,* vol. 2 (Saint Petersburg: Tovarishchestvo M.O. Volfa, 1905), 1792.

25 Richard Taylor, "Soviet Cinema as Popular Culture: Or the Extraordinary Adventures of Mr Nepman in the Land of the Silver Screen," *Revolutionary Russia* 1, no. 1 (1988): 36.

26 V.N. Shulgin, *Pamyatnye vstrechi* (Moscow: Gosudartsvennoe izdatelstvo politicheskoi literatury, 1958), 17–18.

1. Lunacharsky and the Power of Laughter

1 Lunacharsky, "O smekhe," 538.
2 Lunacharsky was the first commissar of the Narkompros, the People's Commissariat of Enlightenment, created on 26 October 1917, the day following the October Revolution. The areas that fell under the purview of the Narkompros included education, propaganda, and the arts. See Sheila Fitzpatrick, *The Commissariat of Enlightenment: Soviet Organization of Education and the Arts under Lunacharsky* (Cambridge: Cambridge University Press, 1970).
3 Lunacharsky was appointed to the Academy in early February 1930. The committee met for the first time on 28 February 1930. Russian State Archive of Socio-political History (RGASPI), f. 142, op. 1, del. 576.
4 RGASPI, f. 142, op. 1, del. 583, st. 8–9.
5 *Literaturnaya gazeta* was created in 1929 to foster debates in the literary field. On its back cover, the "Club of the Twelve Chairs" rubric was particularly popular among its readers. It was named as an homage to Ilf and Petrov's eponymous satirical novel of 1928 and featured satirical short stories, jokes, and caricatures.
6 Lunacharsky, "Pismo v redaktsiu," *Literaturnaya gazeta*, no. 15 (6 March 1931): 4. The polemic on satire will be addressed in chapter 6.
7 Mikhail Bakhtin, *Rabelais and His World* [1965], trans. Helen Iswolsky (Bloomington: Indiana University Press, 2009), 73. See also D.S. Likhachev, A.M. Panchenko, and N.V. Ponyrko, *Smekh drevnei rusi* (Leningrad: Nauka, 1984).
8 Bakhtin, *Rabelais and His World*, 89.
9 Dianne Ecklund Farrell, "Popular Humor in Russian Eighteenth Century Lubki," *Slavic Review* 50, no. 3 (1991): 552.
10 Ernest Zitser, *The Transfigured Kingdom: Sacred Parody and Charismatic Authority at the Court of Peter the Great* (Ithaca: Cornell University Press, 2004), 3.
11 Ibid., 5.
12 Bakhtin, *Rabelais and His World*, 11–2.
13 See Dianne Ecklund Farrell, "Laughter Transformed: The Shift from Medieval to Enlightenment Humour in Russian Popular Prints," in *Russia and the World of the Eighteenth Century*, ed. Roger P. Bartlett, A.G. Gross, and Karen Rasmussen, 157–76 (Columbus: Slavica, 1988).
14 Michael E. Gardiner, "Post-Romantic Irony in Bakhtin and Lefebvre," *History of the Human Sciences* 23, no. 3 (2012): 54.
15 Matthew Cullerne Bown, *Socialist Realist Painting* (New Haven: Yale University Press, 1998), 4–5.

16 Eighteen issues of the journal were published. L.B. Lekhtblau, *Russkie satiricheskie zhurnaly XVIII veka* (Moscow: Uchebno-pedagogicheskoe izdatelstvo Narkomprosa RSFSR, 1940), 3–40; Richard Pipes, *Russia Under the Old Regime* (London: Penguin, 1974), 253–9.

17 Charles Moser, ed., *The Cambridge History of Russian Literature* (Cambridge: Cambridge University Press, 1992), 71.

18 These topics nevertheless found their way into private, hand-drawn satirical albums such as that described by Ernest Zitser in "A Full Frontal History of the Romanov Dynasty: Pictorial 'Political Pornography' in Pre-Reform Russia," *Russian Review* 70 (October 2011): 557–83.

19 Belinsky credits Mikhail Lomonosov as the founder of Russian literature. Vissarion G. Belinsky, "Portretnaya gallereya russkikh pisatelei" [1854], in *Polnoe sobranie sochinenii v 12 tomakh*, vol. 8 (Moscow: Khudozhestvennaya literatura, 1955), 615.

20 Nikolai G. Chernyshevsky, "Ocherki gogolevskogo perioda russkoi literatury" [1855], in *Izbrannye estetitcheskie proizvedeniya*, vol. 3 (Moscow: Iskusstvo, 1978), 419.

21 Nikolai A. Dobrolyubov, "Russkaya satira ekaterinskogo vremini" [1859], in *Sobranie sochinenii v 9 tomakh*, vol. 5 (Moscow: Khudozhestvennaya literatura, 1962), 314.

22 Aleksandr I. Herzen, "O pisme, kritikuyushchem 'Kolokol'" [1858], in *Sobranie sochinenii v 30 tomakh*, vol. 13 (Moscow: Izd. Akademii nauk SSSR, 1952), 190.

23 The *Peredvizhniki* (The Wanderers) were a group of Russian realist artists who broke, in 1863, with the Imperial Academy of Art in protest at academic restrictions. In 1870, they formed the Society for Travelling Art Exhibitions.

24 Bown, *Socialist Realist Painting*, 11.

25 Louise McReynolds, *Russia at Play: Leisure Activities at the End of the Tsarist Era* (Ithaca: Cornell University Press, 2003), 242.

26 For example, Anatoly V. Lunacharsky, "Frantsuzkaya komediya v nashi dni," *Novyi zhurnal dlya vsekh*, no. 2 (1912): 95–102; "Frantsusskskii kritik ob angliskom komediografe," *Teatr i iskusstvo*, no. 39 (6 September 1912): 724–44; and "Yumor irlandskii i yumor frantsuzkii," *Teatr i iskusstvo*, no. 6 (9 February 1914): 131–2.

27 For example, Anatoly V. Lunacharsky, "Salon yumoristov," *Kievskaya mysl*, no. 90 (1 April 1912): 3; and "Yumor i parizhskie yumoristy karandasha," *Nov*, no. 69 (5 April 1914): 3.

28 In 1930 Lunacharsky filled out a questionnaire indicating that he spoke fluent French, German, and Italian and read English and Spanish.

A.F. Ermakov, *A. Lunacharsky* (Moscow: Novosti Press Agency Publishing House, 1975), 6.

29 Leon Trotsky, "Anatole Vasilievich Lunacharsky" [1934], in *Writings of Leon Trotsky*, vol. 6 (New York: Pathfinder, 1973), 181. First published in *Byulleten oppozitsii*, no. 38–9 (February 1934).

30 François Champarnaud, *Révolution et contre-révolution culturelles en U.R.S.S.: De Lénine à Jdanov* (Paris: Anthropos, 1975), 206.

31 Anatoly V. Lunacharsky, "Marksizm i literatura" [1923], in *Sobranie sochinenii*, vol. 7, 337.

32 Ibid.

33 In his famous treatise on art, Leo Tolstoy explains:

Every work of art causes the receiver to enter into a certain kind of relationship both with him who produced, or is producing, the art, and with all those who, simultaneously, previously, or subsequently, receive the same artistic impression. Speech, transmitting the thoughts and experiences of men, serves as a means of union among them, and art acts in a similar manner. The peculiarity of this latter means of intercourse, distinguishing it from intercourse by means of words, consists in this, that whereas by words a man transmits his thoughts to another, by means of art he transmits his feelings.

See Leo Tolstoy, *What Is Art?* [1898], trans. Aylmer Maude (Indianapolis: Bobbs-Merrill, 1960), 49.

34 Anatoly V. Lunacharsky, "Education of the New Man" [1928], in *On Education,* trans. Ruth English (Moscow: Progress Publishers, 1981), 234.

35 Anatoly V. Lunacharsky, "Lozhka protivoyadiya" [1918], in *Sobranie sochinenii,* vol. 2, 206.

36 Anatoly V. Lunacharsky, "Teatr i revolutsiya" [1921], in *Sobranie sochinenii,* vol. 3, 82.

37 As Lunacharsky explains in his 1931 essay, he uses "laughter" as an umbrella term that encompasses satire, humour, wit, and other comic genres. See Lunacharsky, "O smekhe," 532.

38 Anatoly V. Lunacharsky, "O satire" [1930], in *Sobranie sochinenii,* vol. 8, 185.

39 Anatoly V. Lunacharsky, "Budem smeyatsya," 77.

40 Ibid.

41 Ibid.

42 Lunacharsky, "Chto takoe yumor?" [1930], in *Sobranie sochinenii,* vol. 8, 184.

43 Lunacharsky, "O smekhe," 533.

44 Aymeric Monville, "Préface du traducteur," in *L'esthétique soviétique contre Staline,* by Anatole Lounatcharski, ed. and trans. A. Monville (Paris: Éditions Delga, 2005), 9.

45 Anatoly V. Lunacharsky, "Dzhonatan Svift i ego skazka o bochke" [1930], in *Sobranie sochinenii,* vol. 6, 37–47.
46 Herbert Spencer, "The Physiology of Laughter," in *Essays: Scientific, Political, and Speculative* (London: Williams and Norgate, 1863), 115–16.
47 Lunacharsky, "O smekhe," 533.
48 James Sully, *An Essay on Laughter: Its Forms, Its Causes, Its Development and Its Value* (London: Longman, Green, 1902).
49 Sigmund Freud, *The Joke and Its Relation to the Unconscious* [1905], trans. Joyce Crick (New York: Penguin Classics, 2003).
50 Theodor Lipps, *Komik und Humor* (Hamburg: L. Voss, 1898).
51 Sigmund Freud, "Humour" [1927], *International Journal of Psycho-Analysis* 9, no. 1 (1928): 1–6. For Freud, laughter allows the subject to economize affect, affording a means to shield against exterior frustrations and trauma. Relief, however, is the result of failed expectations. "We shall best understand the genesis of the yield of humorous pleasure if we consider the process in the listener before whom someone else produces humour. He sees this other person in a situation which leads the listener to expect that the other will produce the signs of an affect – that he will get angry, complain, express pain, be frightened or horrified or perhaps even despair; and the onlooker or listener is prepared to follow his lead and to call up the same emotional impulses in himself. But this emotional expectancy is disappointed; the other person expresses no affect but makes a jest. The expenditure of feeling that is economized turns into humorous pleasure in the listener" (1–2).
52 Lunacharsky, "Dzhonatan Svift i ego skazka o bochke," 38.
53 Bergson, *Laughter,* 7–8.
54 Lunacharsky, "Dzhonatan Svift i ego skazka o bochke," 38.
55 Lunacharsky, "O smekhe," 535.
56 Bergson, *Laughter,* 87–8.
57 Lunacharsky, "O smekhe," 536–7.
58 Anatoly V. Lunacharsky, "Kinematograficheskaya komediya i satira" [1931], in *Lunacharsky o kino* (Moscow: Izdatelstvo "Iskusstvo," 1965), 194.
59 Bergson, *Laughter,* 198.
60 Lunacharsky, "O smekhe," 538.
61 Lev Nikulin, "On lyubil i ponimal yumor," Russian State Archive of Literature and Art (RGALI), f. 279, op. 2, del. 736, l. 14–18.
62 Ibid., l. 16. This openness to caricature is also exemplified by the comical drawings Politburo members made of one another throughout the 1920s and early 1930s, reproduced in Alexander Vatlin and Larisa Malashenko, eds, *Piggy Foxy and the Sword of the Revolution: Bolshevik Self-Portraits* (New Haven: Yale University Press, 2006).

63 Irina Lunacharskaya, "Sversheniya i zamysly (A.V. Lunacharsky: Iz pisem i dnevnikov)," *Novyi mir* 11 (1975): 248.

64 RGALI, f. 279, op. 2, del. 240, l. 1–19.

2. Soviet Satirical Print Culture

1 Lunacharsky, "O smekhe," 537.

2 See Charles A. Ruud, *Fighting Words: Imperial Censorship and the Russian Press, 1804–1906* (Toronto: University of Toronto Press, 2009); and Jonanthan W. Daly, "Government, Press and Subversion in Russia, 1906–1917," *Journal of the Historical Society* 9, no. 1 (March 2009), 23–65.

3 Vladimir Ulianov [Lenin], "Dekret o pechati," in *O partiinoi i sovetskoi pechati: Sbornik dokumentov* (Moscow, Izdatelstvo "Pravda," 1954), 173. The decree was originally published in *Pravda,* no. 171, 10 November 1917.

4 Ibid.

5 Ibid.

6 The debate that erupted at the meeting of the All-Russian Central Executive Committee of the Soviet of Workers' and Soldiers' Deputies (TsEK) on 17 November and led to the resignation of five commissars is recounted by John Reed in *Ten Days That Shook the World* (Harmondsworth: Penguin, 1986), 237–43.

7 Most revolutionaries had been journalists in pre-revolutionary times and had been victims of state censorship. As Peter Kenez explains, neither Lenin nor anyone else had envisaged a 1917 victory. They assumed that the Revolution would be carried out over time, through argument and persuasion, waged in a diversified press. The question of repression had simply not arisen. See Peter Kenez, "Lenin and the Freedom of the Press," in *Bolshevik Culture: Experiment and Order in the Russian Revolution,* ed. Abbott Gleason, Peter Kenez, and Richard Stites (Bloomington: Indiana University Press, 1985), 131–59.

8 Anatoly V. Lunacharsky, "Svoboda knigi i revolutsia" [1921], in *Isbrannye stati po estetike* (Moscow: Iskusstvo, 1975), 82–3.

9 Ibid., 82.

10 Ibid., 83.

11 Cited in David King and Cathy Porter, *Blood & Laughter: Caricatures from the 1905 Revolution* (London: Jonathan Cape, 1983), 32.

12 "Zhurnalistika perioda mezhdu dvumya revolyutsiyami (1905–1917)," in *Literaturnaya entsiklopediya,* vol. 4, ed. A.V. Lunacharsky (Moscow: Kom. akad., 1930), 243.

13 After a financial dispute that took place in 1913, *Satirikon*'s main collaborators resigned from the journal and founded *Novyi satirikon*

early in the winter of 1914. The two journals coexisted for a few months. See Lesley Milne, "*Novyi satirikon* 1914–1918: The Patriotic Laughter of the Russian Liberal Intelligentsia during the First World War and the Revolution," *Slavonic and East European Review* 84, no. 4 (2006): 639–65.

14 The Revolutionary Tribunal of the Press was created by decree on 28 January 1918. Its role was to rule on crimes committed against the state and the people by means of the press. Vladimir Ulianov [Lenin], "O revolyutsionnom tribunale pechati" [1918], in *O partiinoi i sovetskoi pechati. Sbornik dokumentov* (Moscow: Izdatelstvo "Pravda," 1954), 175–6. The decree was originally published in *Gazeta rabochego i krestyanskogo pravitelstva*, no. 30 (22 February 1918).

15 Sergei Stykalin, *Sovetskaya satiricheskaya pechat 1917–1963* (Moscow: Gospolizdat, 1963), 11–12.

16 Stephen White, *The Bolshevik Poster* (New Haven: Yale University Press, 1988), 91.

17 ROSTA was created in 1918. It was partially replaced by TASS (Telegraphic Agency of the Soviet Union) in 1925, but remained the news agency of Soviet Russia until 1935.

18 From January 1921, ROSTA windows were published by Glavpolitprosvet, the Political Education Committee of the Narkompros, created in 1920. On ROSTA windows, see Alex Ward, *Power to the People: Early Soviet Propaganda Posters in the Israel Museum* (Jerusalem: The Israel Museum, 2007); White, *The Bolshevik Poster;* and Vladimir V. Mayakovsky, *Mayakovsky: Okna ROSTA i Glavpolitprosveta, 1919–1921*, ed. Aleksei Morozov (Moscow: Kontakt-kultura, 2010). The White Army also possessed a Service for Propaganda and Information (OSVAG), which produced an important number of counter-revolutionary posters during the period. See François-Xavier Coquin, "Une source méconnue: Les affiches contre-révolutionnaires (1918–1920)," in *Russie URSS 1914–1991: Changement de regard,* ed. Wladimir Berelowitch and Laurent Gervereau (Paris: Musée d'histoire contemporaine de la Bibliothèque de documentation internationale contemporaine, 1991), 52–63.

19 Mayakovsky, *Mayakovsky,* 96.

20 Vladimir Mayakovsky, *Groznyi smekh* (Moscow: Gosudarstvennoe izdatelstvo khudozhestvennoy literatury, 1932). The text was first published in 1930 in the journal *Ogonek,* no. 1 (5 January 1930). While Mayakovsky worked on ROSTA windows, he was also an employee of IZO Narkompros, the fine arts section of the Narkompros.

21 Victoria Bonnell, *Iconography of Power: Soviet Political Posters under Lenin and Stalin* (Berkeley: University of California Press, 1997), 38. While the practice became current earlier, the term itself appeared at the end of the 1920s.

22 Anatoly V. Lunacharsky, "Industrialnaya tematika v izobrazitelnom iskusstve," *Brigada khudozhnikov,* no. 5–6 (1931): 13.

23 Lunacharsky, "Dzhonatan Svift i ego skazka o bochke," 39.

24 Bergson, *Laughter*, 87.

25 See Parisa Kolesnikova, *"Okna TASS" 1941/1945: Oruzhie pobedy* (Moscow: Taktika, 2005).

26 Vladimir V. Mayakovsky, "Okna satiry ROSTA" [1930], in *Polnoe sobranie sochinenie v 13 tomakh*, vol. 12 (Moscow: GIKhL, 1959), 210.

27 The *Novaya Ekonomitcheskaya Politika* was a temporary economic measure put in place in 1921. It reintroduced relative market freedom, aiming at stimulating the country's economy, which had been seriously compromised by WWI, the Revolution, the Civil War, and famine. The inauguration of the First Five-Year Plan in 1928 marks the end of the NEP.

28 In 1924, *Krasnyi voron* closed shop due to administrative difficulties and immediately reappeared under the title *Begemot* (*The Hippopotamus,* 1924–28), produced by the same team.

29 Jeffrey Brooks, "Public and Private Values in the Soviet Press, 1921–1928," *Slavic Review* 48, no. 1 (1989): 16–35.

30 Even during the NEP period, satirical journals were not expected to turn a profit. Their managers, however, were compelled to avoid shortfalls.

31 First published under the title *Bezbozhnik* (*Godless*), it was renamed in its first year of existence to avoid confusion with a rival homonymous publication, by which it was later absorbed, in 1932.

32 Vladimir V. Mayakovsky, "Vystuplenie na dispute "Bolnye voprosy sovetskoi pechati': 14 dekabrya 1925 goda" [1925], in *Polnoe sobranie,* vol. 12, 294.

33 Print runs varied constantly. They were, on average, one thousand copies for the smaller journals and forty thousand for the larger ones. See Stykalin, *Sovetskaya satiricheskaya pechat,* 335–52.

34 Central Committee of the Communist Party, "O satiriko-yumoristicheskikh zhurnalakh," in *Krasnaya pechat,* no.11 (1927): 74.

35 Ibid.

36 There were two attempts to revive *Krokodil* under the title *Novyi krokodil* (*The New Crocodile*), from 2001 to 2004, and from 2006 to 2008.

37 It became *Bich* (*The Whip*) in 1927–28.

38 Most of the reader studies were conducted between 1924 and 1926. They were meant to assist in adapting publishing strategies to popular taste and avoiding wasting precious resources on materials that would not be read. See Jeffrey Brooks, "Studies of the Reader of the 1920s," *Russian History/ Histoire russe* 9, no. 2–3 (1982): 187–202.

39 Marian Pehowski suggests that recurrent paper shortages have limited its print run, which could have been even greater. Like most Soviet periodical publications, *Krokodil* was mainly sold through subscription. In the 1970s, 90 per cent of the copies were subscribed, while only 10 per cent were sold in kiosks. Marian Pehowski, "*Krokodil*-Satire for the Soviets," *Journalism Quarterly* 55, no. 4 (1978): 729.

40 NEPmen (feminine, NEPmenka) were businesspeople who benefited from the market conditions created by the NEP. Even though the NEP had been initiated by the party, the entrepreneurial activities and the mere presence of NEPmen were considered by some an affront to the regime.

41 Central Committee of the Communist Party, "O zhurnale 'Krokodil'" [1948], in *O partiinoi i sovetskoi pechati: Sbornik dokumentov* (Moscow: Izdatelstvo "Pravda," 1954), 600. The decree was originally published in *Kultura i zhizn*, no. 26 (11 September 1948).

42 Central Committee of the Communist Party, "O nedostatkakh zhurnala 'Krokodil' i merakh ego uluchsheniya" [1951], in *O partiinoi i sovetskoi pechati*, 621.

43 Alex Inkeles and Kent Geiger, "Critical Letters to the Editors of the Soviet Press: Areas and Modes of Complaint," *American Sociological Review*, vol. 17, no. 6 (December 1952), 694.

44 Karl Marx, *The Eighteenth Brumaire of Louis Bonaparte* (New York: International Publishers, 1963), 19.

45 V.I. Lenin, *Collected Works*, vol. 33 (Moscow: Progress Publishers, 1973), 77, 225.

46 Lunacharsky, "Ilf i Petrov" [1931], in *Sobranie sochinenii*, vol. 2, 522.

47 Lunacharsky, "O smekhe," 533.

48 Bakhtin first broached the theme of laughter (satirical, carnivalesque, and grotesque) in *Problems of Dostoevsky's Poetics*, first published in 1929, and then in *Rabelais and His World*, written in the 1930s but first published in 1965.

3. Laughter in the Ring, in the Street, and on Stage

1 Lunacharsky, "Budem smeyatsya," 76.

2 On the concept of scenes, see Will Straw, "Scenes and Sensibilities," *Public*, no. 22/23 (2002): 245–57.

3 Pamela Kachurin makes a similar argument, that networks and relationships between artists allowed them to shape institutions and eventually caused their demise. The idea of the scene is slightly different, since the scene, as an informal structure, is not limited to a single

organization or discipline. Kachurin, *Making Modernism Soviet: The Russian Avant-Garde in the Early Soviet Era, 1918–1928* (Chicago: Nortwestern University Press, 2013).

4 Miriam Neirick, *When Pigs Could Fly and Bears Could Dance: A History of the Soviet Circus* (Madison: University of Wisconsin Press, 2012), 6.

5 "Khronologiya tsirka i estrady, 1917–1928 g. g," *Tsirk i estrada,* no. 16 (1928): 1.

6 Anatoly V. Lunacharsky, "Zadacha obnovlennogo tsirka," *Vestnik teatra,* no. 3 (1919): 5.

7 Vladimir Ulianov [Lenin], "Dekret ob edinenii teatralnogo dela," *Vestnik teatra,* no. 33 (1919): 2.

8 Yurii Dmitriev, *Sovetskii tsirk, ocherk istorii, 1917–1941* (Moscow: Iskusstvo, 1963), 64–5.

9 Neirick, *When Pigs Could Fly,* 33.

10 František Deák and Vladimir Mayakovsky, "The Championship of the Universal Class Struggle," *The Drama Review* 17, no. 1 (1973): 53–63.

11 Neirick, *When Pigs Could Fly,* 14.

12 "Khronologiya tsirka i estrady," 1.

13 Neirick, *When Pigs Could Fly,* 15.

14 Anatoly V. Lunacharsky, "Rebenek i tsirk," *Tsirk,* no. 3 (1925): 10.

15 Neirick, *When Pigs Could Fly,* 31, 43, 51–7.

16 Neirick, *When Pigs Could Fly,* 64.

17 Lev Kuleshov, "Circus-Cinema-Theatre" [1925], in *Lev Kuleshov, Selected Works: Fifty Years in Films,* trans. Dmitri Agrachev and Nina Belenkaya (Moscow: Raduga, 1987), 62.

18 Norman Swallow, *Eisenstein: A Documentary Portrait* (London: George Allen and Unwin, 1976), 24.

19 Robert Leach, *Revolutionary Theatre* (London: Routledge, 1994), 1–2.

20 Several polemical publications were published between 1905 and 1917 debating the role and nature of theatre, aiming to find new direction for the performing arts, most notably the collections of essays *Kniga o novom teatre* (Saint Peterburg: Sipovnik, 1908), edited by Anatoly Lunacharsky; *Kriziz teatra* (Moscow: Problemy iskusstva, 1908), edited by Yurii M. Steklov; and *V sporakh o teatre* (Moscow: Knigoizdatelstvo pisatelei v Moskve, 1913), edited by Yulii I. Aikhenvald.

21 Konstatin Rudnitsky, *Russian and Soviet Theatre 1905–1932,* trans. Roxane Permar (New York: Harry N. Abrams, 1988), 10.

22 See Vsevolod Meyerhold, "The Actor of the Future and Biomechanics" [1922], in *The Soviet Theatre: A Documentary History,* ed. Laurence Senelick and Sergei Ostrovsky (New Haven: Yale University Press, 2014), 147–9.

23 Futurism appeared in Russia as early as 1909, following the publication in the Parisian newspaper *Le Figaro* of the futurist manifesto, which was translated into Russian later that year. But Russian futurism strayed from its Italian genitor. Aside from a passion for speed and dynamism and an irreverent attitude towards the past and the art that preceded them, they shared little. Russian futurism was anti-war, wickedly funny, and borrowed heavily from primitive forms. The Union of Youth was created in Saint Petersburg in 1909 and lasted until 1917.

24 Lunacharsky is credited with having written at least seventy-two plays, a number of them using the pseudonym Anatoly Anyutin, and several satirical in intent. Many remain unpublished. See Dave Renton, *Dissident Marxism: Past Voices for Present Times* (London: Zed, 2004), 51; and A.L. Tait, "Lunacharsky, the Poet-Commissar," *Slavonic and East European Review* 52, no. 127 (1974), 235. Some of his best known satirical plays include *The King's Barber* (1906), *Faust and the City* (1918), *The Tale of Petrushka* (1920), *Lloyd-George's Dream* (1921), and *Locksmith and Chancellor* (1921), which was turned into a silent film in 1923.

25 In 1918, along with the shift from the Julian to the Gregorian calendar, a series of Soviet holidays were created, with the objective of breaking with traditional or religious celebrations, but also as a means of establishing Soviet historical references and a socialist temporal framework. See Malte Rolf, *Soviet Mass Festivals, 1917–1991,* trans. Cynthia Klohr (Pittsburgh: University of Pittsburgh Press, 2013), 72–8.

26 Pustynin will also be involved, in the 1920s with the *Sinyaya bluza* movement (see later in this section) and the satirical journal *Krokodil*.

27 Lunacharsky, "Budem smeyatsya," 76.

28 J.A.E. Curtis, "Down with the Foxtrot! Concepts of Satire in the Soviet Theatre of the 1920s," in *Russian Theatre in the Age of Modernism*, ed. Robert Russell and Andrew Barratt (New York: St. Martin's Press, 1990), 220.

29 In his memoirs, published in 1933, Benedikt Livshitz testifies to the importance of the futurist cabarets by dedicating a whole chapter to the activities of the Stray Dog. Livshitz, *The One and Half-Eyed Archer* (Newtonville: Oriental Research Partners, 1977).

30 Curtis, "Down with the Foxtrot!," 220–1.

31 A.N. Manteifel, "Teatr revolyutsionnoi satiry (Terevsat)," in *Sovetskii teatr: Dokumenty i materialy 1917–1967*, vol. 1 (Leningrad: Iskusstvo, 1968), 190.

32 David King, *Red Star over Russia: A Visual History of the Soviet Union from the Revolution to the Death of Stalin* (New York: Harry N. Abrams, 2009), 148.

33 The original crew involved several students from the Communist Institute of Journalism. Yurii A. Dmitriev, *Teatralnaya Moskva 1920-e gody* (Moscow: Gosudarstvennyi institut iskusstvoznaniya, 2000), 40.

34 Varlam Chalamov, *Les années vingt: Cahier 2, réflexions d'un étudiant*, trans. Christiane Loré and Nathalie Pighetti-Harrison (Lagrasse: Verdier, 2008), 85.

35 Robert Leach, "Revolutionary Theatre, 1917–1930," in *A History of Russian Theatre*, ed. Robert Leach and Victor Borovsky (Cambridge: Cambridge University Press, 1999), 318.

36 Chalamov, *Les années vingt*, 84–9.

37 "Sinyaya bluza," *Literaturnaya gazeta*, no. 24 (30 September 1929): 2.

38 Anatoly V. Lunacharsky, "Moim opponentam," *Vestnik teatra*, no. 76–77 (14 December 1920), 4.

39 From the libretto printed in the program published for the representation staged for the Third Congress of the Komintern in 1921. Vladimir V. Mayakovsky, "Libretto 'Misterii-buff'" [1921], in *Polnoe sobranie sochinenie*, vol. 2, 359.

40 Ibid.

41 Anatoly V. Lunacharsky, "Teatr RSFSR" [1922], in *Sobranie sochinenii*, vol. 3, 123.

42 Quoted in Rudnitsky, *Russian and Soviet Theatre*, 123

43 Rudnitsky, *Russian and Soviet Theatre*, 139.

44 In the 1930s, some of them would be accused of "Meyerholdism," the usage of Meyerhold's strategies for purely formal or decorative goals. In a speech given in March 1936 at a meeting organized in Leningrad by the *Pravda* editorial staff, Meyerhold defended himself against formalism. The speech has become known as "Meyerhold against Meyerholdism."

45 The *Proletkult*, a movement for proletarian culture that grew out of the party school in Capri and in particular the figures of Bogdanov, Gorky, and Lunacharsky, while remaining at arm's length, scorned professionalism in the arts. Its members believed that arts should develop somewhat organically from the working class and through experimentation with workers. In the early 1920s, the *Proletkult* had about three hundred branches, and approximately half a million people were involved in some way in their various activities. The *Proletkult* was particularly active with regard to theatre. It did not play established repertoire, but attempted to find new ways of engaging the public.

46 Sergei Eisenstein, "Montage of Attraction" [1923], in *The Film Factory: Russian and Soviet Cinema in Documents*, ed. Richard Taylor and Ian Christie (Cambridge, MA: Harvard University Press, 1988), 87–9.

47 Central Committee of the Communist Party, *Kommunisticheskaya partiya sovetskogo soyuza v rezolutsiyakh i retsenziyakh sezdov, konferentsii i plenumov SK*, vol. 1 (Moscow: Politizdat, 1953), 740–1.

48 "Kukryniksy" was the collective name of graphic satirists Mikhail Kupriyanov, Porfiri Krylov, and Nikolai Sokolov. They began drawing caricatures under the joint signature in 1924 and became nationally famous in the 1930s after the rise of fascism, drawing for the satirical journal *Krokodil*. During WWII, they renewed the ROSTA windows tradition by establishing a satirical poster program for TASS, ROSTA's successor. See Parisa Kolesnikova, *"Okna TASS" 1941/1945.*

49 Rudnitsky, *Russian and Soviet Theatre*, 207.

50 Letter by Vladimir Nemirovich-Danchenko quoted in Inna Solovyova, "The Theatre and Socialist Realism," in Leach and Borovsky, *A History of Russian Theatre*, 326.

51 Anatoly V. Lunacharsky, "Neskolko vpechatlenii" [1927], in *Sobranie sochinenii*, vol. 3, 372.

52 Quoted in Solovyova, "The Theatre and Socialist Realism," 327.

53 Curtis, "Down with the Foxtrot!," 229.

54 Central Committee of the Communist Party, "Decree on the Reconstruction of Literary and Artistic Organizations" [1932], in *Art in Theory 1900–2000: An Anthology of Changing Ideas*, ed. Charles Harrison and Paul Wood (London: Blackwell, 2002), 417–18.

4. Laughter on the Silver Screen

1 Anatoli Lunacharsky, "Speech to Film Workers" [1928], in Taylor and Christie, *The Film Factory*, 197.

2 Anatoli Lunacharsky, "Conversation with Lenin. I. Of all the arts ..." [1922], in Taylor and Christie, *The Film Factory*, 57.

3 Quoted in Denise Youngblood, *Movies for the Masses: Popular Cinema and Soviet Society in the 1920s* (Cambridge: Cambridge University Press, 1992), 36. The manifesto focuses on documentary film, barely mentioning entertainment.

4 Lunacharsky, "Kinematograficheskaya komediya i satira," 209.

5 See Patrick Brantlinger, *Bread and Circuses: Theories of Mass Culture as Social Decay* (Ithaca: Cornell University Press, 1983).

6 Richard Stites, *Russian Popular Culture: Entertainment and Society since 1900* (Cambridge: Cambridge University Press, 1992), 38.

7 Lunacharsky, "Kinematograficheskaya komediya i satira," 207.

8 Leon Trotsky, "Vodka, the Church and the Cinema" [1923], in *Problems of Everyday Life and Other Writings on Culture & Science* (New York: Monad, 1973), 32.

9 Lunacharsky, "Kinematograficheskaya komediya i satira," 205.

10 In 1918, Mayakovsky acted in three silent films, for which he had also written scripts. The only surviving one, *The Young Lady and the Hooligan*, was based on the novel *The Workers' Young Schoolmistress*, published in 1895 by Edmondo De Amici. The other two, *Born Not for the Money* and *Shackled by Cinema*, are presumed lost.

11 Birgit Beumers, *A History of Russian Cinema* (Oxford: Berg, 2009), 31.

12 *Agitpoezda* were modified trains that were equipped with presses, stores of books and pamphlets, and portable film studios. On these, public speakers, writers, and film-makers travelled to remote areas of the country, circulating Bolshevik propaganda and producing it while in transit. Aleksandr Medvedkin recounts his experience creating propaganda shorts on the *agitpoezd* in Chris Marker's documentary *Le Tombeau d'Alexandre*, 1992. Medvedkin had previously been involved in satirical agitation theatre. On agitational trains, see Robert Argenbright, "The Soviet Agitational Vehicle: State Power on the Social Frontier," *Political Geography* 17, no. 3 (1998): 253–72.

13 See "Table 2. Film Production 1918–1941" in Taylor and Christie, *The Film Factory*, 424.

14 Sovnarkom of the RSFSR, "Decree of the establishment of Sovkino" [1924], in Taylor and Christie, *The Film Factory*, 114.

15 A number of these have been made available on the DVD compilation *Animated Soviet Propaganda: From the October Revolution to Perestroïka*, Kino Video, 1997. Early animated satirical films such *Interplanetary Revolution* (1924) and *We'll Keep Our Eyes Peeled* (1927) experiment with a remarkable variety of animation techniques, including drawn, cut out, collage, and stop motion.

16 Youngblood, *Movies for the Masses*, 15.

17 Lev Kuleshov, "Americanism" [1922], in Taylor and Christie, *The Film Factory*, 72.

18 Youngblood, *Movies for the Masses*, 15.

19 Ibid., 18.

20 Eisenstein, "Montage of Attraction."

21 Ilya Trainin, quoted by Youngblood, *Movies for the Masses*, 17.

22 Youngblood, *Movies for the Masses*, 17.

23 Anatoli Lunacharsky, "Revolutionary Ideology and Cinema – Theses" [1924], in Taylor and Christie, *The Film Factory*, 109.

24 Lev Kuleshov, "Circus-Cinema-Theatre" [1925], in *Lev Kuleshov, Selected Works: Fifty Years in Films*, trans. Dmitri Agrachev and Nina Belenkaya (Moscow: Raduga, 1987), 62.

25 Peter Christensen, "An Ambivalent NEP Satire of Bourgeois Aspirations: *The Kiss of Mary Pickford*," in *Inside Soviet Film Satire: Laughter with a Lash*, ed. Andrew Horton (Cambridge: Cambridge University Press, 1993), 48.

26 Eileen Whitfield, *Pickford: The Woman Who Made Hollywood* (Lexington: University Press of Kentucky, 1997), 245.
27 Christensen, "An Ambivalent NEP Satire," 53.
28 Lunacharsky, "Kinematograficheskaya komediya i satira," 209.
29 Ibid., 199.
30 Ibid., 201–2.
31 Ibid., 212.
32 Youngblood, *Movies for the Masses*, 33.
33 Osip Brik, "Na podstupakh v sovetskoi komedii," *Kino front,* no. 3 (1927): 14.
34 P. Bliakhin, "K partsoveshchaniiu," *Novyi zritel* (13 December 1927): 4, quoted in Taylor, "Soviet Cinema as Popular Culture," 43.
35 Quoted in Taylor, "Soviet Cinema as Popular Culture," 44.
36 Youngblood, *Movies for the Masses*, 32.
37 Emma Widdis, *Alexander Medvedkin* (London: I.B. Tauris, 2005), 55.
38 Boris Shumyatsky, "A Cinema for the Millions (Extracts)" [1935], in Taylor and Christie, *The Film Factory,* 368.
39 Shumyatsky, "A Cinema for the Millions," 367.
40 On the topic of motherhood and race, see Alison Rowley, "Where Are All the Mother-Heroines? Images of Maternity in Soviet Films of the 1930s," *Canadian Journal of History* 44: 1 (2009): 25–38.
41 A. Surkov, "Untitled," in *Pervyi vsesoyuznyi sezd sovetskikh pisatelei, 1934: Stenograficheskii otchet,* ed. I.K. Luppol, M.M. Rozental, S.M. Tretyakov, and S.L. Lesnevskii (Moscow: Sovetskii pisatel, 1934), 512–13.
42 Sheila Fitzpatrick, "Cultural Revolution in Russia 1928–1932," *Journal of Contemporary History* 9, no. 1 (1974): 36.
43 Boris Shumyatsky, "A Cinema for the Millions," 369.

5. The Strategies and Targets of Satire

1 Lunacharsky, "Kinematograficheskaya komediya i satira," 207.
2 Vladimir V. Mayakovsky, "Mozhno li stat satirikom?" [1923], in *Polnoe sobranie sochinenie,* vol. 12, 31–2.
3 Mayakovsky, "Mozhno li stat satirikom?" 32.
4 According to Gérard Genette, transtextuality, or the textual transcendance of the text, is "all that sets the text in relationship, whether obvious or concealed, with other texts." Genette, *The Architext: An Introduction* (Berkeley: University of California Press, 1992), 83. Here the term "text" can be understood broadly to include all types of communication, including visual arts, the circus, theatre, and cinema, and transtextuality

can be specified in five subtypes: intertextuality, paratextuality, architextuality, metatextuality, and hypertextuality (also known as hypotextuality).

5 Salvatore Attardo, *Linguistic Theories of Humor* (Berlin: Mouton de Gruyter, 1994), 20.

6 Ruch, Attardo, and Raskin, "Towards an Empirical Verification of the General Theory of Verbal Humor."

7 Christian Hempelmann and Andrea Samson, "Cartoons: Drawn Jokes?" in *The Primer of Humor Research*, ed. Victor Raskin (Berlin: Mouton de Gruyter, 2008), 627.

8 Salvatore Attardo, "A Primer for the Linguistics of Humor," in Raskin, *The Primer*, 104.

9 Arvo Krikmann, "Contemporary Linguistic Theories of Humor," *Folklore: Electronic Journal of Folklore*, no. 33 (2006): 28.

10 Paul De Man, "The Rhetoric of Temporality," in *Blindness and Insight: Essays in the Rhetoric of Contemporary Criticism* (Minneapolis: University of Minnesota Press, 1983), 187–228.

11 Attardo, "A Primer," 108.

12 Attardo, "A Primer," 110.

13 For a detailed discussion of how the GTVH can be adapted to the analysis of visual arts, see Annie Gérin, "A Second Look at Laughter: Humor in the Visual Arts," *Humor: International Journal of Humor Research* 26, no. 1 (2013): 155–76.

14 Before the twentieth century, collage existed as a technical trick in advertisement, postcard, posters, magazine illustration, and as a craft technique, most representatively used in domestic scrapbooks and photo albums. But it was only accepted as a valid technique for art production with the advent of synthetic cubism in 1912.

15 Leon Trotsky, "How to Begin," in *Problems of Everyday Life*, 66.

16 Svetlana Boym, *Common Places: Mythologies of Everyday Life in Russia* (Cambridge, MA: Harvard University Press, 1994), 30.

17 Leon Trotsky, "Vodka, the Church and the Cinema," in *Problems of Everyday Life*, 33.

18 Leon Trotsky, "From the Old Family to the New," in *Problems of Everyday Life*, 38.

19 This conception is grounded in Friedrich Engels' seminal 1884 work, *The Origin of the Family, Private Property, and the State*.

20 Elizabeth Wood, *The Baba and the Comrade: Gender and Politics in Revolutionary Russia* (Bloomington: Indiana University Press, 1997), 199.

21 Ibid., 197.

22 Ibid., 195.

23 Leon Trotsky, "Habit and Custom," in *Problems of Everyday Life*, 27.

24 The journal was revived as *Novyi LEF* in 1927–29.

25 Sergei Tretyakov, "Otkuda i kuda?" *LEF,* no. 1 (1923): 200.

26 This utilitarian orientation on the part of avant-garde artists was known as productivism. See Christina Kiaer, *Imagine No Possessions: The Socialist Objects of Russian Constructivism* (Cambridge, MA: MIT Press, 2005).

27 Tretyakov, "Otkuda i kuda?" 200.

28 The sentence was taken from an unfinished poem written earlier in the year. It is thought to be an epilogue to "At the Top of My Voice," 1929–30. Vladimir V. Mayakovsky, "Neokonchennoe," in *Polnoe sobranie sochinenie*, vol. 10, 287.

29 Anatoly V. Lunacharsky, "Tezisy o zadachakh marksistkoi kritiki" [1928], in *Sobranie sochinenii,* vol. 8, 7–8.

30 A.V. Lunacharsky, *Meshchanstvo i individualism* (Moscow: Gosudarstvennoe izdatelstvo, 1923), 69.

31 Marietta Shaginyan, *Novyi byt i iskusstvo* (Moscow: Zakkniga, 1926), 32–8.

32 Ibid., 17.

33 This section presents a much-condensed version of Annie Gérin, *Godless at the Workbench: Soviet Illustrated Humoristic Antireligious Propaganda* (Regina: Dunlop Art Gallery, 2003). The term "antireligious" (*bezbozhnyi*) differs from the term "atheist" (*ateist*) in that it suggests an overtly militant attitude.

34 Karl Marx, "A Contribution to the Critique of Hegel's Philosophy of Right: Introduction" [1843], in *Early Writings*, trans. Rodney Livingstone and Gregor Benton (London: Penguin, 1992), 244.

35 This echoed Marx's argument that in order to emancipate themselves in the social and private spheres, humans need to remove all religion from political practice. See Karl Marx, "On the Jewish Question" [1843], in *Early Writings*, 211–41.

36 Russian S.F.S.R., *Constitution of the Russian Socialist Federal Soviet Republic. Order of the Fifth All-Russia Congress of Soviets Passed on the 10th of July, 1918* (London: People's Russian Information Bureau, 1919), n.p.

37 Lewis Siegelbaum, *Soviet State and Society between Revolutions* (Cambridge: Cambridge University Press, 1992), 157. Lunacharsky was very much opposed to the destruction of Russia's religious heritage. Having heard rumours that Moscow's Cathedral of Saint Basil the Blessed and the Cathedral of the Assumption were under fire, Lunacharsky resigned from his newly granted position as People's Commissar of Enlightenment in a letter published in *Pravda* on 15 November 1917. The rumours were false

and Lunacharsky revoked his resignation. The episode is recounted in
John Reed, *Ten Days That Shook the World* (London: Penguin, 1986), 220–1.

38 See Daniel Peris, *Storming the Heavens: The Soviet League of the Militant
Godless* (Ithaca: Cornell University Press, 1998).

39 Furthermore, all Soviet satirical journals mentioned in chapter 2
participated in the propaganda crusade. *Krokodil, Krasnyi perets,* and
Krasnyi voron, to name just a few, routinely depicted the clergy as
alcoholics, avaricious parasites, warmongers, or sadists.

40 Bergson, *Laughter*, 29–30.

41 Nicholas Timasheff, "The Inner Life of the Orthodox Church," in *The
Transformation of Russian Society,* ed. Cyril Black (Cambridge: Cambridge
University Press, 1960), 426.

42 Dmitrii Moor, unpublished manuscript written in 1934. TSGALI, f. 1988,
op. 2.

43 From the First All-Union Russian Congress of Women in 1918, quoted
in Richard Stites, *The Woman's Liberation Movement in Russia: Feminism,
Nihilism, Bolshevism 1860–1930* (Princeton: Princeton University Press,
1978), 330.

44 Soyuz voinstvuyushchikh bezbozhnikov, *Kak ustroit ugolok bezbozhnika*
(Moscow: Bezbozhnik u stanka, 1924).

45 On Lenin corners, see Nina Tumarkin, *Lenin Lives! The Lenin Cult in Soviet
Russia* (Cambridge: Cambridge University Press, 1983), 183.

46 On the winding down of the antireligious campaign in the late 1930s, see
Gérin, *Godless at the Workbench,* 44–6.

47 David King documents the doctoring of photographs during the Stalinist
period in *The Commissar Vanishes: The Falsification of Photographs and Art in
Stalin's Russia* (London: Metropolitan Books, 1997).

48 Stuart Hall, "The Work of Representation," in *Representation: Cultural
Representations and Signifying Practices,* ed. Stuart Hall (London: Sage,
1997), 45.

49 Philippe Saltel, *Les philosophes et la haine* (Paris: Ellipses, 2001), 27.

6. The Rhetorics of Satire

1 Lunacharsky, "Kinematograficheskaya komediya i satira," 203.

2 Andrei Bubnov, a supporter of Stalin's policies, replaced Lunacharsky as
People's Commissar of Enlightenment in 1929. Bubnov was not known as
a great intellectual, and he shifted the work on the Narkompros towards
education and technical training, with less emphasis on the arts. His tenure
was short lived. In 1937, he was declared an enemy of the people, expelled

from the Central Committee of the Communist Party, and arrested. He perished in a labour camp in 1940.

3 Ilya Ehrenburg, *Memoirs: 1921–1941*, trans. Tatania Shebunina and Yvonne Kapp (New York: World Publishing, 1964), 209.

4 Mandelstam, *Hope Abandoned*, 108. See also Boris Briker, "Anti-Stalinist Humor of the 1930s: Life-Death Jokes," *Przegląd Rusycystyczny* 4, no. 120 (2007): 33–43; and Ben Lewis, *Hammer and Tickle: The Story of Communism, a Political System Almost Laughed Out of Existence* (New York: Pegasus, 2009).

5 Ehrenburg, *Memoirs*, 209.

6 Vladimir Blum, cited in Lewis, *Hammer and Tickle*, 42.

7 Graeme Gill defines the metanarrative as "a body of discourse which presents a simplified form of the ideology and which is the communication between the regime and those who live under it; it is the principal form of cultural mediation between regime and people." Gill, *Symbols and Legitimacy in Soviet Politics* (Cambridge: Cambridge University Press, 2011), 3. On the formation and the transformation of the Soviet metanarrative from 1917 to 1929, see ibid., 26–88.

8 Ibid., 36–7.

9 This is the title of a decree originally published in *Pravda*, no. 32, 1918. See Vladimir I. Lenin, "The Socialist State is in Danger" [1918], in *Collected Works*, vol. 27 (Moscow: Progress Publishers, 1973), 30–3.

10 Joseph Stalin, "Oktyabrskaya revolyutsiya i taktika russkikh kommunistov," in *Voprosy leninizma* (Moscow: Gosudarstvennoe sotsialnoe ekonomicheskoe izdatelstvo, 1931), 107–14. Not all agreed with this proposition. Most notably Leon Trotsky and Anatoly Lunacharsky believed the revolutionary period would certainly last decades, mainly because mentalities needed to be transformed through a complex process of acculturation.

11 In 1928, a group of engineers were arrested by the Soviet secret police (OGPU) in the North Caucasus town of Shakhty. They were publicly accused of conspiring with former owners of coal mines (living abroad since the Revolution) to sabotage the Soviet economy. The Shakhty trials marked the beginning of the use of accusations of sabotage against real and imagined class enemies, opening the way to the Great Purge of the 1930s.

12 "Constitution (Fundamental Law) of the Union of Socialist Republics" [1936], in Aryeh Unger, *Constitutional Development in the USSR: A Guide to the Soviet Constitutions* (London: Methuen, 1981), 140–58.

13 Abram Lezhnev, "Na puti k vozrozhdeniyu satiry," *Literaturnaya gazeta*, no. 1 (15 April 1929): 2.

14 Vladimir Blum, "Vozroditsya li satira?" *Literaturnaya gazeta,* no. 6 (27 May 1929): 2.

15 Georgii Yakubovsky, "O satire nashikh dnei," *Literaturnaya gazeta,* no. 11 (8 July 1929): 3.

16 "O putyakh sovetskoy satiry," *Literaturnaya gazeta,* no. 12 (15 July 1929): 1.

17 Ibid.

18 M. Rogi, "Puti sovetskoy satiry," *Literaturnaya gazeta,* no. 14 (22 July 1929): 3.

19 Mayakovsky's intervention can be read in his "Vystuplenie na dispute 'Nuzhna li nam satira?' 8 yanvarya 1930 goda" [1930], in *Polnoe sobranie sochinenie,* vol. 12, 512.

20 Efim Zozulya, "Nuzhna li nam satira?" *Literaturnaya gazeta,* no. 2 (13 January 1930): 3.

21 Ibid.

22 Articles that follow speak to the fact that satire keeps being produced and is well received – at least by the editors and readership of *Literaturnaya gazeta.* See Aleksandr Deitch, "Satira kotoraya nam nuzhna," *Literaturnaya gazeta,* no. 2 (14 January 1931): 2–3; Gr. Roze, "Ot parodii k satire," *Literaturnaya gazeta,* no. 21 (12 May 1932): 3; Mikh. Ts., "Lushche vybirat mishen – Za kachestvo sovetskoi satiry!" *Literaturnaya gazeta,* no. 25 (5 June 1932): 2; and Aleksei Selivanovsky, "Smekh Ilfa i Petrova," *Literaturnaya gazeta,* no. 38 (23 August 1932): 3.

23 Anatoly V. Lunacharsky, "Pismo v redaktsiu," *Literaturnaya gazeta,* no. 15 (6 March 1931): 4.

24 Ilya Erenburg, "Untitled," in Luppol, Rozental, Tretyakov, and Lesnevskii, *Pervyi vsesoyuznyi sezd,* 182.

25 *Ideinost* (ideological commitment) concerns the ideological motivation behind a given work and that of its author; *partiinost* (party-mindedness) marks how it can contribute to the construction of socialism according to party guidance; and *narodnost* (popular spirit) relates to the need to express the will and expectation of the people.

26 Drawing on contemporary and historical scholarship, Thomas Lahusen demonstrates how socialist realism was in fact a system open to change and reinterpretation. Lahusen, "Socialist Realism in Search of Its Shores: Some Historical Remarks on the 'Historically Open Aesthetic System of the Truthful Representation of Life,'" in *Socialist Realism without Shores,* ed. Thomas Lahusen and Evgeny Dobrenko (Durham: Duke University Press, 1997), 5–26. On the debates around the question of realism in the 1920s and 1930s, see Bown, *Socialist Realist Painting.*

27 Hayden White, *Metahistory: The Historical Imagination in Nineteenth-Century Europe* (Baltimore: Johns Hopkins University Press, 1973), 46.

28 Leon Trotsky, "Revolutionary and Socialist Art" [1923], in *Literature and Revolution,* ed. William Keach, trans. Rose Strunsky (New York: Haymarket, 2005), 234.

29 Cited in Bown, *Socialist Realist Painting,* 87.

30 The Society of Easel Painters (Obshchestvo Khudozhnikov-Stankovistov) arose in 1924 and was established formally in 1925. Its founding members had been linked to the avant-garde, and several had produced satirical work for early Soviet journals, most notably Aleksandr Deineka, Yurii Pimenov, Yurii Annenkov, David Shterenberg, Nikolai Denisovsky, and Pyotr Vilyams. See OST [Society of Easel Artists], "Platform, 1929," in *Russian Art of the Avant-Garde: Theory and Criticism 1902–1934,* ed. John Bowlt (London: Thames & Hudson, 1988), 279–81.

31 Contemporaneous with the Society of Easel Painters, the Four Arts Society grouped artists such as Lev Bruni, Vladimir Favorsky, Pavel Kuznetsov, Vladimir Lebedev, Pyotr Miturich, Kuzma Petrov-Vodkin, and El Lissistsky. It was particularly interested in the decorative and lyrical aspects of art. See Four Arts Society of Artists, "Declaration, 1929" in Bowlt, *Russian Art,* 281–284.

32 The group emerged shortly after the forty-seventh exhibition of the Wanderers, in January 1922, and included several members of that group. Its primary aim was to present revolutionary Russia in a realist manner that was grounded in nineteenth century realist traditions. Their opposition to the avant-garde was clearly articulated. See AKhRR, "Declaration of the Association of Artists of Revolutionary Russia, 1922" in Bowlt, *Russian Art,* 265. As Matthew Cullerne Bown argues, the efficiency and the energy of the artists who formed the group, and their ability to connect with the centres of bureaucratic power and attract official commissions, transformed them into the most powerful artists' group in the country, with a membership of over a thousand in 1924 and filial groups across the country. Bown, *Socialist Realist Painting,* 72, 75.

33 October was founded in 1928 and held only one exhibition, in the summer of 1930. It grouped various artists who had been linked to the avant-garde, and several who had been active in the "satirical scene": Aleksandr Deineka, Dmitrii Moor, Aleksandr Rodchenko, Varvara Stepanova, Sergei Eisenstein, Diego Rivera (in Moscow in 1927–28), and many others. October – Association of Artistic Labour, "Declaration, 1928," in Bowlt, *Russian Art,* 277.

34 This can be understood in opposition to formalism, which focuses on intrinsic, formal exploration rather than extrinsic concerns.

35 The speech, titled "More Left than LEF," was partly reproduced in I.
Terentev, "Mayakovskii 'Levee Lefa,'" *Novyi LEF,* no. 9
(1928): 47–8.

36 Cited in Bown, *Socialist Realist Painting,* 87.

37 Cited in ibid., 119.

38 In 1932 all literary and artistic groups were dissolved by the "Decree on
the Reconstruction of Literary and Artistic Organisations," which was
passed 23 April 1932. The direct result of this decree was the creation of
the Union of Soviet Writers. Although the proposed single Union of Soviet
Artists was not convoked until 1957, a special committee in charge of all
art affairs (except those involving architecture and cinema) was organized
in 1936.

39 "Obespechim vse usloviya tvorcheskoi raboty literaturnykh kruzhkov:
Na sobranii aktiva litkruzhkov Moskvy," *Literaturnaya gazeta,* no. 23 (23
May 1932): 1. This was a report of the meeting a few days earlier at which
Gronsky's speech was given.

40 Anatoly V. Lunacharsky, "Sotsialisticheskii realism" [1933], in *Sobranie
sochinenii,* vol. 8, 501.

41 Anatoli Lunacharsky, "Synopsis of a Report on the Tasks of Dramaturgy
(Extract)" [1933], inTaylor and Christie, *The Film Factory,* 327.

42 Andrei Zhdanov, "Soviet Literature – The Richest in Ideas, the Most
Advanced Literature," in *Soviet Writers' Congress 1934: The Debate on
Socialist Realism and Modernism in the Soviet Union* (London: Lawrence and
Wishart, 1977), 21.

43 Boris Romashov, "Untitled," in Luppol, Rozental, Tretyakov, and
Lesnevskii, *Pervyi vsesoyuznyi sezd,* 428.

44 He was also the brother of Boris Efimov, a prolific graphic satirist who
would contribute regularly to *Pravda* and *Krokodil* until the journal closed
following the collapse of the Soviet Union in 1991. Efimov received the
Stalin Prize for his satirical work in 1950 and in 1951.

45 Mikhail E. Koltsov, "Untitled," in Luppol, Rozental, Tretyakov, and
Lesnevskii, *Pervyi vsesoyuznyi sezd,* 221–2.

46 Ibid., 223.

47 Lunacharsky, "Chto takoe yumor?" 182–4.

48 Boris Groys makes the provocative argument that socialist realism
realized the project left incomplete by the avant-garde of producing
world-transformative art. See Groys, *The Total Art of Stalinism: Avant-garde,
Aesthetic Dictatorship, and Beyond,* trans. Charles Rougle (London:
Verso, 2011).

Conclusion

1 Lunacharsky, "O smekhe," 535.
2 Clement Greenberg, "Modernist Painting" [1960], in *Art in Theory 1900–2000: An Anthology of Changing Ideas,* ed. Charles Harrison and Paul Wood (London: Blackwell, 2002), 774.
3 Kazimir Malevich, "From Cubism and Futurism to Suprematism: The New Painterly Realism"[1915], in *Russian Art of the Avant-Garde: Theory and Criticism 1902–1934,* ed. John Bowlt (London: Thames & Hudson, 1988), 116–35.
4 Groys, *The Total Art of Stalinism:,* 36.
5 Henri Lefebvre, *Introduction to Modernity: Twelve Preludes: September 1959–May 1961,* trans. John Moore (London: Verso, 1995), 3.
6 Mikhail E. Koltsov, "Untitled," in Luppol, Rozental, Tretyakov, and Lesnevskii, *Pervyi vsesoyuznyi sezd,* 223.
7 *Anekdoty* are short topical stories. After 1917, the word *anekdot* took on a more specific meaning, referring to jokes or short stories with punchlines circulating through word of mouth, and often oppositional to the regime.
8 Alexei Yurchak, *Everything Was Forever, Until It Was No More: The Last Soviet Generation* (Princeton: Princeton University Press, 2005), 273.
9 Groys, *Total Art of Stalinism,* 75.
10 Yurchak, *Everything Was Forever,* 1.
11 Pussy Riot's satirical punk prayer can be seen on You Tube: https://www.youtube.com/watch?v=Yr0jNui5Qw8 (accessed 5 October 2017).

Appendix

1 Lunacharsky, "O smekhe," 531–8.

Bibliography

Aikhenvald, Yulii I., ed. *V sporakh o teatre*. Moscow: Knigoizdatelstvo pisatelei v Moskve, 1913.

AKhRR. "Declaration of the Association of Artists of Revolutionary Russia, 1922." In *Russian Art of the Avant-Garde: Theory and Criticism 1902–1934*, edited by John Bowlt, 265–7. London: Thames & Hudson, 1988.

Argenbright, Robert. "The Soviet Agitational Vehicle: State Power on the Social Frontier." *Political Geography* 17, no. 3 (1998): 253–72.

Aristotle. *Poetics* [c. 350 BCE]. Translated by Gerald F. Else. Ann Arbour: University of Michigan Press, 1967.

Attardo, Salvatore. *Linguistic Theories of Humor*. Berlin: Mouton de Gruyter, 1994.

– "A Primer for the Linguistics of Humor." In *The Primer of Humor Research*, edited by Victor Raskin, 101–55. Berlin: Mouton de Gruyter, 2008.

Bakhtin, Mikhail. *Problems of Dostoevsky's Poetics* [1929]. Translated by Caryl Emerson. Minneapolis: University of Minnesota Press, 1984.

– *Rabelais and His World* [1965]. Translated by Helen Iswolsky. Bloomington: Indiana University Press, 2009.

Belinsky, Vissarion G. "Portretnaya gallereya russkikh pisatelei" [1854]. In *Polnoe sobranie sochinenii v 12 tomakh*, vol. 8, 613–34. Moscow: Khudozhestvennaya literatura, 1955.

Bergson, Henri. *The Creative Mind: An Introduction to Metaphysics* [1934]. Translated by Mabelle L. Audison. New York: Philosophical Library, 1946.

– *Laughter: An Essay on the Meaning of the Comic* [1900]. Translated by Cloudesley Brereton and Fred Rothwell. New York: Macmillan, 1911.

– *Matter and Memory* [1896]. Translated by N.M. Paul and W.S. Palmer. New York: Zone, 1988.

Berstein, David, Ekaterina Bobrinskaya, Natalia Kozyreva, Elena Vasilyevskaya, and Lyudmila Vostretsova. *Collage in Russia, XX Century.* Saint Petersburg: Palace Editions, 2005.

Beumers, Birgit. *A History of Russian Cinema.* Oxford: Berg, 2009.

Billig, Michael. *Laughter and Ridicule: Towards a Social Critique of Humour.* London: Sage, 2005.

Blakesley, Rosalind Polly. *Russian Genre Painting in the Nineteenth Century.* Oxford: Clarendon Press, 2000.

Blum, Vladimir. "Vozroditsya li satira?" *Literaturnaya gazeta,* no. 6 (27 May 1929): 2.

Bonnell, Victoria. *Iconography of Power: Soviet Political Posters under Lenin and Stalin.* Berkeley: University of California Press, 1997.

Borev, Yury. *Lunacharsky.* Moscow: Molodaya gvardiya, 2010.

Bown, Matthew Cullerne. *Art under Stalin.* Oxford: Phaidon, 1991.

– *Socialist Realist Painting.* New Haven: Yale University Press, 1998.

Boym, Svetlana. *Common Places: Mythologies of Everyday Life in Russia.* Cambridge, MA: Harvard University Press, 1994.

Brantlinger, Patrick. *Bread and Circuses: Theories of Mass Culture as Social Decay.* Ithaca: Cornell University Press, 1983.

Brik, Osip. "Na podstupakh v sovetskoi komedii." *Kino front,* no. 3 (1927): 14.

Briker, Boris. "Anti-Stalinist Humor of the 1930s: Life-Death Jokes." *Przegląd rusycystycny* 4, no. 120 (2007): 33–43.

Brooks, Jeffrey. "Public and Private Values in the Soviet Press, 1921–1928." *Slavic Review* 48, no. 1 (1989): 16–35.

– "Studies of the Reader of the 1920s." *Russian History/Histoire russe* 9, no. 2–3 (1982): 187–202.

– *Thank You, Comrade Stalin! Soviet Public Culture from Revolution to Cold War.* Princeton: Princeton University Press, 2000.

Central Committee of the Communist Party. "Decree on the Reconstruction of Literary and Artistic Organizations" [1932]. In *Art in Theory 1900–2000: An Anthology of Changing Ideas,* edited by Charles Harrison and Paul Wood, 417–18. London: Blackwell, 2002.

–*Kommunisticheskaya partiya sovetskogo soyuza v rezolutsiyakh i retsenziyakh sezdov, konferentsii i plenumov SK,* vol. 1. Moscow: Politizdat, 1953.

– "O nedostatkakh zhurnala 'Krokodil' i merakh ego uluchsheniya" [1951]. In *O partiinoi i sovetskoi pechati: Sbornik dokumentov,* 621–22. Moscow: Izdatelstvo "Pravda," 1954.

– "O zhurnale 'Krokodil'" [1948]. In *O partiinoi i sovetskoi pechati: Sbornik dokumentov,* 599–600. Moscow: Izdatelstvo "Pravda," 1954.

Chalamov, Varlam. *Les années vingt: Cahier 2, réflexions d'un étudiant*. Translated by Christiane Loré and Nathalie Pighetti-Harrison. Lagrasse: Verdier, 2008.

Champarnaud, François. *Révolution et contre-révolution culturelles en U.R.S.S.: De Lénine à Jdanov*. Paris: Anthropos, 1975.

Chernyshevsky, Nikolai G. "Ocherki gogolevskogo perioda russkoi literatury" [1855]. In *Izbrannye estetitcheskie proizvedeniya*, 418–516. Moscow: Iskusstvo, 1978.

Christensen, Peter. "An Ambivalent NEP Satire of Bourgeois Aspirations: *The Kiss of Mary Pickford*." In *Inside Soviet Film Satire: Laughter with a Lash*, edited by Andrew Horton, 48–57. Cambridge: Cambridge University Press, 1993.

Coquin, François-Xavier. "Une source méconnue: Les affiches contre-révolutionnaires (1918–1920)." In *Russie URSS 1914–1991: Changement de regard*, edited by Wladimir Berelowitch and Laurent Gervereau, 52–63. Paris: Musée d'histoire contemporaine de la Bibliothèque de documentation internationale contemporaine, 1991.

Curtis, J.A.E. "Down with the Foxtrot! Concepts of Satire in the Soviet Theatre of the 1920s." In *Russian Theatre in the Age of Modernism*, edited by Robert Russell and Andrew Barratt, 219–35. New York: St. Martin's Press, 1990.

Dal, Vladimir, ed. *Tolkovyi slovar zhivogo velikorusskogo yazyka*, vol. 2, 3rd ed. Saint Peterburg: Tovarishchestvo M.O. Volfa, 1905.

Daly, Jonanthan W. "Government, Press and Subversion in Russia, 1906–1917." *Journal of the Historical Society* 9, no. 1 (2009): 23–65.

Deák, František. "The Agitprop and Circus Plays of Vladimir Mayakovsky." *Drama Review* 17, no. 1 (1973): 47–52.

Deák, František, and Vladimir Mayakovsky. "The Championship of the Universal Class Struggle." *Drama Review* 17, no. 1 (1973): 53–63.

Deitch, Aleksandr. "Satira kotoraya nam nuzhna." *Literaturnaya gazeta*, no. 2 (14 January 1931): 2–3.

Deleuze, Gilles, and Félix Gattari. *A Thousand Plateaus: Capitalism and Schizophrenia* [1980]. Translated by Brian Massumi. Minneapolis: University of Minnesota Press, 1987.

De Man, Paul. "The Rhetoric of Temporality." In *Blindness and Insight: Essays in the Rhetoric of Contemporary Criticism*, 187–228. Minneapolis: University of Minnesota Press, 1983.

Deutscher, Isaac. *The Prophet: Trotsky, 1879–1940*. 3 vols. London: Verso, 2009.

Dmitriev, Yurii A. *Sovetskii tsirk, ocherk istorii, 1917–1941*. Moscow: Iskusstvo, 1963.

– *Teatralnaya Moskva 1920-e gody*. Moscow: Gosudarstvennyi institut iskusstvoznaniya, 2000.

Dobrenko, Evgeny. "Soviet Comedy Film; or, The Carnival of Authority."
    Discourse 17, no. 3 (1995): 49–57.

Dobrolyubov, Nikolai A. "Russkaya satira ekaterinskogo vremini" [1859].
    Sobranie sochinenii v 9 tomakh, vol. 5, 313–401. Moscow: Khudozhestvennaya
    literatura, 1962.

Eco, Umberto. "The Frames of Comic Freedom." In *Carnival!,* edited by
    Umberto Eco, V.V. Ivanov, and Monica Rector, 1–9. Berlin: Mouton de
    Gruyter, 1984.

Ehrenburg, Ilya. *Memoirs: 1921–1941.* Translated by Tatania Shebunina and
    Yvonne Kapp. New York: World Publishing, 1964.

– "Untitled." In *Pervyi vsesoyuznyi sezd sovetskikh pisatelei, 1934.
    Stenograficheskii otchet,* edited by I.K. Luppol, M.M. Rozental, S.M.
    Tretyakov, and S.L. Lesnevskii, 182–3. Moscow: Sovetskii pisatel, 1934.

Eisenstein, Sergei. "A Few Thoughts about Soviet Comedy" [1937]. In *Notes of
    a Film Director,* translated by X. Danko, 106–12. New York: Dover, 1970.

– "Montage of Attraction" [1923]. In *The Film Factory: Russian and Soviet
    Cinema in Documents,* edited by Richard Taylor and Ian Christie, 87–9.
    Cambridge, MA: Harvard University Press, 1988.

Engels, Friedrich. *The Origin of the Family, Private Property, and the State.* New
    York: International Publishers, 1972.

Ermakov, A.F. *A. Lunacharsky.* Moscow: Novosti Press Agency Publishing
    House, 1975.

Evreïnoff, Nicolas. *Histoire du théâtre russe.* Paris: Éditions du Chêne, 1947.

Farrell, Dianne Ecklund. "Laughter Transformed: The Shift from Medieval to
    Enlightenment Humour in Russian Popular Prints." In *Russia and the World
    of the Eighteenth Century,* edited by Roger P. Bartlett, A.G. Gross, and Karen
    Rasmussen, 157–76. Columbus: Slavica, 1988.

– "Popular Humor in Russian Eighteenth Century Lubki." *Slavic Review* 50,
    no. 3 (1991): 551–65.

Fink, Hillary. *Bergson and Russian Modernism 1900–1930.* Evanston:
    Northwestern University Press, 1999.

Fitzpatrick, Sheila. *The Commissariat of Enlightenment: Soviet Organization of
    Education and the Arts under Lunacharsky.* Cambridge: Cambridge University
    Press, 1970.

– "Cultural Revolution in Russia 1928–1932." *Journal of Contemporary History* 9,
    no. 1 (1974): 33–52.

– "Review: Lunacharsky." *Soviet Studies* 20, no. 4 (1969): 527–35.

Four Arts Society of Artists. "Declaration, 1929." In *Russian Art of the
    Avant-Garde: Theory and Criticism 1902–1934,* edited by John Bowlt, 281–4.
    London: Thames & Hudson, 1988.

Freud, Sigmund. "Humour" [1927]. *International Journal of Psycho-Analysis* 9, no. 1 (1928): 1–6.
– *The Joke and Its Relation to the Unconscious* [1905]. Translated by Joyce Crick. New York: Penguin Classics, 2003.
Gardiner, Michael E. "Post-Romantic Irony in Bakhtin and Lefebvre." *History of the Human Science* 23, no. 3 (2012): 51–69.
Genette, Gérard. *The Architext: An Introduction.* Berkeley: University of California Press, 1992.
Gérin, Annie. *Godless at the Workbench: Soviet Illustrated Humoristic Antireligious Propaganda.* Regina: Dunlop Art Gallery, 2003.
– "On rit au *Narkompros*: Anatoli Lounatcharski et la théorie du rire soviétique." *RACAR: Revue d'art canadienne/Canadian Art Review* 37, no. 1 (2012): 41–52.
– "Rire rouge: La presse satirique en Russie soviétique." *Ridiculosa* (special issue, 2013): 56–93.
– "A Second Look at Laughter: Humor in the Visual Arts." *Humor: International Journal of Humor Research* 26, no.1 (2013): 155–76.
Gerould, Daniel. "Lunacharsky on Revolutionary Laughter." *Slavic and East European Performance* 26, no. 1 (2006): 58–62.
Gill, Graeme. *Symbols and Legitimacy in Soviet Politics.* Cambridge: Cambridge University Press, 2011.
Greenberg, Clement. "Modernist Painting" [1960]. In *Art in Theory 1900–2000: An Anthology of Changing Ideas,* edited by Charles Harrison and Paul Wood, 773–9. London: Blackwell, 2002.
Groys, Boris. *The Total Art of Stalinism: Avant-garde, Aesthetic Dictatorship, and Beyond.* Translated by Charles Rougle. London: Verso, 2011.
Hall, Stuart. "The Work of Representation." In *Representation. Cultural Representations and Signifying Practices,* edited by Stuart Hall, 13–74. London: Sage, 1997.
Hempelmann, Christian, and Andrea Samson. "Cartoons: Drawn Jokes?" In *The Primer of Humor Research,* edited by Victor Raskin, 613–44. Berlin: Mouton de Gruyter, 2008.
Herzen, Aleksandr I. "O pisme, kritikuyushchem 'Kolokol'" [1858]. In *Sobranie sochinenii v 30 tomakh,* vol. 13, 189–91. Moscow: Izd. Akademii nauk SSSR, 1952.
Hobbes, Thomas. *Leviathan, or the Matter, Forme & Power of a Common-wealth Ecclesiaticall and Civill* [1651], edited by Richard Tuck. Cambridge: Cambridge University Press, 1996.
Hutcheon, Linda. "Ironie, satire, parodie: Une approche pragmatique de l'ironie." *Poétique: Revue de théorie et d'analyse littéraires* 12, no. 46 (1981): 140–55.

Inkeles, Alex, and Kent Geiger. "Critical Letters to the Editors of the Soviet Press: Areas and Modes of Complaint." *American Sociological Review* 17, no. 6 (1952): 694–703.

Kachurin, Pamela. *Making Modernism Soviet: The Russian Avant-Garde in the Early Soviet Era, 1918–1928.* Chicago: Northwestern University Press, 2013.

Kenez, Peter. *Cinema & Soviet Society 1917–1953.* Cambridge: Cambridge University Press, 1992.

– "Lenin and the Freedom of the Press." In *Bolshevik Culture: Experiment and Order in the Russian Revolution,* edited by Abbott Gleason, Peter Kenez, and Richard Stites, 131–59. Bloomington: Indiana University Press, 1985.

"Khronologiya tsirka i estrady, 1917–1928 g. g." *Tsirk i estrada,* no. 16 (1928): 1.

Kiaer, Christina. *Imagine No Possessions: The Socialist Objects of Russian Constructivism.* Cambridge, MA: MIT Press, 2005.

King, David. *The Commissar Vanishes: The Falsification of Photographs and Art in Stalin's Russia.* London: Metropolitan Books, 1997.

– *Red Star over Russia: A Visual History of the Soviet Union from the Revolution to the Death of Stalin.* New York: Harry N. Abrams, 2009.

King, David, and Cathy Porter. *Blood & Laughter: Caricatures from the 1905 Revolution.* London: Jonathan Cape, 1983.

Kleberg, Lars. "The Nature of the Soviet Audience: Theatrical Ideology and Audience Research in the 1920s." In *Russian Theatre in the Age of Modernism,* edited by Robert Russell and Andrew Barratt, 173–95. New York: St. Martin's Press, 1990.

Kolesnikova, Parisa. *"Okna TASS" 1941/1945: Oruzhie pobedy.* Moscow: Taktika, 2005.

Koltsov, Mikhail E. "Untitled." In *Pervyi vsesoyuznyi sezd sovetskikh pisatelei, 1934. Stenograficheskii otchet,* edited by I.K. Luppol, M.M. Rozental, S.M. Tretyakov, and S.L. Lesnevskii, 221–4. Moscow: Sovetskii pisatel, 1934.

Krikmann, Arvo. "Contemporary Linguistic Theories of Humor." *Folklore: Electronic Journal of Folklore,* no. 33 (2006): 27–58.

Kuleshov, Lev. "Americanism" [1922]. In *The Film Factory: Russian and Soviet Cinema in Documents,* edited by Richard Taylor and Ian Christie, 72–3. Cambridge, MA: Harvard University Press, 1988.

– "Circus-Cinema-Theatre" [1925]. In *Lev Kuleshov: Selected Works: Fifty Years in Films,* translated by Dmitri Agrachev and Nina Belenkaya, 62–3. Moscow: Raduga, 1987.

Lahusen, Thomas. "Socialist Realism in Search of Its Shores: Some Historical Remarks on the 'Historically Open Aesthetic System of the Truthful Representation of Life.'" In *Socialist Realism without Shores,* edited by Thomas Lahusen and Evgeny Dobrenko, 5–26. Durham: Duke University Press, 1997.

Leach, Robert. *Revolutionary Theatre*. London: Routledge, 1994.

– "Revolutionary Theatre, 1917–1930." In *A History of Russian Theatre*, edited by Robert Leach and Victor Borovsky, 302–24. Cambridge: Cambridge University Press, 1999.

Lefebvre, Henri. *Introduction to Modernity: Twelve Preludes, September 1959–May 1961*. Translated by John Moore. London: Verso, 1995.

Lekhtblau, L.B. *Russkie satiricheskie zhurnaly XVIII veka*. Moscow: Gosudarstvennoe uchebno-pedagogicheskoe izdatelstvo Narkomprosa RSFSR, 1940.

Lenin, V.I. *Collected Works*. Moscow: Progress Publishers, 1973.

Levinson, Jerrold. "The Concept of Humor." In *Contemplating Art: Essays in Aesthetics*, 589–400. Oxford: Oxford University Press, 2006.

Lewis, Ben. *Hammer and Tickle: The Story of Communism, a Political System Almost Laughed Out of Existence*. New York: Pegasus, 2009.

Leys, Ruth. "How Did Fear Become a Scientific Object and What Kind of Object Is It?" *Representation*, no. 110 (2010): 66–104.

– "The Turn to Affect: A Critique." *Critical Inquiry* 37, no. 3 (2011): 434–72.

Lezhnev, Abram. "Na puti k vozrozhdeniyu satiry." *Literaturnaya gazeta*, no. 1 (15 April 1929): 2.

Likhachev, D.S., A.M. Panchenko, and N.V. Ponyrko. *Smekh drevnei rusi*. Leningrad: Nauka, 1984.

Lipps, Theodor. *Komik und Humor*. Hamburg: L. Voss, 1898.

Livshitz, Benedikt. *The One and Half-Eyed Archer* [1933]. Newtonville: Oriental Research Partners, 1977.

Lounatcharski, Anatole. *L'esthétique soviétique contre Staline*. Edited and translated by Aymeric Monville. Paris: Éditions Delga, 2005.

Lunacharskaya, Irina. "Sversheniya i zamysly (A.V. Lunacharsky: Iz pisem i dnevnikov)." *Novyi mir*, no. 11 (1975): 244–59.

Lunacharsky, Anatoli V. "Budem smeyatsya" [1920]. In *Sobranie sochinenii v 8 tomakh*, vol. 3, 76–9. Moscow: Khudozhestvennaya literatura, 1964.

– "Chto takoe yumor?" [1930]. In *Sobranie sochinenii v 8 tomakh*, vol. 8, 182–4. Moscow: Khudozhestvennaya literatura, 1967.

– "Conversation with Lenin. I. Of all the arts ..." [1922]. In *The Film Factory: Russian and Soviet Cinema in Documents*, edited by Richard Taylor and Ian Christie, 56–7. Cambridge, MA: Harvard University Press, 1988.

– "Dzhonatan Svift i ego skazka o bochke" [1930]. In *Sobranie sochinenii v 8 tomakh*, vol. 6, 37–47. Moscow: Khudozhestvennaya literatura, 1965.

– "Education of the New Man" [1928]. In *On Education*, translated by Ruth English, 217–41. Moscow: Progress Publishers, 1981.

– "Frantsuzkaya komediya v nashi dni." *Novyi zhurnal dlya vsekh*, no. 2 (1912): 95–102.

– "Frantsuzkii kritik ob angliskom komediografe." *Teatr i iskusstvo,* no. 39 (6 September 1912): 724–44.

– "Industrialnaya tematika v izobrazitelnom iskusstve." *Brigada khudozhnikov,* nos. 5–6 (1931): 13.

– "Ilf i Petrov" [1931]. In *Sobranie sochinenii v 8 tomakh,* vol. 2, 519-25. Moscow: Khudozhestvennaya literatura, 1964.

– "Kinematograficheskaya komediya i satira" [1931]. In *Lunacharsky o kino,* 192–212. Moscow: Izdatelstvo "Iskusstvo," 1965.

–"Kino – Orudie massovoy agitatsii i propagandy" [1930]. In *Lunacharsky o kino,* 170–5. Moscow: Izdatelstvo "Iskusstvo," 1965.

– "Lozhka protivoyadiya" [1918]. In *Sobranie sochinenii v 8 tomakh,* vol. 2, 206–8. Moscow: Khudozhestvennaya literatura, 1964.

– "Marksizm i literatura" [1923]. In *Sobranie sochinenii v 8 tomakh,* vol. 7, 331–40. Moscow: Khudozhestvennaya literatura, 1967.

– *Meshchanstvo i individualism.* Moscow: Gosudarstvennoe izdatelstvo, 1923.

– "Moim opponentam." *Vestnik teatra,* no. 76–7 (14 December 1920): 4–5.

– "Neskolko vpechatlenii" [1927]. *Sobranie sochinenii v 8 tomakh,* vol. 3, 371–4. Moscow: Khudozhestvennaya literatura, 1964.

– "O satire" [1930]. In *Sobranie sochinenii v 8 tomakh,* vol. 8, 185–7. Moscow: Khudozhestvennaya literatura, 1967.

– "O smekhe" [1931]. In *Sobranie sochinenii v 8 tomakh,* vol. 8, 531–8. Moscow: Khudozhestvennaya literatura, 1967.

– "O sotsialisticheskom realisme" [1933]. In *Sobranie sochinenii v 8 tomakh,* vol. 8, 524–8. Moscow: Khudozhestvennaya literatura, 1964.

– "Pismo v redaktsiu." *Literaturnaya gazeta,* no. 15 (6 March 1931): 4.

– "Rebenek i tsirk." *Tsirk,* no. 3 (1925): 10.

– "Revolutionary Ideology and Cinema – Theses" [1924]. In *The Film Factory: Russian and Soviet Cinema in Documents,* edited by Richard Taylor and Ian Christie, 109–10. Cambridge, MA: Harvard University Press, 1988.

– "Salon yumoristov." *Kievskaya mysl,* no. 90 (1 April 1912): 3.

– "Sotsialisticheskii realism" [1933]. In *Sobranie sochinenii v 8 tomakh,* vol. 8, 491–523. Moscow: Khudozhestvennaya literatura, 1964.

– "Speech to Film Workers" [1928]. In *The Film Factory: Russian and Soviet Cinema in Documents,* edited by Richard Taylor and Ian Christie, 195–7. Cambridge, MA: Harvard University Press, 1988.

– "Svoboda knigi i revolutsia" [1921]. In *Isbrannye stati po estetike,* 82-3. Moscow: Iskusstvo, 1975

– "Synopsis of a Report on the Tasks of Dramaturgy (Extract)" [1933]. In *The Film Factory: Russian and Soviet Cinema in Documents*, edited by Richard Taylor and Ian Christie, 327. Cambridge, MA: Harvard University Press, 1988.

– "Teatr i revolutsiya" [1921]. In *Sobranie sochinenii v 8 tomakh*, vol. 3, 80–105. Moscow: Khudozhestvennaya literatura, 1964.

– "Teatr RSFSR" [1922]. In *Sobranie sochinenii v 8 tomakh*, vol. 3, 115–28. Moscow: Khudozhestvennaya literatura, 1964.

– "Tezisy o zadachakh marksistkoi kritiki" [1928]. In *Sobranie sochinenii v 8 tomakh*, vol. 8, 7–18. Moscow: Khudozhestvennaya literatura, 1964.

– "Yumor i parizhskie yumoristy karandasha." *Nov*, no. 69 (5 April 1914): 3.

– "Yumor irlandskii i yumor frantsuzkii." *Teatr i iskusstvo*, no. 6 (9 February 1914): 131–2.

– "Zadacha obnovlennogo tsirka." *Vestnik teatra*, no. 3 (1919): 5.

Lunacharsky, Anatoly V., ed. *Kniga o novom teatre*. Saint Peterburg: Sipovnik, 1908.

Luppol, I.K., M.M. Rozental, S.M. Tretyakov, and S.L. Lesnevskii, eds. *Pervyi vsesoyuznyi sezd sovetskikh pisatelei, 1934: Stenograficheskii otchet*. Moscow: Sovetskii pisatel, 1934.

Malevich, Kazimir. "From Cubism and Futurism to Suprematism: The New Painterly Realism" [1915]. In *Russian Art of the Avant-Garde: Theory and Criticism 1902–1934*, edited by John Bowlt, 116–35. London: Thames & Hudson, 1988.

Marx, Karl. "A Contribution to the Critique of Hegel's Philosophy of Right: Introduction" [1843]. In *Early Writings*, translated by Rodney Livingstone and Gregor Benton, 243–57. London: Penguin, 1992.

– *The Eighteenth Brumaire of Louis Bonaparte* [1869]. New York: International Publishers, 1963.

– "On the Jewish Question" [1843]. In *Early Writings*, translated by Rodney Livingstone and Gregor Benton, 211–41. London: Penguin, 1992.

Mayakovsky, Vladimir V. "Libretto 'Misterii-buff'" [1921]. In *Polnoe sobranie sochinenie v 13 tomakh*, vol. 2, 359–60. Moscow: GIKhL, 1959.

– *Mayakovsky: Okna ROSTA i Glavpolitprosveta, 1919–1921*. Edited by Aleksei Morozov. Moscow: Kontakt-Kultura, 2010.

– "Mozhno li stat satirikom?" [1923]. In *Polnoe sobranie sochinenie v 13 tomakh*, vol. 12, 30–2. Moscow: GIKhL, 1959.

– "Neokonchennoe." In *Polnoe sobranie sochinenie v 13 tomakh*, vol. 10, 286–7. Moscow: GIKhL, 1959.

– "Okna satiry ROSTA" [1930]. In *Polnoe sobranie sochinenie v 13 tomakh*, vol. 12, 210. Moscow: GIKhL, 1959.

– "Predipolslovie" [1923]. In *Polnoe sobranie sochinenie v 13 tomakh*, vol. 12, 51–3. Moscow: GIKhL, 1959.

– "Vystuplenie na dispute 'Bolnye voprosy sovetskoi pechati': 14 dekabrya 1925 goda" [1925]. In *Polnoe sobranie sochinenie v 13 tomakh*, vol. 12, 292–4. Moscow: GIKhL, 1959.

– "Vystuplenie na dispute 'Nuzhna li nam satira?': 8 yanvarya 1930 goda" [1930]. In *Polnoe sobranie sochinenie v 13 tomakh*, vol. 12, 512. Moscow: GIKhL, 1959.

Mandelstam, Nadezhda. *Hope Abandoned* [1974]. Translated by Max Hayward. New York: Atheneum, 1981.

Mandelstam, Osip. *Complete Poetry of Osip Emilevich Mandelstam*. Translated by Burton Raffel and Alla Burago. Albany: State University of New York Press, 1973.

Manteifel, A.N. "Teatr revolyutsionnoi satiry (Terevsat)." In *Sovetskii teatr: Dokumenty i materialy 1917–1967*, edited by A.Z. Yufit and A.Ya. Altshuller, vol. 1, 181–90. Leningrad: Iskusstvo, 1968.

Massumi, Brian. "The Autonomy of Affect." *Cultural Critique*, no. 31 (1995): 83–109.

McReynolds, Louise. *Russia at Play: Leisure Activities at the End of the Tsarist Era*. Ithaca: Cornell University Press, 2003.

Meyerhold, Vsevolod. "The Actor of the Future and Biomechanics" [1922]. In *The Soviet Theatre: A Documentary History*, edited by Laurence Senelick and Sergei Ostrovsky, 147–9. New Haven: Yale University Press, 2014.

Milne, Lesley. "*Novyi satirikon* 1914–1918: The Patriotic Laughter of the Russian Liberal Intelligentsia during the First World War and the Revolution." *Slavonic and East European Review* 84, no. 4 (2006): 639–65.

Moor, Dmitrii S. "Moskovskie mastera satiry" [1938]. In *"Ya – bolshevik!" Sbornik statei*, 87–101. Moscow: Sovetskii khudozhnik, 1967.

Moser, Charles, ed. *The Cambridge History of Russian Literature*. Cambridge: Cambridge University Press, 1992.

Neirick, Miriam. *When Pigs Could Fly and Bears Could Dance: A History of the Soviet Circus*. Madison: University of Wisconsin Press, 2012.

Nemchinskii, Maksimilian. *Tsirk Rossii naperegonki so vremenem: Modeli tsirkovykh spektaklei, 1920–1990kh godov*. Moscow: GITIS, 2001.

Nikulin, Lev V. "On lyubil i ponimal yumor." Russian State Archive of Literature and Art (RGALI), f. 279, op. 2, del. 736, l. 14–18.

"Obespechim vse usloviya tvorcheskoi raboty literaturnykh kruzhkov: Na sobranii aktiva litkruzhkov Moskvy." *Literaturnaya gazeta*, no 23 (23 May 1932): 1.

October – Association of Artistic Labour. "Declaration, 1928." In *Russian Art of the Avant-Garde: Theory and Criticism 1902–1934*, edited by John Bowlt, 273–9. London: Thames &Hudson, 1988.

"O putyakh sovetskoy satiry." *Literaturnaya gazeta*, no. 12 (15 July 1929): 1.

OST [Society of Easel Artists]. "Platform, 1929." In *Russian Art of the Avant-Garde: Theory and Criticism 1902–1934*, edited by John Bowlt, 279–81. London: Thames & Hudson, 1988.

O'Sullivan, Simon. "The Aesthetics of Affect: Thinking Art beyond Representation." *Angelaki: Journal of Theoretical Humanities* 6, no. 3 (2001): 125–35.

Pehowski, Marian. "*Krokodil*-Satire for the Soviets." *Journalism Quarterly* 55, no. 4 (1978): 729.

Peris, Daniel. *Storming the Heavens: The Soviet League of the Militant Godless.* Ithaca: Cornell University Press, 1998.

Polimeni, Joseph, and Jeffrey Reiss. "The First Joke: Exploring the Evolutionary Origins of Humor." *Evolutionary Psychology* 4 (2006): 347–66.

Propp, Vladimir. *On the Comic and Laughter.* Edited and translated by Jean-Patrick Debbèche and Paul Perron. Toronto: Toronto University Press, 2009.

Quintilian. *The Institutio Oratoria* [95 CE]. Translated by H.E. Butler. Cambridge, MA: Harvard University Press, 1977.

Raskin, Victor, ed. *The Primer of Humor Research.* Berlin: Mouton de Gruyter, 2008.

Reed, John. *Ten Days That Shook the World* [1919]. London: Penguin, 1986.

Renton, Dave. *Dissident Marxism: Past Voices for Present Times.* London: Zed, 2004.

Rogi, M. "Puti sovetskoy satiry." *Literaturnaya gazeta*, no. 14 (22 July 1929): 3.

Rolf, Malte. *Soviet Mass Festivals, 1917–1991.* Translated by Cynthia Klohr. Pittsburgh: University of Pittsburgh Press, 2013.

Romashov, Boris S. "Untitled." In *Pervyi vsesoyuznyi sezd sovetskikh pisatelei, 1934. Stenograficheskii otchet*, edited by I.K. Luppol, M.M. Rozental, S.M. Tretyakov, and S.L. Lesnevskii, 426–8. Moscow: Sovetskii pisatel, 1934.

Rowley, Alison. "Where Are All the Mother-Heroines? Images of Maternity in Soviet Films of the 1930s." *Canadian Journal of History* 44, no. 1 (2009): 25–38.

Roze, Gr. "Ot parodii k satire." *Literaturnaya gazeta*, no. 21 (12 May 1932): 3.

Ruch, Willibald, Salvatore Attardo, and Victor Raskin. "Towards an Empirical Verification of the General Theory of Verbal Humor." *Humor: International Journal of Humor Research* 6, no. 2 (1993): 123–36.

Rudnitsky, Konstatin. *Russian and Soviet Theatre 1905–1932.* Translated by Roxane Permar. New York: Harry N. Abrams, 1988.

Russell, Robert. "The First Soviet Plays." In *Russian Theatre in the Age of Modernism,* edited by Robert Russell and Andrew Barratt, 148–71. New York: St. Martin's Press, 1990.

Russian Socialist Federal Soviet Republic. *Constitution of the Russian Socialist Federal Soviet Republic. Order of the Fifth All-Russia Congress of Soviets Passed on the 10th of July, 1918.* London: People's Russian Information Bureau, 1919.

Ruud, Charles A. *Fighting Words: Imperial Censorship and the Russian Press, 1804–1906.* Toronto: University of Toronto Press, 2009.

Salys, Rimgaila. *The Musical Comedy Films of Grigorii Aleksandrov: Laughing Matters.* Bristol: Intellect, 2009.

Schopenhauer, Arthur. *The World as Will and Representation* [1818]. Translated by E.F.J. Payne. New York: Dover, 1966.

Shaginyan, Marietta. *Novyi byt i iskusstvo.* Moscow: Zakkniga, 1926.

Shulgin, V.N. *Pamyatnye vstrechi.* Moscow: Gosudartsvennoe izdatelstvo politicheskoi literatury, 1958.

Shumyatsky, Boris. "A Cinema for the Millions (Extracts)" [1935]. In *The Film Factory: Russian and Soviet Cinema in Documents,* edited by Richard Taylor and Ian Christie, 358–69. Cambridge, MA: Harvard University Press, 1988.

Selivanovsky, Aleksei. "Smekh Ilfa i Petrova." *Literaturnaya gazeta,* no. 38 (23 August 1932): 3.

Senelick, Laurence, and Sergei Ostrovsky, eds. *The Soviet Theatre: A Documentary History.* New Haven: Yale University Press, 2014.

Service, Robert. *Trotsky: A Biography.* Cambridge, MA: Harvard University Press, 2011.

"Sinyaya bluza." *Literaturnaya gazeta,* no. 24 (30 September 1929): 2.

Solovyova, Inna. "The Theatre and Socialist Realism." In *A History of Russian Theatre,* edited by Robert Leach and Victor Borovsky, 325–57. Cambridge: Cambridge University Press, 1999.

Sovnarkom of the RSFSR. "Decree on the Establishment of Sovkino" [1924]. In *The Film Factory: Russian and Soviet Cinema in Documents,* edited by Richard Taylor and Ian Christie, 114–15. Cambridge, MA: Harvard University Press, 1988.

Soyuz voinstvuyushchikh bezbozhnikov. *Kak ustroit ugolok bezbozhnika.* Moscow: Bezbozhnik u stanka, 1924.

Spencer, Herbert. "The Physiology of Laughter." In *Essays: Scientific, Political, and Speculative,* 105–19. London: Williams and Norgate, 1863.

Stalin, Joseph. *Voprosy leninizma*. Moscow: Gosudarstvennoe sotsialnoe ekonomicheskoe izdatelstvo, 1931.

Steklov, Yurii M., ed., *Kriziz teatra*. Moscow: Problemy iskusstva, 1908.

Stites, Richard. *Russian Popular Culture: Entertainment and Society since 1900.* Cambridge: Cambridge University Press, 1992.

– *The Woman's Liberation Movement in Russia: Feminism, Nihilism, Bolshevism 1860–1930*. Princeton: Princeton University Press, 1978.

Stourac, Richard, and Kathleen McCreery, eds. *Theatre as a Weapon: Workers' Theatre in the Soviet Union, Germany and Britain, 1917–1934*. London: Routledge & Kegan Paul, 1986.

Straw, Will. "Scenes and Sensibilities." *Public*, no. 22/23 (2002): 245–57.

Stykalin, Sergei. *Sovetskaya satiricheskaya pechat 1917–1963*. Moscow: Gospolizdat, 1963.

Sully, James. *An Essay on Laughter: Its Forms, Its Causes, Its Development and Its Value*. London: Longman, Green, 1902.

Surkov, A. "Untitled." In *Pervyi vsesoyuznyi sezd sovetskikh pisatelei, 1934. Stenograficheskii otchet*, edited by I.K. Luppol, M.M. Rozental, S.M. Tretyakov, and S.L. Lesnevskii, 512–15. Moscow: Sovetskii pisatel, 1934.

Swallow, Norman. *Eisenstein: A Documentary Portrait*. London: George Allen and Unwin, 1976.

Tait, A.L. "Lunacharsky, the Poet-Commissar." *Slavonic and East European Review* 52, no. 127 (1974): 234–51.

Taylor, Richard. "Soviet Cinema as Popular Culture: Or the Extraordinary Adventures of Mr Nepman in the Land of the Silver Screen." *Revolutionary Russia* 1, no. 1 (1988): 36–56.

Taylor, Richard, and Ian Christie, eds. *The Film Factory: Russian and Soviet Cinema in Documents*. Cambridge, MA: Harvard University Press, 1988.

Terentev, I. "Mayakovskii 'Levee Lefa.'" *Novyi LEF*, no. 9 (1928): 47–8.

Timasheff, Nicholas. "The Inner Life of the Orthodox Church." In *The Transformation of Russian Society*, edited by Cyril Black, 425–37. Cambridge: Cambridge University Press, 1960.

Tolstoy, Leo. *What Is Art?* [1898]. Translated by Aylmer Maude. Indianapolis: Bobbs-Merrill, 1960.

Tretyakov, Sergei. "Otkuda i kuda?" *LEF*, no. 1 (1923): 192–203.

Trotsky, Leon. "Anatole Vasilievich Lunacharsky" [1934]. In *Writings of Leon Trotsky*, vol. 6, 181–90. New York: Pathfinder, 1973.

– *Literature and Revolution* [1925]. Edited by William Keach, translated by Rose Strunsky. New York: Haymarket, 2005.

– *Problems of Everyday Life and Other Writings on Culture & Science*. New York: Monad, 1973.

Ts, Mikh. "Lushche vybirat mishen – Za kachestvo sovetskoi satiry!" *Literaturnaya gazeta*, no. 25 (5 June 1932): 2.

Tumarkin, Nina. *Lenin Lives!: The Lenin Cult in Soviet Russia*. Cambridge: Cambridge University Press, 1983.

Ulianov, Vladimir [Lenin]. "Dekret ob edinenii teatralnogo dela." *Vestnik teatra*, no. 33 (August 1919): 2.

– "Dekret o pechati." In *O partiinoi i sovetskoi pechati: Sbornik dokumentov*, 173. Moscow: Izdatelstvo "Pravda," 1954.

– "O revolyutsionnom tribunale pechati" [1918]. In *O partiinoi i sovetskoi pechati: Sbornik dokumentov*, 175–6. Moscow: Izdatelstvo "Pravda," 1954.

Unger, Aryeh. *Constitutional Development in the USSR: A Guide to the Soviet Constitutions*. London: Methuen, 1981.

Vatlin, Alexander, and Larisa Malashenko, eds. *Piggy Foxy and the Sword of the Revolution: Bolshevik Self-Portraits*. New Haven: Yale University Press, 2006.

Ward, Alex. *Power to the People: Early Soviet Propaganda Posters in the Israel Museum, Jerusalem*. Jerusalem and Burlington: The Israel Museum and Aldershot & Lund Humphries, 2007.

Waterlow, Jonathan. "Sanctioning Laughter in Stalin's Soviet Union." *History Workshop Journal* 79, no. 1 (2015): 198–214.

White, Hayden. *Metahistory: The Historical Imagination in Nineteenth-Century Europe*. Baltimore: Johns Hopkins University Press, 1973.

White, Stephen. *The Bolshevik Poster*. New Haven: Yale University Press, 1988.

Whitfield, Eileen. *Pickford: The Woman Who Made Hollywood*. Lexington: University Press of Kentucky, 1997.

Widdis, Emma. *Alexander Medvedkin*. London: I.B. Tauris, 2005.

Wood, Elizabeth. *The Baba and the Comrade: Gender and Politics in Revolutionary Russia*. Bloomington: Indiana University Press, 1997.

Yakubovsky, Georgii. "O satire nashikh dnei." *Literaturnaya gazeta*, no. 11 (8 July 1929): 3.

Youngblood, Denise. *Movies for the Masses: Popular Cinema and Soviet Society in the 1920s*. Cambridge: Cambridge University Press, 1992.

Yurchak, Alexei. *Everything Was Forever, Until It Was No More: The Last Soviet Generation*. Princeton: Princeton University Press, 2005.

Zhdanov, Andrei. "Soviet Literature – The Richest in Ideas, the Most Advanced Literature." In *Soviet Writers' Congress 1934: The Debate on Socialist Realism and Modernism in the Soviet Union*, 15–24. London: Lawrence and Wishart, 1977.

Zitser, Ernest. "A Full Frontal History of the Romanov Dynasty: Pictorial 'Political Pornography' in Pre-Reform Russia." *Russian Review* 70 (2011): 557–83.

– *The Transfigured Kingdom: Sacred Parody and Charismatic Authority at the Court of Peter the Great*. Ithaca: Cornell University Press, 2004.

Zozulya, Efim. "Nuzhna li nam satira?" *Literaturnaya gazeta*, no. 2 (13 January 1930): 3.

Index